# Global Environmental Politics

PROBLEMS, POLICY, AND PRACTICE

Concern about humanity's impact on the planet has never been greater, but what are the drivers of environmental change? This wide-ranging introductory textbook outlines the competing explanations of why environmental problems occur and examines the different political approaches taken to address them. Adopting a case study approach, Hayley Stevenson enables students to gain a detailed understanding of how theories and concepts are applied in practice. Diverse perspectives on a variety of contemporary environmental challenges, from climate change to hazardous waste, as well as various responses, from multilateral diplomacy to consumer-focused campaigns, provide students with an in-depth understanding of the merits and limitations of different forms of political action. Refined on the basis of classroom feedback, features include textboxes, key points, a Glossary of key terms, questions, further reading suggestions, and supplementary online resources. This lively book is an essential resource for advanced undergraduate and postgraduate courses on global environmental politics and environmental policy.

**Hayley Stevenson** is Associate Professor in International Relations at the Universidad Torcuato Di Tella, Argentina, and Reader in Politics at the University of Sheffield. She is the author of *Institutionalizing Unsustainability: The Paradox of Global Climate Governance* (2012) and *Democratizing Global Climate Governance* (with John S. Dryzek, 2014), and co-editor of *Traditions and Trends in Global Environmental Politics: International Relations and the Earth* (with Olaf Corry, 2017).

# Global Environmental Politics

## PROBLEMS, POLICY, AND PRACTICE

Hayley Stevenson

# CAMBRIDGE
## UNIVERSITY PRESS

University Printing House, Cambridge CB2 8BS, United Kingdom

One Liberty Plaza, 20th Floor, New York, NY 10006, USA

477 Williamstown Road, Port Melbourne, VIC 3207, Australia

4843/24, 2nd Floor, Ansari Road, Daryaganj, Delhi – 110002, India

79 Anson Road, #06–04/06, Singapore 079906

Cambridge University Press is part of the University of Cambridge.

It furthers the University's mission by disseminating knowledge in the pursuit of education, learning, and research at the highest international levels of excellence.

www.cambridge.org
Information on this title: www.cambridge.org/9781107121836
DOI: 10.1017/9781316344354

First published 2018

Printed in the United Kingdom by TJ International Ltd. Padstow Cornwall

*A catalogue record for this publication is available from the British Library.*

ISBN 978-1-107-12183-6 Hardback
ISBN 978-1-107-54753-7 Paperback

Additional resources for this title can be found at www.cambridge.org/stevenson

# Table of Contents

List of Figures                                                *page* xi
List of Tables                                                      xii
List of Maps                                                       xiii
List of Boxes                                                      xiv
Preface                                                             xv
List of Abbreviations                                             xviii

**1  Global Politics and the Environment**                          1
Summary of Key Points                                               1
Introduction                                                        2
State of the Planet                                                 3
The Politics of Environmental Change                                7
Outline of this Book                                               10
Discussion Questions                                               16

**PART 1:  WHY DO ENVIRONMENTAL
              PROBLEMS OCCUR?**                                     17

**2  The Tragedy of the Commons**                                  19
Summary of Key Points                                              19
Introduction                                                       19
Core Assumptions Underpinning the 'Tragedy'                        22
    Human Beings are Self-regarding and Short-sighted              22
    'The Commons' are Unmanaged and Freely Accessible              22
    Privatisation and Socialism are the Only Possible Solutions
        to Avoid Degradation                                       23
Critiques and Corrections                                          25
    Human Nature and the Commons                                   25
    Historical Inaccuracies                                        26
    Alternative Governance Options                                 27
The Global Commons                                                 30
    What are the Global Commons?                                   30
    Managing the Global Commons                                    31

Conclusion                                                          35
Discussion Questions                                                35

**3**  **Population and Poverty**                                   37
Summary of Key Points                                               37
Introduction                                                        38
The Malthusian Renaissance                                          39
Solving the Population Problem                                      40
Trends in Population Growth                                         41
Is Population Control the Answer?                                   45
Is Poverty the Main Driver of Environmental Degradation?           46
    The Environmental Kuznets Curve (EKC)      48
    Questioning the Validity of the EKC        50
    Outsourcing Production and Pollution       52
    Do Wealthier People Care More About the Environment?    53
Conclusion                                                          56
Discussion Questions                                                57

**4**  **Capitalism**                                              58
Summary of Key Points                                               58
Introduction                                                        58
The Contradictions of Capitalism                                   60
    The Traditional Contradiction             60
    The Ecological Contradiction              61
Capitalism's Rifts                                                 63
    Alienation from Nature                    64
    Metabolic Rift                            64
    Ecological Rift                           65
Ecological Imperialism                                             66
Over-consumption                                                   68
Is Sustainable Capitalism the Solution?                            70
Eco-socialism                                                      72
Steady-state Economy and Degrowth                                  74
Conclusion                                                         75
Discussion Questions                                               77

**PART 2:  RESPONDING TO GLOBAL ENVIRONMENTAL
PROBLEMS**                                                         79

**5**  **Conflict and Securitisation**  *Water Scarcity*          81
Summary of Key Points                                              81

Introduction                                                          82
Conflict and the Natural Environment                                  83
   Conflicts Over Natural Resources                     84
Water and Conflict                                                    88
   State of the World's Water                           88
   Water Wars: Theory and Evidence                      92
   Weaknesses in International Cooperation               99
Securitising the Environment                                         102
Conclusion                                                           105
Discussion Questions                                                 106

6  **Multilateral Diplomacy**   *Sustainable Development*             107
Summary of Key Points                                                107
Introduction                                                         108
Multilateral Diplomacy                                               109
Environmental Multilateralism                                        112
   The Environmental Movement                          112
   The Birth of Environmental Multilateralism          112
   North–South Tensions Emerge                         114
   The Golden Age of Environmental Multilateralism      116
   Environmental Multilateralism in the Twenty-first Century  117
   Legal and Political Status of MEAs                   119
Sustainable Development                                               120
   The Concept of Sustainable Development               120
   Institutionalising Sustainable Development:
      Earth Summit, 1992                  122
   Reality Check: World Summit on Sustainable
      Development, 2002                   127
   Facing Up to Unmet Promises: Rio+20 and Beyond       129
Conclusion                                                           137
Discussion Questions                                                 138

7  **Transnational Governance Experiments**   *Climate Change*        140
Summary of Key Points                                                140
Introduction                                                         141
Transnational Governance                                             142
Climate Change                                                       145
   The Science of Climate Change                       146
   A 'Wicked' Policy Problem                            147
   Multilateral Cooperation on Climate Change          149
   Transnational Climate Change Governance             156
   Governance Experiments                              156

Virtues of Transnational Climate Governance                        162
Limitations of Transnational Climate Governance                    163
Coordinating Governance Experiments: NAZCA                         164
Conclusion                                                         165
Discussion Questions                                               166

**8    Aid and Finance    *Deforestation***                        167
Summary of Key Points                                              167
Introduction                                                       168
Aid and Financial Assistance                                       169
Multilateral Environmental Agreements                              169
The Environmental Impact of ODA                                    171
Debt-for-Nature Swaps                                              176
Payment for Ecosystem Services                                     179
Finance and Deforestation                                          183
The Nature of the Problem                                          183
Drivers of Deforestation                                           185
Global Forestry Governance                                         187
Deforestation and the Global Climate Regime                        189
REDD+                                                              191
Conclusion                                                         195
Discussion Questions                                               196

**9    Individualising Responsibility    *Unsustainable Consumption***  197
Summary of Key Points                                              197
Introduction                                                       198
Consumption and Its Environmental Impact                           199
Mobile Phones                                                      202
Fashion                                                            204
Sustainable Consumption: Intergovernmental Initiatives             206
Private Sector and Civil Society Initiatives: Individualising
Responsibility                                                     209
Voluntary Simplicity                                               210
Ecological Footprint                                               211
Carbon Neutrality                                                  213
Eco-labelling                                                      214
The Limits of Individualising Responsibility                       215
Over-stating Consumer Sovereignty                                  216
'Greenwash'                                                        217
Attitude–Behaviour Gap                                             218
Depoliticising Unsustainability                                    219

Defending Individual Responsibility                                         220
Conclusion                                                                  222
Discussion Questions                                                        223

**10  Problem Displacement**   *Hazardous Substances*                       224
Summary of Key Points                                                       224
Introduction                                                                225
Toxic Elements                                                              226
  Mercury                                                         228
  Lead                                                            229
  Cadmium                                                         231
  Dioxins and Dioxin-like Substances                             232
Global Governance of Chemicals and Hazardous Waste                         233
  Fragmented Global Chemical Governance: Overlaps and Gaps        240
Displacing the Problem                                                      242
  The *Khian Sea*                                                 243
  Environmental Injustice                                         244
  Understanding Environmental Injustice                           245
  The Basel Convention: Weaknesses and Limitations               248
  E-waste Dumping or Much Needed Trade?                           251
Conclusion                                                                  253
Discussion Questions                                                        254

**11  Resistance and Localisation**   *Unsustainable Agriculture*           256
Summary of Key Points                                                       256
Introduction                                                                257
Social Movements and Resistance                                            258
Globalisation and the Environment                                          260
Agriculture and the Environment                                            261
  The Rise of Modern Agriculture                                  262
  The Relationship Between the Environment and Agriculture        267
Resisting Unsustainable Agriculture                                         272
  Demanding Sustainable Agriculture                               273
  Practising Sustainable Agriculture                              275
  Brazil and the Landless Rural Workers Movement                  276
  Campesino a Campesino, Central America                          277
  Cuba and Organic Agriculture                                    278
  Questioning Agroecology                                         279
Conclusion                                                                  280
Discussion Questions                                                        281

**12  Appraising Global Environmental Governance**                282
   Summary of Key Points                                          282
   Introduction                                                   282
   The Nature of Environmental Problems                           283
   Evaluating Policy and Practice                                 286
   Distributing Environmental Harm                                290
      Temporal Inequality                                         290
      Social Inequality                                           290
      Geographic Inequality                                       292
   Towards Effective and Equitable Governance                     292
   Discussion Questions                                           293

   Glossary                                                       295
   References                                                     313
   Index                                                          343

# List of Figures

| | | |
|---|---|---|
| 1.1 | Socio-economic trends from 1750 to 2010 | *page* 4 |
| 1.2 | Earth system trends from 1750 to 2010 | 5 |
| 3.1 | World population growth rates, 1950–2050 | 42 |
| 3.2 | World population, 1950–2050 | 43 |
| 3.3 | The Environmental Kuznets Curve | 48 |
| 3.4 | Relationship between environmental problems and wealth: The N-shaped curve | 51 |
| 3.5 | Alternative depiction of the relationship between environmental problems and wealth | 52 |
| 4.1 | Planetary boundaries | 66 |
| 4.2 | Waste generation by economic activity and households, EU-28 | 69 |
| 5.1 | Different relationships between rivers and state borders | 96 |
| 5.2 | The Basins at Risk (BAR) Scale | 97 |
| 5.3 | Pattern of interactions over water | 98 |
| 7.1 | The governance triangle | 144 |
| 8.1 | Growth of environmental aid, 1980–99 | 170 |
| 8.2 | Falling ratio of dirty aid to environmental aid, 1980–99 | 172 |
| 8.3 | Comparing 'green' aid and 'brown' aid | 174 |
| 8.4 | Top recipients of environmental aid | 175 |
| 8.5 | The process of debt-for-nature swaps | 177 |
| 8.6 | Declining rate of tropical deforestation | 184 |
| 9.1 | Mobile phone replacement cycle (in months) | 203 |
| 10.1 | Fragmented governance of hazardous substances | 241 |
| 11.1 | Elements of agricultural biodiversity | 270 |

# List of Tables

6.1   Evaluating Progress on Agenda 21: 1992–2012      *page* 131

10.1   Chemicals and Chemical Compounds Controlled by the Main Multilateral Agreements      236

# List of Maps

3.1  By 2050, nine countries will be home to 50 per cent of the
     world's population                                      *page* 44
3.2  Protecting environment vs. Economic growth                    54
3.3  Protecting environment vs. Economic growth                    55
5.1  Transnational river basins                                    90
5.2  The Jordan River Basin                                        94

# List of Boxes

| | | |
|---|---|---|
| 6.1 | The Rio Declaration on Environment and Development | *page* 124 |
| 6.2 | Agenda 21 | 124 |
| 6.3 | Sustainable Development Goals | 136 |
| 7.1 | Climate Change Risks | 148 |
| 9.1 | Five Things You Can Do To Help | 212 |
| 9.2 | Ten Signs of Greenwash | 217 |
| 10.1 | Global Chemical Agreements | 234 |
| 11.1 | The Six Pillars of Food Sovereignty | 274 |
| 11.2 | Features of Agroecosystems | 276 |

# Preface

In the first few days of my PhD programme at the University of Adelaide, Australia, I stumbled across a public seminar organised by Friends of the Earth. The topic was 'climate refugees'. As I listened to the speakers I was filled with a growing sense of anger: anger at the injustice that those who had contributed least to the problem of climate change were facing its greatest impacts; and anger that I had gotten so far in my education while learning so little about environmental problems. At that moment I made a decision that would set off alarm bells for any PhD supervisor – I completely changed the topic of my research. I am grateful (and lucky) that my own supervisors allowed me to drop my research proposal on post-conflict peacebuilding and pick up the topic of global climate change governance, one I knew almost nothing about at that time!

One of the great luxuries of being a PhD student is the time to read, and read, and read some more. New worlds open up as one realises that the more one reads, the more there is to learn! I came to understand that climate change is implicated in so many other environmental issues, and that many environmental issues fail to get any attention at all as we increasingly focus on climate change. Several years later, as a new lecturer at the University of Sheffield, I had my first opportunity to design a course on global environmental politics. Having never studied such a course myself, I didn't have a model to follow. Instead I thought about how I would have liked to study this topic as a student. I would have liked to become familiar with classic contributions to the literature, including the insights of people whose names I'd heard, like Rachel Carson, Garrett Hardin, and Paul Ehrlich. I would have liked to develop an understanding of many different environmental problems, including those that don't always get a lot of media attention. And I would have liked to learn about what governments, citizens, and others are doing to address all these issues.

Once I'd identified these priorities I set out to find a textbook for my course. There are many books on climate change and environmental issues; some books on environmental politics; and a few books on international environmental politics. Some of these are excellent resources, and you will find recommendations and references to them scattered throughout this book. But I didn't find any book that ticked all my boxes. As I designed my course I created long bibliographies for my students from existing journal articles, book chapters, news material, reports, and videos. But there is a limit to the pre-seminar reading we can expect from even the most diligent student. What I needed – and couldn't find – was a single book that covered the most important details on each topic so that students could come to class adequately informed and ready to discuss, debate, apply new concepts, and build on their knowledge. What you have before you is the book I was looking for.

There are several ways to use this book. It is intended mainly for students enrolled in undergraduate and postgraduate university courses on Global Environmental Politics. Each chapter provides a topic that can be covered in one week of a semester-long course. It doesn't require existing knowledge about environmental sciences, economics, international relations, or political economy. It uses concepts from each of these disciplines but these are all clearly explained for the non-specialist reader. This book contains a glossary providing definitions of around 150 core terms and concepts used in the book. The glossary terms are also provided for reference as part of the online resources hosted at www.cambridge.org/stevenson.

If you're using this as a course book, it is best to read the chapters in the order that they are written. The three chapters in Part 1 cover different explanations for why environmental problems occur. The seven chapters in Part 2 then examine different approaches taken by the international community to respond to important contemporary environmental problems. Different responses are paired up with different problems in each chapter. This structure is designed to deepen the reader's understanding of a range of environmental problems, and to allow them to see how international political processes are applied in different contexts.

Each of the chapters in Part 2 would be fully coherent if read in isolation, or in an alternative order. But careful thought was given to the order of these chapters. Reading them in the existing order is the most effective way to appreciate how different political responses (like diplomacy, governance experiments, environmental aid, and problem displacement) relate to one another. Reading the chapters in this order will also develop your cumulative knowledge about how environmental problems emerge from or exacerbate other problems.

Key points appear at the start of each chapter, and suggested discussion questions conclude each chapter. In the online resources you will find lists of recommended reading on each topic, as well as links to specially selected videos that provide additional case studies, interviews with experts and practitioners, and other empirical material.

The book is certainly not suitable only for university students. If you're picking up this book because you're concerned about environmental issues, then it will help you to develop your awareness of why environmental problems occur, and deepen your understanding of the political action that is taking place. If you're working through the book on your own, the discussion questions at the end of each chapter will guide your independent reflections and perhaps stimulate future research projects.

As you make your way through this book you'll uncover some grim circumstances. By helping you to understand these problems I do not wish to only fill your minds with information and knowledge. I also wish to inspire a range of emotions: *indignation* and *anger* to drive you to raise awareness and push for more fair and effective political action; and *hope* to spark your creativity in finding ways to make our societies more sustainable and just. Ignorance may at times be bliss, but this doesn't mean that insight must be misery. Each of us has our own role to play in improving our planetary predicament. I hope this book helps you to identify your own role, however small and humble. There's a lot to do, and the world is waiting for you.

Hayley Stevenson
*Sheffield, United Kingdom, December 2016*

# List of Abbreviations

| | |
|---|---|
| 1OYFP | Ten-year framework of programmes on sustainable consumption and production |
| APP | Asia-Pacific Partnership on Clean Development and Climate |
| AUC | Autodefensas Unidas de Colombia (United Self-Defense of Colombia) |
| BAN | Basel Action Network |
| BAR | Basins at Risk |
| BRICS | Brazil, Russia, India, China, and South Africa |
| CBDR | Common but differentiated responsibilities and respective capabilities |
| CDM | Clean Development Mechanism |
| CDP | Carbon Disclosure Project |
| CFCs | Chlorofluorocarbon compounds |
| $CO_2$ | Carbon dioxide |
| CSD | Commission on Sustainable Development |
| DDT | Dichlorodiphenyltrichloroethane |
| ECOSOC | Economic and Social Council |
| EKC | Environmental Kuznets Curve |
| ELN | Ejército de Liberación Nacional, Colombia (National Liberation Army) |
| EU | European Union |
| EZLN | Ejército Zapatista de Liberación Nacional, Mexico (Zapatista Army of National Liberation) |
| FAO | Food and Agricultural Organization |
| FARC | Fuerzas Armadas Revolucionarias de Colombia (Revolutionary Armed Forces of Colombia) |
| FSC | Forest Stewardship Council |
| GCF | Green Climate Fund |
| GDP | Gross Domestic Product |
| GEF | Global Environment Facility |
| GHG | Greenhouse gas emissions |
| GM | Genetic engineering or manipulation |

| | |
|---|---|
| IFF | Intergovernmental Forum on Forests |
| IMF | International Monetary Fund |
| IO | International organisation |
| IPCC | Intergovernmental Panel on Climate Change |
| IPEN | International POPS Elimination Network |
| IPF | Intergovernmental Panel on Forests |
| ITTO | International Tropical Timber Organization |
| IUCN | International Union for Conservation of Nature |
| JUSCANZ | Japan, the United States, Canada, Australia, and New Zealand |
| LDC | Least developed country |
| MEA | Multilateral environmental agreement |
| MST | Movimento dos Trabalhadores Rurais Sem Terra (Landless Rural Workers Movement, Brazil) |
| NAFTA | North American Free Trade Agreement |
| NATO | North Atlantic Treaty Organization |
| NAZCA | Non-State Actor Zone for Climate Action |
| NGOs | Non-governmental organisations |
| NIMBY | Not In My Back Yard |
| $NO_x$ | Nitrogen dioxide and nitric oxide |
| ODA | Official development assistance |
| OECD | Organization for Economic Cooperation and Development |
| OPEC | Organization of the Petroleum Exporting Countries |
| PCBs | Polychlorinated biphenyls |
| PCDDs | Polychlorinated dibenzodioxins |
| PDCFs | Polychlorinated dibenzofurans |
| PES | Payments for ecosystem services |
| PIC | Prior Informed Consent |
| PLAID | Project-Level Aid |
| POPs | Persistent organic pollutants |
| PPM | Parts per million |
| PVC | Polyvinyl chloride |
| REDD+ | Reducing greenhouse gas Emissions from Deforestation and forest Degradation, forest stock conservation, sustainable forest management, and the enhancement of forest stock. |
| RIO+20 | UN Conference on Sustainable Development (UNCSD) |
| SAICM | Strategic Approach to International Chemicals Management |
| SCP | Sustainable consumption and production |

| | |
|---|---|
| SDGs | Sustainable Development Goals |
| $SO_2$ | Sulphur dioxide |
| TEEB | The Economics of Ecosystems and Biodiversity |
| UN | United Nations |
| UNCBD | United Nations Convention on Biological Diversity |
| UNCCD | United Nations Convention to Combat Desertification |
| UNCED | United Nations Conference on Environment and Development |
| UNCTAD | United Nations Commission on Trade and Development |
| UN DESA | United Nations Department of Economic and Social Affairs |
| UNDP | United Nations Development Programme |
| UNEP | United Nations Environment Programme |
| UNESCO | United Nations Educational, Scientific and Cultural Organization |
| UNFCCC | United Nations Framework Convention on Climate Change |
| US | United States of America |
| USAID | United States Agency for International Development |
| VCS | Verified Carbon Standard |
| WAVES | Wealth Accounting and the Valuation of Ecosystem Services |
| WHO | World Health Organization |
| WSSD | World Summit on Sustainable Development |
| WTO | World Trade Organization |
| WWF | World Wildlife Fund |

# 1 Global Politics and the Environment

**key points**

- Scientists say that an epochal shift took place in the mid-twentieth century. We are no longer in the Holocene, but rather the Anthropocene.
- Local, regional, and international policies have been put into place to address environmental problems but the scale and ambition of action rarely matches the scale of the problems.
- Capturing and holding public attention remains a big challenge for those concerned about environmental change and its impact on people.
- Environmental problems are complex political problems without straightforward solutions. People disagree on the nature of problems; their seriousness and priority; who should take responsibility; and what kind of action is appropriate.
- Many actors play a role in political processes aiming to improve environmental conditions; the main ones are states, scientists, civil society, and business.

# Introduction

'Breathing in poison'

'More plastic than fish in oceans by 2050'

'The climate refugees of the Arctic'

'How humans are driving the sixth mass extinction'

'Deforestation may threaten majority of Amazon tree species'

'August ties July for hottest month on record'[1]

It is surely a defining characteristic of our times that headlines such as these have become commonplace in the media. Perhaps they no longer even shock most readers. The fact that you have picked up this book is a good indicator that this kind of news concerns you. But if you do find yourself rather unalarmed by those headlines, think for a moment of how your father or grandmother may have reacted if they were reading the same news at your age (here's a hint: plastic only really entered consumer markets after World War Two). Today many of us could recite a long list of problems that ail the earth: climate change, species extinction, deforestation, air and water pollution, resource depletion, etcetera. But what drives these problems? What are their **underlying causes**? What are governments, the United Nations, corporations, and individuals doing to ameliorate these problems? Are their actions making any difference? The aim of this book is to take you behind the headlines of environmental news stories and find answers to these questions.

We begin this chapter by taking a look at the current state of the planet. Human activity has had such a massive impact on the environment that scientists now say that we have provoked an epochal shift: the planet is no longer in the Holocene but the **Anthropocene**, the era of the human. We will look at the socio-economic trends and earth system trends that underpin this claim. We then consider the ways in which global environmental issues are *political* issues, and what this means for our capacity to resolve problems like **climate change**, **deforestation**, and **hazardous waste**. Various actors are involved in the political processes that aim to improve environmental conditions (states, scientists, **civil society**, and business), and we briefly review the roles they play. Finally, you'll find an outline of the book, including summaries of each chapter.

# State of the Planet

Humans are just one of the 8 million species that occupy the earth (UNEP 2011). But our collective impact on the planet has been far greater than any other species. On 29 August 2016, an expert committee of earth scientists travelled to the South African city of Cape Town to make an important announcement to the International Geological Congress. For the past seven years, they had been examining the case for naming a new epoch of geological time, an epoch marked by the impact of human activity. Are we still in the Holocene – an epoch that has endured for over eleven millennia – or have we entered the Anthropocene? Their finding was almost unanimous: the idea of the Anthropocene, first suggested in 2000, is 'geologically real' (University of Leicester 2016). We entered this 'era of the human' in 1950.

Humans have left many marks on the planet's 'stratigraphic record' over thousands of years, and together these have changed earth systems in long-lasting (and in some cases irreversible) ways. But it is the acceleration of human activity since 1950 that has had the most discernible impact: accelerated rates of erosion and sedimentation, chemical changes in the atmosphere (such as carbon cycles), changes in the global climate and sea levels, and unprecedented movement of species across the planet (University of Leicester 2016). A set of interlinked socio-economic and earth-systemic trends mark what scientists call the 'Great Acceleration' that began in 1950 (Steffen et al. 2015: 82). We can see some of these trends in Figures 1.1 and 1.2. On the socio-economic front, among the changes we see are significant increases in population, GDP, water and energy use, paper production, and international tourism. On the earth system front, among the changes we see are massive growth in emissions of carbon dioxide, methane, and nitrous oxide, **ocean acidification**, and marine life capture.

Some of these social and environmental changes are well known, others less so. The UN's environmental agency **UNEP** has been working hard to make citizens and policy-makers aware of these changes for some time. Every five years they release a Global Environment Outlook, providing an update on the state of the planet. And every five years the findings are grimmer. Although local, regional, and international policies have been put into place to address problems like climate change, **biodiversity** loss, and water scarcity, the scale and ambition of action never seems to match the scale of the problems. On most of the global environmental issues that UNEP reports on, we see continuous

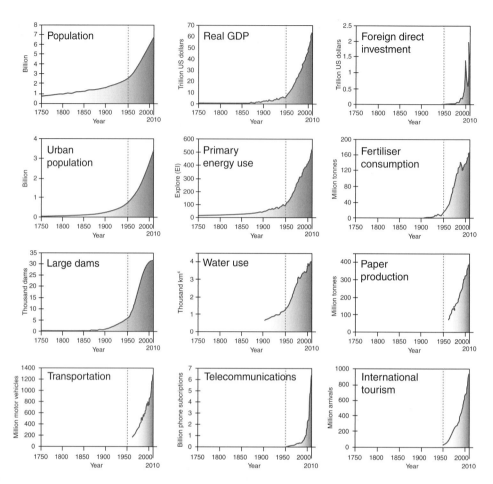

**Figure 1.1:** Socio-economic trends from 1750 to 2010
Source: Steffen et al. 2015: 84

decline. Some of these issues will be explored in depth in Part 2 of this book. But let's take a brief look here at some of the concerning trends:

- Urban living is damaging people's health: 98 per cent of cities in low- and middle-income countries have dangerous levels of air pollution. In high-income countries, the figure is 56 per cent. This makes city dwellers more vulnerable to stroke, heart disease, lung cancer, and respiratory problems like asthma (WHO 2016c). Risks are almost never equally distributed, and the poorest tend to suffer the most: they tend to live in the dirtiest neighbourhoods and spend a higher proportion of their time outdoors exposed to car fumes and fine particles in the air. This reflects 'environmental injustice' (Boyce and Shrivastava 2016).

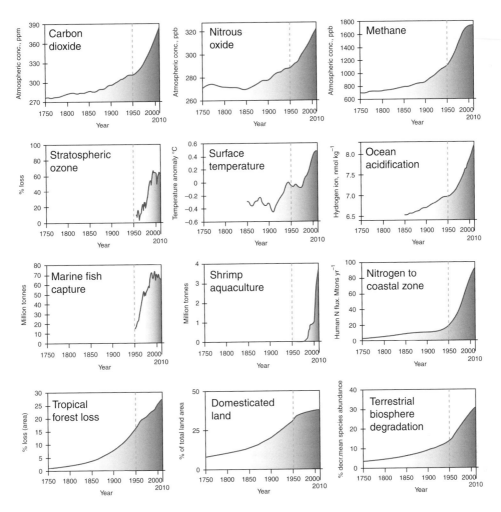

**Figure 1.2:** Earth system trends from 1750 to 2010
Source: Steffen et al. 2015: 87

- We are losing biodiversity at rapid rates: The WWF Living Planet Index monitors the population of 3,706 vertebrate species across the globe. Since 1970 numbers have declined by 58 per cent, primarily as a result of human activity and resource use. By 2020 they expect average declines of 67 per cent (WWF 2016: 12). This has knock-on effects for human wellbeing. Environmental scientist, Tim Newbold, explains that 'If ecosystem functions don't continue … it affects the ability of agriculture to sustain human populations and we simply don't know at which point that will be reached' (quoted in Vaughan 2016).
- Pressures on land undermine future productivity: growing populations and global markets lead to increased demands for food, fibre, fuel, and livestock

feed. These demands exceed the 'biophysical limits to productivity', which means the earth cannot replenish itself to continue meeting human demands (UNEP 2012b: 66). This leaves many people in a position of food insecurity, which will be worse for future generations. Although rates of deforestation are declining, annual forest loss is still extremely high at 13 million hectares in 2010 (UNEP 2012b: 72).

- Freshwater demands have tripled since the mid-twentieth century: many regions are already exceeding sustainable limits of water use from surface and groundwater. Developing countries are particularly vulnerable to water scarcity; some 80 per cent of the world's population live in areas that cannot provide adequate water for drinking, sanitation, and production – most of these people are in developing countries (UNEP 2012b: 128).
- Global chemical consumption is growing: the chemical industry contributes to economic growth and development, but chemical pollution has a damaging impact on human health and the environment. Hazardous waste is often mixed with municipal waste and then dumped or burned. Millions of people die each year from exposure to chemicals, and it has further impacts on land and water quality (UNEP 2012b: 168). Such disruptions to **ecosystems** have complex impacts that scientists don't fully understand.

Few may understand the complex causes and effects of environmental change and degradation, but there is now widespread recognition that environmental problems are serious. American planetary scientist David Grinspoon sees this awareness as the hallmark of the Anthropocene. Not only are humans changing the earth in far-reaching and irreversible ways – we are aware that we are doing so. 'Self-conscious global change' is what is completely new, according to Grinspoon (2016).

Surveys on public attitudes to the environment don't reveal neat trends of growing concern. Concern can wax and wane as other issues vie for public attention (e.g., terrorism and economic recession), as 'climate fatigue' sets in, and when popular media misrepresents scientific certainty (Capstick et al. 2015: 36). Concern tends to be highest in wealthy countries (Dalton and Rohrschneider 2015), but large numbers of citizens in developing countries show concern for environmental problems and climate change even if these don't rank as their highest priority (Smith 2013). This awareness is important, and is perhaps a reason to be optimistic. But capturing and holding public attention remains a big challenge for those concerned about environmental change and its impact on people. The concept of the Anthropocene packs a powerful punch – it is a concept with the potential to further raise awareness of our impact on the planet, why it matters, and what we might do about it. Climatologist Chris Rapley explains that by entering the Anthropocene we have effectively fiddled with the planet's machinery with no way of knowing what the effects will be:

Since the planet is our life support system – we are essentially the crew of a largish spaceship – interference with its functioning at this level and on this scale is highly significant. If you or I were crew on a smaller spacecraft, it would be unthinkable to interfere with the systems that provide us with air, water, fodder and climate control. But the shift into the Anthropocene tells us that we are playing with fire, a potentially reckless mode of behaviour which we are likely to come to regret unless we get a grip on the situation.

(Rapley quoted in Carrington 2016a)

But how precisely do we 'get a grip on the situation'? What will it take to seriously address our environmental predicament? Are there solutions? Or does action just generate more problems of its own? Who needs to take this action? Which actors have the authority or capacity to do so? Can we be optimistic that those actors *will* take responsibility? Should existing political action give us confidence? These are some of the questions we will explore in this book.

## The Politics of Environmental Change

The issues that we look at in this book don't have any single technical solutions. Images of protesters demanding environmental action frequently show placards with slogans such as 'Take Action', 'Climate Action Now!', or perhaps the slightly more precise 'Cut Carbon Pollution'. Such public demands are important. Sometimes these events raise public awareness and apply pressure on government. But let's say that suddenly every citizen and politician agreed that climate change is important and action needs to be taken. Could we be confident that the problem of climate change would be solved? The answer is no, because climate change – just like every other environmental issue we examine in this book – is a *political* problem. There is no solution because people disagree on the nature of the problem; its seriousness and priority compared to other problems; the division of responsibility for taking action; and the type of action that would be appropriate to take. This doesn't mean that action is not possible. But it does mean that we should be attentive to the ways in which an issue is defined as a problem, which aspects are emphasised or overlooked, who or what is identified as the cause, what kinds of actions are considered (or overlooked) and agreed upon, and how the costs and benefits are distributed when action is taken. Disagreement or conflict is often prominent at each of these stages. We would probably see elements of disagreement if we brought together the neighbours on our street to resolve a common concern. The potential for disagreement and the difficulty of resolving disagreements are amplified at the global level where there are many affected parties, and where authority, power, and capacity are diffuse.

The subtitle of this book is *Problems, Policy, and Practice*. It is an unfortunate reality of global environmental politics that these three elements are rarely aligned. The health of the planet would undoubtedly be in better shape if it were possible to identify a problem, decide on a plan of action, and then change our practices accordingly. But what in fact often happens is that environmental change and degradation occur for a long time before political actors treat it as a serious problem; plans of action to control, reduce, eliminate, or adapt to the problem are generally too weak or unambitious to achieve their intended aims; and policies often fail to change behaviour because their implementation is partial, delayed, or even abandoned.

Various actors contribute to global environmental politics. Let's take a look at the types of actors that we will see throughout this book.

- *States*: The main actor in international relations remains the state. No other actor has the same authority to pass and enforce laws, and to create international law in collaboration with other states. States often delegate power to international organisations like the UN to facilitate cooperation and implement multilateral agreements. These organisations may allow non-state actors to participate in certain ways, but states are the primary members of these organisations. As we saw above, in debates about environmental problems actors often disagree about the nature and seriousness of a problem; about who should take action; and about what sort of action they should take. States have established diplomatic processes to try to work through these disagreements. Diplomatic outcomes may not reflect shared understandings but rather compromises. Diplomats like to quote Henry Kissinger in claiming that the best outcome of an international negotiation is one in which all parties are equally unhappy! This is because they have all had to concede more than initially intended, or take on more responsibility than they initially intended. Disagreements in international negotiations often appear along North–South lines. These terms refer very broadly to developed and developing countries (all such terms have their problems and limitations but they are still often analytically useful). The environmental concerns and priorities of developing countries are often very different to those of developed countries. Moreover, developing countries are more limited in the capacity to resolve or adapt to environmental change. For some issues, like climate change, the most vulnerable are often those who have contributed least to the problem.

- *Scientists*: Sometimes we hear the argument that science and politics should be kept separate. But in practice the two intersect more than we might hope. Scientific research is not a value-free endeavour. The issues that scientists choose to study, or the issues that funding bodies choose to prioritise, all push research in certain directions. Many scientists carry out their studies of environmental change without social or political objectives in mind. But some scientists are so concerned by their evidence that they undertake awareness raising and advocacy. This is when scientists most clearly become political actors. Academics refer to such scientists as 'knowledge brokers' or 'epistemic communities' who aim to translate scientific knowledge into public and policy-making circles, and to push for particular action. When scientists shift from saying 'evidence shows that X is occurring' to 'we must do Y', they are taking on a political role. Governments often try to exert some control over the way scientific evidence is translated into policy recommendations. For example, the Intergovernmental Panel on Climate Change (IPCC, which reviews and summarises climate science) is comprised of government-nominated and -approved scientists, although the scientists work independently once appointed. The International Union for Conservation of Nature (IUCN) is a non-governmental organisation (NGO) but it was created by governments to develop understanding of nature conservation and promote international cooperation.

- *Civil society*: non-governmental organisations, social movements, and community groups often play a key role in drawing the public's attention to environmental issues, and in mounting campaigns to push for collective action. In multilateral negotiations, the United Nations organises civil society into nine '**major groups**', which are intended to reflect all sectors of society: women, children and youth, indigenous peoples, non-governmental organisations, local authorities, workers and trade unions, business and industry, scientific and research organisations, and farmers. There are often overlaps in affiliation, but this provides a way for the UN to manage and coordinate the involvement of non-state actors in multilateral diplomacy. Stanley W. Burgiel and Peter Wood, two long-term observers of multilateral environmental negotiations, identify three roles that NGOs play: *witnesses* (monitoring and documenting progress); *architects* (influencing policy frameworks and promoting certain ideas and issues); and *detractors* (critiquing processes and questioning their legitimacy, and shaming countries to change their positions) (Burgiel and Wood 2012: 128–9). Civil society also plays an active role outside multilateral settings by helping citizens and the private sector to become more sustainable (e.g., establishing reporting and monitoring systems for businesses to reduce greenhouse gas emissions (GHG), and creating tools for people to measure their personal 'ecological footprint').

- *Business*: Businesses are involved in global environmental politics in several different ways. For some, the profit and growth motives that drive business in a capitalist system are the main source of environmental degradation. This puts many businesses in a defensive position: lobbying to water down environmental regulations and obstruct international environmental negotiations. Some types of business see themselves as vulnerable to global environmental change, or see opportunities to profit from sustainable development policies. These sectors often lobby governments to take more ambitious action. The insurance and renewable energy sectors are key examples in the area of climate change. An additional trend is for business actors to voluntarily create their own forms of environmental governance, sometimes with other businesses, and sometimes in cooperation with civil society or states. This trend has been growing since the mid-2000s, and is especially prominent in climate change. For example, we see business-initiated schemes for measuring and reporting greenhouse gas emissions, as well as schemes for offsetting greenhouse gas emissions through investments in renewable energy or energy efficiency in developing countries.

## Outline of this Book

This book is organised into two parts. Part 1 develops your understanding of why environmental problems occur. Part 2 then examines different approaches taken by the international community to respond to important contemporary environmental problems.

## Part 1: Why Do Environmental Problems Occur?

Imagine you're sitting on a bus on the way to your first seminar on global environmental politics. An inquisitive lady beside you asks about your studies, and then poses a deceptively simple question: 'Why do we have so many environmental problems?' What would your answer be? Perhaps you are already committed to a specific understanding about why environmental degradation occurs. Or perhaps you haven't questioned this too deeply but have some readily available assumptions that you can draw on to respond to our hypothetical passenger: there are too many people; people are too selfish; we consume too much 'stuff'; corporations are exploiting people and the environment; we don't have the right markets in place to value nature. Whatever your existing assumptions may be, the aim of Part 1 is to expose you to different explanations. This may help to sharpen and reinforce your existing position, or it may help you to develop new and nuanced explanations for why environmental problems occur.

The chapters in Part 1 (Chapters 2–4) introduce you to the work of some of the most influential environmental thinkers of the nineteenth and twentieth centuries. Of course we can't encounter all of those philosophers, economists, ecologists, and political theorists who shaped contemporary environmental thought. But you will be introduced to the work of many key scholars, including Karl Marx, Thomas Malthus, Garrett Hardin, Elinor Ostrom, Paul and Anne Ehrlich, and James O'Connor. Through their work we will examine arguments that environmental degradation occurs because of weak **governance** and management ('**tragedy of the commons**'), over-population, poverty and under-development, capitalism, affluence, and economic growth. Each argument has its strengths and weaknesses, and understanding these will equip you to develop your own well-reasoned explanation for environmental degradation.

Developing an argument about why environmental degradation occurs usually also entails sketching out a solution. So Part 1 will also briefly introduce you to arguments that have been advanced over time for solving environmental problems. These include privatisation and marketisation, population control, collective action institutions, poverty reduction and development, and eco-socialism.

## Part 1: Chapter Outlines

Chapter 2 examines Garrett Hardin's influential 1968 essay on the 'tragedy of the commons'. Hardin saw the combination of human freedoms and freely available resources as inevitably destructive. Three assumptions underpinned his position: that humans are self-regarding and short-sighted; that 'the commons' are unmanaged and freely accessible; and that privatisation and socialism are the only solutions to avoid degradation. Many share these assumptions, but many others – most prominently Elinor Ostrom – have critiqued them. We will examine the counter-evidence that decentralised, citizen-controlled governance can produce more environmentally effective and socially just outcomes than privatisation and centralised regulation. This chapter concludes by reflecting on how the insights of 'commons' research can help us to understand contemporary global environmental problems.

Chapter 3 turns to the question of whether over-population and poverty are the main drivers of environmental degradation. Concerns about the earth's capacity to support an ever growing number of people have been around for centuries. Thomas Malthus pondered the problems of procreation in the eighteenth century, and his ideas found a welcome audience in the 1960s when the popular movement of environmentalism emerged. But others critique this focus on *numbers* of people. They insist that the *conditions* in which people live have a greater impact on the environment. We examine this position and consider whether bringing countries out of poverty reduces their impact on the environment.

Chapter 4 examines whether environmental degradation is an inevitable consequence of capitalism. Although Karl Marx himself probably wouldn't have identified as an environmentalist, Marxist theory contains several concepts and insights that help to understand ecological crises. Contemporary ecological Marxists argue that capitalism suffers from an inherent **ecological contradiction**: the earth is a closed system that cannot support infinite growth, but capitalism cannot survive without continual growth. In addition, capitalism alienates people from nature by reducing them to labourers and consumers, and by undermining their natural cooperative tendencies. We examine these and other arguments advanced by eco-socialists and reflect on the social and ecological merits of non-capitalist forms of society.

## Part 2: Responding to Global Environmental Problems

In Part 2 we examine different solutions in greater depth and focus. In these chapters (Chapters 5–11) we explore the diverse approaches the international community has taken in response to important environmental problems. Each chapter focuses on a different environmental problem and a different response. Pairing up problems and responses in this way will deepen your understanding of several environmental issues, as well as the diversity of approaches that are taken with the aim of resolving environmental problems. This also allows you to see very clearly how international political processes are applied in different contexts. For example, rather than learning about the micro-processes involved in multilateral negotiations in a purely theoretical or abstract way, you will see how states engage in negotiations on a particular issue (sustainable development). By deepening your understanding of different problems and existing responses, you will develop the capacity to question whether there are alternative or additional ways that states, international organisations, citizens, and/or business can respond to problems at global, national, and local levels.

## Part 2: Chapter Outlines

Chapter 5 examines the 'common wisdom' that resource scarcity inevitably (or at least very likely) leads to **conflict**. Conflict is a very broad concept. It looks very different depending on the actors involved, the measures they take, and the intensity of actions. But when politicians and pundits talk about natural resource scarcity, they usually have the risk of violent conflict or even war in mind. In this chapter we look at whether evidence supports the claim that resource scarcity drives violent conflict. 'Water wars' have attracted more attention than most resource-based conflicts, and the case of freshwater scarcity provides the focus of Chapter 5. We scrutinise the rhetoric and reality of 'water wars'. Although it turns out that cooperation over water is far more prevalent than conflict, we see that cooperation doesn't necessarily deliver fair and effective outcomes for everyone involved.

Chapter 6 deepens our exploration of international cooperation by examining how states have built multilateral institutions for reducing transnational pollution and conserving the environment. Environmental multilateralism emerged in the mid-twentieth century and by the end of the century states had negotiated hundreds of multilateral environmental agreements (MEAs). In Chapter 6 we examine the political and legal status of these agreements, and the divisions between the global **North** and global **South** that have emerged during negotiations. The case we focus on in this chapter is **sustainable development**, which has been a central concern on the global environmental agenda since the late 1980s. Over several decades states have gathered in global summits to establish principles, set goals, pledge action, and review progress on sustainable development. We will see a pervasive mismatch between promises and performance, and reflect on the future potential for multilateral efforts to deliver fair and sustainable outcomes.

Chapter 7 takes account of the increasing **fragmentation** of global environmental governance. In recent decades **non-state actors** (businesses, NGOs, philanthropic foundations, community groups) and sub-national actors (provincial governments and city councils) have challenged the supreme authority of the state. Dwindling confidence in national governments' capacity and political will to address global environmental problems has pushed these other actors to establish alternative governance mechanisms and processes. Sometimes these are complementary; other times they are competitive. Multilateral UN processes are now just one part of global environmental governance. The global regime for climate change is particularly fragmented, and this issue provides the focus of Chapter 7. There are now hundreds of climate **governance 'experiments'**, including **carbon markets, emissions trading** schemes, information-sharing networks, and voluntary GHG reduction programmes. We will look at the different types of governance experiments and their dominant characteristics, and reflect on the virtues and limitations of this approach to addressing climate change.

Chapter 8 examines how governmental aid and financial support have been used to prevent environmental degradation and facilitate international cooperation on environmental problems. Financial promises have been central to efforts to diffuse the tensions that frequently emerge between the global North and global South in multilateral environmental negotiations. In this chapter we will examine different forms of environmental finance, including bilateral and multilateral environmental aid, and innovative and experimental forms of financial assistance, including **'debt-for-nature swaps'** and **'payments for ecosystem services'**. Deforestation is the primary focus of this chapter. This is an issue that reveals many of the tensions that exist between wealthy and developing countries, including differences in capacity and national priorities. We will examine the various drivers of deforestation before looking at the institutions and financial mechanisms that have been designed as part of efforts to reduce deforestation.

Chapter 9 explores the issue of unsustainable consumption. Multilateral institutions have largely failed to address the impact of modern lifestyles on the environment. Although the UN has a sustainable consumption agenda, there has been no serious and sustained attempt to promote changes in individual consumption patterns. Instead it has become quite common to 'individualise responsibility' for unsustainability. In Chapter 9 we will look at the environmental impact of high-volume **luxury consumption,** by focusing on two popular goods: mobile phones and fashion. We will look at the voluntary initiatives that the private sector and civil society groups have established to encourage people to change their consumption habits. Not everyone agrees that focusing on individual responsibility and change is appropriate or effective for addressing problems like over-consumption. We will examine the arguments that support a focus on the individual, as well as the problems and limitations of such an approach.

Chapter 10 examines a particularly insidious response to environmental problems that we see play out at the international level. It is called 'problem displacement' whereby privileged groups enjoy the material benefits of modernity while casting the negative consequences onto less privileged groups. This is a form of shifting responsibility for resolving an environmental problem that has arisen during industrial development. The issue we focus on in Chapter 10 is hazardous substances (chemicals, metals, and toxic wastes). We look at the central role chemicals and metals play in modern production and industrial development, and the impacts they have on environmental and human health. The international community has tried to control the production, use, and export of hazardous substances through multilateral agreements and public-private initiatives. But the limited success of these efforts has resulted in international export of hazardous wastes. We will reflect on whether this is a case of environmental injustice (as critics claim), or a legitimate form of international trade that supports development in the global South (as others claim).

Chapter 11 focuses on the efforts of social movements to bring about progressive change in the face of environmental degradation and social injustice. Through processes of resistance, social movements have rejected the assumption that environmental protection is compatible with existing systems of international trade, capitalist accumulation, and economic growth. In this chapter we examine how protest and alternative practices have been used to promote fairer and more sustainable forms of agriculture. We chart the rise of the modern industrialised agricultural system, and unpack the relationship between environmental change and modern agriculture. We then look at alternative practices of sustainable agriculture based on agroecology and the localisation of food production and trade, and reflect on whether these are viable ways of meeting our food needs in the twenty-first century.

Chapter 12 concludes the book with a reflection on two of its recurring themes: effectiveness of responses, and the distribution of environmental harm. This chapter summarises the strengths and weaknesses of the responses that have been explored in the book, and draws conclusions about their potential for resolving the most serious environmental problems of contemporary times.

In this chapter we also reflect on the ways in which the costs of environmental harm are inequitably distributed in temporal, social, and geographic terms. Finally, we will consider the prospects for more effective and equitable responses to global environmental problems in the future.

## Discussion Questions

1. What does the 'Anthropocene' refer to, and what global changes reflect this planetary shift?
2. Which environmental problems do you find most concerning? Why?
3. What do you assume are the main reasons for environmental change and degradation?
4. What do you think are the greatest obstacles to international environmental cooperation?
5. What factors do you expect would make effective and fair environmental cooperation possible at the international level?

## Note

1. References in respective order: Toppa 2016; Kotasova 2016; *The New York Times* 2016; Hance 2015; St. Fleur 2015; and Workman 2016.

# PART 1

## Why Do Environmental Problems Occur?

# 2    The Tragedy of the Commons

**key points**

- Garrett Hardin's 1968 essay 'The Tragedy of the Commons' has shaped popular and political assumptions about how to manage shared natural resources.
- Hardin argued that resources must be controlled by markets or states to avoid degradation.
- Some critics argue that Hardin's work is historically inaccurate, unduly pessimistic, and simplistic and narrow-minded in its prescriptions.
- Cooperative management schemes have enjoyed some success at the local level, but it remains unclear if this approach can be scaled up to the global level.
- The absence of a global government doesn't make degradation of global commons inevitable; it is difficult but possible to establish institutions and mechanisms for regulating access to global commons.

## Introduction

In 1968, American ecologist Garrett Hardin penned a short lecture that would come to have a profound impact on environmental debates for decades to come. Titled 'The Tragedy of the Commons', Hardin's lecture outlined a simple (some say simplistic) parable of environmental degradation under conditions of human freedom:

Picture a pasture open to all. It is to be expected that each herdsman will try to keep as many cattle as possible on the commons … As a rational being, each herdsman seeks to maximize his gain. Explicitly or implicitly … he asks, 'What is the utility to me of adding one more animal to my herd?'

The herdsman in Hardin's parable knows that if he adds one more animal to his herd, he will receive all the profits from the sale of this animal. He also reasons that the additional grazing by just one additional animal would have an insignificant impact on the pasture. As a result, Hardin continues:

the rational herdsman concludes that the only sensible course for him to pursue is to add another animal to his herd. And another; and another … But this is the conclusion reached by each and every rational herdsman sharing a commons. Therein is the tragedy. Each man is locked into a system that compels him to increase his herd without limit – in a world that is limited. Ruin is the destination toward which all men rush, each pursuing his own best interest in a society that believes in the freedom of the commons. Freedom in a commons brings ruin to all.

(Hardin 1968)

The tragedy of this situation lay in its unhappy inevitability: so long as human freedom was respected, and land and natural resources were freely available for anyone to use, they would slowly but inevitably be destroyed. The earth's 'carrying capacity' would be eroded (Hardin 1968). In the short term, the benefits of adding additional cattle would accrue to the individual herdsmen, but in the long term the depleted common resource would benefit no one. The situation is exacerbated by population growth because the more people there are, the more users there are. In remote and sparsely populated areas it may not matter if the commons were 'used as a cesspool' or if wildlife or resources were lavishly consumed because there are few people to share with and plenty to go around (Hardin 1968: 1245).

Hardin was not the first person to make this argument: he simply resurrected, extended, and popularised an observation made over a century before by the English economist, William Forster Lloyd. Lloyd observed that common land was 'bare-worn' and over-cropped, with 'puny' and 'stunted' cattle, while on enclosed land (namely, land with recognised property rights) the natural limits or 'point of saturation' was prudently respected (1832: 30–1).

Hardin intended to shine a light on a topic he was greatly concerned about: population growth. But this was not the main impact of his lecture. Concerns about the environmental impact of over-population certainly began to grow during the latter half of the twentieth century. But since its publication in

*Science* magazine (Hardin 1968), Hardin's lecture has had a much greater impact on our understanding of how we can and should *manage* environmental degradation. This is perhaps because the parable that Hardin so memorably described focused not on population but on the degradation of land and natural resources that results from weak governance or management. Hardin had several modern commons in mind: rivers, parklands, oceans, and air. He presented us with just two options for avoiding and mitigating the further degradation of these commons. We could bring natural resources under the control of either market forces (privatisation) or the state (socialisation). Both of these regimes could provide the necessary enforceable limits on people's access to natural resources.

Hardin's short, six-page article was really more a reflective essay than a scientific article, which makes its impact particularly surprising. Its arguments have been cited – often uncritically – by students and scholars across environmental studies, resources science, economics, ecology, and political science. Throughout the 1960s and 1970s, Hardin's warnings were heeded by governments and international organisations, whose policy innovations are still widely felt (Dietz et al. 2009a: 10–11). As George Monbiot explains,

For ... the World Bank and Western governments it provided a rational basis for the widespread privatization of land. In Africa, among newly-independent governments ... it encouraged the massive transfer of land from tribal peoples to the state or to individuals. In Africa, Asia, Europe and the Americas, developers hurried to remove land from commoners and give it to people they felt could manage it.

(1994)

Given the legacy of Hardin's lecture, in this chapter we review the governance aspects of 'the tragedy of the commons', and save our discussion of population for Chapter 3. First we examine three key assumptions that underpin Hardin's parable, namely, that humans are self-regarding and short-sighted; that 'the commons' are unmanaged and freely accessible; and that privatisation and socialism are the only solutions to avoid degradation. We then consider a set of critiques and counter-arguments that have been directed at Hardin over the years, including the suggestion that his parable is historically inaccurate, unduly pessimistic, and simplistic and narrow-minded in its prescriptions. Based on this reading of Hardin's arguments and its critiques, we then explore how the insights of '**commons**' research can help us to understand contemporary global environmental problems.

# Core Assumptions Underpinning the 'Tragedy'

Three key assumptions underpin the argument that environmental degradation results from weak management and the lack of enforceable limits on access to natural resources. Social scientists have questioned each of these assumptions, and we will examine their counter-arguments in the next section. First let's look at the three assumptions.

## Human Beings are Self-regarding and Short-sighted

In Hardin's parable, tragedy is inevitable because individual herdsmen are primarily motivated to maximise their own short-term profits without regard for the long-term effects this imposes on either the wider community or their own future livelihood. Any future costs will be shared, while the present gains can be enjoyed alone. This assessment of human nature dates back at least as far as Thucydides and Aristotle. Thucydides lamented that people 'devote a very small fraction of time to the consideration of any public object, most of it to the prosecution of their own objects. Meanwhile each fancies that no harm will come to his neglect, that it is the business of somebody else to look after this or that for him; and so . . . the common cause imperceptibly decays' (c. 460 BC, quoted in Lipp 2001: 92). Economists and philosophers have echoed this sentiment ever since. Aristotle argued that 'what is common to the greatest number has the least care bestowed upon it. Everyone thinks chiefly of his own, hardly at all of the common interest' (350 BC) (Aristotle, *Politics*, Book II, chapter 3). Austrian economist and champion of private property, Ludwig von Mises, later warned that 'If land is not owned by anybody . . . it is used without any regard to the disadvantages resulting. Those who are in a position to appropriate to themselves the returns – lumber and game of the forests, fish of the water areas, and mineral deposits of the subsoil – do not bother about the later effects of their mode of exploitation' (1949: 652).

## 'The Commons' are Unmanaged and Freely Accessible

The term 'commons' is widely used to refer to resources that are not exclusively owned: resources that are freely available for humans to use. Think of air, rivers, oceans, and land that is either collectively owned or set aside for public use. Scientists and scholars generally refer to these as **'common pool resources'**, and they highlight two key characteristics that these resources share. The first is *excludability*, which means that it is difficult or costly to control access to the resource: it is difficult to exclude any potential users or even limit their access. Migratory species of birds and other wildlife are characterised in this way, as are the atmosphere, freshwater, and large tracts of forest or land. The second characteristic is *subtractability*, which means that when one person uses the resources it reduces the quantity or quality for others: if a factory emits pollution into the atmosphere it increases pollution concentration and thus reduces air quality for others; a fisherman's daily catch reduces fish stocks available to others (Feeny et al. 1990: 3–4).

Garrett Hardin's parable dealt with a hypothetical grazing environment in which some land was shared. He didn't elaborate on the reasons for this arrangement; he didn't explain whether or why it would have been difficult or costly to control access to land. Instead, he only focused on the *subtractable* quality of this resource, observing that when a herdsman added cattle to his herd, it reduced the quality of land available to everyone. Hardin implicitly assumed that joint ownership entails a complete absence of regulation. He assumed that each herdsman had complete autonomy and freedom to act as he wished, with no way of influencing the actions of other herdsmen. Three decades later, Hardin acknowledged that this was a mistake:

> To judge from the critical literature, the weightiest mistake in my … paper was the omission of the modifying adjective 'unmanaged.' In correcting this omission, one can generalize the practical conclusion in this way: 'A "managed commons" describes either socialism or the privatism of free enterprise. Either one may work; either one may fail: "The devil is in the details." But with an unmanaged commons, you can forget about the devil: As overuse of resources reduces carrying capacity, ruin is inevitable'.
>
> (Hardin 1998: 683)

Despite this acknowledgement that commons are not necessarily open access, the parable of the 'tragedy of the commons' largely remains common wisdom. The assumption that commons equates to open access, and thereby degradation, has stuck.

## Privatisation and Socialism are the Only Possible Solutions to Avoid Degradation

Hardin assumed that a non-interventionist approach to controlling population and preserving resources would ultimately fail to protect the common interest because it is inconsistent with human nature. Adam Smith's idea of the 'invisible hand', whereby the public interest is promoted by individuals acting in their own interest, was, in Hardin's judgment, fundamentally unsound. The parable of the 'tragedy of the commons' served to rebut this idea and its associated assumption that a laissez-faire policy is best for all. Instead, Hardin argued that what is required to avoid the degradation of open access is 'mutual coercion, mutually agreed upon' (1968: 1247). As we also saw in Hardin's quote above, he assumed that two types of 'mutually agreed coercion' were feasible: socialism and privatisation. He didn't necessarily see these as *just* or fair regimes, merely workable – and potentially effective – ones. And, ultimately, he reasoned, 'injustice is preferable to total ruin' (1968: 1247). What Hardin called 'socialism' was simply the idea of bringing common pool resources under the ownership of a centralised government. The government could then determine rules about who can access the resources, for what purposes, and how much they can use. This would not always be possible (e.g., for resources that cross jurisdictions), but some resources could certainly be centrally managed to restrict access through permits, fines, or other regulatory tools. Maybe you can think of examples in your own country where the government regulates (or tries to regulate) access to a lake, forest, or park.

Hardin was sceptical about centralised control because he thought distant bureaucrats could hide their mistakes and be less accountable for their conservation efforts. He placed more hope in the opposite approach to managing the commons, which he called 'privatism' (now generally called privatisation). This would see resources subdivided into private property with responsibility for conservation invested in the private owner. For Hardin, this would change the terms of the calculation we saw above: under a private property regime, the owner enjoys the profits generated by her resources, but she also incurs the costs of any damage. Responsible owners prosper; short-sighted ones suffer (Hardin 1994: 105–6). In recent years this position has been labelled 'free market environmentalism'. Its proponents assume that privatisation not only provides the right incentives for environmental stewardship; it also better harnesses knowledge about environmental conditions. Free Market Environmentalists Terry Anderson and Donald Leal argue that 'individual property owners, who are in a position and have an incentive to obtain time- and place-specific information about their resource endowments, are better suited than centralized bureaucracies to manage resources' (1996: 245).

# Critiques and Corrections

Since 'The Tragedy of the Commons' was published in 1968, environmentalists, anthropologists, and political scientists have scrutinised Hardin's arguments. They point to three key weaknesses in his work.

## Human Nature and the Commons

Earlier we saw that the argument of 'tragedy of the commons' assumes that human beings are selfish by nature. This is a core assumption underpinning rational choice theory more generally. But this understanding of human nature is hardly an objective truth. Critics of the 'tragedy' hypothesis point to evolutionary theory to support an alternative account of human nature (Richerson et al. 2009). It is too simplistic to say that humans are either inherently selfish or inherently cooperative. But anthropological and historical research reveals that at different times and in different places humans have cooperated in diverse and extensive ways. Contrary to the assumptions of rational choice theorists, there is evidence that humans do have cooperative sentiments. But in societies where cooperative institutions are absent, or have been dismantled or neglected, it can take considerable time to develop these. Cooperation is not counter to human nature, but neither does it necessarily come about easily (Richerson et al. 2009: 404). Much of our understanding of humans' cooperative tendencies comes from experimental research, such as 'prisoners' dilemma' games. These show that people will often cooperate, even with strangers, especially when they are given the opportunity to communicate and thereby build some trust (Richerson et al. 2009: 404). Peter Richerson and his colleagues reviewed a range of theories and evidence and concluded that:

People behave in experiments and in the field as if they have strong – perhaps innate – dispositions to cooperate, although dispositions vary considerably from person to person, society to society, and time to time. The variation is best explained by the existence of complex cultural traditions of social behavior, the collective results of which we call social institutions. Our ability to organize cooperation on a scale considerably larger than predicted by theory based on unconstrained selfish rationality, or by most evolutionary mechanisms, is one of the most striking features of our species.

(2009: 432)

What insights should we take from this? These findings remind us that people come with all sorts of personalities and dispositions: some will consistently behave in self-interested ways and refuse to cooperate (these people are called 'free riders'); some will cooperate if they can be assured that they won't be exploited and that free riders will be dealt with; some will initiate cooperation in the hope that others will come on board; and some will altruistically put the collective good above their own self-interests irrespective of what others decide to do (Ostrom et al. 1999). Does this ring true to you? Think of the people you know – your relatives, friends, colleagues, sports team – they are likely to display various different dispositions, and perhaps behave differently in different contexts. This should warn us against accepting simplistic statements about human nature. As we will see below (and in many of the chapters that follow in Part 2 of this book), the human capacity for cooperation has actually led to a range of governance arrangements for conserving natural resources. Privatisation and socialism are evidently not the only two options for responding to environmental degradation.

## Historical Inaccuracies

In his 1968 lecture, Hardin avoided alluding to any particular historical time or place: his arguments were discussed in a hypothetical setting free of any particular context. Where he used examples, they were drawn from resource use and environmental pollution on the national rangelands and national parks of the United States. Nevertheless, over the years, his work has often been quoted with reference to medieval and pre-industrial England where pasture was frequently set aside for public use (Buck 1985: 51–3). In a 1977 paper, Hardin reinforced the association between 'tragedy of the commons' and these historical periods in England by referring to the Enclosures Acts of the eighteenth and nineteenth century as a successful (though unjust) means of avoiding over-grazing (Hardin 1977). But some question the historical accuracy of this account of the 'destruction of common pastures of English country towns' (Falk 1971: 48). Environmental historian Susan Buck argues that the commons system declined not because it proved destructive but because land reforms were passed in the favour of wealthy landowners. She calls these reforms 'nothing more than a sophisticated land-grab' (Buck 1985: 59).

Critics also question the assumption that the degradation that did occur on commons land was the result of selfish and short-sighted herdsmen. Susan Buck's reading of manor court rolls from the mid-thirteenth century suggested that open fields were actually closely monitored and when they did degrade it was more a result of illegal activity or the oppression of poorer tenants. She also highlights that the land made available for commons use was typically of poorer quality (e.g., reclaimed from forests and marsh), while the lords kept the best land enclosed for their private use (Buck 1985: 55–60). Under such circumstances, degradation of the common land is unsurprising. Those relying on the commons had few resources to invest in improving the land and adopting new technologies. But once the land was enclosed, wealthier landholders would invest to improve productivity. On this account, the observed differences between the common and enclosed land derived from inequalities rather than from free access and selfish over-grazing.

## Alternative Governance Options

Political scientists and institutional economists have learnt a great deal about the diverse ways in which communities actually deal with shared natural resources. This knowledge has come through observations 'in the field' as well as experiments with human subjects in controlled settings. It turns out that privatisation and central government control are just two possible systems for attempting to sustainably manage natural resources and avoid environmental degradation. To maintain common resources in a sustainable way, two things need to be in place: (1) a way of controlling access (i.e., rules to permit some people to use the resource while excluding others); and (2) a way of regulating the use of those people who are permitted access (Ostrom et al. 1999). If neither access nor use is controlled, we call a resource '**open access**'.

As we saw above, access is generally controlled through property rights: individual property rights in the case of privatisation, and government property rights in the case of centrally controlled systems. But an alternative to private and government property regimes is *communal property*. One of Hardin's fundamental errors was that he implicitly assumed that communal property is the same as open access. Communal property means that a resource (an area of forest, a fishery, range lands, etc.) is owned and controlled by a group of people. The group's rights to this resource may be legally recognised (*de jure*) or simply recognised and respected in practice (*de facto*) (Feeny et al. 1990: 4–5). Communities in many different places and at many different times in history have successfully managed to both *exclude* non-members from gaining access to a resource and to *regulate* community members' use of that resource. Let's look at some examples.

The indigenous Cree community in Quebec communally managed fishing and hunting in a sustainable way for hundreds of years before their communal property rights were legally recognised in the 1930s. Legal recognition and enforcement only became necessary when an influx of non-natives disrupted communal systems. These settlers introduced the fur trade into the area and started hunting beavers on a scale never practised by the indigenous communities, and thereby pushed the beaver populations to an all time low. Numbers only began to stabilise once access was restricted to the original Amerindian community (Berkes et al. 1989: 91–2). Examples of sustainable communal management are not unique to indigenous communities. The leading scholar in the study of how commons resources are governed is the late American political scientist, Elinor Ostrom. Ostrom explains that 'Field studies in all parts of the world have found that local groups of resource users, sometimes by themselves and sometimes with the assistance of external authorities, have created a wide diversity of institutional arrangements for coping with common-pool resources' (1999: 494–5). Among many others, Ostrom documents cases of communal tenure of meadows and forests in Switzerland and Japan; and communal irrigation institutions in Spain and the Philippines (2015: 61–87). The details of these arrangements are all context-specific, but these successful and enduring communal institutions do share one important similarity and that is that the communities have endured over a long period of time. They are, in the words of Ostrom, made up of individuals 'who have shared a past and expect to share a future'. This creates trust and reliability, norms about appropriate ways of behaving, and an interest in the next generation who will inherit the land (2015: 88–9).

There is plenty of evidence to support the claim that keeping commons resources under communal management (without private property or state regulation) is ecologically rational. These systems have often been replaced with either centralised (government) rules or market-based institutions (private property) because outsiders have assumed that they are environmentally unsustainable. But many authors suggest that this is a reflection not of reality but of outsiders' lack of understanding of local conditions and communal institutions (see Wall 2014: 37–8). African commons systems have been particularly vulnerable to misguided interventions. According to environmental historians and anthropologists, what has often appeared to outsiders as environmental degradation from over-use was actually evidence of environmental change (Beinart 2000: 277–9). Nuanced understandings of ecological cycles often develop over generations, and this has allowed African pastoralists to rotate between periods of heavy stocking and light stocking of animals to get through periods of drought and allow pastures to recover. If outsiders only observe these practices at one moment in time, rather than across their cycles, they may misinterpret them as unsustainable (Beinart 2000: 279).

Interventions and the imposition of centralised rules or private property regimes have sometimes led to environmentally and socially tragic outcomes. We can see this in the case of the Turkana people in north-west Kenya. There, goat farmers relied on the pods of acacia trees to feed their animals. Access to the acacia woods was tightly regulated by community elders to ensure that the pods weren't over-exploited. Those farmers who violated the communal rules would be punished and potentially killed. During a period of drought in the 1960s, the Kenyan government intervened with the support of United Nations agencies (UNDP and FAO) to settle nomadic herdsmen on private plots of land, and install irrigation systems. Populations swelled with labourers and traders, but the subsequent drought saw the irrigation system collapse and settlers revert to herding animals. But without the elder-controlled communal system for regulating access to acacia trees, the resource was destroyed along with the herdsmen's principal source of survival (Monbiot 1994).

It is important to recognise that communities of people have often successfully managed common pool resources without relying on either the enforcement of the state or the market. But we should also be careful not to romanticise self-governed institutions. What lessons should we take from these studies of commons institutions? Perhaps the most important lesson is that there is no 'one size fits all'. In some contexts, privatisation measures may be effective, in other cases centralised rules or communal management may be more suitable. The precise conditions under which different institutions will perform most effectively remain uncertain. Indeed, Elinor Ostrom suggested that we cannot possibly ever know when a change in rules (e.g., the introduction of a market mechanism or a government regulation) will improve environmental conditions (1999: 497). Her advice was to treat policy proposals as experiments and be open to different communities experimenting in different ways: rather than everyone putting their hopes in government regulation, or markets, or communal management, we ought to experiment with all of these institutions when confronting different environmental problems. In different contexts and for different problems, some types of rules may be better than others at changing incentives, or providing information and feedback, or monitoring and ensuring compliance (Dietz et al. 2009b: 1910). This vision of **'polycentric governance systems'** takes us well beyond Hardin's narrow vision of tragedy or privatisation.

# The Global Commons

Since we have no global government to centrally control access and use of global resources, is Hardin's 'tragedy' inevitable at the global level? Not necessarily. As we saw above, Hardin argued that degradation was inevitable in a regulatory vacuum. But even without a central government, the international community has managed to establish some institutions and mechanisms for regulating who has access to global resources, and how much they can use. This is not to say that these institutions and mechanisms are always easy to establish or that they are always effective once they are in place. Throughout this book we will encounter many cases in which the international community is failing to sustainably govern global resources. But it remains far from certain that the destruction of the global environment is inevitable.

Hardin's original article triggered much debate and further research. Most studies deal with experiences at the local level. So what lessons can we take from local-level common pool resources to understand governance of global-level resources? To answer this question, let's first look at what is meant by the term 'global commons'.

## What are the Global Commons?

The oceans, atmosphere, outer space, and celestial bodies like the moon are often referred to as 'global commons'. But international law makes an important distinction between two Latin terms: *res nullius* and *res communis*. This distinction serves to remind us that not all un-owned resources are common resources. *Res nullius* (nobody's property) refers to parts of nature over which no state has recognised ownership, and all are legally free to use as they wish (i.e., 'open access'). *Res communis* (common property) refers to parts of nature over which no state can claim ownership but for which rules have been agreed to regulate all states' use of the resource, and to ensure that their use does not undermine the ability of other states to also use it. *Res communis* therefore refers to resources that are governed in common (Milun 2011: 57–8). In practice the distinction can become blurred. Matters are further complicated by the tendency for scholars of international relations to use the term 'global commons' for resources that are legally *res nullius*. The case of Antarctica reveals the ambiguity about drawing a clear distinction between these terms. Although some states have claimed ownership over parts of Antarctica, a treaty signed in 1959 prohibited new claims and neither recognised nor denied existing claims to ownership. The Antarctica treaty also stipulated that all states are permitted access for research that is carried out in an open way. A follow-up **protocol** signed in 1991 established a moratorium on oil exploration and exploitation for fifty years (Soroos 2005: 39–40).

## Managing the Global Commons

Efforts by states to cooperate and avoid a 'tragedy of the global commons' have had mixed results. The high seas are one important part of the global environment that states have largely managed to transform from *res nullius* to *res communis*. A patchwork of agreements limits sovereignty claims over the seas, and aims to protect the marine environment in the interests of all humanity. Coastal states can claim sovereignty up to 12 nautical miles beyond the shoreline, but all states retain a right of passage along these waters. Coastal states can further claim exclusive economic use of waters within 200 nautical miles, which secures their legal right to catch fish and extract natural gas and crude oil from below the seabed, yet still with the obligation to protect and preserve the marine environment. In practice, the precise boundaries of many 'economic exclusive zones' have been disputed since this international law was agreed in the mid-twentieth century. Waters beyond these zones are called 'high seas' and are open to all states equally for trade, commerce, communication, etcetera, while seabed resources have the status of 'common heritage of humankind' and its use is governed by an International Seabed Authority (Anderson 2012).[1]

As we saw earlier, government regulation is just one of the ways we can attempt to control who accesses resources and how much they can use. Other options are to privatise resources and apply market mechanisms, or to create voluntary communal arrangements. Are these options also available at the global level to avoid 'tragedy'? There has been some experimentation with global environmental markets without resorting to full privatisation. These are most advanced in the global regime for governing climate change where transnational emissions trading schemes have been created. These are designed to force companies to internalise the costs of their pollution by either selling surplus pollution credits or purchasing additional credits. Markets generally cannot function without some governmental involvement. But it is widely accepted that the role of governments should be limited to establishing markets and maintaining general conditions of law and order that give businesses the confidence to participate. As we will see in Chapter 7, the most advanced environmental markets have been established to limit emissions of greenhouse gases. Some of these markets have sprung up voluntarily, and others have been created by states. But even voluntary markets rely somewhat on governments to send clear signals that give buyers and sellers more confidence in participating.

Hardin's critics have tried to show that communities can regulate shared resources without resorting to either private markets or governmental rules. Is this also possible at the global level? Globalisation creates ever greater and stronger connections between communities around the world. These connections might facilitate the sort of communal cooperation we have seen in many places at the local level. Indeed, as we will see in Chapter 7, voluntary governance networks are an increasingly common feature in global climate change politics. Whereas communal arrangements for managing local common pool resources tend to involve communities of local citizens, at the global level they tend to involve civil society groups and the private sector. One example is the **Forest Stewardship Council** (FSC), led by the non-governmental organisation, the World Wildlife Fund. This was established in the early 1990s to fill a gap in global forest governance. As we will see in Chapter 8, states have struggled to develop a robust and effective multilateral regime to protect the world's remaining forests, and tropical forests in particular. Frustrated with the slow pace of governmental talks, civil society and the private sector created the FSC as a voluntary certification scheme (an 'eco-label') to help customers choose products from sustainably managed forests. Over the years, many other competing **certification schemes** have been created with the aim of preventing deforestation. While the results have been less than satisfactory, this does show that voluntary governance arrangements are alive and well in forestry and other areas.

One lesson that we can take from the experience of governing local common pool resources is that different regimes are needed for different contexts and different problems: there is no single solution for all contexts and all problems. Sometimes intergovernmental regulation will be politically feasible and effective; sometimes market mechanisms will be more promising; and other times voluntary governance networks will prove more plausible or effective.

Sceptical readers may be wondering whether we really can apply lessons from the local level to the global level. Surely the differences are greater than the similarities? It is unquestionably harder to sustainably manage resources at the global level than at the local level, but why is this so? Pause here to think of the most obvious differences between local socio-ecological systems and global socio-ecological systems. How might these differences make it harder to sustainably manage global resources than local resources?

I suggest that three factors are potentially relevant here: *size and scale*, *complexity*, and *enforceability*.

*Size and scale*: Perhaps the most obvious difference between global and local resources is their scale, as well their number of users. The oceans and atmosphere are of a much greater scale than a local fishery or pasture. Many more people also need to be involved in trying to control their access and use. This is true not just of global-scale resources, but also transnational ones like rivers. For some international relations scholars, it is common wisdom that the difficulty of reaching agreement increases with the size and diversity of the group. The fact that multilateral negotiations typically involve close to 200 countries is seen as one of the main obstacles to creating international environmental agreements that can successfully regulate the use of global resources. But we have seen successful common pool resource governance at the local level, and it would be a mistake to assume that these necessarily involve fewer actors than at the international level. Studies carried out by Elinor Ostrom and her collaborators point to successful decision-making among hundreds and even thousands of actors at the local level – a much larger number than directly involved in multilateral negotiations. A recurring finding in these studies is that the *size* of the group matters less for reaching a decision than issue-specific factors (discount rates), institutional factors (transaction costs), and communicative factors (common understanding of interests). In fact, while it might be assumed that cultural homogeneity at the local level makes cooperation and decision-making easier than at the global level, this overlooks the positive role that diversity can play in negotiations. Sometimes a diversity of interests and preferences facilitates decision-making by presenting more positive-sum options (Stevenson 2016a: 405–6). Cooperation at the global level is not easy, but it is possible. As we'll see in Chapter 6, hundreds of multilateral environmental agreements have been successfully negotiated with the aim of avoiding further degradation of shared resources.

*Complexity*: Understanding natural cycles and processes at the global level is a significant challenge for scientists. This is exacerbated by the ways in which common pool resources interact and affect one another. For example, concentrations of greenhouse gases in the atmosphere affect ocean acidity, which in turn affects the health of marine life and biodiversity. Understanding the global environment is difficult for scientists, but it is even more difficult for ordinary people. Globalisation is creating tighter networks of people across the globe and, in many cases, building shared understandings and values. But – globalisation is also making it immensely difficult to perceive and understand the impacts of our actions on the natural world. People's lives are increasingly reliant on activities that take place very far from where they live. Think of the production of food, the extraction of petroleum, and the manufacture of goods. Very few people take the time to understand what these entail. As we'll see in Chapter 10, spatial and temporal 'distance' makes it easy to remain ignorant of human impacts on natural resources. In other words, the impact of people's choices will often be felt in other places in the world, or in future years. When people do take the time to determine and reduce their '**ecological footprint**' (see Chapter 9), the complexity of production processes can make it very difficult to understand.

*Enforceability*: The international system is 'anarchical'. While there is a patchwork of institutions and norms that give some order to this system, there is no higher authority than the nation-state. This makes managing the global commons very difficult. The United Nations provides the architecture for negotiating agreements, but its capacity to monitor let alone enforce agreements is not always strong enough to ensure compliance. International environmental law expert Daniel Bodansky notes that there is a blurring of 'politics' and 'law' in this context. While **treaties** and protocols are legally binding, many other international environmental agreements are only declarations, guidelines, and codes of conduct. These are referred to as 'soft law' because they are not legally binding on the states that sign them (Bodansky 2010: 14–15). We will examine the distinction between **hard and soft law** in more detail in Chapter 6. But we should be cautious about drawing too sharp a distinction between the enforceability of local and international agreements. Robert Keohane and Elinor Ostrom once suggested that many countries are barely less anarchical than the international system (1995). In poor and weakly governed countries, many people simply cannot rely on state authorities (like police and courts) to enforce agreements. This is especially true for remote communities in which people are entirely reliant on common pool resources for their livelihoods. This is where the importance of voluntary cooperation becomes particularly important.

# Conclusion

We began this chapter with Garrett Hardin's captivatingly simple fable about the selfishness and short-sightedness of humankind. We unpacked his assumptions about human nature, the openness of common resources, and the limited options for sustainably managing common resources. We saw that there is considerable evidence that humans are capable of cooperation. Indeed, under the right conditions, people are disposed to cooperate. Recognising this point is important, and I deliberately stress it early on in the book. It serves to remind us that our inherited assumptions about the world are often weak or incomplete; any student of politics has an intellectual duty to question these assumptions. The idea that people are selfish and conflict-prone runs deep. We will see this in Chapter 5 where assumptions of 'water wars' are pervasive. In fact, evidence suggests that communities are more likely to cooperate than fight over trans-national water resources.

The insight that no 'one size fits all' when it comes to designing sustainability institutions and mechanisms is also important. Environmental problems are numerous and complex. We need to think creatively about the best approaches – and combination of approaches – for improving environmental conditions and social outcomes. We do ourselves and the planet a great disservice if we cling uncritically to assumptions that solutions lie only in markets, or centralised control, or voluntary cooperative schemes.

In the next chapter, we take a closer look at whether over-population and poverty are the main drivers of environmental degradation.

## Discussion Questions

1. What factors do you think explain the popularity and impact of the 'tragedy of the commons' parable?
2. What assumptions underpin Hardin's parable? How have these been critiqued? Do you find the critiques persuasive?
3. If 'open access' resources are environmentally dangerous, how should common resources be managed? Consider the strengths and weaknesses

of different management systems, and how these might be better suited to some contexts more than others.

4. In what ways is Hardin's parable useful for understanding global problems like climate change?

5. To what extent can we rely on voluntary constraint in protecting locally and globally shared resources?

## Note

1. Although some states can also claim jurisdiction within this area on the basis of their underwater landmass, known as the continental shelf.

# 3 Population and Poverty

## key points

- Concern about the sustainability of a growing population dates back centuries. Today this position is called '**neo-Malthusianism**' after the eighteenth-century cleric, Thomas Malthus.
- The concept of 'doubling time' is central to the concerns of neo-Malthusians: the time it takes for the human population to double has been shrinking throughout most of human history.
- Some argue that conditions in which people live have a greater impact on the environment than the size of the population.
- Poverty is widely accepted as a driver of environmental problems. International environmental policy is often based on the assumption that environmental conditions will improve as countries develop.
- Global trade complicates the relationship between development and pollution reduction. Wealthy countries often show signs of improved sustainability because they are outsourcing production and pollution to poorer countries.
- The assumption that environmental concerns are a luxury that only the wealthy can afford is simplistic and overlooks differences in environmental priorities.

# Introduction

Concerns about over-population trace back to Babylonian times. Babylonian mythology was first recorded in about 1600 BC and those inscribed tablets reveal the gods' annoyance at multiplying humans and their noisy ways. Plagues, floods, and finally infertility were supposedly inflicted on humans to control their numbers and leave the gods in peace and quiet (Cohen 1995: 5–6). The idea that natural catastrophes would provide a check on human populations is more commonly associated with the eighteenth-century writings of English cleric Thomas Robert Malthus. While many of his contemporaries were engaging in 'speculations about the perfectibility of man and of society' (Malthus 1798: 3), Malthus could not share their optimism. Instead, he focused on the 'unconquerable difficulties' in realising their rosy pictures of the future. He was mostly concerned about a tension he saw in two fixed laws of nature: one, the necessity of food for man's existence, and two, the 'passion between the sexes' (1798: 4). These laws exist in tension, he argued, because food and population cannot possibly grow at the same rate: 'Population, when unchecked, increases in a geometrical ratio. Subsistence increases only in an arithmetical ratio' (1798: 4). Without any social controls on population growth, the natural world imposes its own limits in ways that produce significant human suffering: families are forced to abandon children, and disease, malnourishment, and ultimately famine would suppress procreation and eliminate vast numbers.

An ever increasing population simply could not be sustained on a planet with finite limits. Malthus contemplated the possibility that liberal, educated men of limited financial means would avoid or delay marriage to avoid sharing their wealth and descending the social ladder. Fewer marriages would, in that era, necessarily mean fewer births (1798: 24–5). But the vast majority of men could not be relied upon to exercise such judgment or restraint. So minimising marriages could provide only a limited social check on population (1798: 24–5). Recognising their limited means, poorer people might prudently limit their family size. But Malthus observed that this was rare. Indeed, he rejected the 'Poor Laws' on the grounds that child support payments to poor labourers would further discourage smaller families. So although it might improve the condition of the poor in the short term, it would lead to scarcer resources in the long term (1798: 42).

Malthus' fears made a resurgence in the 1960s when environmentalism took shape as a popular movement. US environmentalist Barry Commoner observed that in the lead up to the Earth Day in 1970, it seemed that 'almost every writer, almost every speaker, on the college campuses, in the streets and on television and radio broadcasts, was ready to fix the blame and pronounce a cure for the environmental crisis' (1971: 1). One of the loudest voices in these debates was that of those who became known as the 'neo-Malthusians'. They echoed Malthus' eighteenth-century fears that unchecked population growth would cause suffering for everyone in the long run. In this chapter we examine whether population should be considered the main driver of environmental problems. After reviewing the arguments and evidence in support of a focus on population, we will consider the counter-argument that the *conditions* in which people live are of much greater relevance than the *numbers* of such people. In particular, we will examine whether bringing countries out of conditions of poverty reduces their impact on the environment.

# The Malthusian Renaissance

Two books mark the renaissance of Malthusian ideas in the twentieth century. One is *The Population Bomb*, published in 1968. The other is *The Limits to Growth*, published soon after in 1972. Although credit (and criticism) for *The Population Bomb* is attributed only to Paul Ehrlich, it was in fact co-written with his wife, Anne Ehrlich, an accomplished ecological scientist in her own right. The Ehrlichs later explained that the publisher imposed two unfortunate conditions: they would only name a single author on the book, and they would use the polemical *Bomb* title instead of the Ehrlichs' preferred *Population, Resources, and Environment* (Ehrlich and Ehrlich 2009: 63).[1] As a result, Paul Ehrlich became known among his critics as the 'population bomber'. For the Ehrlichs, over-population is a simple question of mathematics: if people were willing 'to do simple math' they would have to conclude that 'the capacity of Earth to produce food and support people is finite' (2009: 64, 68). This, they maintain, was true in the 1960s and remains true today.

This message of natural limits was also central to *The Limits to Growth*, which was written by an international group of economists, industrialists, and scientists known as the '**Club of Rome**'. Gathering for the first time in 1968, their aim was to promote understanding of the economic, political, natural, and social dimensions of the global system. The Club analysed population growth as part of a global system in which industrialism, pollution, food production, and resource depletion were bringing the planet dangerously close to its 'limits' (Meadows et al. 1972: 23). In particular, they examined how population growth and economic growth were, in tandem, undermining the earth's support systems. Even with advancements in technology and efficiency, they argued, at some point the planet would be unable to produce sufficient food to support ever larger populations and economies. Their explanation for this built on Malthus' earlier observation that 'Population . . . increases in a geometrical ratio. Subsistence increases only in an arithmetical ratio'. The distinction is better known as *exponential* growth and *linear* growth. What's the difference? Perhaps as a child you had a 'piggy bank' or 'money box'. If you placed your weekly pocket money of $5 into the piggy bank, over time your savings would have grown *linearly*. If, however, you'd deposit your $5 into a bank account with a 5 per cent interest rate, your savings would've grow *exponentially*. The size of growth in the piggy bank is constant (fixed) and independent of the amount of the savings already accumulated. The size of growth in the bank account varies (and increases) each month because it does depend on the amount of savings already accumulated. What does this mean for population? Well, like the money in the bank account, population grows *exponentially*: for example, an adult bears three children, who in turn bear two or three children each, who each bear another few children, and so on. Economies grow in the same way (or at least that is the intention).

## Solving the Population Problem

Echoing Malthus, the Ehrlichs warned that the 'population problem' has two kinds of solutions: 'a "birth rate solution," in which we find ways to lower the birth rate . . . (and) a "death rate solution," in which ways to raise the death rate – war, famine, pestilence – *find us*' (Ehrlich 1968: 17, emphasis in original). The Club of Rome agreed: they understood the problem of over-population as partly a result of our success in reducing worldwide mortality. The balance between birth rates and death rates was disrupted because investments in health and human development have postponed death for large numbers of people, but similar efforts have not been made to reduce births (Meadows et al. 1972: 158–9). A sustainable environment would require setting the birth rate to equal the death rate (as well as stabilising industrial growth, which we will examine in more detail in Chapter 4). Failure to do so would invite 'nature-imposed limits to growth', resulting in 'an uncontrollable decrease in population and capital' (Meadows et al. 1972: 169). Precisely when and how this might occur was left open: it might be sudden or gradual, worldwide or localised. In any case, the prospect was grim: 'Certainly whatever fraction of the human population remained at the end of the process would have very little left with which to build a new society in any form we can now envision' (Meadows et al. 1972: 170).

The Ehrlichs were equally pessimistic but rather bolder in their predictions. Back in 1968, they predicted that it was already too late to completely avoid nature's own solutions to over-population. In a bold tone generally avoided by scientists, the Ehrlichs predicted that 'In the 1970s and 1980s hundreds of millions of people will starve to death' (Ehrlich 1968). In fact, deaths from famine began to drop significantly in the 1970s as a result of increased food production (*The Economist* 2013). In Chapter 11 we will examine the sustainability of the agricultural techniques used to achieve this increase in food production. For now, though, we can see an apparent flaw in the Ehrlichs' analysis. Writing forty years after the publication of *The Population Bomb*, the authors acknowledged that the book had its flaws, but that the thrust of their argument remains relevant (Ehrlich and Ehrlich 2009). They argued that whether or not famines, plagues, water shortages, etcetera occurred on the precise schedule anticipated by their scenarios, these threats remain on the horizon (2009). The Club of Rome shared the Ehrlichs' pessimism but argued that the extent of the problems facing human societies could be obscured because nature has delayed feedback mechanisms. So while it might be possible to increase food production in the short term to feed a larger population, over time this is decreasing 'the carrying capacity of the environment', which will eventually intensify declines in population and capital (Meadows et al. 1972: 156).

# Trends in Population Growth

The concept of '**doubling time**' is central to the concerns of neo-Malthusians. This refers to the time it takes for a population to double in size, and it provides a useful reminder that apparently small annual growth rates have a significant impact over a longer time span. From 10,000 years ago until AD 1650, global population grew at an estimated rate of 0.1 per cent per year, which meant that it took over 1,000 years to double. But the time it takes for the human population to double has been shrinking throughout most of human history. Annual growth rates rose to 0.46 per cent in the seventeenth and eighteenth centuries, and to 0.54 per cent in the nineteenth and early twentieth centuries. By the 1960s and 1970s, annual growth rates had risen to about 2 per cent, which meant that the world's population was doubling within a period of about thirty-five years (McKinney et al. 2012: 39). Doubling our numbers at such a fast rate would mean that in another 900 years, there would be sixty million billion people on the planet: an almost unimaginably high number (60,000,000,000,000,000).

British physicist J.H. Fremlin imagined the impossibility of sustaining so many lives on earth. He suggested that this would require a 2,000-story building covering the entire planet (oceans included): half of this would be devoted to food production machinery and the other half to housing; each person would have 7.5 square metres of space (about the size of an average prison cell) and would receive a daily supply of liquid 'food' piped into their 'home' (Fremlin 1964).

Some find optimism in the fact that the *rate* of population growth has been declining since about 1970. This is largely a result of greater education and economic opportunities for women, as well as greater availability of contraceptives. But as long as growth rates remain above zero (i.e., as long as birth rates exceed death rates), the global population will continue to increase, and this concerns those who believe it is already far too large for the planet to sustain. Figures 3.1 and 3.2 illustrate the magnitude of estimated population expansion, in spite of declining annual growth rates.

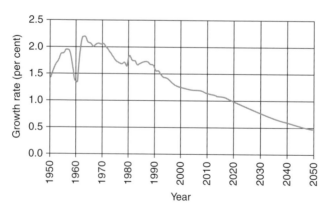

**Figure 3.1:** World population growth rates, 1950–2050

Source: US Census Bureau 2016a

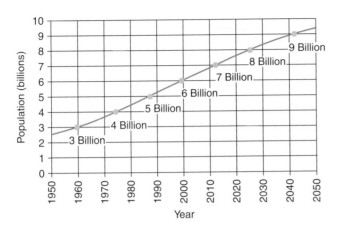

**Figure 3.2:** World population, 1950–2050

Source: US Census Bureau 2016b

Rather than finding comfort in declining growth rates, neo-Malthusians argue that we should focus our attention on determining what a sustainable population would be, and figuring out how we can achieve this. As we saw in Chapter 1, our collective human impact on the planet is already significant. If the number of people on the planet is the greatest determinant of environmental impact, what would be a sustainable number? Demographers and environmentalists sometimes use the term 'carrying capacity' to refer to the maximum number of people the earth can support in a sustainable fashion. Over the years, dozens of estimates have been suggested; ranging from as few as about 1 billion to as many as 100 billion. Most estimates, however, fall somewhere in the range of 7.7 and 12 billion (Cohen 1995). But we shouldn't assume that these estimates are value-free scientific calculations. Estimating carrying capacity requires making implicit or explicit assumptions about the sort of living conditions that are appropriate or desirable. After all, few would want to live like a human battery hen in the sort of dystopic conditions described by Fremlin in the 1960s.

Rather than thinking about the maximum number of people the planet could sustain, some demographers suggest that we should focus on determining the *optimum population*. This is calculated as 'a function of the desired quality of life and the resultant per-capita impacts of attaining that lifestyle on the planet's life support systems' (Daily et al. 1994: 470). This forces us to think about the *best* size population, not the largest one possible. For the Ehrlichs, the best size would be small enough to preserve large areas of wilderness but large enough to ensure vibrant urban centres with diverse and creative communities. They put the number at about 1.5 to 2 billion people (Ehrlich 1968).

Today we are already well beyond the Ehrlichs' estimate of an optimum population. In about 2011, the world's population reached 7 billion. This means

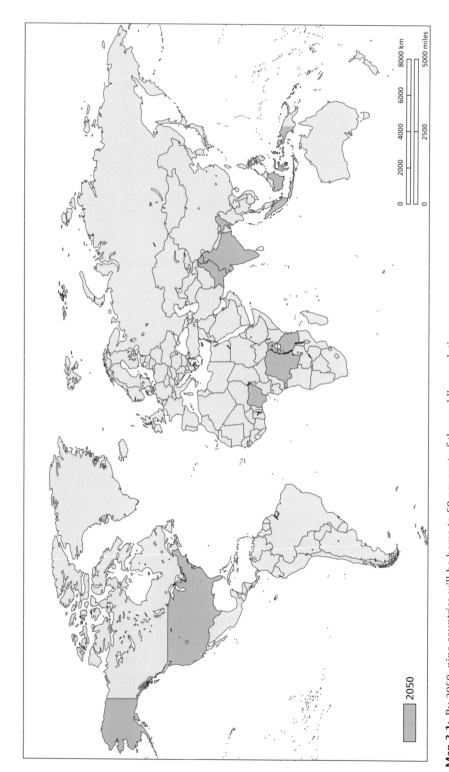

**Map 3.1:** By 2050, nine countries will be home to 50 per cent of the world's population

that 'roughly 14% of all of the human beings that have ever existed are still alive today' (Bradshaw and Brook 2014: 16610). This also makes humans the most populous organism on earth. But although the world's population is growing, this growth is distributed unevenly across countries. When the United Nations forecasts that the world's population will grow to 9 billion by 2050 it is not suggesting that the populations of all countries will significantly expand. Instead, most of the increase in world population will take place in a small number of high-fertility countries that already have large populations. African countries will account for about half of the population increase up to 2050. In fact, by 2050, just nine countries will be home to half the world's population: India, Nigeria, Pakistan, the Congo, Ethiopia, Tanzania, United States of America, Indonesia, and Uganda (UN 2015). Map 3.1 shows just how concentrated and skewed such a distribution of population will be: the shading represents a small proportion of the world's territory, but this area will hold half of the world's population in 2050.

## Is Population Control the Answer?

In the mid-twentieth century, interest in controlling global population growth began to grow. The United Nations created a UN Population Fund, and this multilateral agency worked closely with US administrations, as well as US-based research institutions and think tanks (such as the Rockefeller Foundation) to promote birth control in developing countries. Throughout the 1970s and 1980s, common wisdom held that population should be limited by setting demographic goals and goals for the uptake of women's contraceptives, and promoting the use of incentives and disincentives to change people's reproductive behaviour (Eager 2004). In some parts of the world, women welcomed the availability of the contraceptive pill as an opportunity to avoid unwanted pregnancies. In other parts it became part of government-led (and often US-funded) population control programmes (Hartmann 1995). Concerted campaigns by feminists and human rights movements succeeded in shifting attention away from population control to women's empowerment. They did so partly by arguing that 'development was the best contraceptive': women with access to education, health and social services, secure livelihoods, freedom from violence have more control over their own bodies. Such women generally have fewer children than those who have limited control over their bodies (Eager 2004: 153; Hartmann et al. 2015). As a result, since the mid-1990s, global population policy has focused less on draconian population control measures and more on respecting women's human rights and autonomy over reproduction.

## Is Poverty the Main Driver of Environmental Degradation?

The shift from controlling population to empowering women through development reflects a broader shift towards 'sustainable development' in the 1980s and 1990s. Feminists were not the only ones objecting to population-centric explanations for environmental problems. Ever since the issue of the environment moved onto the international agenda, developing countries have resisted efforts to blame large populations for environmental degradation (Najam 1996). It might appear self-evident that the greater the number of people, the heavier the environmental impact: people need food, fibre, and fuel to sustain their lives, and more people use up more of these resources. But developing countries argue that it is not the number of people in their countries that is the problem, but rather the poor conditions in which they live. They echoed the feminists in arguing that development is the best solution to modern maladies.

In fact, some argue that the neo-Malthusians are confusing their concern of over-population with a concern for poverty. This is perhaps evident in the opening chapter of *The Population Bomb* where the Ehrlichs evoke a 'hellish' street scene in the busy Indian city of Delhi. It was while travelling by taxi in this city for the first time in the mid-1960s that the Ehrlichs came to 'emotionally' understand the 'population explosion':

The seats were hopping with fleas ... As we crawled through the city, we entered a crowded slum area. The temperature was well over 100, and the air was a haze of dust and smoke. The streets seemed alive with people. People eating, people washing, people sleeping. People visiting, arguing, and screaming. People thrusting their hands through the taxi window, begging. People defecating and urinating. People clinging to buses. People herding animals. People, people, people, people ... since that night I've known the feel of overpopulation.

(Ehrlich 1968: 15–16)

Some critics have pointed out that the Ehrlichs didn't have to travel to Delhi to 'feel over-population': a trip to Manhattan would have exposed them to a similar density of people! What they were witnessing (though not 'feeling') was poverty: people were carrying out their lives in the streets instead of behind doors as they would in a wealthy city (see Greer 1985: 402). By describing the feeling of crowds in Delhi rather than in Manhattan, the Ehrlichs opened themselves up to charges of racism. Indeed, many scholars identify a strong racist undercurrent in the work of Malthus and his contemporary followers. Historian Allen Chase argues that Malthus sowed the seeds of scientific racism (1977: 36), although this was implicit rather than explicit in his work (Fluehr-Lobban 2006: 165). While we should be careful about attributing racist convictions to all neo-Malthusians, it is important to acknowledge that population concerns can quickly descend into (and are sometimes a cover for) racist demands and eugenic thinking (whereby the poor are deemed genetically inferior) (see Ehrlich et al. 1995; Foster 1998; Lohmann 2005; Angus and Butler 2011; Robertson 2012).

The idea that poverty is the enemy of the environment was first proposed at the UN **Conference on Environment and Development** in Stockholm in 1972, and gradually attracted support during the following years. In Stockholm, India's prime minister, Indira Gandhi, gave an impassioned speech in which she argued that poverty and deprivation are 'the greatest polluters' (quoted in Rajan 1997: 25–6). This assumption came to underpin the idea of 'sustainable development', which acknowledges the importance of clean and efficient economic development, particularly in developing countries. *Our Common Future* was the first high-profile international report to promote this vision of development. It was published in 1987 by a group of policy elites and economists who formed the UN Commission on Environment and Development (dubbed the '**Brundtland Commission**' after its chair Gro Harlem Brundtland, former prime minister of Norway). Reflecting on the writing process, Brundtland acknowledged that among the most difficult questions they addressed in the report were those concerning population pressure and the relationship between poverty, environment, and development (World Commission on Environment and Development 1987: 7). Nevertheless, they came to an unequivocal conclusion: 'Poverty is a major cause and effect of global environmental problems … A world in which poverty is endemic will always be prone to ecological and other catastrophes' (1987: 12, 16). The Commission further highlighted that over-population indeed poses a threat to ecological sustainability, but that 'the issue is not just numbers of people, but how those numbers relate to available resources' (1987: 18). Extreme rates of population would need to be limited while making great strides in industrial innovation to ensure that current and future generations could live well.

A few years later, the World Bank's 1992 *World Development Report* echoed this message that poverty drives environmental degradation (World Bank 1992). The key message was that poor environmental conditions undermine human health, productivity, and future development opportunities. Accelerated economic development could help to improve environmental conditions, the authors argued (World Bank 1992).[2] In Chapter 6 we will examine in more detail precisely how the framework of 'sustainable development' has been politically constructed at the international level. For now, let's look in greater depth at the logic underpinning the assumption that economic development can improve environmental conditions.

## The Environmental Kuznets Curve (EKC)

Many resource economists claim that the relationship between environmental pollution and economic growth takes the shape of an inverted U curve. This curve is called the **Environmental Kuznets Curve** (EKC).[3] It suggests that environmental quality deteriorates as a country's economy grows but starts to improve when the country reaches a certain level of development (Grossman and Krueger 1991, 1996). This inverted U is shown in Figure 3.3.

In this Figure 3.3 we see growing levels of sulphur emissions in the early stages of income growth, followed by a sharp and enduring decline as wealth increases beyond about $4,000 or $5,000 per capita income (although at early

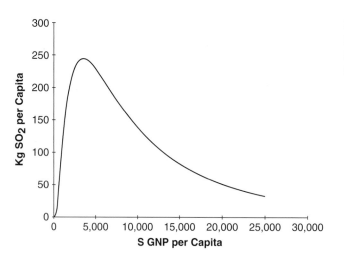

**Figure 3.3:** The Environmental Kuznets Curve
Source: Stern et al. 1996: 1152

1980s values). American economists Gene Grossman and Alan Krueger first introduced the EKC in the early 1990s. In many quarters, it became common wisdom that economic growth is beneficial for the environment. This impact is somewhat surprising. Grossman and Krueger's hypothesis inspired hundreds of further studies, many of which pointed to flaws and limitations in the assumed inverted-U curve. But before we refer to the critics, let's take a closer look at the evidence that Grossman, Krueger, and others point to in support of the EKC.

Grossman and Krueger wanted to dispel the claims by environmentalists that a free trade agreement between the United States and Mexico would be environmentally detrimental. Environmentalists raised multiple concerns: that the expansion of international markets and economic activity inevitably depletes natural resources and increases pollution; that Mexico's regulatory system was too weak to handle further industrialisation, and that unregulated expansion would result in even more pollution; and that the US's own environmental regulatory standards would be driven down by the push to protect industry competitiveness. Grossman and Krueger accused environmentalists of relying on anecdotal evidence and criticised their failure to understand the relationship between stages of economic development, trade liberalisation, pollution, and natural resources (1991: 1–3). They acknowledged that economic development does have an impact on the environment. 'Some pollutants', they wrote, 'are a natural by-product of economic activities such as electricity generation and the operation of motor vehicles' (1991: 6). But as countries modernise and grow richer, they have the option to use cleaner technologies. Moreover, as citizens become wealthier they are more likely to call on their government to protect the environment (1991: 6–7). Buoyed by this possibility, they analysed urban pollution data for dozens of countries during the 1970s and 1980s. They found that sulphur dioxide ($SO_2$) emissions grew at lower levels of development, but began to fall at higher levels of development. Countries varied in their precise turning point but averaged out at just over \$4,000 per capita GDP. Some countries saw improvements in pollution with incomes as low as \$5,000, and others as high as \$14,000 (1985 values). Concentrations of smoke pollution in the atmosphere showed a similar pattern. Another pollutant, 'suspended particles', fell as incomes grew even at low levels: this means that economic growth was correlated with less pollution without any delay period (1991: 14–18). What was the apparent take-home message? Environmentalists were wrong to be concerned about a free trade agreement. NAFTA, Grossman and Krueger argued, would probably drive economic growth in Mexico, and once they reached a per capita income of about \$5,000, they would likely see improvements in environment conditions (1991: 19–20).

## Questioning the Validity of the EKC

Some follow-up studies into the relationship between pollution and stages of development confirmed the existence of an Environmental Kuznets Curve. But others cast doubt on this. What became clear was that there is no single stage of development at which environmental conditions begin to improve. For a few pollutants, improvements are seen when incomes are still quite low. Dissolved oxygen (affecting water) is one of these, so is arsenic. But others, like nitrates, nitrogen dioxide, and nitric oxide (associated with acid rain and air pollution) continue rising even when countries reach a middle-income level of development. Importantly, even when researchers are looking at the same pollutant, they usually reach wildly different figures about the incomes at which pollution begins to improve. Sulphur dioxide has been the 'poster child' of EKC studies (Carson 2010: 15), and more attention has been paid to this than any other pollutant. But this flurry of research activity has not produced consistent results. For policy purposes, it makes a significant difference whether $SO_2$ pollution can be expected to drop off when per capita income reaches $3,670 or $18,039. More recent evidence suggests that it might be as high as $50,000 (Stern 2006).

What explains such divergent findings? Critics suggest that the studies are based on patchy and poor-quality data. Many countries, especially low-income ones, do not have complete and accurate records of their pollution levels at any one point in time, let alone data over a period of time. Different methods and procedures may also be used in different countries, and at different times. So the data used may bear little resemblance to reality (Carson 2010; Kaika and Zervas 2013). Other critics point out that the data that is available not only produces inconsistent estimates of pollutant turning points; it also casts doubt on whether a U-shaped turning point generally exists. This question is important because the argument that poverty drives environmental degradation rests largely on the assumption that environmental quality improves when countries reach a certain level of development. Some studies point not to a U-shaped curve but an N-shaped curve, as broadly depicted in Figure 3.4.

The N-shaped curve suggests that improvements in environmental quality are sometimes only temporary. Once a country reaches a certain level of development, governments and business are willing to invest in cleaner and more efficient technologies. But the decline in environmental impact may be temporary if abatement costs are too high for a middle-income country to sustain, or if technological innovation cannot keep up with growth in demand. This latter prospect is called the 'Jevons Paradox'. In the mid-nineteenth century, English

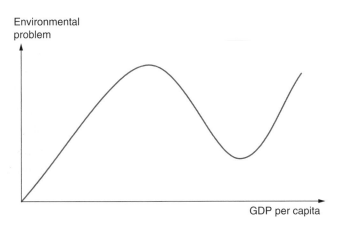

Environmental problem

GDP per capita

**Figure 3.4:** Relationship between environmental problems and wealth: The N-shaped curve

economist William Stanley Jevons was concerned about the sustainability of England's coal supplies (back then it wasn't the environmental sustainability that concerned him, but rather its potential to sustain national prosperity and progress). He argued that measures introduced to make coal use more efficient would likely have a rebound effect: efficiency drives down the unit cost of production, which in turn drives industrialists to increase production (Jevons 1866). Efficiency measures can only work if they are coupled with caps on production. The same trend has been observed at the consumer level. A fuel-efficient car allows one to drive more while spending the same amount on fuel. Cutting down meat consumption frees up income to spend on travel. In this case, environmental savings in one area are cancelled out by greater environmental impact in another area (Tainter 2008: ix). This is actually a core principle of mainstream economic theory: 'any time one reduces the cost of consuming a valued resource, people will respond by consuming more of it ... Or ... people will consume more of something else, perhaps resulting in no net savings or even greater overall consumption' (Tainter 2008: ix).

Other studies that cast doubt on the EKC reveal neither an inverted U-shaped curve nor an N-shaped curve, but rather a single growing line, as depicted in Figure 3.5. This suggests that affluence and pollution continue growing together.

This single line represents what economists call monotonous growth. The rate at which pollution emissions increase may slow, but the total amount of pollution continues to increase. This is the case with carbon dioxide ($CO_2$) and urban waste, which continue growing in wealthy countries (Stern 2015: 3–4; Shafik 1994). It is also true of other environmental issues like biodiversity loss.

So when does economic growth drive reductions in pollution? It appears to be the case that an Environmental Kuznets Curve exists for problems that are

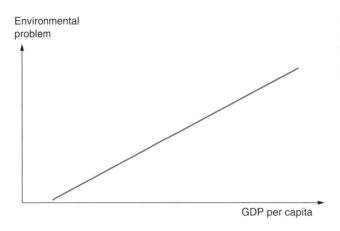

Environmental problem

GDP per capita

**Figure 3.5:** Alternative depiction of the relationship between environmental problems and wealth

visible in the short term and are relatively affordable to address (e.g., urban air pollution, urban sanitation, and water pollution). Pollution that is not immediately visible or has little or no impact on the most people's lives in the short term, and is costly to reduce, tends to continue rising as incomes rise. In other words, there is no Environmental Kuznets Curve (Kaika and Zervas 2013: 1405–6).

## Outsourcing Production and Pollution

Other critics argue that any evidence of an Environmental Kuznets Curve reflects changes in the global economy, rather than any positive relationship between growth and environmental quality. Consumption patterns in wealthy countries haven't changed: people still buy cars, electronic goods, furniture, and household appliances. The only difference now is that these goods are rarely produced in wealthy countries. As wealthy countries have shifted to service-based economies, they have 'outsourced' the production of resource-intensive goods. The energy and resources that go into producing these goods – and the pollution that comes out in the production process – now appear on the accounting sheets of developing countries. These haven't necessarily disappeared or declined, they have simply shifted. What's more, some argue, the weaker environmental regulation of developing countries makes them an attractive investment option for dirty industries. In Chapter 10 we will see how international trade has provided opportunities for wealthy countries to export the hazardous waste associated with luxury consumption. The environmental consequences of consumption are hidden in this way. Trade creates what Rothman calls 'an illusion of sustainability' (1998: 186).

This should dampen, or at least moderate, our optimism. It calls into question the potential for economic growth to drive future improvements in environmental quality. If today's wealthy countries have become richer and cleaner by exporting their dirty industries to poorer countries, then developing countries will not have this option in the future. Eventually there will be no other countries to pick up the dirty industry. This exposes a deeper flaw in EKC theory: it assumes that developing countries will follow the same development path as developed countries.

The EKC-concept presupposes that the production base of an economy shifts (gradually and over time) from agriculture to industry and consequently to services. The primary sector (agriculture) is the least polluting sector. The secondary sector (industry) generates pollution due to the extraction of natural resources and the generation of wastes. The tertiary sector (services) is more 'information'-intensive and goods are non-material, so services are considered to generate less pollution.

(Kaika and Zervas 2013: 1407)

This idea of 'stages of development' becomes doubtful when we recognise that today's poorer countries are developing in a very different context to the historical context in which Western countries developed. For a start there are new pollutants and modern technology is capable of extracting resources much more rapidly than in the nineteenth and early twentieth centuries. Trade allows for importing existing technologies rather than developing them domestically, which could be environmentally beneficial if efficiency is prioritised. But trade also allows '**pollution havens**' to emerge. Many of today's developing countries are former colonies. Western countries developed by extracting raw materials from their colonies. Many of these now-independent countries remain locked into an extractionist development model. They can only seek higher incomes through expanded extraction and export of natural resources, not by moving towards another 'stage' of development (see Winslow 2005: 9–10; Kaika and Zervas 2013: 1405). Some wonder whether China is becoming a 'colonial power' in its quest for growth (Grammaticas 2012), but most developing countries do not have this option. We should therefore be very cautious about using the West's experience to anticipate the development paths of today's poorer countries.

## Do Wealthier People Care More About the Environment?

Let's consider one final assumption embodied in the EKC literature. The idea that poverty reduction drives environmental protection is partly based on the assumption that wealthy people care more about the environment than poor people do. This assumption is widely and intuitively accepted, but is it true? Are environmental concerns a luxury that citizens can only indulge in once they reach a certain level of income? Wilfred Beckerman, an economist and strong critic of 'sustainability as constraint', states this plainly: 'As people become richer, their priorities change and the environment moves up in the hierarchy of human needs. When basic needs for food, water, clothing and shelter are satisfied, then people can begin to attach importance to other ingredients in total welfare, including, eventually, the environment' (Beckerman 1992: 7).

The World Values Survey, the most comprehensive and robust international survey of social values, casts doubt on this assumption. Since 1999 it has asked respondents whether environmental protection is a greater priority than economic growth and job protection. It turns out that a large number of people believe it is, and whether they live in a poor or rich country has little bearing on this attitude. Map 3.2 illustrates the countries in which more than 50 per cent agree that 'Protecting the environment should be given priority even if it causes slower economic growth and some loss of jobs'. This includes high-income countries like Australia, Sweden, and Qatar; and middle-income countries like Argentina, Malaysia, and Brazil. While the survey data does not include the world's poorest

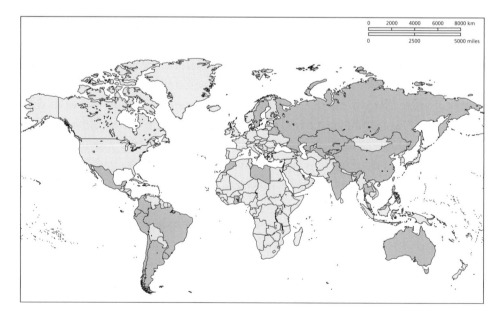

**Map 3.2**: Protecting environment vs. Economic growth.
Countries (shown in darker shading) in which more than 50% agree that 'Protecting the environment should be given priority even if it causes slower economic growth and some loss of jobs'.
2010–14 data

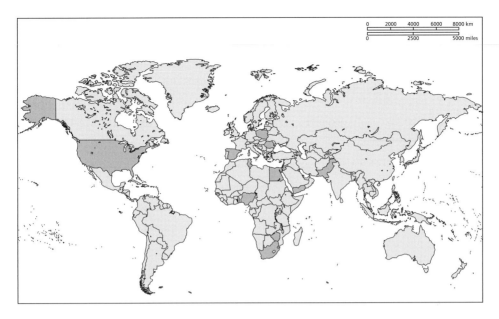

**Map 3.3:** Protecting environment vs. Economic growth
Countries (shown in darker shading) in which more than 50% agree that 'Economic growth and creating jobs should be the priority, even if the environment suffers to some extent'.
2010–14 data

countries, it does include lower-middle-income countries like India and Morocco, which both appear in this group of environmental-prioritising countries.

When we look at those countries that explicitly prioritise economic growth and jobs, we also see a mix of income levels. Map 3.3 shows the countries in which more than 50 per cent agree that 'Economic growth and creating jobs should be the priority, even if the environment suffers to some extent'. This group includes high-income countries like the United States, Kuwait, and Singapore; middle-income countries like Jordan and Bahrain; lower-middle-income countries like Pakistan, and Zimbabwe, a low-income country.[4]

This survey data suggests that the 'too poor to care' thesis is too simplistic. But what it doesn't reveal is the precise character of environmental concerns and values. As American environmental economist Margrethe Winslow points out, it is rational to assume that poor people care at least about those aspects of environmental quality that affect human health and livelihoods. 'One would expect poor fishermen to care about water pollution that kills fish, and rice farmers to care about deforestation that affects the hydraulic cycle where they grow their rice. Deteriorating environmental quality can also have direct consequences on human health, and certainly poor people care about their children dying from diarrhea or asthma' (2005: 13–14). Ramachandra Guha and Joan

Martínez Alier argue that there are wide 'varieties of environmentalism' (1997). Among subordinated social groups in the global South, nature has considerable significance; it is certainly not a 'luxury good' for which they don't earn enough to value. Instead, nature is inextricably bound up with livelihoods, social conflict, and political power. Environmentalism for these groups is about securing access to natural resources, and resisting the powerful efforts of the state and market to take control of these resources (1997).

## Conclusion

The argument that development is the best solution to environmental problems has often been summoned with good intentions. Feminists used this argument to defend themselves against draconian and intrusive population control policies. Developing countries have used it to defend efforts to blame their large populations for global environmental problems. It is safe to conclude that women's empowerment has the added benefit of reducing birth rates. But the relationship between economic growth and environmental improvement is much less clear. Some pollutants do decline as incomes rise, other pollutants rise and fall and rise again, and other pollutants continue rising even beyond very high levels of income. Different pollutants show different trends, and studies haven't even been able to produce consistent findings when looking at the same pollutants. As attractive as the idea may be, we can't simply conclude that poverty is bad for the environment, and affluence is good. Neither can we assume that contemporary developing countries will follow the same development patterns as contemporary wealthy countries. Political economic conditions dictate otherwise. Finally, we must also be cautious about the seductively simple argument that environmental concern is a luxury of the rich. Environmental problems are complex and diverse; they affect people in different ways and at different times. Different groups may have different environmental priorities, and it is important to recognise whose priorities are reflected in international environmental agendas.

In the next chapter we turn to arguments that capitalism is at the root of environmental degradation. This gives us a very different perspective to what we've already seen in Chapters 2 and 3. It also gives us a deeper insight into the complex relationship between development and the environment, which we began looking at in this chapter.

## Discussion Questions

1. What factors would we have to take into account to determine the global 'optimum population'?
2. Is population control likely to be an effective way of addressing global environmental problems? Why or why not?
3. How have feminists critiqued neo-Malthusian arguments about over-population? Do you find their critique persuasive?
4. In what ways is it helpful or unhelpful to treat poverty as one of the principal drivers of environmental problems?
5. What is the relationship between income and environmental values? What evidence can you find to support your argument?

## Notes

1. Perhaps more than any other environmentalist perspective, the neo-Malthusians tend to resort to highly polemic language: in addition to the imagery of a population 'bomb', people have been represented in this tradition as a 'disease', 'a cancer', and 'a menace' (Lovelock 2006; Ehrlich 1968; Brower 1968). This may serve to attract attention, but it also serves to attract the wrong kind of attention. Neo-Malthusian itself has become a term of derision in some quarters where Ehrlich and his colleagues are dismissed as doomsayers and environmental alarmists. No derision is implied in my use of the term neo-Malthusian.
2. The annual World Development Reports present studies by World Bank staff but they are considered an intellectual exercise to stimulate debate. They do not reflect World Bank policy or the agreed position of the Board.
3. This name comes from the original "Kuznet's curve", which influenced resource economists' thinking about the relationship between development and the environment. In 1955, Simon Kuznets observed that income inequality rises in the early stages of development, but then gradually reduces once a certain level of economic growth is reached (Kuznets 1955).
4. Country Income Groups (World Bank Classification), 2011, The World Bank Group, http://data.worldbank.org/about/country-classifications/country-and-lending-groups (accessed 5 May 2016).

# 4 Capitalism

## key points

- Marxist theory contains several concepts and insights that help to understand contemporary ecological crises.
- Ecological Marxists argue that there is a tension between the planet's natural limits and the limitless material expansion required in a capitalist system.
- Critics of capitalism argue that it dulls people's natural cooperative tendencies, and alienates them from nature and the natural world that sustains life.
- Critics of contemporary capitalism disagree on whether 'sustainable capitalism' is a viable vision or a contradiction in terms.
- Some scholars argue that the only sustainable economic system is one that is not based on exponential economic growth.

## Introduction

Is sustainability possible within a global capitalist system? Marxist-inspired scholars are convinced that efforts to address problems like climate change, deforestation, biodiversity loss, and hazardous waste are bound to fail unless we acknowledge the role of global capitalism. In this chapter we will explore the argument that environmental problems are driven by the capitalist system. From this perspective, it's not the size of the population, conditions of poverty, or selfish misuse of common areas that drive environmental degradation. Focusing on these factors is seen as merely a distraction. Consider this quote from ecological socialists Ian Angus and Simon Butler who plead with us to recognise the destructive nature of capitalism, and the imperialism inherent to the global capitalist system.

> Those who claim slowing population growth will stop or slow environmental destruction are ignoring [the] real and immediate threats to life on our planet. Corporations and armies aren't polluting the world and destroying ecosystems because there are 'too many people' . . . If Afghan women have fewer babies, the US military won't stop firing shells made of depleted uranium into their villages. Nor will military bases in Afghanistan stop dumping toxic wastes into open burn pits. If Iraq's birth rate falls to zero, the US military will not use one gallon of oil less. If the United States and Australia block immigration, energy companies will continue burning coal to produce electricity.
>
> (Angus and Butler 2011: 176)

These are hard-hitting and angry words. Perhaps they shock you into attention. Perhaps they alienate you with their directness. Whatever your initial reaction, the aim of this chapter is for you to understand the assumptions that underpin the ecological critique of capitalism. Together with your reading of Chapters 2 and 3, you will then be in a position to articulate your own arguments for why global environmental problems occur.

The Marxist tradition offers the most comprehensive ecological critique of capitalism. But not all green critics of capitalism identify as Marxists. Among many greens there is a lingering 'Marxist allergy' (Soper 1996: 82). Some scholars have critiqued the '**economism**' of our modern liberal democratic systems without any mention of Karl. Economism refers to the fact that GDP is the primary measure of progress in almost all countries, and exponential economic growth is the overarching goal of nearly all governments. However, whether such thinkers identify with Marxism or not, their arguments are largely compatible with – and influenced by – Marxist theory. Resistance to the Marxist label tends to have a political rather than theoretical source: Marxist-inspired socialist experiments have had devastating social and ecological consequences so it is unsurprising that many people don't wish to be associated with them. Often, though, regimes have adopted the name of socialism despite bearing little resemblance to the theoretical ideal. So we should be cautious about judging the theory's value by comparing it to existing and historical regimes. After all, you probably wouldn't judge the value of democratic theory by observing the experience of the Democratic People's Republic of Korea (otherwise known as North Korea)!

Most contemporary Marxist scholars acknowledge that traditional Marxist theory is inadequate for making sense of contemporary ecological predicaments. Marx himself was not 'green' in the way we would recognise today. He lived during a time when nature was valued almost exclusively in materialist terms (as 'natural resources'). Traditional Marxism is avowedly anthropocentric: nature is not inherently valuable; instead it is valued only insofar as it is valuable for human welfare. But, as we will see, with some contemporary ecological revisions traditional Marxist theory can help us to understand why environmental problems occur.

We begin by examining the argument that environmental degradation is an inevitable consequence of capitalism. Anti-capitalist ecological thought is rich in concepts that can help us to understand the logic of this argument. We will explore the concepts of **metabolic rift** and **ecological rift**; the contradictions of capitalism; **economic Malthusianism**; **alienation**; and the **'core' and 'periphery'** of the capitalist world system. We will then examine the implications of a capitalist critique for finding solutions to the environmental crisis. Some say it is possible to create a **sustainable capitalism**', while critics of capitalism argue that we need more radical changes such as a move to a steady-state economy or degrowth. We will consider the merits and limitations of each of these ideas.

# The Contradictions of Capitalism

From a Marxist perspective, capitalism is a system ravaged by 'dialectical contradictions'. This means that its internal elements are inconsistent or opposed to one another. David Harvey recently identified no fewer than seventeen contradictions in capitalism (Harvey 2014).

## The Traditional Contradiction

Marxists traditionally identify the central contradiction as between production and consumption. This means that there is a tension between the *forces* of production (the combination of tools, technology, and human labour) and the *relations* of production (how it is socially organised, e.g., slavery, feudalism, capitalism, socialism). Tension emerges between these two elements in a capitalist society where an owning class employs a working class to produce goods for consumption. The main goal of the owning class is to generate a profit, which is achieved by selling goods at a higher rate than what it cost to produce them. Every commodity has a 'use value' and 'exchange value'; the difference between them is the 'surplus value', or profit. Sustaining a certain level of profit requires keeping production costs low by investing in efficient tools or technology, and avoiding wage increases. In theory this eventually generates a crisis of over-production because the labour force cannot afford to purchase the commodities it is producing. The capitalist system cannot perpetually sustain both consumer demand and profit. Marx assumed that the system would eventually self-destruct because profits would collapse and workers disgruntled by under-consumption would organise into a labour movement, which in turn would build pressure for social change. The end result, it was assumed, would be a revolution in which the relations of production are socialised. But in practice this tension or contradiction is sustained by state interventions (and non-state interventions permitted by the state): governments maintain budget deficits and develop business-friendly foreign trade and investment policies; consumer credit and mortgages are widely available; and businesses borrow money.

## The Ecological Contradiction

Ecological Marxists argue that a 'second contradiction' becomes apparent when we acknowledge the role that nature plays in sustaining all economic activity. This second contradiction has a material dimension, as well as political and social dimensions. Materially there is a tension between the planet's natural limits and the limitless material expansion required in a capitalist system. The earth is a 'closed system' that cannot support infinite growth, but capitalism cannot survive without continual growth. The laws of thermodynamics help us to understand this tension:

The first law of thermodynamics (or conservation law) states quite simply that energy is neither created nor destroyed as it is changed from one form to another (heat, light, motion, etc.). The second law of thermodynamics states that the availability of that energy to perform useful work is reduced as it passes through successive transformations. This is sometimes described as the law of entropy – entropy being a measure of the amount of energy no longer capable of further conversions to perform useful work. Entropy within any closed system inevitably increases over time.

(Porritt 2007: 58)

So when natural resources are used for productive purposes (like fossil fuels for energy) they aren't used in the sense that they disappear; they are simply converted into less useful or valuable matter. This matter often takes the form of waste or pollution. Biophysical systems may eventually convert this waste into a more useful resource, but these natural processes are out of sync with capitalist production processes. As a result, capitalism undermines its own 'productive conditions'.

Capitalism relies on the availability of land, minerals, water, clean air, and a stable climatic system, etc. These provide resources and sustain human life (i.e., the labour force). But economic activities often create environmental problems that damage these natural conditions. Consider the case of **acid rain**: coal-fired power plants emit sulphur dioxide, which is converted to acid in the air, which then falls as acid rain destroying forests and arable land, killing marine life, damaging buildings, eroding the paint on cars, etc. These problems in turn reduce profits and undermine future productive potential.

Capitalism also requires and promotes competition. This acts as an additional driver of environmental degradation and resource depletion. Competing with other firms or states requires keeping immediate production costs as low as possible. This means that individual capitalists will use the highest-quality resources or most easily accessible resources first, whether or not this is a productive strategy in the long term. Market rationality is in this way out of kilter with ecological rationality. This material tension that is inherent to capitalism cannot be maintained forever. Eventually, Marxists argue, environmental degradation and resource depletion will bring about the demise of capitalism.

Some Marxist scholars, most notably James O'Connor, argue that the material dimension of capitalism's ecological contradiction introduces additional political and social tensions. All of these tensions weaken the long-term viability of the capitalist system, they argue. The political tension emerges because the short-term competitive logic of capitalism undermines its own long-term sustainability. The only way to ensure that longer-term considerations are internalised into the current costs of production is to introduce interventions that go against the logic of capitalism. In other words, governments need to introduce regulations. O'Connor, an ecological Marxist, argues that by introducing regulations governments are politicising the conditions of capitalist production. For O'Connor, intervention from the state is a sign of the socialisation of productive relations. Notice here the analogy with classical Marxist theory of the inevitable transition from capitalism to socialism. In the classic account, it is a crisis of over-production or under-consumption that undermines the capitalist system from within. The emergence of ecological crises, O'Connor argues, 'brings into being new forms of flexible planning and planned flexibility, which increases tensions between a more flexible capitalism and a more planned capitalism'

(O'Connor 1998: 210). When the state intervenes, the relations of production are altered: they become more socialised. This, in turn, has the effect of 'making socialism at least more imaginable' (O'Connor 1998: 210).

But sympathetic critics point out that state involvement does not necessarily weaken the hold of capitalism. The state can reinforce capitalism by acting in market-friendly ways that protect the capitalist system (but may come at the expense of individual capitalists). Introducing emissions trading systems, for example, imposes demands on industry but does not undermine the overall functioning of capitalism. It may reduce the profits of fossil fuel intensive firms but increase the profits of those with a stake in renewable energy and alternative technologies. Similarly, restricting the release of waste into lakes and rivers may undermine the interests of heavy-industry capitalists, but serve the interests of capitalists in the agricultural or tourism industries (Vlacho 1996: 232). Can you think of other ways in which governmental intervention for environmental protection can protect some industries while putting a burden on others?

The introduction of environmental regulation was one way that O'Connor thought the capitalist system might be weakened. The other way was through social movements. He argued that the ecological crisis generates a 'social tension' because social movements tend to form when people recognise the risks of environmental problems. Social movements in turn may push capitalist production conditions in a more social direction. The analogy with classic Marxist theory is evident in O'Connor's thinking: 'Labor exploitation . . . engendered a labor movement which during particular times and places turned itself into a "social barrier" to capital. Nature exploitation . . . engenders an environmental movement (environmentalism, public health movement, occupational health and safety movements, women's movement organised around the politics of the body, etc.) which may also constitute a "social barrier" to capital' (O'Connor 1998: 211). The emergence of new social movements therefore presents a potential 'route to socialism' (Benton 1996: 188).

## Capitalism's Rifts

It is only in recent decades that Marxists have begun elaborating on the ecological contradictions of capitalism. But we can identify the seeds of an ecological critique in Marx's own nineteenth-century writings. This work presented concepts like alienation, metabolic rift, and **ecological rift**. These concepts are useful for understanding the relationship between capitalist development and environmental degradation.

## Alienation from Nature

Marx understood that humans are part of nature and deeply dependent on it:

Nature is man's inorganic body, that is to say nature in so far as it is not the human body. Man lives from nature, i.e., nature is his body, and he must maintain a continuing dialogue with it if he is not to die. To say that man's physical and mental life is linked to nature simply means that nature is linked to itself, for man is part of nature.

(quoted in Dickens 1992: 64)

Marx saw that the capitalist mode of production alienates people from nature in two ways. It alienates people from their human nature by reducing them to providers of labour to meet the goals set by the bourgeoisie. This mode of production alienates workers from their cooperative tendencies. This prevents them from fulfilling their own potential and directing their own destiny. This is the classic understanding of alienation. But an ecological form of alienation was also detected by Marx. He argued that people lose their conscious connection with nature when they are engaged in mechanistic and industrialised production. Once people lose this connection, they are less likely to behave in ways that sustain the natural world that sustains the lives.

## Metabolic Rift

The ecological conceptualisation of alienation was further theorised in Marx's work on the metabolic rift. His concept of the metabolic rift was influenced by German chemist, Justus von Liebig's work on metabolism. This concept allowed Marx to sharpen his critique of industrialised agriculture within capitalist society. The term 'metabolism' was initially used by scientists to refer to 'the complex biochemical process of exchange, through which an organism . . . draws upon materials and energy from its environment and converts these . . . into the building blocks of growth' (Foster et al. 2010: 402). Given that humans are dependent on nature, Marx believed that the idea of metabolism could be extended to the social world. This would help to capture 'the complex, dynamic interchange [of matter and energy] between human beings and nature' (Foster 2000: 158). Marx observed that capitalism interrupted the natural dynamic processes that connected humans with the earth. He called this disruption a 'metabolic rift', and observed it in soil degradation in the countryside, and specifically in the loss of nitrogen, phosphorus, and potassium. During earlier times when production and consumption occurred within close proximity, crops and natural wastage were returned to the land as fertilizer, thus sustaining its nutrient base and productive capacity. Marx saw that the accumulative imperative of capitalism concentrated land ownership, depopulated rural areas, increased the density of urban living, and ultimately created an urban–rural divide that resulted in soil nutrients accumulating as urban waste (Foster et al. 2010: 77).

## Ecological Rift

Contemporary ecological Marxists like John Bellamy Foster, Brett Clark, and Richard York have drawn on the concept of 'metabolic rift' to critique the global economic system and understand ecological degradation. They argue that the 'ecological rift' that Marx observed has expanded and globalised because governments and corporations are promoting 'technological fixes' to environmental problems. For example, large industrial farms are using large amounts of artificial nitrogen fertiliser to compensate for the loss of organic soil nutrients. A side effect of this is the release of nitrogen compounds into the atmosphere, which contribute to global warming. Another side effect is that soil run-off increases the concentration of nutrients in waterways causing **eutrophication** and marine 'dead zones' (Foster et al. 2010: 81–2).

In 2009, Swedish sustainability scientist Johan Rockström and his colleagues released an influential study on the '**planetary boundaries**' that 'define the safe operating space for humanity with respect to the Earth system and are associated with the planet's biophysical subsystems or processes' (Rockström et al. 2009).

Three of these boundaries have already been exceeded: the nitrogen cycle, rate of biodiversity loss, and climate change (see Figure 4.1). What this means is that the earth system moves into a new state that can have highly adverse consequences for humans. Rockström and his colleagues do not identify with ecological Marxists, but their work has influenced ecological Marxists who see this research as evidence of planetary-scale 'ecological rifts'. From this perspective, climate change is understood as an ecological rift in the carbon cycle: the carbon cycle is ruptured by social forces that drive an over-accumulation of carbon dioxide in the atmosphere (Foster et al. 2010: 126–32). Problems of planetary-scale rifts arise because capitalism does not recognise natural

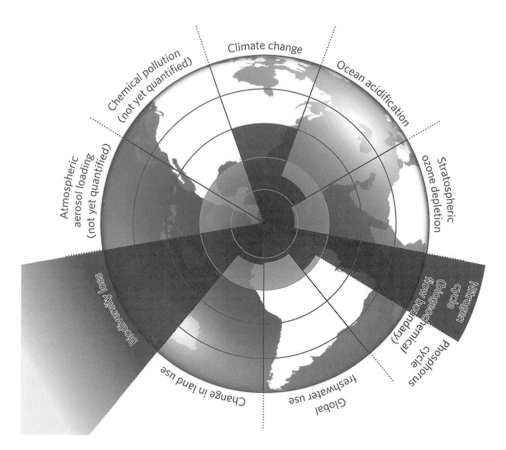

**Figure 4.1:** Planetary boundaries
(Credit: Azote Images/Stockholm Resilience Centre)
Source: Rockström et al. 2009

boundaries or planetary limits. Nature is treated as limitless, so any problems that arise are merely barriers to be overcome by using new technologies (Foster et al. 2010: 40).

## Ecological Imperialism

Ecological Marxists argue that to understand contemporary environmental problems we need to understand the ecological dimensions of European colonisation and capitalist expansion. Taking a longer perspective allows us to see how the 'metabolic rift' emerges not only from an urban–rural divide (as Marx himself saw), but also from a divide between a global core (i.e., Europe) and its periphery (i.e., colonised lands). This is referred to as **'ecological imperialism'**. Marxist scholars argue that the pursuit of profit at the 'core' has destroyed social and ecological systems at the 'periphery' for several centuries. Historically we can see this with commodities like sugar and silver, which Jason Moore refers to as the great 'commodity frontiers' of early modern capitalism (2003: 308). Moore argues that these commodities have been both economically and eco-logically central to the emergence of a global economy based on endless capital accumulation. Economically, the exploitation of distant lands for these com-modities fuelled capital expansion in Europe's urban centres. Environmental degradation wasn't just a consequence of intensively producing these commod-ities for international trade. Instead, environmental degradation also promoted European expansion and thus the globalisation of a capitalist economy. Moore explains: 'Degradation and relative exhaustion in one region after another were followed by recurrent waves of global expansion aimed at securing fresh supplies of land and labor, and thence to renewed and extended cycles of unsustainable development on a world-scale' (Moore 2003: 309).

Other ecological Marxists have shown how the nineteenth-century inter-national trade in *guano* (seabird excrement) was exemplary ecological imperial-ism and a 'global metabolic rift'. This involved direct transfer of *guano*, a phosphate- and nitrogen-rich resource, from South America to Britain to help deal with the declining fertility of British soil, which had itself been caused by capitalist modes of agriculture. Accomplishing this transfer at minimal cost to the imperial power required various interventions with social, economic, and military consequences. Cheap Chinese labour was transferred to Peru to deal with local labour shortages (shortages themselves caused by the expansion of plantations and mines). Under terrible labour conditions, the Chinese workers (who Marx and Engels likened to slaves) then extracted the *guano* for export to Britain. This resulted in greater prosperity in Europe at the expense of distant environmental degradation in South America. A resource that had richly accu-mulated over thousands of years was depleted far more rapidly than it could be replenished. Through this process, Peru was transformed into a country depend-ent on the global market for *guano*. In less than twenty years, the commodity's contribution to Peruvian GDP rose from 5 per cent to 80 per cent (Foster et al. 2010: 357–8). As global demand for *guano* grew, so did tensions between Peru, Chile, and Bolivia, who disputed the sovereignty of the Pacific islands on which *guano* was most abundant. The resulting 'War of the Pacific' was thereby provoked (and, it is suggested, covertly supported) by imperial powers and their 'environmental overdraft' (Foster et al. 2010: 347–55).

Ecological Marxists insist that such exploitation continues to this day. Ecological imperialism is not just an historic phenomenon. The global South tends to provide much of the cheap labour for manufacturing goods that generate profits for Northern-based corporations. In addition, many developing countries continue to depend on the export of primary natural resources to industrialised countries where the lion's share of profit is obtained through refinement or 'value adding' (converting primary commodities into consumer products). This contemporary form of 'ecological imperialism' is sometimes referred to as 'ecologically unequal exchange'.

## Over-consumption

Capitalist societies are characterised by growing levels of consumption. So should we as consumers accept our share of the blame for pushing the planet into its current state? It seems almost self-evident that we should, but ecological Marxists urge us to reject this misguided view. Drawing an analogy with traditional Malthusian concerns about population growth, they label this perspective 'economic Malthusianism' (Foster et al. 2010: 178). We encountered Thomas Malthus and his modern-day followers in Chapter 3. Traditional Malthusian concerns arise from the idea that the planet can support only a limited number of people; they are therefore concerned about overall population levels. Economic Malthusians shift focus from the overall number of 'the masses' to the consumption habits of 'the masses'. Calls for population control are replaced with calls for restraints on consumption: we should shop less or buy only 'green' products.

Marxists accept that consumption is an important driver of environmental degradation. But they criticise the failure of consumption critics to recognise the class dimension of consumption in a capitalist society. They argue that focusing on the habits of individual consumers leads to a mistaken diagnosis of the role of consumption in ecological problems. To focus on household or individual consumption as a driver of environmental degradation is to lose sight of the role of investment. Investment is a form of consumption that has a far greater impact than individual consumption. The environmentally conscious household that

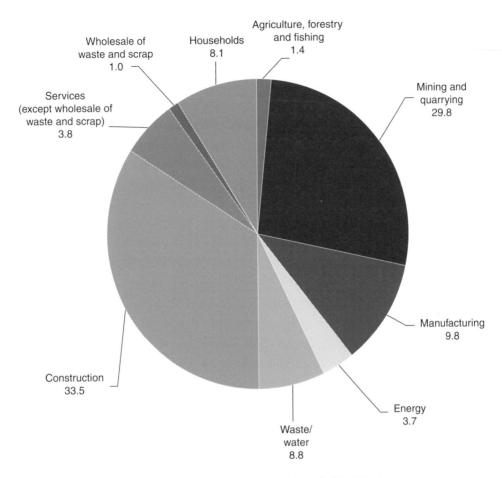

**Figure 4.2:** Waste generation by economic activity and households, EU-28
Source: Eurostat 2014

responsibly reduces its consumption and minimises its waste will have a minuscule impact. Even if every single household follows their lead, the reduction in waste will be minimal. The reason for this is revealed in Figure 4.2.

The graph in Figure 4.2 shows the contribution of different sectors to overall waste in the European Union. Household waste is just 8.1 per cent of the total. Foster and his colleagues estimate that in the United States the contribution of all municipal solid waste is just 2.5 per cent of the total (2010: 383). The vast majority of waste in our societies comes from sources over which individuals and households have very little influence: construction, mining, manufacturing, water supply, and waste management. 'The masses' have little control over the volume of waste generated in these sectors, or on the way it is treated (reused, recycled, sent to landfill, etc.).

Now, it may be argued that much of the waste generated in these various sectors of the economy is indirectly connected to consumer demand. After all, resources are mined and goods are manufactured because people are buying the final products: food, clothing, cars, gadgets, etc. But ecological Marxists argue that this also fails to recognise how personal consumption is shaped in capitalist societies by forces beyond individual control. As critics of 'economic Malthusianism' point out, an enormous and growing amount of money is spent on advertising campaigns to convince people to buy things they didn't previously need or want. In 2013, $516.47 billion was spent globally on advertising (Statistica 2016).

Harvard economist John Kenneth Galbraith recognised the power of the advertising industry back in the 1950s. He noted that its 'central function is to create desires – to bring into being wants that previously did not exist' (Galbraith 1958: 127). The power of this industry is far greater today than when Galbraith expressed these concerns. In the 1940s, only about $33 was 'invested' each year in shaping the consumption habits of each American. Now this figure is almost seventeen times higher, at $554 per American, per year (Statistica 2016). What this reflects is the myth of consumer sovereignty (Princen et al. 2002b: 325). Thomas Princen and his colleagues argue that to confront the role of consumption in environmental degradation we need to debunk this myth:

It is a myth convenient for those who would locate responsibility for social and environmental problems squarely on the backs of consumers. It makes the idea of unlimited economic growth appear both natural and inevitable. But consumers do not have perfect information and they are not insulated from the influence of marketers. Their consumption choices seem broad but are in fact rightly constrained (one chooses, in today's marketplace, between a red car and a blue one, not between an automobile-based transport system and a mass-transit based one, and this is no accident).

(Princen et al. 2002b: 325)

## Is Sustainable Capitalism the Solution?

Can capitalism ever become ecologically sustainable, or is this a contradiction in terms? Many people are optimistic that traditional capitalism can be transformed into sustainable capitalism. They see ecological sustainability and business profitability as compatible. Hawken and the Lovins advance such a view in their book *Natural Capitalism*, as does Jonathon Porritt in his book *Capitalism as if the World Matters*. The solution, they argue, is to be found in expanding our understanding of 'capital'. 'Capital', writes Porritt, 'is a stock of anything that has the capacity to generate a flow of benefits which are valued by humans' (2007: 138). Financial capital and manufactured capital, they suggest, are just two types of capital. Equally important is growth in the value of human capital (health, knowledge, skills, motivation, emotional/spiritual capacities), social capital (families, communities, businesses, trade unions, voluntary organisations, legal/political systems, education and health bodies – all of which enable people to mutually develop their human capital), and natural capital (renewable and non-renewable resources, seas and forests that act as pollution 'sinks', and natural systems that regulate the climate) (Porritt 2007: 139). Based on these forms of capital, Hawken and the Lovins describe 'a future in which business and environmental interests increasingly overlap, and in which businesses can better satisfy their customers' needs, increase profits, and help solve environmental problems all at the same time' (1999). They argue that this can be achieved in three steps. First, by radically increasing resource productivity, and using the savings to finance a shift towards closed-loop production. Closed-loop production is sometimes called a '**circular economy**'. It involves the use of waste as a resource so that there are no by-products from production. Second, by shifting from product provision to service provision. And third by reinvesting in the ecosystems that support life and business (i.e., '**natural capital**').

Hopes that we can transition to a sustainable form of capitalism have been buoyed by the efficiency gains achieved throughout the 2000s. If we can achieve the same goods and services while continuously decreasing use of energy and resources, then economic growth can become more sustainable. This is referred to as '**dematerialisation**'. On a global scale, about 33 per cent less energy was used per unit of GDP in 2008 than in 1970 (Jackson 2009). This means that the global economy was less 'energy intensive'. By 2015, many countries were improving the 'energy intensity' of their economies by at least 2 per cent per year (International Energy Agency 2016: 13). Critics warn against conflating efficiency and sustainability. As long as we aim for bigger economies, then our consumption of energy and resources will continue to grow in absolute terms, even if our use is more efficient (see Stevenson 2016b: 4–8). Critics point to 'Jevons paradox', which we saw in Chapter 3, as evidence that sustainable capitalism is not possible.

Ecological Marxists see 'sustainable capitalism' as an oxymoron. Overcoming the contradictions of capitalism, they argue, would require such extensive changes to the state that it would simply cease to function as a capitalist state. It would require considerable central planning and coordination rather than leaving social and economic processes to be determined by the market. So James O'Connor's response to the question 'Is an ecologically sustainable capitalism possible?' is 'Not unless and until capital changes its face in ways that would make it unrecognizable to bankers, money managers, venture capitalists, and CEOs looking at themselves in the mirror today' (1998: 239).

For many Marxists the key question is not whether capitalism can ever become sustainable. Martin O'Connor acknowledges that global capitalism may remain viable for quite some time. But he argues that viable shouldn't be confused with desirable because 'the prices to be paid in terms of both human conflicts and lost human, cultural, and ecological riches will be very great' (1994: 2). For O'Connor and others, capitalism can never be either sustainable in the long term or sustaining in the short term, if we take this to mean providing the necessities of human life (1994: 2).

# Eco-socialism

For many anti-capitalist ecological thinkers, the solution to our environmental crises lies in some form of socialism. In a socialist society, the forces of production would be publicly owned, and the relations of production would be based on cooperation. Eco-socialists see this as a necessary though not sufficient condition for sustainability. Replacing capitalism with socialism, they argue, would remove the inherent drive towards endless accumulation, and ease the tensions that alienate people from the natural world. It's important to recognise that while many anti-capitalist thinkers point towards socialist solutions to the environmental crisis they do not necessarily support any existing or historical socialist or communist experiments. In fact, most are very quick to point out that the USSR left a devastating environmental legacy, and China's environmental record has on balance been appalling. Socialism would need to be infused with ecological principles to be sustainable.

Different schools of ecological Marxists offer different visions of ecologically sustainable socialism. Robyn Eckersley distinguishes between orthodox eco-Marxism and humanist eco-Marxism (1992: 75–96). The former maintains Marx's anthropocentric worldview. It aims to liberate nature from the domination of the bourgeoisie so that nature can instead service the material needs and desires of the working class. Environmental conservation for reasons other than human welfare has no place in this version of eco-Marxism. Eckersley explains that 'orthodox eco-Marxists simply seek to replace the private and socially inequitable mastery of nature under capitalism with the public and socially equitable mastery of nature under communism' (1992: 85). Humanist eco-Marxism places humans in the role of nature's stewards, which carries a responsibility of care and avoids treating nature in a purely instrumental fashion. In Donald Lee's humanist elaboration, eco-socialism would feature 'socially useful production, the reduction of labor time, maximum creative leisure, wise use of resources, rational population control, and solidarity between all living things' (see Eckersley 1992: 88).

We can already see many ideas and experiments in cooperation. These are not usually explicitly presented as socialist experiments, but they are informed by socialist principles. Consider the 'sharing economy'. Even if you haven't heard of this idea you've probably heard of popular sharing initiatives like Airbnb (owners and tenants offering guests temporary accommodation) and Zipcar (a car-sharing club). The idea behind the sharing economy is simple: most of the time we don't need to own something to get what we want from it. You need a hole in the wall, not a power drill. You need to get from home to work; you don't need to own a car. You want to read the latest Nordic noir bestseller; you don't need to own another book.

The environmental benefit of sharing initiatives is that less ownership means less use of resources and less generation of waste and pollution. Numerous social sharing enterprises have sprung up in recent years to reduce consumption and ownership by connecting citizens and their belongings. Some of these have been absorbed into the capitalist system, and blur the line between sharing and profit seeking. Others, like Uber and Airbnb, reveal the tensions that can emerge when informal initiatives exist in parallel to the formal economy (where taxis and hotels are regulated and taxed). The case of South Korea's capital Seoul shows us how governments can foster and regulate social sharing to reduce these tensions. Seoul's Metropolitan Government defines sharing as 'activities that create social, economic and environmental values by jointly using resources, such as space, goods, information, talent and experience' (Seoul Metropolitan Government 2014). Under the leadership of Seoul's mayor Park Won-soon, sharing has become part of the city's sustainability plans. Policies introduced in 2014 ensure that sharing activities function in the public interest, rather than for the private benefit of a few. These policies ensure that citizens have the opportunity to share cars, books, tools, housing, meals, clothes, hobbies, labour, and ideas. 'Sharing enterprises' have access to subsidies and public credit to expand their initiatives; and the mayor and citizens share responsibility for raising awareness of sharing and promoting a 'sharing culture' (Seoul Metropolitan Government 2014, 2016).

# Steady-state Economy and Degrowth

Many non-capitalist visions of sustainable society are based on post-growth principles. Sometimes these are presented as '**steady state–economics**' and other times as '**degrowth**' societies.

A steady-state economy is one that maintains a stable size in terms of both population and material consumption. It is sometimes referred to as a 'stationary state economy'. The most prominent advocate of this approach is Herman Daly. Daly distinguishes between 'development' and 'growth', arguing that a steady-state economy provides for 'development without growth' (2014: viii). Daly does not believe that growth is always bad: he acknowledges that countries with widespread poverty will need to continue growing for some time. Freeing up the resources and 'atmospheric space' to do so demands a rapid transition to steady-state economies in already wealthy countries (2014: ix). For Daly and his many followers, a steady-state economy does not mean returning to the dark ages. Wealthy countries could continue to *progress* through production that meets basic needs, and increases leisure time, family time, and cooperation.

The idea of a 'steady-state economy' certainly does not promise that the planet will be able to support human life into eternity: the law of entropy still applies and eventually resources will run out. Instead, the idea is based on the ethical assumption that it is better to fairly share the planet's resources over as long a period of time as possible. We can choose between 'sufficiency with longevity' or 'extravagance with impatience' (2014: ix).

Today the size of the global economy relies on a level of resource consumption that is highly unsustainable. This means that the transition to sustainable steady-state economies would have to entail what is called 'degrowth', which is the equitable downsizing of production and consumption. Proponents of degrowth have developed the basic idea of material downsizing into a vision of deeper democracy, shorter working hours, equitable sharing of resources, cooperative human relations replacing market relations, and ecosystem protection (Schneider et al. 2010). This has moved beyond an academic interest to a growing social movement, especially in European countries. Thinking through the details of a degrowth transition is still in its infancy. Advocates are quick to point out that an immediate abandonment of growth would be socially disastrous, resulting in recession, depression, unemployment, and poverty that would hit the poorest the hardest (Schneider et al. 2010: 512).

Advocates of the steady-state economy and degrowth acknowledge that moving to such a post-capitalist system will be neither quick nor easy. Some demand that nothing short of ecological revolution is required. Others are more realistic and point to the importance of taking ameliorative steps in the short term to reduce the impact of capitalism on the environment. This would include national and international policies such as greater regulation, high taxes on natural resources and certain consumer products, heavy subsidies on solar and alternative energy, public investment in mass transit, and stronger restrictions on pollution and deforestation. The reduction of poverty and inequality is also often cited as important in the short term. Victor Lippit explains that this is important because

For those living in poverty, or even for those not in poverty but feeling materially deprived compared to their neighbours, the promise of economic growth is a bright one. For the transition ... to be feasible there must be a great diminution in inequality and a complete eradication of poverty. For this reason the entire world has an interest in the successful development of the Third World, as well as in measures that lead to significant reduction in inequality within individual nation-states.

(2005: 137–8)

## Conclusion

In this chapter we've examined the argument regarding whether environmental degradation is an inevitable consequence of capitalism. We saw that although not all critics of growth-centric economics are Marxists, the ecological Marxist tradition offers the most comprehensive environmentalist critique of capitalism. The concepts of capitalist contradictions, alienation, the metabolic rift, ecological rift, and ecological imperialism all help us understand how the capitalist economic system might be responsible for producing ecological degradation. You may not agree with the conclusions that ecological Marxists draw from their analysis of global capitalism, but understanding these concepts should at least help you to understand these arguments.

Familiar with various explanations for why environmental problems occur, you are now better equipped to respond to that hypothetical bus passenger we met in Chapter 1: 'Why do we have so many environmental problems?' Is it because humans are short-sighted and selfish; because resources are often left open and unmanaged; because there are too many people in the world; because many countries are still living in poverty and too poor to prioritise a clean environment; because countries continue to grow even once they're 'developed'; because the capitalism system requires continuous growth and competition; or because people have become alienated from the natural world?

Perhaps some readers are impatient to move on to discover more about the options for responding to environmental problems. If the ecological crisis is as serious as we saw in Chapter 1, then surely it's poor use of our time to dwell on the reasons for the problems. There is a pragmatic appeal to this, a certain schoolyard common sense: 'I don't care how the mess was made, I just want it cleaned up now!' But for political issues, we do have to devote attention to figuring out why problems occur. Even once 'solutions' are well underway, it is vital that we continue analysing the underlying drivers of environmental problems. Without this deeper understanding of causes, solutions become mere Band-Aids.

Responses to environmental problems are shaped by understandings of their causes. As we will see in Part 2 of this book, the international community is largely unwilling to question the capitalist economic system. This forms the backdrop to much international interaction. Occasionally we see actors like the European Commission develop alternative measures of progress like the 'enlarged GDP', which adjusts GDP to reflect the impact on national wealth of resource depletion, environmental degradation, and income inequality. But there is generally little questioning of the benefits of exponential economic growth and market-based approaches to environmental problems. Instead we see frameworks and mechanisms developed that try to make economic growth environmentally sustainable (examples include 'sustainable development', which we'll see in Chapter 6, and 'emissions offsetting', which we'll see in Chapter 7).

By understanding different explanations for why environmental problems occur, you will be able to reflect more critically on existing international responses to environmental problems. You will be better placed to identify which 'problematisations' are taken seriously, which aspects of a problem are acknowledged and overlooked, and what alternative responses might look like. We will return to these concerns in Chapter 12. But now let's turn to the first of our empirical chapters, which looks at freshwater scarcity and responses of conflict and cooperation.

## Discussion Questions

1. What do Marxists traditionally mean by the contradictions of capitalists? How have ecological Marxists elaborated on these insights to understand environmental degradation?
2. Is there still a 'core' and 'periphery' in the global economic system? In what ways has this historically and/or presently produced environmental degradation and injustice?
3. Is sustainable capitalism possible and/or desirable? Why or why not?
4. Do you see non-capitalist economic systems as potentially viable? What social and political factors make them viable or unviable?
5. Why do environmental problems occur?

# PART 2

## Responding to Global Environmental Problems

# 5 Conflict and Securitisation
## Water Scarcity

**key points**

- Conflict takes many forms depending on the actors involved, the measures they take, and the intensity of the events that unfold.
- Environmental factors alone are neither a necessary nor sufficient cause for violent conflict, when they do play a causal role they do so in combination with other physical and social factors.
- The world's freshwater resources are highly transnational and increasingly scarce. These two conditions underpin assumptions that violent conflict is either prevalent or likely.
- Cooperation over water is much more prevalent than conflict. But cooperation doesn't always ensure fair and effective outcomes.
- Scholars disagree about whether we should treat environment problems as security threats.

# Introduction

One of the greatest impediments to environmental sustainability is the mismatch between people's material desires and the world's natural resources. Human needs and desires are constantly expanding. No state really considers itself as 'developed': all states aim to expand their economies and improve the living conditions of their citizens. The advertising industry spends enormous amounts of money to ensure that needs and desires continue expanding in all countries (see Chapter 4). So although we tend to divide the world into developed and developing countries, all countries are effectively developing countries.

But the planet's natural resources are not expanding to meet these needs and demands: some renewable resources maintain a stable level of supply while many non-renewable resources are being depleted. Irrespective of whether the supply is stable or shrinking, under conditions of growing demands, both renewable and non-renewable resources become scarce to some degree. The common wisdom accompanying this dilemma tends to be that states (and perhaps individuals) will resort to conflict to secure their own access to scarce resources. Water is perhaps the archetype resource in these narratives. The alliteratively appealing phrase of 'water wars' has rolled off the tongue of many politicians, past and present:

The next war in the Middle East will be fought over water, not politics.

(Boutros Boutros-Ghali, former UN Secretary General, 1988)

The wars of the next century will be over water.

(Ismail Serageldin, former vice president of the World Bank, 1995)

Fierce competition for freshwater may well become a source of conflict and wars in the future.

(Kofi Annan, former UN Secretary General, 2001)

In this chapter we examine how the international community has responded to resource scarcity, with a particular focus on freshwater. Given the prevalent assumption that conflict over natural resources is somehow inevitable, pervasive, or highly likely in the future, the chapter begins with an analysis of the relationship between conflict and the natural environment. In this section we define the concept of conflict and review the existing research into whether resource abundance or resource scarcity tend to drive violent conflict. We find that there is no simple answer: all violent conflicts have multiple causes, and in some circumstances the availability of resources can contribute to the onset of violent conflict, or affect the duration of existing conflicts. We then move on to our case study of freshwater. Here we see how the world's freshwater resources are both highly transnational and increasingly scarce, and these two conditions underpin assumptions that violent conflict is either prevalent or likely. The rhetoric and the reality of 'water wars' then come under scrutiny. We see that while states have sometimes maintained tense relations over shared water resources, modern history features no cases of war over water. In fact, cooperation over water turns out to be much more prevalent than conflict. Nevertheless, cooperation doesn't necessarily deliver fair and effective outcomes for everyone involved. International relations over water are inherently political and they generate winners and losers among and within states. Irrespective of the extent of actual and historical conflict over water and other natural resources, there are increasing calls to treat the environment as an issue of security. In the final section of the chapter we examine the reasons underpinning this 'securitisation' agenda, and consider the possible negative effects of securitising the environment.

# Conflict and the Natural Environment

To understand how environmental degradation and resource scarcity can lead to situations of conflict we need to begin with an understanding of the concept of conflict. Conflict emerges whenever two or more actors confront one another over diverging values or interests at stake in a particular issue. This can then manifest in a variety of ways depending on the actors involved, the measures they take, and the intensity of the events that unfold (Heidelberg Institute for International Conflict Research 2014: 8–9). The actors involved might be states, international alliances like NATO and the Arab League, or non-state actors such as mobilised citizens, rebel groups, and terrorist organisations. Conflict measures range from peaceful regulatory procedures like elections, courts, and mediation through to the threat or use of physical violence. The intensity of a conflict can be measured along a scale from low-intensity non-violent disputes through to high-intensity all-out war. The Heidelberg Institute for International Conflict Research defines five types of conflict along this scale: dispute, non-violent crisis, violent crisis, limited war, and war (Heidelberg Institute for

International Conflict Research 2014: 9). A particular situation is likely to move back and forth along this scale at different stages of a conflict. Determining where any particular situation is located along the scale at any particular time requires measuring the numbers of people involved, the numbers of casualties, the types of weapons used, the degree of destruction, and the numbers of people displaced internally or abroad (Heidelberg Institute for International Conflict Research 2014: 9). We could expect a low-intensity conflict to involve no weapons or light use of light weapons, a small number of actors involved, no or few casualties, low levels of damage to the economy, society, and civilian infrastructure, and to produce little or no displacement. A high-intensity conflict, by contrast, might involve the deployment of heavy weapons, high numbers of personnel, high casualty numbers, a high level of destruction, and high levels of displacement. All of these considerations are subjective and scholars disagree on what defines a high number of fatalities: some place the figure as low as sixty (Heidelberg Institute for International Conflict Research 2014: 9) while others set the war threshold at 1,000 deaths (Ramsbotham et al. 2011: 64).

## Conflicts Over Natural Resources

French geographer Philippe le Billon observes that 'Natural resources have played a conspicuous role in the history of armed conflicts' (2001: 562). Two competing hypotheses define the relationship between resources and conflict. One camp of scholars highlights the potential for resource scarcity to drive conflict, while another camp highlights the potential for conflict to emerge in areas of resource abundance. The assumption underlying the resource scarcity hypothesis is simple and perhaps intuitive: when a resource necessary for human survival is scare, people will fight to secure their own access to it. During the 1970s and 1980s, scholars began speculating on the conditions under which such violent conflict might occur. International war might emerge from environmental change that altered the balance of power among states; poorer countries might confront wealthier countries to secure a share of the dwindling resources required for development; state stability could be undermined by the movement of '**environmental refugees**'; diminishing arable land could aggravate existing class and ethnic tensions and lead to civil conflict (Homer-Dixon 1999).

In the late 1980s, a Toronto-based team of researchers led by Thomas Homer-Dixon began to move beyond speculation and investigate the relationship between resources and conflict more systematically (see Homer-Dixon 1999). Homer-Dixon and his colleagues examined the incidence of conflict in contexts where a resource had become scarce through either a reduction in supply, an increase in demand, or reduced access brought about by structural changes such as privatisation of the resource (Homer-Dixon 1999: 8–9). They have found that under certain social conditions, resource scarcity and environmental change increase the likelihood of violent conflict. Threatening factors included climate change, soil depletion, desertification, forest loss, freshwater depletion and pollution, and fisheries depletion (Floyd and Matthew 2013: 6). Reflecting on his research in 1999, Homer-Dixon wrote:

I believe that in coming decades the world will probably see a steady increase in the incidence of violent conflict that is caused, at least in part, by environmental scarcity. Developing countries are likely to be affected sooner and more severely than developed countries. They tend to be much more dependent on environmental goods and services for their economic well-being; they often do not have the financial, material, and human capital resources to buffer themselves from the effects of environmental scarcities; and their economic and political institutions tend to be fragile and riven with discord.

(1999: 4)

Homer-Dixon and his colleagues have been careful to stress that violent conflicts never have a single cause. Environmental factors alone are neither a necessary nor sufficient cause for violent conflict; when they do play a causal role they do so in combination with other physical and social factors (1999: 7). Nevertheless, Homer-Dixon does maintain that many conflicts cannot be properly understood without taking environmental factors into account. The rise of terrorist group Sendero Luminoso in Peru in the 1980s, for example, cannot be understood without taking into account the impact of a growing population and land degradation. Incidences of communal violence between Hindus and Muslims in urban India in the 1990s can be partly attributed to tensions relating to large-scale migration of the rural poor, which in turn is partly attributable to land degradation and rural resource scarcity (1999: 18–20). An environmental dimension has also been identified in the 2011 violent uprising in Syria that escalated into civil and international war. While clearly only one of several social and political factors (poverty, unemployment, political suppression, inequality, etc.), drought, researchers in the United States argued, was one of the conflict triggers (Kelley et al. 2015). Syria experienced its worst drought on record in the years 2007–10. Based on 100 years of records on precipitation, temperature, and sea-level pressure, the researchers argued that the drought was very likely the result of anthropogenic global warming. The drought led to widespread crop failure in the north-eastern 'breadbasket' and the migration of 1.5 million rural residents to Syrian cities. This added to the strains on urban resources that had been building up over several years of Iraqi refugee arrivals. By the end of 2010, internally displaced people and refugees accounted for 20 per cent of the Syrian population, and the unrest developed in the urban peripheries where they had settled (Kelley et al. 2015).

Le Billon offers several reasons that theoretically challenge the resource scarcity hypothesis. Firstly, in the face of dwindling resource supplies or increasing human demands, a society has the option of becoming more innovative in how it uses a particular resource, and diversifying its economy to develop human capital. Secondly, local scarcities can be mitigated by international trade or managed with market mechanisms. Thirdly, resource-poor countries are dependent on the non-resource revenue generated by citizens, this in turn makes them more likely to be accountable to citizens, which in turn makes them less likely to be violently conflictual (this reasoning resembles the 'democratic peace' thesis) (Le Billon 2001: 564). What these arguments show is that conflict is not inevitable under conditions of resource scarcity. However, what the arguments do not disprove is that environmental factors can play a causal role in triggering or exacerbating violent conflicts. Certainly many countries will often not be in a position to innovate and diversify their economies; international trade will not always mitigate the loss of livelihoods resulting from scarcity; and many resource-dependent countries are not shining examples of democracy.

The resource abundance hypothesis focuses on the potential for conflict to arise over access to abundant primary commodities. Resource abundant countries are said to have a '**resource curse**' because citizens are vulnerable to the violence, human rights abuse, and environmental degradation that accompany struggles among rebel groups and oppressive governments for the control of valuable resources. Some researchers see these patterns in conflicts in Sierra Leone and the Congo where rebel groups have violently confronted the state not necessarily to take over the government but to secure control of resources like diamonds, gold, cobalt, copper, and oil (Renner 2005: 96). In other cases like Afghanistan, Angola, Cambodia, Colombia, and Sudan, researchers have argued that violent conflicts were triggered by secessionist motives, but that access to valuable resources provided secessionist groups with significant revenue that prolonged conflict (Renner 2005: 96). In the case of Colombia, researchers have shown how the insurgent groups FARC (Revolutionary Armed Forces of Colombia), AUC (United Self-Defense of Colombia), and ELN (National Liberation Army) were able to finance their operations by gaining control of oil reserves and mines for coal, gold, and emeralds. Moreover, natural resources and infrastructure not under rebel control such as oil pipelines, freshwater, and forests have been threatened or damaged to weaken the state (Lavaux 2006/2007). It must be remembered, though, that all cases of conflict are highly contextual and highly complex. In each of the cases above, scholars have disagreed about the relationship between power, conflict, and resources. In particular, scholars often disagree about whether secessionist groups are motivated more by a general desire to take power, or by a specific desire to control certain resources.

Paul Collier and Anke Hoeffler at the University of Oxford have spent two decades studying the relationship between resource abundance, underdevelopment, and civil conflict. By analysing large-scale civil wars in over eighty countries between 1960 and 2004, they have shown that 'the risk of conflict is substantially increased when primary commodity exports (that is, commodities in their raw or unprocessed state) make up a higher share of gross domestic product (GDP) ... The risk of civil war is at its highest point when primary commodity exports make up about 25 percent of GDP; at still higher levels, the risk decreases' (Collier and Hoeffler 2012: 298). They also showed that this relationship is significantly affected by per capita income: vulnerability to conflict subsides at higher levels of per capita income. This explains why countries such as Australia and Norway have not experienced civil conflict despite high levels of resource dependence.

The precise causal mechanisms linking resource abundance and violent conflict in any particular context will be complex. Researchers have highlighted two mechanisms: greed and grievance. In the past these were treated as competing explanations for conflict, but today it is increasingly recognised that these motives often overlap in practice. Again, we need to remain sensitive to the fact that individual conflicts are complex and neat analytical distinctions have limitations.

Greed can manifest as a causal mechanism when the confronting party has no clear political agenda and appears to be seeking to enrich themselves and their followers. Collier and Hoeffler suggest that cases of pure greed are rare, although they acknowledge that it can be difficult to determine when it is a predominant factor in a conflict (2012: 299–300). International greed can also manifest as a causal mechanism. Liberian president Charles Taylor supported and helped to organise the invasion by the Revolutionary United Front (RUF) of Sierra Leone from Liberia with the objective of overthrowing the Sierra Leonean government. During the decade-long conflict, Taylor received millions of dollars in diamonds, and facilitated their illegal trade to Europe thereby generating hundreds of millions of dollars in revenue (UN Panel of Experts 2000). Desire to secure a share of the Congo's significant natural resources also saw the Rwandan and Ugandan governments support rebellions in Congo in the 1990s. This is what Michael Ross calls the 'booty futures' mechanism because rebel groups were securing support from neighbouring countries and foreign firms by selling future mineral rights (Ross 2004: 57–58).

The other widely cited causal link between resource abundance and conflict is grievance. The grievance might be related predominantly to resource extraction itself, or it might be wrapped up with a bundle of grievances relating to widespread inequalities, political suppression, or communal divisions. Seeking control of lucrative resources can then finance a secessionist or revolutionary campaign, and help to redress the material sources of grievance.

In summary, two decades of research into environment and conflict has generated important but not conclusive insights into the conditions under which environmental factors can trigger or affect civil and international conflicts. What is clear is that environmental factors are only ever one part of a bundle of causal factors leading to conflict: conflict certainly does not directly and inevitably emerge from conditions of resource scarcity or resource abundance. In the next two sections of this chapter we focus on one particular resource, freshwater, to understand whether conflict is a common or dominant response to environmental change and scarcity.

# Water and Conflict

In this section we will first look at the state of the world's water, which is both highly transnational and increasingly scarce. We then scrutinise the common assumption that freshwater has been, and is increasingly likely to be, a source of war. We will see that cooperation over water is actually quite common, but that this doesn't always ensure fair and effective outcomes.

## State of the World's Water

Like many of the natural resources that support human wellbeing and economic development, water is transnational and increasingly scarce: two characteristics that sit uncomfortably together. On the one hand, the transnational nature of water resources condemns states to interact with one another to secure access. On the other hand, the scarce nature of water resources makes such interactions sensitive and potentially volatile.

What do you think it means to say that water is transnational and scarce? Perhaps these sound like counter-intuitive assertions: surely water is global and plentiful? It is true that over 70 per cent of the earth's surface is covered in water, making it a global and plentiful element. But as a resource for human use, water availability is much more limited. Oceans hold the lion's share of the world's water (U.S. Geological Survey 2015). It would be a mistake to under-value this water, after all oceans do provide important 'ecosystem services' such as absorbing carbon dioxide, and supporting fish populations that provide human livelihoods and protein. Nevertheless, saline water is not the resource that most directly and profoundly affects people's day-to-day lives.

Freshwater accounts for just 2.5 per cent of the world's water, and less than one-third of this is actually available for human use (the rest being locked in glaciers and permanent snow cover) (Bernauer and Kalbhenn 2010). So while water itself is plentiful, the amount available as freshwater is very limited indeed. It is estimated that just 0.007 per cent of the earth's water is accessible for human consumption (MacQuarrie and Wolf 2013: 169). It is freshwater that is an essential resource for human survival (e.g., for drinking water and sanitation), and supports all sectors of the economy from agriculture (food and fibre production), energy production (hydropower, and cooling power plants), and tourism (aesthetic pleasure and natural beauty) (Russi et al. 2013: 7). The importance of water is recognised in UN Resolution 64/292, which defines access to safe drinking water and sanitation as a human right, and in the Rio+20 agreement, which recognises water as at the core of sustainable development.

Freshwater can be characterised as a transnational resource because the basins from which it emerges and the rivers through which it flows are rarely confined to sovereign borders. Global river flow is by and large a transnational phenomenon. On the most recent count, there are 286 international **river basins** and 145 states have territory lying within one of these basins. This means that more than three-quarters of the world's countries share a source of freshwater with at least one neighbouring country (Wolf et al. 2005; MacQuarrie and Wolf 2013: 170; UNEP-DHI and UNEP 2016).[1] Not all of this freshwater is visible to the naked eye: streams and lakes form systems of surface water, which are connected to vast systems of underground water (called 'groundwater'). Map 5.1 shows the disjuncture between sovereign boundaries and river basin boundaries.

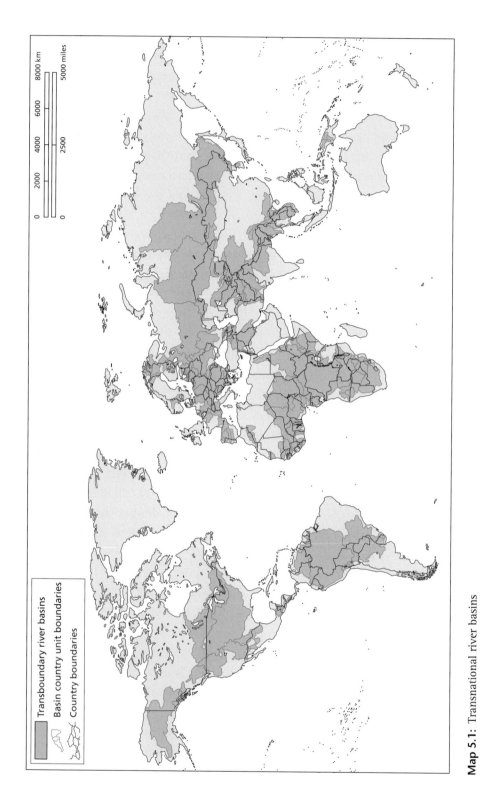

**Map 5.1:** Transnational river basins

Source: GEF–TWAP River Basins Assessment © 2015 http://twap-rivers.org (UNEP-DHI and UNEP 2016)

Freshwater can be characterised as scarce because human demand for this resource increasingly exceeds supply. The UN defines water scarcity as 'the point at which the aggregate impact of all users impinges on the supply or quality of water under prevailing institutional arrangements to the extent that the demand by all sectors, including the environment, cannot be satisfied fully' (UN-Water 2006). Global freshwater availability is fairly stable but there are fears that climate change will affect this. Temperature rises are expected to increase the rate of water evaporation in some areas, and reduce rainfall in dry subtropical areas thereby reducing the availability of water (IPCC 2014: chapter 3).

The most prominent and direct factors that contribute to freshwater scarcity are increasing demands and declining quality. Demand for freshwater rises with economic development. Even if water use is becoming more efficient in some countries and sectors, overall consumption continues to increase. This points to the limits of efficiency that we saw in Chapters 3 and 4. Many of our consumption choices have a hidden water footprint, which we'll examine more closely in Chapter 9. Agriculture is the thirstiest economic sector, accounting for over 90 per cent of global freshwater use (Gerbens-Leenes et al. 2013: 25). We'll see in Chapter 11 that modern agriculture techniques rely on extensive irrigation. The rise of a global consuming class (see Chapter 9) is shifting eating habits away from cereal-based diets towards diets heavy in meat and animal products. The result is increased stress on freshwater sources because meat production requires twenty times more water per calorie than cereals and root vegetables (Mekonnen and Hoekstra 2012: 401). Once we add population growth to the equation, we can see that the water required for food production in the years ahead will be very great indeed. Preferences for larger homes, private cars, and electronic goods all entail greater demands for freshwater. There is certainly no 'Environmental Kuznets Curve' for water: countries consume more water as they become wealthier.

The problem of excessive demand is compounded by the environmental impact it has on water quality. As groundwater levels decline, aquifers become vulnerable to salt intrusion, which in turn diminishes the supply of freshwater. Further environmental contamination results from agricultural fertilisers, industrial waste, and untreated water entering rivers and waterways.

Freshwater scarcity is not a problem we can anticipate only in the future. Demands on freshwater sources are already unsustainable in many parts of the world, and many people already experience water scarcity in their daily lives. In a moderately developed country, the minimum amount of water an individual requires for a decent quality of life is assumed to be about 1,000,000 litres

(1,000 cubic metres) per year (MacQuarrie and Wolf 2013: 169). The most water scarce region of the world is the Middle East: Israel has less than 300 cubic metres of water available per person per year; Jordan has about 100 cubic metres, and Gaza and the West Bank have even less than this (Jägerskog 2005: 86). It is also important to recognise that scarcity is a social problem rather than purely an objective measure of supply. Unequal distribution of freshwater means that some people experience this as a scarce resource, and others do not. Rapid urbanisation and the proliferation of slums in many cities in the South mean that hundreds of millions of people do not have access to adequate clean water, even though those cities may not be classified as water scarce or water stressed. Water scarcity, then, is also an issue of environmental injustice.

## Water Wars: Theory and Evidence

The spectre of water wars looms large in popular and political rhetoric. This is evident in the quotes presented in the introduction to this chapter. Perhaps more than any other natural resource, politicians, scholars, and other observers have warned of the potential for violent conflict to emerge from freshwater scarcity. Even humourist Mark Twain has been attributed with forecasting the threat back in the nineteenth century, supposedly quipping that 'Whiskey is for drinking. Water is for fightin over' (Ricks 2011).

For some scholars, such as Michael Klare, the risk of conflict inevitably grows when states that share scarce water supplies wish to increase their allocated supplies (2001). Peter Gleick's 1993 article 'Water and Conflict' was one of the first to back up this assumption with historical analysis. He predicted that growth in population and demand, combined with uncertain supply, would increase the likelihood of water and water infrastructure becoming objectives of international military action and instruments of war (Gleick 1993).

The Middle East and southern and central Asia are identified as particularly vulnerable to water-related violence. Gleick saw water as a likely objective of military action when it can provide a country with a source of political or economic strength: 'Under these conditions, ensuring access to water provides a justification for going to war, and water-supply systems can become a goal of military conquest' (1993: 84). This idea is supported with cases from the Middle East. As we saw earlier, the Middle East is the most water scarce region in the world. There is no major river in the region that respects sovereign borders. Gleick found historic and contemporary examples to support his argument that water is a likely instrument of war there. Fourteen centuries ago, the King of Assyria reportedly 'seized control of water wells as part of his strategy of desert warfare against Arabia' (1993: 85). More recent conflicts have emerged over control of the Jordan River basin shown in Map 5.2.

Animosities in this region had already been running high since Israel was formed in 1948. But it was Arab countries' attempt to divert the headwaters of the Jordan River away from Israel in the 1960s that pushed them towards violent conflict. Statements by political leaders in the Middle East support the suggestion that water was a causal factor. In 1967, shortly before the onset of war between Israel and its neighbours (Jordan, Syria, and Egypt) the Israeli prime minister warned that water is essential for the country's survival and 'Israel will use all means necessary to secure that the water continues to flow'. The Crown Prince of Jordan later claimed that the war 'was brought on very largely over water related matters' (quoted in Toset et al. 2000: 927). Over a period of six days, Israel bombed a Jordanian dam on an important tributary to the Jordan River and seized territory spanning the West Bank, Gaza Strip, Golan Heights, and the Sinai Peninsula as far as the Suez Canal. Return of the Sinai Peninsula to Egypt was negotiated a decade later, but Israel significantly expanded its access to freshwater by maintaining control of the upstream territories. This enhanced its 'hydrostrategic position' (Toset et al. 2000: 978).

In addition to providing a reason for going to war, Gleick argued that freshwater has long been a target and tool of war. Examples from major international wars in the twentieth century, as well as regional conflicts in the Middle East, support this claim. Dams were bombed during World War Two and the Korean War. Conflicts between and within Iran, Iraq, and Kuwait featured extensive destruction of water infrastructure: electricity supplies in Iraq were cut when Iran bombed a hydroelectric dam in Iraqi Kurdistan during the 1981 Iran–Iraq War; during the 1990–1 Persian Gulf War dams, desalination plants, and water-supply and sanitation systems were bombed in Kuwait and Iraq; and Iraqi president Saddam Hussein reportedly suppressed civil unrest in Shiite regions of the country by poisoning and draining their water supplies (Gleick 1993: 87–8).

Beyond actual cases of water being used as a weapon, the threat that it might be used in this way raises concerns throughout many regions of the world. Writing again about the Middle East, Gleick explained:

It is sometimes only a short step from capability to implementation. The ability of Turkey to shut off the flow of the Euphrates, even temporarily, was noted by political and military strategists at the beginning of the Persian Gulf conflict. In the early days of

**Map 5.2:** The Jordan River Basin
Source: UN 2004

the war, there were behind-the-scenes discussions at the United Nations about using Turkish dams on the Euphrates River to deprive Iraq of a significant fraction of its fresh water supply in response to its invasion of Kuwait. While no such action was ever taken, the threat of the 'water weapon' was again made clear.

(1993: 89)

Gleick's analysis chimed with post-cold war thinking about the significance of non-traditional threats to security. But while the prospect of water wars has been a salient narrative in political and popular discourse, scholars have often been sceptical. Some have questioned whether it is merely media sensationalism and political hyperbole, or whether there is evidence to support the concern.

Scholars have tested the water war hypothesis via two lines of investigation. The first examines whether sharing a freshwater source increases the probability of armed conflict between countries. The second focuses on water-related events or interactions and examines whether conflict is more prevalent than cooperation (Bernauer and Kalbhenn 2010). Scholars in Norway have led the first research agenda, producing several large-N studies over the past two decades (Toset et al. 2000; Gleditsch et al. 2006; Brochmann and Gleditsch 2012). The first study, published in 2000, was based on data spanning the years 1880–1992 (Toset et al. 2000). Toset and his colleagues were somewhat sceptical about Gleick's findings. They point out that most of the fifty-four conflicts that Gleick identified were only verbal conflicts, threats of violence, or water-related violence in already occurring wars. In other words, they were not cases of water scarcity triggering armed conflict. Moreover, in most cases, water was only an instrument of war or a strategic target, not the objective of fighting in the first place (Toset et al. 2000). Toset and his colleagues began by pointing to the different types of conflict that can emerge depending on the nature of the shared water source. Rivers can run along an international border thereby separating two countries (a *river boundary* relationship); they can run from one country into another (an *upstream/downstream* relationship), or they can do both (a *mixed* relationship). This is depicted in Figure 5.1.

In upstream/downstream relationships, problems relating to the sharing of water resources are more serious. The upstream country is generally in a stronger position because it has the power to divert water for its own advantage. In river boundary relationships, the most likely problems are those relating to 'fuzzy boundaries': rivers are inherently susceptible to change; they erode the landscape and change shape. This can create disputes over the ownership of territory and when national and natural boundaries should be reconsidered (Toset et al. 2000: 980–1). Their study indicated 'that a joint river does indeed

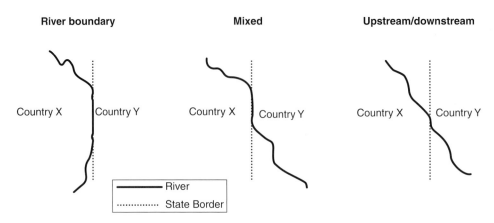

**Figure 5.1:** Different relationships between rivers and state borders
Source: Toset et al. 2000: 980

increase the probability of militarised disputes and armed conflict over and above mere contiguity' (Toset et al. 2000: 972). In other words, it is not the mere fact that neighbouring countries have more opportunities to fight that makes river dyads more likely to engage in armed conflict: the shared resource exacerbates the likelihood of conflict beyond that fact alone.

Water scarcity was found to be one factor contributing to disputes in upstream/downstream relationships, but it was not the only factor: others included 'friction over navigation, pollution, fishing rights, or territorial issues' (Toset et al. 2000: 992). A 2006 study building on this research reiterated that 'countries that share rivers have a higher risk of military disputes'. In fact, a shared basin doubles the risk of a fatal military dispute (Gleditsch et al. 2006: 373). The risk of 'fuzzy boundary' conflicts was found to be minimal, but the size of the river basin turned out to be significant: 'While acute conflicts over individual rivers are rare, the presence of a large shared river basin provides a resource worth fighting for' (Gleditsch et al. 2006: 373).

The second major research agenda on water and conflict has examined not whether a shared water resource increases the risk of conflict among neighbouring countries, but whether and when interactions between water-sharing countries are more likely to be conflictual or cooperative. To help identify patterns of conflict and cooperation a water event intensity scale called the Basins at Risk (BAR) Scale was established for defining situations as one of fifteen types of interaction. Lying at the polar ends of the scale are 'formal declaration of war' and 'voluntary unification into one nation' with thirteen forms of interaction lying between (as shown in Figure 5.2).

| BAR scale | COPDAB scale | BAR event description |
|---|---|---|
| -7 | 15 | Formal declaration of war; extensive war acts causing deaths, dislocation, or high strategic costs |
| -6 | 14 | Extensive military acts |
| -5 | 13 | Small-scale military acts |
| -4 | 12 | Political-military hostile actions |
| -3 | 11 | Diplomatic-economic hostile actions |
| -2 | 10 | Strong verbal expressions displaying hostility in interaction |
| -1 | 9 | Mild verbal expressions displaying discord in interaction |
| 0 | 8 | Neutral or non-significant acts for the inter-nation situation |
| 1 | 7 | Minor official exchanges, talks, or policy expressions–mild verbal support |
| 2 | 6 | Official verbal support of goals, values, or regime |
| 3 | 5 | Cultural or scientific agreement or support (non-strategic) |
| 4 | 4 | Non-military economic, technological, or industrial agreement |
| 5 | 3 | Military economic or strategic support |
| 6 | 2 | International freshwater treaty: major strategic alliance (regional or international) |
| 7 | 1 | Voluntary unification into one nation |

**Figure 5.2:** The Basins at Risk (BAR) Scale
Source: Wolf et al. 2003: 34

Using this scale, Wolf and his colleagues categorised 'all reported events of either conflict or cooperation between nations over water resources' between the years 1948 and 2000 (Wolf et al. 2003: 29). They found that the physical aspects of a water system (such as where it is located, how big it is, and how scarce the supplies are) matter less than the institutional capacity within a water basin (such as whether there are water management bodies or treaties, and whether the countries involved generally have positive political relations) (Wolf et al. 2003: 29). Conflict, it turned out, was most likely to occur in situations where sovereignty was nascent (i.e., new states) or where one country unilaterally developed water projects in the absence of a cooperative regime. Each of these factors can out-strain institutional capacity and lead to conflict.

The periods of 1948–80 and 1987–2000 were relatively conflictual because this is when the British Empire and the Soviet Union were breaking up: 'Conflicts in the world's most tense basins – the Jordan, Nile, Tigris–Euphrates, Indus and Aral – were all precipitated by these break-ups' (Wolf et al. 2003: 44). Newly independent states by their very nature have weak institutional capacity to absorb stresses: they may be economically weak, but more importantly they lack water management bodies and international agreements, general experiences of friendship and cooperation with other countries, and stable democratic regimes (Wolf et al. 2003: 42).

However, the headline finding of the study was that 'the record of acute conflict over international water resources is overwhelmed by the record of cooperation' (Wolf et al. 2003: 30). Of the almost 2,000 events that took place in this fifty-year period, just over 25 per cent were conflictive (lying between -1

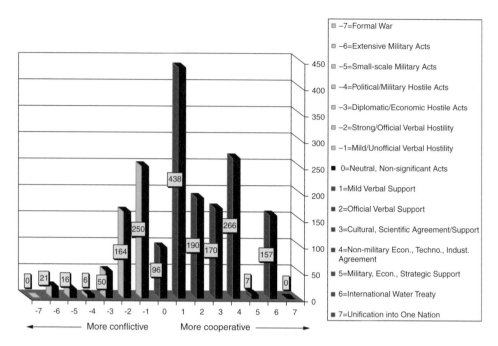

**Figure 5.3:** Pattern of interactions over water
Source: Wolf et al. 2003: 40

and -7 on the BAR scale), about 5 per cent were neutral or non-significant, and the remaining nearly 70 per cent were cooperative (lying between 1 and 7 on the BAR scale).[2] We can see the pattern of categorisation in the researchers' graph in Figure 5.3.

A noteworthy finding of the study was that there were no actual wars over freshwater resources during this period. The authors noted that 'one has to go back 4500 years to find the single historical example of a true "water war". This was a dispute between the city-states of Lagash and Umma on the Tigris–Euphrates' (Wolf et al. 2003: 38–9). Only thirty-seven cases were categorised as 'acute conflict' lying at -5 or -6 on the BAR scale, and thirty of these were between Israel and one of its neighbours. Violent conflict over water, it turns out, is a fairly rare and isolated phenomenon (Wolf et al. 2003). Wolf and his colleagues assume that based on these findings we should be able to identify and monitor 'basins at risks'. One 'red flag' to watch out for would be public calls for tender for future water infrastructure projects that have been planned outside the context of an international water body or treaty. Another would be the rise of nationalist movements that, if successful in their attempts to secede, could have an impact on regional water relations (Wolf et al. 2003: 47–8).

Research shows that the factors most conducive to cooperation over shared water resources are democracy, international trade relations, and membership of multilateral organisations (Kalbhenn 2011). Dense political, economic, and social relations among states makes them more 'integrated', which makes cooperation more likely in general, and in relation to shared water resources in particular (Bernauer and Kalbhenn 2010). Such relations make it easier for countries to trust one another and make credible commitments. Recall that in Chapter 2 we learned that trust and reliability were important for the success of cooperative arrangements over shared resources. These qualities build up over time as different groups develop shared expectations and interests (Chapter 2). This is also the case in transnational water regimes. Once they are established, water regimes turn out to be quite resilient even in the face of conflict over other issues. Wolf lists a number of cooperative water bodies that survived conflict and even war between water-sharing countries (1998: 260):

- the Indus River Commission has survived two wars and ongoing tensions between India and Pakistan;
- agreements between China and Hong Kong on the supply of water from the Dongjiang River have held up throughout tense relations between these countries;
- the Mekong Committee (later renamed Mekong River Commission) governing water between Cambodia, Laos, Thailand, and Vietnam survived the Vietnam War.

## Weaknesses in International Cooperation

When trying to gauge the potential for future cooperation, scholars and political actors tend to be guided by the past. They draw lessons from the prevalence of cooperation in the past and the conditions under which this was achieved. But the past is not necessarily an accurate guide to the future. It is impossible to make certain predictions about the future, and projections are made difficult by the fact that some institutional, technological, and geophysical factors have the potential to reduce the risk of conflict while others have the potential to increase it. Taking an optimistic angle, we can see how new modelling, monitoring, and remote sensing technologies can provide a more transparent basis on which to negotiate agreements between water-sharing states. In addition, other technologies can reduce demands on water supplies by improving the efficiency of consumption.

From a more pessimistic perspective, however, irrespective of whether scarcity was a driver of historical conflicts it may well be a driver of future conflict because unprecedented demands on this limited resource are projected. Water is non-substitutable in agriculture, human wellbeing, and some manufacturing and electricity generation. So long as these demands increase, water will become ever scarcer, thereby creating conditions that we have not seen in the past (Postel and Wolf 2009). Even more concerning is that we still have a fairly limited understanding of the nature and prevalence of sub-national conflicts over freshwater. Based on the broader literature on conflict and natural resources that we reviewed in the previous section, there is certainly good reason to anticipate sub-national conflict over water in developing countries, especially where ethnic and regional tensions are already present.

A further problem should be kept in mind when we consider the limitations of international water law. Cooperation between neighbouring countries over the use of shared water resources might create its own forms of conflicts or injustice at the sub-national level. International legal norms and institutions provide no recourse to justice or resolution to these sub-national groups, nor to significantly affected people like the Palestinians on the Jordan River or the Kurds on the Euphrates River. The International Court of Justice arbitrates only between sovereign states (Wolf 1998: 252–3).

Sub-national conflict in the context of international cooperation can be seen in plans between Sudan and Egypt to build a canal on swamps of the Nile River to release an additional 4.7 cubic kilometres of water each year. In 1983, the Sudan People's Liberation Army destroyed canal construction equipment because they believed the project would benefit Northern Sudan and Egypt at the expense of local populations in South Sudan where the swamps were located (Mason et al. 2009: 331). Similar tensions can be seen in South Asia. The Indus Water Treaty gives Pakistan control of the Indus River, but in exercising these rights, inter-provincial tension has been provoked. In Pakistan, the wealthier northern province of Punjab is seen to unfairly benefit from legal water rights at the expense of more disadvantaged provinces (Sindh, Balochistan, and North-West Frontier Province). Tensions came to a head in 2004 when President Musharraf announced that the Kalabagh Dam would be built along the Indus River to support agriculture and electricity generation. Residents of Sindh and the North-West Frontier Province opposed this development because they feared that they would bear the brunt of environmental impact (including increased salinity and loss of water) while the Punjab would receive most of the benefits. By the time it was decided to put the project on hold, conflict had been limited to street protests and verbal exchanges between provincial governments. But some observers worry that population pressures and economic expansion will push the project forward and intensify inter-provincial tensions and potentially more serious conflict (Markey 2011: 90–1).

One of the limits of international multilateral institutions for promoting cooperation over water is that they don't protect sub-national groups. At the domestic level there are all sorts of competing interests that can provoke tension over how water is used and distributed: farmers might want water for irrigation; citizens might want it for recreational and aesthetic reasons as well as for essential wellbeing; industry might want it for electricity generation; environmentalists might want it to protect ecosystems, etc. When water-sharing governments negotiate over international access and conservation, the chances of satisfying all these interests are low. Even when cooperation is secured through international processes involving a non-sovereign actor, the existing power imbalances might be simply reinforced. This is what Jan Selby sees in the Oslo 'peace process' involving Israel and Palestine. Selby disputes the claim that cooperative mechanisms for managing the West Bank's water resources were a major success of the Oslo process. Instead, he argues, 'Much of what had previously been patron–client relations under occupation were suddenly discursively repackaged and represented as instances of Israeli–Palestinian "co operation"'. The result was little more than domination dressed up as cooperation (Selby 2003: 123).

These sub-national experiences serve as a reminder that arrangements of conflict and cooperation are complex: we should not assume that conflict is always 'bad' and cooperation is always 'good'. Mark Zeitoun and Naho Mirumachi have called on scholars to completely rethink their assumptions about conflict and cooperation as alternative processes. Because transnational interactions over shared water are inherently political processes, elements of conflict will often be present alongside processes of cooperation: the two coexist (Zeitoun and Mirumachi 2008: 299). The dominant ways of analysing conflict and cooperation along a continuum (such as the BAR scale discussed above) do not allow us to consider that conflict and cooperation may be present at any one time. These continuums also preclude analysis of how dynamics of cooperation and conflict change over time. The practical danger of this analytical blindspot is that conflict resolution might be pursued by pushing processes along towards the cooperation end of the spectrum and thereby losing sight of the context as a whole (Zeitoun and Mirumachi 2008: 301–2). When this happens there might be a tendency to celebrate the cooperation that is occurring and neglect the sensitive issues that are kept off the negotiating table. Reaching agreement on data-sharing, and following through on such an agreement, might be seen as a positive sign. This has been the case in water relations between India and Bangladesh over the Ganges River, for example. When Bangladesh has pushed for cooperation to deal with the effects of drought and floods, the Indian response has been 'but, we *are* cooperating'. The value and impact of that cooperation must remain open to critical analysis to ensure that power relations and their effects are fully recognised (Zeitoun and Mirumachi 2008: 305).

## Securitising the Environment

Political rhetoric about resource wars and studies of resource conflict reflect wider trends in the practice and study of international politics. With the end of the cold war, and the spectre of nuclear strikes lifted, political actors and scholars became increasingly concerned about non-traditional threats to peace and security. We saw this reflected in the security doctrines of the US, post-Soviet Russia, and other countries. The Clinton administration in the US was particularly receptive to the idea that environmental factors could become security threats. Robert Kaplan, a foreign affairs commentator, proved especially influential in this respect. His 1994 article 'The Coming Anarchy' depicted a dystopian future in which 'surging populations, spreading disease, deforestation and soil erosion, water depletion, air pollution, and, possibly, rising sea levels' would incite violent conflict and mass migration (Kaplan 1994). Following its publication in *The Atlantic*, the article was praised by the Clinton administration and reportedly faxed to all US embassies around the world. A series of actions followed in recognition of the potential impact of transnational environmental issues on international security and American strategy. The role of Deputy Under Secretary for Environmental Security was created within the Defense Department in 1993; an Environmental Task Force was established within the US intelligence network; and non-military threats such as environmental degradation and population growth featured prominently in the 1994 National Security Strategy (Wolf et al. 2005: 81). Later, in 1996, US Secretary of Defense William Parry introduced the concept of 'preventive diplomacy'. Drawing on an analogy with preventive medicine, preventive diplomacy was a doctrine based on acting early to prevent conditions like environmental degradation escalating into serious security threats.

In more recent times, it has become common for states and international institutions to express concern over the potential security threats arising from climate change. In 2007, Britain used its presidency of the UN Security Council to convene a one-day debate on the security implications of climate change. Some countries, including China, were doubtful about whether the Security Council was the appropriate site for such talks, arguing that climate change was fundamentally an issue of sustainable development not security. Vulnerable countries, meanwhile, were adamant that climate change should be treated as a security issue, with Papua New Guinea's representative arguing that 'the impact of climate change on small islands was no less threatening than the dangers guns and bombs posed to large nations' (UN 2007a). Debates about the relationship between security and climate change were repeated in the UN Security Council in 2009, 2011, 2013, and 2015. It is hard to gauge the actual impact of these debates on international responses to climate change, but they are generally seen as injecting a sense of urgency into annual negotiations on climate change held under the auspices of the UNFCCC.

Debates among states about whether the UN Security Council is the appropriate site for debating an issue like climate change reflect debates among scholars about whether the environment ought to be 'securitised'. As we saw earlier, scholars were already analysing the relationship between violent conflict and the environment back in the 1970s. But debates about 'environmental security' only began to develop within the discipline of 'security studies' in the late 1980s and early 1990s. The cold war came to an end at this time just as planning got underway for the 1992 Rio Earth Summit (an important multilateral event that we'll examine in Chapter 6). The coincidence of these two events prompted some scholars to begin reflecting on the links between security and the environment. As a result, the field of environmental security studies was born (Floyd and Matthew 2013: 1). Even as far back as the 1970s, some pioneer scholars had begun to frame the environment in security terms. American scholar of international law, Robert Falk, warned in 1971 that 'We need to revamp our entire concept of "national security" and "economic growth" if we are to solve the problems of environmental decay' (Falk 1971: 185). These sentiments were echoed in 1985 by another prominent American scholar, George Kennan. Writing in the widely read journal *Foreign Affairs*, Kennan presented resource scarcity as an unprecedented and 'supreme danger' on a par with nuclear war (Kennan 1985). But it was not until the end of the cold war that such warnings attracted any serious attention. Scholars like Barry Buzan and his 'Copenhagen School' colleagues argued that there was analytical value in treating non-military issues as existential threats, and therefore as issues of security (Buzan et al. 1998). For scholars concerned about environmental degradation, 'securitisation' holds the potential to push the issue up the political agenda. As Peter Hough explains, 'The meaning of "security" is not just an arcane matter of academic semantics. The term carries significant weight in "real-world" political affairs since threats to the security of states have to be a priority for governments and threats to the lives of people are increasingly accepted as more important than other matters of contention' (Hough 2014: 140–1).

By upgrading environmental degradation to the status of security threat there is a possibility that states will allocate greater resources to resolving environmental problems. But some worry that the potential negative effects of securitisation outweigh the potential positive effects. The main danger here is the dominant association of *security* and *military*. Treating environmental change and resource scarcity as security threats might plausibly justify the use of force and other emergency measures: armies might be deployed to protect scarce resources, or borders might be closed to environmental refugees. Given the claims of scientists that the Syrian refugee crisis of 2015 was driven in part by climate change, it is not a far stretch to consider the 1 million Syrians who arrived in Europe that year as 'climate refugees'.[3] In fact, *Time* magazine presented the 'surge of migrants' in precisely this light (Baker 2015). The Syrian conflict has coincided with a rise of nationalism across much of the world, and growing hostility towards both immigrants and refugees. In this context, several European countries responded to the Syrian refugees by closing borders and deploying armies to manage the movements of refugees. By redefining an issue as a security matter, the normal political and democratic processes for handling it no longer apply: drastic and urgent measures are justified.

Even if securitisation doesn't lead to militarisation of the environment, it might still work against the interests of marginalised groups and local communities. This is because national security issues are by definition the responsibility of the nation-state. As we saw in Chapter 2, central government control is not always the most appropriate response to environmental problems. There might be social and environmental reasons for devolving responsibility for water management to the regional and local level. But this becomes unlikely when issues are securitised (MacQuarrie and Wolf 2013: 171).

Some scholars see value in adopting a security approach to environmental problems, but prefer to frame this in terms of 'human security' (Barnett et al. 2010: 6–7). Scholars of human security argue that the 'referent object' of security should be the individual. This means that it is the individual that should be secured. This directs attention away from militarisation and protection of the state, and focuses primarily on the wellbeing of individuals. Understood in a narrow sense, human security might focus attention on the ways in which human lives are directly threatened by environmental change and resource scarcity. In its broadest sense, human security might highlight the many ways in which human wellbeing is undermined by environmental factors (Barnett et al. 2010: 8). Debate over the merits and limitations of environmental securitisation continue to play out in the scholarly journals. This is likely to continue as the effects of problems like climate change become more evident, and as states struggle to find ways to respond.

## Conclusion

It is a geopolitical reality that many of the natural resources that support human lives do not fall neatly within sovereign borders. The transnational character of many resources requires that states interact with one another to determine who gets access and under what conditions. When resources are also characterised by growing scarcity, interactions become particularly sensitive. Political leaders and pundits alike have widely assumed that violent conflict is likely under such conditions. Perhaps it's an intuitively sensible idea: when access to a basic and essential resource is threatened, people are likely to take drastic measures to secure their existence and livelihoods. But studies over several decades show that the relationship between resources and conflict is very complex. At times it has been one of several factors contributing to – or sustaining – violent conflict.

But when we look closely at freshwater, we see that international interactions are usually more cooperative than conflictive. In modern history, there has been no international war over water. States are more likely to avoid threatening behaviour and instead look for diplomatic ways to manage shared resources. It is important to remember, though, that cooperation is difficult and often generates winners and losers. We have seen in this chapter that cooperative arrangements can leave some states and sub-national groups in a disadvantaged position. This means that when we reflect on the effectiveness of a particular response to environmental issues, we need to consider whether it is effective for some actors and not others, and whether there are questions of environmental injustices at stake.

In the next chapter we examine multilateral diplomacy in more detail, and turn our attention to the issue of sustainable development.

## Discussion Questions

1. What explains the discrepancy between the rhetoric and reality of 'water wars'?
2. Are we likely to see more violent conflicts over natural resources in the future? Which resources are most likely to be the object of conflict?
3. In what ways could the international community intervene to fairly and effectively resolve a conflict between two more countries over water natural resources?
4. Is conflict always 'bad' and cooperation always 'good'?
5. Should we be concerned about efforts to 'securitise' the environment? Can you identify 'real world' examples that offer reasons to be optimistic or concerned about the effects of securitisation?

## Notes

1. It is not uncommon to see alternative figures to these. The number is periodically reviewed on the basis of (a) self-determination and the creation of new states, and (b) technological advances that allow more precise detection of natural boundaries.
2. The precise figures are: 1,831 events: 507 conflictive; 1,228 cooperative; and 96 neutral or non-significant.
3. The 1 million figure is an estimate from the International Organization for Migration.

# 6 Multilateral Diplomacy
## Sustainable Development

**key points**

- Multilateral institutions proliferated throughout the latter half of the twentieth century. But in recent years **multilateralism** has been strained by fragmentation and the growth of '**minilateralism**'.
- The international community began to take a political interest in environmental issues in the 1960s and 1970s. North–South divisions have been a feature of environmental multilateralism since this time.
- There are different types of multilateral agreements including resolutions, conference declarations, framework conventions, and protocols. Some agreements constitute 'soft' law and others constitute 'hard' law.
- The international community placed development at the centre of the environmental agenda to protect economic growth and ensure participation from developing countries.
- Since 1992, states have met in a series of high-level summits to promote sustainable development. Many promises have been made but progress has been poor.

# Introduction

On 7 December 1972, astronauts aboard the *Apollo 17* spacecraft captured an image that would have a profound effect on people's perceptions of planet earth. It is now so pervasive and familiar that, for most, it perhaps triggers no reaction at all. But this image allowed people to see the earth in full view for the very first time. Perfectly illuminated, it appeared as a blue marble floating in an empty sea of darkness. 'Tiny', 'fragile', and 'unified' are words that came to be associated with this image of earth. Commander Eugene Cernan described how national boundaries disappeared when he viewed the planet from this perspective. His words capture a sentiment that spread widely at this time, when Western environmentalist movements were gathering momentum and demanding political action. Commander Cernan wrote: 'I think the view from 100,000 miles could be invaluable in getting people to work out joint solutions, by causing them to realize that the planet we share unites us in a way far more basic and far more important than the differences in skin colour or religion or economic system' (quoted in White 1998: 37). The timing of the 'blue marble' photograph was politically advantageous. As we will see in this chapter, it coincided with the 'birth' of environmental multilateralism. International cooperation experienced a boom in the post World War Two period, with hundreds of intergovernmental institutions created by the end of the twentieth century. It was in the 1960s and 1970s that the environment made it onto the international agenda. Resource use and environmental degradation were gradually recognised as common problems that would require collective and coordinated action.

In this chapter we will first examine the concept and practice of multilateralism, and see how it has been changing since the mid-twentieth century. We then trace the development of environmental multilateralism and identify the factors that have promoted, strengthened, and challenged diplomatic efforts to address the causes and consequences of environmental change. Here we will discuss different types of multilateral environmental agreements (MEAs) and their political and legal status. Since its inception, environmental multilateralism has been characterised by divisions between the North and the South. Diplomats resolved this division by placing development at the centre of international environmental cooperation, which led to the idea of 'sustainable development'. After our general overview of environmental multilateralism we will zoom in on multilateral efforts to promote sustainable development. We will see that this has taken the form of summit-based multilateralism whereby states gather every ten years to establish principles, set goals, pledge action, and review progress. What emerges is a fairly bleak record of summit-based diplomacy for sustainable development. Promises proliferate, but performance has been generally poor.

# Multilateral Diplomacy

To define multilateralism, scholars usually turn to John Ruggie's seminal IR text, *Multilateralism Matters* (Ruggie 1993). Multilateralism, Ruggie writes, 'is an institutional form that coordinates relations among three or more states on the basis of generalized principles of conduct: that is, principles which specify appropriate conduct ... without regard to the particularistic interests or the strategic exigencies that may exist' (Ruggie 1993: 11). The most important principle that governs relations among states is sovereignty: despite differences in power, the principle of sovereignty requires that states recognise each other as equals with an inviolable right to manage their own internal affairs free of external influence. Multilateralism doesn't override sovereignty, but instead recognises coordination as mutually beneficial.

Ruggie's definition refers to 'principles of conduct' that underpin multilateralism. But just as state sovereignty is often violated, these principles of conduct are not always observed. But in theory three principles define multilateralism (Ruggie 1993: 11–12; Heywood 2015). The first is indivisibility, whereby states identify and act as a single international community; this means they seek to address common issues as a unified actor with common interests. States will have differences of opinion and some diverging interests, but these differences are, in principle, subordinate. For example, states perceive a common interest in protecting the ozone layer, and they present themselves as a single international community against this threat. The second principle is non-discrimination, meaning that states mustn't favour or privilege any single state or group of states. For example, if states are establishing a carbon market to trade pollution permits, Japan cannot make private arrangements to buy permits only from South Korea; nor can it arrange to buy permits from any country except South Korea. The third principle is diffuse reciprocity, meaning that states can expect cooperation to be enduring, and to extend into other areas of interaction. This promotes give-and-take, and pushes states to cooperate on issues that they would prefer to neglect – they do so because they believe it will benefit them in other ways in the future. For example, Russia may cooperate on efforts to establish an environmental agreement because they believe their cooperation will be reciprocated in future trade talks.

Instances of international cooperation appeared before the twentieth century, but it was in the aftermath of World War Two that multilateralism bloomed. In 1879, there were just nine international organisations (IOs); by 1914 this number had grown to 49, and by 1949 there were 123 IOs. The number of international organisations continued to grow until the mid-1980s, peaking at 380 but then declining to 240 in 2010 (Rittberger et al. 2012: 67–8). The number of treaties and agreements created by these organisations is much larger, amounting to over 2,000 today (Union of International Associations 2016). These organisations and agreements cover many different issues of common interest or concern, such as security, migration, human rights, environmental degradation and pollution, and development. Some multilateral organisations restrict membership to a geographical area (such as the European Union and the Association of Southeast Asian Nations), others impose restrictions based on domestic regime traits (such as the World Trade Organization), and others have open membership (such as the United Nations). The common feature is that only states can be members of multilateral institutions (Keohane 1990).

The UN has been described as 'the global symbol and embodiment of multilateralism and all of its promise and limitations' (Newman et al. 2006: 6–7). Its inclusivity and treatment of all states as equals (with the important exception of the UN Security Council) have come to define legitimate multilateral arrangements in the eyes of many states and observers. In the UN General Assembly, and in the hundreds of negotiations conducted under the UN's auspices, inclusivity and equality are crucial. The tiny island state of Tuvalu has the same status as superpowers like China or the US. This explains why middle powers and small states constantly struggle to keep the UN as the main negotiating arena: they stand a greater chance of reaching agreements that favour their interests than if such negotiations were conducted bilaterally or in more exclusive institutions. The UN has experienced highs and lows as powerful states' commitment to inclusive multilateralism has fluctuated. The rise in number and importance of 'minilateral' institutions has posed the biggest challenge to the UN's authority. Unlike multilateral institutions that restrict membership to a geographical region or regime trait, minilateral institutions restrict membership to powerful states (such as the G7 and G20), or to like-minded states dissatisfied with the UN (such as the short-lived **Asia–Pacific Partnership on Clean Development and Climate**).

The legitimacy of minilateralism is sometimes questioned due to its exclusivity. This reflects the extent to which the UN shapes understandings of what is legitimate in multilateralism. Minilateral institutions not only exclude most states, but they also have very stringent (or non-existent) arrangements for civil society involvement. This runs against evolving multilateralism in the United Nations. While UN membership is restricted to states, it is increasingly open to civil society participation in meetings, negotiations, and summits. Civil society inclusion in UN processes was anticipated from its very inception. Article 71 of the UN Charter states that 'The Economic and Social Council may make suitable arrangements for consultation with non-governmental organizations which are concerned with matters within its competence. Such arrangements may be made with international organizations and, where appropriate, with national organizations after consultation with the Member of the United Nations concerned'. Provisions for civil society involvement were strengthened in 1996 to extend accreditation to regional, subregional, and national non-governmental organisations (NGOs), and to explicitly encourage greater participation from NGOs in developing countries (UN 1996). All UN bodies have their own specific rules for NGO participation, but they typically allow NGOs to observe some meetings, access reports, and submit written or oral statements.

The rise of minilateralism is just one way in which multilateralism has been changing during the twenty-first century. Global governance has become increasingly complex. Whereas in the 1990s, a single UN institution may have enjoyed primary authority on a particular issue, now it may share authority with several other institutions – including other UN institutions, other intergovernmental institutions, and private institutions created by non-state actors. This is referred to as the fragmentation of global governance. On the issue of health, for example, the UN's World Health Organization was the only significant global authority for several decades. Now the WHO shares (or competes for) authority with other institutions including the World Bank and the Global Fund. We will examine fragmentation in closer detail in Chapter 7 because it has had a remarkable impact on the way the international community responds to global environmental problems, especially climate change.

## Environmental Multilateralism

While some may dispute the relevance and effectiveness of inclusive institutions, the UN's role in shaping global environmental governance is undeniable. Here we look at how environmental multilateralism emerged and has developed over the past sixty years, and the legal and political status of multilateral environmental agreements.

### The Environmental Movement

Before there was environmental multilateralism there were environmental movements. Early but very marginal nature protection groups appeared in Britain and the US in the late nineteenth century and early twentieth century. But popular environmentalism is predominantly a post World War Two trend (McCormick 1989: vii–viii). The growth of environmental movements in Western Europe and North America in the 1960s is an important factor in explaining how international institutions like the UN began to respond to environmental problems. They did so because governments began to take notice of environmental protests, and states including Germany and Sweden then urged other states to cooperate.

Environmental movements of the 1960s and 1970s were not just concerned about preserving pristine wilderness (although some focused on this). The popular environmentalist movement encompassed concerns about industrial development, technology such as nuclear energy, resource depletion, and the impact of chemicals on the land and human health (as we'll see in Chapter 10). Carter explains that 'Modern environmentalism came of age on 22 April 1970 when millions of Americans celebrated and protested on Earth Day, which remains the largest environmental demonstration in history' (Carter 2001: 4).

### The Birth of Environmental Multilateralism

The first multilateral organisation to take an interest in environmental issues was the United Nations Educational, Scientific and Cultural Organization. UNESCO was created in 1945 with a mandate to promote scientific cooperation and intercultural understanding. As the UN's 'intellectual agency', it is fitting that UNESCO took responsibility for promoting international understanding about the relationship between humans and the natural world (or, more accurately, humans' place in the natural world) (UNESCO 2016).

Oceans dominated UNESCO's environmental research agenda in its early years, but the subject of sustainable resource use was taken up in the mid-1960s. It was in 1968 that the first international environmental conference took place. The Intergovernmental Conference for Rational Use and Conservation of the Biosphere was organised by UNESCO in collaboration with the UN, FAO, and WHO, and brought together sixty-three states. For the first time, governments were convening to develop common understandings of humans and the environment. Given the North–South divide that later emerged in environmental multilateralism, it is significant that participants included wealthy countries like the US and Australia, and poor countries like Vietnam and Somalia. The aim was to reflect on existing scientific knowledge of how humans use natural resources (soil, water, marine life, vegetation, animals); how resource use impacts and degrades ecosystems; and to consider how scientific research can better help 'man' to achieve 'a dynamic balance with the environment, satisfying physical, economic, social and spiritual needs' (UNESCO 1968: 1–3). Deforestation, over-hunting, over-fishing, wetland drainage, species extinction, and pollution were identified as problems, but the conference struck a positive tone with optimism in humans' capacity to improve environmental quality (UNESCO 1968: 4).

As preparations for the 1968 Biosphere Conference were underway, Sweden requested the UN's Economic and Social Council (ECOSOC) to debate the 'question of convening an international conference on the problems of the human environment' (UN 1968). Environmental awareness was developing in Sweden earlier than in other countries, and the government was eager to host a UN conference to address the social impacts of emerging problems such as air and water pollution, industrial pollution, and solid waste. ECOSOC approved a resolution highlighting the importance of international cooperation to protect the environment for human wellbeing and economic development, and calling on the UN General Assembly to consider the possibility of holding such a conference, and determining its scope and timing. The recommendations of both ECOSOC and UNESCO pushed the environment up the international agenda, and led to the UN General Assembly's decision to convene the United Nations Conference on the Human Environment four years later (UNGA 1968). The conference was held in Stockholm, in 1972.

## North–South Tensions Emerge

During preparations for the **Stockholm Conference**, divisions began to appear. As developing countries voiced reservations it was not even clear that the conference would go ahead. Some developing countries threatened to boycott the conference; they feared that an international agenda on environmental protection would curtail their economic development aspirations. A concerted diplomatic effort was launched to secure the commitment of developing countries; it was clear that without their participation the conference would fail and the nascent environmental agenda would lose momentum.

Maurice Strong was assigned the role of Secretary-General of the Stockholm Conference. At the time, Strong was a Canadian businessman but he went on to become an influential environmental diplomat. His efforts were pivotal in bringing developing countries on board. Strong convened a group of developing country economists and diplomats in the Swiss city of Founex in 1971 to find a way of framing environmental challenges such that they would serve the interests of developing countries. The product of this meeting, the Founex Report on Development and Environment, was much more political in its tone and substance than earlier UN reports on the environment (Founex 1971). The Founex report distinguished between the environmental problems of developed countries and those of developing countries. Industrialised countries were concerned with problems of industrial pollution arising from high levels of development. Developing countries were concerned with problems endangering the very lives of their citizens: natural disasters, disease, and lack of clean water, sanitation, housing, and nutrition. In comparing the two types of environmental problems, the report insinuates that 'human environment' concerns of the time reflected the North's priorities while overlooking the priorities of the South. The report sought to make the concept of development more central to concerns of human environment, and specifically to the theme of the Stockholm Conference. It stated that 'the kind of environmental problems that are of importance in developing countries are those that can be overcome by the process of development itself'. Development was the 'cure' for their problems. But integrating concern for environmental conservation into development plans would be costly, so developed countries would have to be willing to shoulder the additional financial burden, and to ensure that their own conservation measures (such as trade restrictions and higher prices on exported goods) did not impose further costs on developing countries.

With development now at the centre of the human development agenda, many poorer countries agreed to participate in the Stockholm Conference.

In the end, over 100 states participated. The absence of heads of state (only two attended) was a sign that although environmental issues were now on the political agenda, they were still a low priority. The sentiments of Founex were reflected throughout the conference and in the documents it produced, and were memorably echoed by India's prime minister, Indira Gandhi, in her conference speech:

We do not wish to impoverish the environment any further and yet we cannot for a moment forget the grim poverty of large numbers of people. Are not poverty and need the greatest polluters? . . . How can we speak to those who live in villages and in slums about keeping the oceans, the rivers and the air clean when their own lives are contaminated at the source? The environment cannot be improved in conditions of poverty.

(quoted in Rajan 1997: 25–6)

The Declaration of the United Nations Conference on the Human Environment reinforced the distinction between environmental problems experienced by developed and developing countries, and validated developing countries' priority to develop. It also reiterated the importance of transferring 'substantial quantities of financial and technological assistance' from developed to developing countries, and of ensuring that environmental policies do not negatively impact other states. But the declaration also advanced principles consistent with the original aims of preserving and improving the environment for future generations; halting excessive emissions of toxic substances; preventing sea pollution; implementing plans for the rational management of natural resources; and promoting environmental research and education in all countries (UNCHE 1972). As Steven Bernstein observes, the Stockholm Conference documents didn't resolve North–South tensions but 'simply juxtaposed the interest in environmental protection promoted in the North with development concerns in the South' (2000: 469).

The 'Stockholm Principles' were non-binding, meaning that signatory states were under no obligation to adhere to them. Below we will examine the legal nature of multilateral environmental agreements in more detail. Here it is important to recognise that although the Stockholm Principles were not legally binding, they were not legally irrelevant. The principles were institutionalised in subsequent MEAs, and many scholars point to the Stockholm Conference declaration as providing the foundation on which international environmental law was built (Chan 2015: 278).

An important legacy of the Stockholm Conference was the first intergovernmental body dedicated to the environment. Participants debated whether this should be a new organisation, a body of the General Assembly, or a commission attached to ECOSOC (UNCHE 1972: 47). The conference itself did not have the authority to establish this new body, but instead issued a recommendation to the General Assembly, which was swiftly accepted (UNGA 1972). The appropriate form and function of this body has been a contentious point ever since. The General Assembly created the United Nations Environment Programme (UNEP) as a subsidiary organ. This institutional status significantly shaped the strength and ambition of UNEP. It was not created as a specialised agency like FAO or UNESCO, and it has little authority within the UN system. UNEP has also consistently been allocated a relatively small budget, which has further limited its reach and activity (Ivanova 2010: 48–50). This is a further reminder that while the international community accepts the need for environmental cooperation, it remains a fairly low priority for most states.

In the years following the Stockholm Conference, states carried forward their environmental concerns and negotiated agreements on issues as diverse as waterfowl habitats, whaling, drought control, and trade in endangered plants and animals. By the end of the 1970s, close to 150 multilateral environmental agreements were in place (data from Mitchell 2002–2016). At this time, environmental concerns were still mainly limited to issues with immediate and localised effects. Most MEAs at this time were between a handful of neighbouring or nearby states rather than the entire international community. It was only later that planetary-scale issues attracted sufficient concern to merit significant investment of diplomatic time and resources.

## The Golden Age of Environmental Multilateralism

The 1972 Stockholm Conference on environment marked the birth of environmental multilateralism, but it was the early to mid-1990s that mark the 'golden age' of environmental multilateralism. This was a period in which states negotiated hundreds of new regional and global agreements, amendments to agreements, and new protocols. Among these were agreements on climate change, biological diversity, marine pollution, sea life, mining, and the hazardous waste trade (data from Mitchell 2002–2016). What can explain the proliferation of MEAs during this period? One factor is the general international mood in the early 1990s: the cold war had ended, the bipolar tensions that hamstrung multilateral efforts for four decades disappeared as the United States emerged as the sole superpower. Optimism in the UN was generally high, as was interest in environmental degradation. As we saw in the previous chapter, the end of the cold war had led to new ways of conceptualising security, and human security directed attention to non-military threats. In 1989, Jessica Mathews (who would later assume a position in the US administration) wrote an influential article in *Foreign Affairs* arguing that environmental, resource, and demographic issues should be central to definitions of national security (Mathews 1989). In 1992, Bill Clinton made the environment an important part of his US presidential election campaign. With Al Gore as his running mate, Clinton championed the idea that environmental protection, economic growth, and job creation could be compatible. During the campaign period, Gore published one of his first books, *Earth in the Balance*, and cemented his credentials among many US environmentalists (Schneider 1992).

Another factor explaining the proliferation of MEAs during this period was the successful negotiation of the **Vienna Convention** and **Montreal Protocol** for ozone protection in the 1980s. This encouraged the international community to expand environmental multilateralism in the 1980s and 1990s. The ozone agreements were significant for the efficiency with which they were negotiated, and for being the first agreements addressing a global-scale problem. Stratospheric ozone protects the earth's surface from excessive amounts of ultraviolet radiation. In the 1970s, scientists began accumulating evidence that synthetic chemicals called chlorofluorocarbon compounds (CFCs) were depleting the ozone layer and exposing the biosphere to increasingly dangerous levels of ultraviolet radiation. CFCs were used mainly in refrigerators and air conditioners, but also in solvents, aerosol cans, and in the production of foam products (such as disposable cups). Scientists warned that this exposure would probably increase cases of skin cancer, cataracts, and immunity deficiencies in humans, and undermine **food security** through reduced crop yields and reduced populations of marine organisms that play a crucial role in food chains (Manahan 2008: 623). This was a classic example of what Kofi Annan would later call 'problems without passports': using CFCs in one country would harm citizens in other countries; effectively resolving the problem would require agreement from all governments to phase out CFCs. Detection of an atmospheric 'hole' in the Southern hemisphere spurred governments into action in the 1980s. The Vienna Convention and Montreal Protocol created mutually agreed rules to phase out the production and use of CFCs, and they came into force in 1988 and 1989 respectively.

## Environmental Multilateralism in the Twenty-first Century

Environmental multilateralism doesn't occur in a bubble; it is influenced by the international mood, geopolitical tensions, and major world events. US politics tends to cast a long shadow over global environmental governance. Environmental multilateralism was weakened when George W. Bush became president with no interest in foreign affairs and an openly hostile view of international cooperation (Dietrich 2015: 12–13). US interest in environmental cooperation had been in decline since the mid-1990s. Under the Clinton administration, US diplomats continued to actively participate in the negotiation of MEAs, but their negotiating mandate was often at odds with the majority view of Congress. This meant that agreements were negotiated and signed at the international level, but not ratified at the domestic level. Over time, the United States' reputation as an environmental laggard grew. The election of Bush Jr. and his republican administration consolidated this position. By March 2001, within three months of becoming president, Bush had announced his intention to withdraw the US from the Kyoto Protocol. Other important agreements on biodiversity and hazardous wastes were also ignored.

The terror attacks of September 11, 2001, and the subsequent war on terror, fundamentally reconfigured the international agenda, pushing environmental issues well down the priority list. US participation in environmental multilateralism became even more marginal. The Democratic Party's return to power in 2009, under the leadership of Barack Obama, generated some hope that the US would become a more cooperative partner in environmental diplomacy. Climate and energy were key themes of his election campaign, with Obama committing to cutting domestic GHG emissions, and stressing his belief in global cooperation on climate change (Broder 2008; Revkin et al. 2008). Of course, his ability to deliver on these promises was constrained by the US Congress. The progress he did make is now being dismantled under Donald Trump's presidency (2017–20).

In large part due to US recalcitrance, climate change negotiations stalled in the first decade of the twenty-first century. Since climate change had become the defining issue of the environment agenda, lack of progress on this front called into question the viability of inclusive environmental multilateralism. States began looking for minilateral options, or relying on voluntary action from the private sector. The European Union tried to use the opportunity to promote its own leadership in multilateral environmentalism, and did so with some success. It persuaded enough countries to ratify the **Kyoto Protocol**, allowing the instrument to come into force in 2005 without the US. EU leadership was also fundamental in initiating a new negotiation process to reduce GHG emissions beyond 2012 when the Kyoto Protocol would expire. We will examine climate change politics in Chapter 7, and will see that leadership from the US and China has been far more important for securing recent global climate agreements than EU leadership.

## Legal and Political Status of MEAs

So far we have seen four different types of diplomatic agreements: resolutions, conference declarations, framework conventions, and protocols. Each has a different political and legal status. To appreciate these differences we need to understand the nature of international law, and the distinction between hard and soft law. Not all legal scholars accept this distinction; some argue that there is law and there is non-law, and the latter should only be called political or moral norms (Bodansky 2010: 13–14). Others question whether the very idea of international law is an oxymoron: despite multilateral developments throughout the twentieth century there remains no higher authority than the state. This means that there is no international authority that can enforce the rules that states collectively create; and without such an authority, some argue, there can be no law. Nevertheless, the strength of multilateral agreements is frequently distinguished in terms of soft law and hard law.

Soft law includes resolutions, guidelines, declarations, action plans, and roadmaps that emerge from high-level meetings where governmental ministers or heads of state represent their countries. Soft law agreements show that states see an issue as important. They often provide a set of principles explaining an issue's importance, and outline a set of actions regarded as appropriate for tackling the issue in a coordinated or collective way. These texts are not binding; they simply reflect the actions that states intend to take. They are voluntary but if states fail to comply there may be political consequences. What do we mean by political consequences? Failure to comply with stated intentions may invite criticism from other states or international institutions, which may sound insignificant but many states do wish to be seen as good international citizens and will try to act in ways that protect this reputation. Their motivations might be domestic (e.g., citizens want their governments to act honourably in multilateral arenas), or international (e.g., small and middle power states can gain international influence from their reputation). A further political consequence of failing to comply with soft law can be a weakening of a state's negotiating position in future talks. The non-complying state may be seen as untrustworthy in future negotiations, and less worthy of special consideration.

International treaties do have a legal basis and they are referred to as hard law. Unlike soft law, treaties include legally binding obligations. States recognise the negotiating processes that produce treaties as law-making processes, and they approach these processes differently to a conference that is intended to produce a declaration. In the US, a treaty has to receive approval from two-thirds of the country's senators before it can be ratified. No such process is required for the US president to sign a conference declaration. A common approach to developing hard environmental law is the convention/protocol approach (or framework/protocol approach). We saw this earlier in the **ozone depletion** agreements, and the approach has also been used for climate change, biodiversity, hazardous chemicals, and conservation of Antarctica. The convention (or framework) establishes common understandings and collective commitments, and the protocol establishes tighter and more specific obligations for each state, as well as instruments for meeting them (Hunter 2014: 126). This offers a step-by-step approach in which states can respond to changing circumstances (such as new scientific evidence or public demands).

Let's now look more closely at specific practices of environmental multilateralism by zooming in on the issue of sustainable development.

# Sustainable Development

Now that we are familiar with the evolution of environmental multilateralism and the different diplomatic instruments it produces, we will focus our attention on multilateral efforts to promote sustainable development. We'll first examine the concept of sustainable development, and then trace its institutionalisation through a series of multilateral **summits** between 1992 and 2012.

## The Concept of Sustainable Development

The 1972 Stockholm Conference prompted a flurry of negotiations on environmental issues. But it also prompted a deeper conceptual questioning about how to reconcile economic development and environmental protection. UNEP, under the leadership of Maurice Strong, promoted the concept of '**eco-development**' in the early 1970s. At UNEP's first meeting, Strong presented eco-development as a style of development that takes into account the growth needs of current generations as well as the natural resource needs of future generations. But the concept quickly took on a more radical tone. Developing countries gathering in the Mexican city of Cocoyoc for a meeting of UNEP and the United Nations Commission on Trade and Development (UNCTAD) cited eco-development in the conference declaration. The declaration attributed environmental problems to inequality and unequal economic relationships, mal-distribution of resources, 'extravagant' consumption of under-priced materials, and 'careless rapacity'. It called for a new equitable international economic order that provided for the needs of the poorest while restraining over-consumption (Cocoyoc Declaration 1974). If you recall the discussion of ecological Marxism in Chapter 4, you'll see a remarkable resemblance with the demands of developing countries in Cocoyoc. But the declaration met with a scathing rebuke from the US, and the concept of eco-development was swiftly abandoned (Gómez-Baggethun and Naredo 2015; Bernstein 2000).

At the same time that the concept of eco-development was taking a radical turn, the OECD was developing an understanding of environmental protection that was not only compatible with economic growth, but actually dependent on it. This idea was advanced at a 1985 conference of OECD country ministers, business leaders, and environmentalists. The OECD's Environment Director, Jim MacNeill, took these insights into the Brundtland Commission, which developed them into the concept of 'sustainable development' (Bernstein 2000: 495–6).

The Brundtland Commission is the commonly used name for the World Commission on Environment and Development, which was established by the UN General Assembly in the mid-1980s, with the former (and subsequent) Norwegian prime minister, Gro Harlem Brundtland, as its head. The Brundtland Commission's objectives were defined by its UN mandate (UNGA 1983):

- to propose long-term environmental strategies for achieving sustainable development to the year 2000 and beyond;
- to recommend ways in which concern for the environment may be translated into greater co-operation among developing countries and between countries at different stages of economic and social development and lead to the achievement of common and mutually supportive objectives which take account of the interrelationships between people, resources, environment and development;
- to consider ways and means by which the international community can deal more effectively with environmental concerns. . .;
- to help to define shared perceptions of long-term environmental issues and of the appropriate efforts needed to deal successfully with the problems of protecting and enhancing the environment, a long-term agenda for action during the coming decades, and aspirational goals for the world community.

The Commission published its report in 1987 under the heading *Our Common Future*. It is this report that popularised the concept of sustainable development, defined as 'development that meets the needs of the present without compromising the ability of future generations to meet their own needs' (World Commission on Environment and Development 1987: chapter 2.1). The Commission emphasized that meeting humans' basic needs is the primary goal of development, but that people legitimately aspire to a better quality of life beyond food, clothing, shelter, and jobs. These aspirations, it stressed, must be limited to what is 'ecologically possible and to which all can reasonably aspire', and noted that 'many of us live beyond the world's ecological means' (WCED 1987: chapters 2.4 and 2.5). Those of us who do live 'profligately' are only able to do so because we are using resources and ecological space that in more equitable arrangements would be reserved for future generations and current generations living in poverty. Cast your eye back to the Brundtland definition of sustainable development and you'll see that living in this way is unsustainable: excessive lifestyles compromise the ability of present and future generations to meet their needs.

## Institutionalising Sustainable Development: Earth Summit, 1992

In June 1992, some 30,000 people from across the globe made their way to the Brazilian city of Rio de Janeiro. They were environmentalists, activists, journalists, development practitioners, and representatives of governments and international organisations, and they were there to talk about the planet. The **Earth Summit**, formally called the UN Conference on Environment and Development (UNCED), was the largest conference to have ever taken place. Scenes and sound bites were broadcast across the world, attaching even greater importance to the occasion. In total, 172 states participated, including 108 heads of state or government (UN 1992c). The mood was cautiously optimistic; cold war tensions had ended, there were no major geopolitical cleavages to upset efforts at cooperation, public interest was high, and there were plenty of items on the agenda to ensure that some important steps would be taken (Park et al. 2008: 2–3). It was here that the international community adopted the concept of 'sustainable development' as a policy goal, and consolidated its place in future global environmental governance. Whereas the Brundtland Report proposed a 'pathway' for pursuing sustainable development and identified the broad areas that would need to be addressed, it was in Rio that states agreed on guiding principles and a policy framework for sustainable development.

Little can be achieved in a two-week summit unless a lot of preparation takes place beforehand. Diplomats typically invest hundreds of hours in discussion, negotiation, drafting, and redrafting before the official conference begins. Over two years, negotiators met in four preparatory committee (PreCom) meetings to prepare the texts for Rio. Much is usually agreed during this time, but this doesn't mean that summits are purely symbolic. Typically only a few contentious issues are left for negotiation at a summit, because this allows higher-level officials (such as ministers) to lend more weight and authority to negotiations, and ideally settle disputes.

The importance given to pre-negotiation sessions generates another source of North–South inequality in global environmental governance. Wealthy countries have the capacity and resources to send large and highly skilled negotiating teams to these sessions, which generally cover many scientific and political issues. Poorer countries cannot match this capacity; their representatives may be talented and knowledgeable about some technical issues or some political issues, but they rarely have teams to cover all facets of the negotiations. Non-Anglophone developing countries are also at a further disadvantage because simultaneous interpretation is typically only provided in formal sessions but the most important decisions and negotiations take place outside these settings. It is little wonder, then, that the South frequently complains that multilateral environmental agreements favour developed countries' interests. This problem remains acute today, as a glance at the participation list of any environmental conference will quickly reveal. The participation of delegates from the least developed countries is generally subsidised by UN secretariats, but this only ensures a bare minimum of representation; it doesn't overcome inequalities in participation.

The main documents to come out of the Earth Summit were the Rio Declaration on Environment and Development and **Agenda 21** (see Box 6.1 and Box 6.2), as well as three MEAs that had been completed in time to be signed at the landmark conference: United Nations Framework Convention on Climate Change (UNFCCC), the United Nations Convention on Biological Diversity (UNCBD), and the United Nations Convention to Combat Desertification (UNCCD). Each of these texts was influenced by the 1987 Brundtland Report, both in terms of how the problems were understood and how they should be tackled. States also agreed to establish a new body, the UN **Commission on Sustainable Development** (CSD), as a subsidiary to ECOSOC. The CSD's role was to monitor implementation of Agenda 21 (across national, regional, and international levels), and promote further multilateral cooperation on sustainable development.

---

> **Box 6.1: The Rio Declaration on Environment and Development**
>
> - The Rio Declaration was the first internationally negotiated statement on 'sustainable development'. It comprises twenty-seven principles.
> - The Declaration text was finalised at a pre-UNCED negotiating session in April 1992; adopted at UNCED (the Earth Summit) in June 1992; and endorsed by the UN General Assembly in December 1992.
> - The Declaration reflects some of the language and ideas introduced in the 1987 Brundtland Report, *Our Common Future*; it seeks to harmonise development and environmental protection.
> - Many states and civil society actors hoped the Rio Declaration would constitute a 'Charter' (similar in status to the Universal Declaration of Human Rights) but developing countries rejected a binding Earth Charter (hard law) in favour of a conference declaration (soft law).

> **Box 6.2: Agenda 21**
>
> - Agenda 21 was adopted at the Rio Earth Summit (UNCED) in June 1992.
> - The Agenda was produced as a non-binding, voluntary 'action plan' to guide states in implementing sustainable development.
> - Its forty chapters cover issues related to the social and economic dimensions of development; conservation and resource management; participation of civil society and local governments in sustainable development policy; and implantation (finance, technology, education, etc.).
> - Particularly controversial topics were finance, technology transfer, climate, biodiversity, international institutions, poverty, consumption, fisheries, and biotechnology. These were the hardest to negotiate (Dodds 1997: 4).
> - Chapter 28 encouraged sub-national authorities to consult their citizens in creating Local Agendas to institutionalise sustainable development at lower levels of governance. Within five years, over 2000 local agendas were developed.

Farley and Smith identify six common ideas in the Rio Declaration, Agenda 21, and the other agreements signed at Rio. These are all associated with the concept of 'sustainable development' (Farley and Smith 2014: 38):

1. Humans are the central concern for sustainable development.
2. Humans must make changes to live in harmony with the natural environment.
3. Eradication of poverty in developing nations and reduction of excessive consumption in affluent countries are indispensable requirements for sustainable development.
4. Developing nations require special attention and accommodation to ensure parity across nations.
5. The protection of the environment and increasing development are interconnected and can be mutually supportive rather than adversarial goals.
6. Sustainable development is a mechanism for meeting the needs of both the current and future generations.

Others offer more critical interpretations that stress the influence of industry and free market environmentalism. Pratap Chatterjee and Matthias Finger were scathing in their assessment of UNCED. Rather than questioning the global forces of social and ecological destruction, they argued, UNCED reinforced the capitalist model of industrial development that empowers business and industry, and reduces the state to facilitating their expansion (Chatterjee and Finger 1994). Timothy Doyle agreed. He saw the Rio outcomes not as a step towards social and ecological sustainability but as deepening an exploitative international economic system that serves the interests of global capital over those of nature and the majority of the world's people. We can see this reflected in Principle 12 of the Rio Declaration, which predicates sustainable development on an open international system and economic growth, and which warned against restricting international trade under the guise of environmental protection. Principle 16 called on states to develop economic instruments for minimising pollution but 'without distorting international trade and investment'. We can also see the privileging of business and industry in what is *not* included in the Rio documents; the mining and energy sectors are notable exclusions.

Doyle lamented that the Rio sustainable development agenda co-opted the environmental movement and managed to 'almost completely dismantle active environmental critiques of existing political and market systems' (Doyle 1998: 771). By the end of Rio, to be an environmentalist meant to be in favour of economic growth. Of course, critique has not disappeared, but the close association between continued economic growth and environmental protection became dominant. US President, George H.W. Bush, made this clear when he concluded the summit by saying 'Twenty years ago some spoke of the limits to growth, and today we realize that growth is the engine of change and a friend of the environment' (Bush 1992).

As we saw in Chapter 4, our capitalist system relies on continued consumption, so it's tricky to address unsustainable consumption without questioning assumptions on which our economic systems are based. Principle 8 of the Rio Declaration asserted that states 'should' (note the flexible and non-compulsory language) 'reduce and eliminate unsustainable patterns of production and consumption'. This was notable for being the first time that a multilaterally agreed text referred to reducing consumption. Agenda 21 followed this up with a chapter on changing consumption patterns. This reflected the language and tone of the Brundtland Report, which called on states to address profligate lifestyles. But the US ensured that the issue of consumption would stay on the political margins, at Rio and beyond. During preparatory negotiations, US delegates repeatedly insisted that 'the American life-style is not up for negotiation' (quoted in Elmer-DeWitt 1992). As we will see in Chapter 9, multilateral efforts at addressing consumption have since been weak and ineffective.

Scholars tend to call the Rio version of sustainable development 'weak sustainability'. Harriet Bulkeley and her colleagues describe weak sustainability as focusing 'on enhanced efficiencies in consumption and production, the innovation and commercialization of a new generation of technologies, together with policies incentivizing individuals to make more environmentally friendly choices'. By focusing on adjustments that are possible within a capitalist economy, weak sustainability seeks to offer 'win–win solutions' that benefit the economy, allow economic growth to continue, and create new market opportunities (Bulkeley et al. 2013: 964). Critics who focus on the failure of Rio to address the drivers of ecological damage and social inequality offer a 'strong' version of sustainability. From this perspective, win–win solutions are merely papering over problems to protect powerful interests. A 'strong sustainability' approach to environmental governance would fundamentally reform economic and social systems. We saw such examples in Chapter 4 with the 'degrowth' and 'steady-state economy' movements. These weak and strong variants are two ends of a sustainability spectrum. Some readers may find their own judgments falling somewhere in the middle, recognising the inadequacies of Rio-style sustainability, but seeing this as an important step towards more ambitious action over time.

In evaluating the achievements of the Earth Summit we need to recognise that the main documents of the conference (the Rio Declaration and Agenda 21) are soft law. As we saw earlier, states are not legally bound by soft international law: they interpret the documents as recommendations rather than obligations, and they are not required to transpose the principles into national law. One could argue that the concept of sustainable development is too broad and all encompassing to be the subject of a global treaty (i.e., hard law); one could argue that the various aspects of sustainable development are more effectively addressed in separate focused treaties. Similarly, one could argue that separate environmental agreements are more likely to be effective and compatible if they are held together by an overarching treaty that recognises the limits and interconnectedness of ecological systems. This points to the dilemma of 'fragmentation' in global environmental governance, which we will examine in Chapter 7. Whether a soft or hard law approach is likely to be more effective for sustainable development, the fact remains that states opted for the flexible option of a declaration and action plan, together with a commitment to continue cooperation. The global governance of sustainable development has taken the form of summit-based multilateralism whereby states meet every ten years to reflect on progress and set new goals. Below we will see that this approach is failing to generate the ambition and action necessary to achieve sustainable development.

## Reality Check: World Summit on Sustainable Development, 2002

Ten years after Rio, the international community reconvened to assess progress and discuss new ways of advancing sustainable development. Over 20,000 participants, including 191 governments (and 104 heads of state) gathered in Johannesburg in August 2002 for the **World Summit on Sustainable Development** (International Institute for Sustainable Development 2002). But the international mood wasn't auspicious for environmental diplomacy. As we saw above, the early twenty-first century was a challenging period for environmental multilateralism. With a hostile US administration now in power (and the US president refusing to participate in Johannesburg), together with the preoccupation with terrorism, environmental issues were a low priority.

US politics wasn't the only factor dampening excitement and ambition in the run-up to Johannesburg. Many developing countries were coming to the 2002 World Summit poorer than they had been in 1992. There was an even deeper resentment that globalisation and the international trade system were working against the poor. The South came to the summit determined to push this agenda. The resulting Johannesburg Plan of Implementation includes a chapter on 'Sustainable Development in a Globalizing World', which focuses exclusively on promoting more open and equitable multilateral trading and financial systems, and opening up new opportunities for international trade and investment. Precisely how this would promote environmentally sustainable development was left unspecified; in fact, the word 'environment' appears just once in that chapter (UN 2002a).

The shift between 1992 and 2002 was partly captured by UNEP's executive director, Klaus Toepfer:

We had the fall of the Berlin Wall and the end of the Cold War. Today we have a new realism as a result of globalization. So the action plan, agreed here in Johannesburg, is less visionary and more workmanlike, reflecting perhaps the feeling among many nations that they no longer want to promise the earth and fail – that they would rather step forward than run too fast.

(quoted in James 2002)

The decision to hold the summit was made by the UN General Assembly, in February 2001, with the aim of reviewing implementation of Agenda 21 and 'reinvigorat[ing] the global commitment to sustainable development' (UNGA 2001). But in reality states had done little over the past decade to implement promised actions on sustainable development. This pattern of non-implementation was repeated in the ten years following the Johannesburg summit, so we will save our assessment of implementation for the next section on Rio+20. Here let's look at the mark that Johannesburg left on environmental multilateralism. Some observers suggest that the whole summit was rather forgettable. Steinar Andresen reduces the outcomes to a rehashing of the **Millennium Development Goals** (Andresen 2012: 89–90). For Jacob Park and his colleagues, the Johannesburg summit marked the 'death of Rio environmentalism' (Park et al. 2008: 5). Unable to report on any significant accomplishments, governments turned their attention to creating 'partnerships', which in practice delegated much of the responsibility for sustainable development to the private sector and civil society.

The partnership turn in environmental multilateralism reflected the UN's broader interest in promoting cooperation between governments, business, and NGOs. Throughout 2000 and 2001, the UN passed several resolutions stressing the importance of 'global partnerships' for pursuing development and poverty eradication. Resolution 56/76, passed in December 2001, 'invites the United Nations system to adhere to a common approach to partnership' (UNGA 2001). The World Summit on Sustainable Development became, as Marc Pallermaerts describes, 'the first large-scale testing ground for the new partnership approach' (2005: 381). This was not without controversy. Many NGOs and developing countries alike were concerned that the partnership approach would (by design or in effect) allow developed countries to avoid responsibility (Whitfield 2005: 359). Pallermaerts, a long-standing observer of environmental multilateralism, captures this preoccupation with his observation that while 'partnership events' at the summit were promoting and generating interest in multi-stakeholder 'coalitions of the willing', 'in the real-world intergovernmental negotiating arena ... coalitions of the *unwilling* were effectively preventing meaningful multilateral agreement on concrete and time-bound political commitments' (Pallermaerts 2005: 384).

The summit produced two outcome documents: the Johannesburg Declaration on Sustainable Development (UN 2002a) and the Johannesburg Plan of Implementation (UN 2002b). The new commitment to partnerships appears in the declaration in lofty language referring to the 'rich tapestry of people', 'partnership among all the people of our planet', and 'constructive partnership for change'. Like the Rio Declaration, the Johannesburg Declaration is a political expression rather than a legal document that binds states to actions. Soft law can have important consequences. But in light of the lack of progress made in the decade since Rio, the 2002 declaration inevitably rang hollow. Those reading the document at the time would have justifiably raised a sceptical eyebrow at the final principle that 'solemnly pledge[s] to the peoples of the world and the generations that will surely inherit this Earth that we are determined to ensure that our collective hope for sustainable development is realized' (UN 2002b).

The Plan of Implementation (also a soft law document) offered more concrete ideas for 'promoting', 'facilitating', 'creating', 'developing', and 'strengthening' partnerships. But notably absent was any discussion about the criteria for establishing a partnership, or how they would be monitored to ensure that sustainable development objectives would be met. A list of 220 voluntary partnership initiatives published by the WSSD after the summit raised concerns that partnerships would mainly be repackaged 'business as usual'. One was a 'WTO capacity-building initiative' proposed by Japan. Another was a hygiene campaign involving soap-producing companies to promote soap in the Indian state of Kerala. This one was abandoned when 'Indian health campaigners point[ed] out that the hygiene and health situation in Kerala is comparable to some Western countries and that corporate soap advertisements have nothing to do with sustainable development' (Corporate Europe Observatory 2002). These point to questions about the effectiveness, legitimacy, and accountability of sustainable development partnerships, a theme we will return to in the next chapter.

The rise of partnerships in environmental multilateralism reflects the fragmentation of global environmental governance. Our discussion here serves to place this trend in the political and historical context of environmental diplomacy. We will examine partnerships in more detail in Chapter 7, with a particular focus on the experience of using partnerships for governing climate change.

## Facing Up to Unmet Promises: Rio+20 and Beyond

The political climate was no more conducive to environmental cooperation in 2012 than it had been in 2002. Maintaining the tradition of sustainable development summits – rather than political ambition or optimism – appeared to be the main reason for organising the 2012 UN Conference on Sustainable

Development (UNCSD, or **Rio+20**). Leading up to the summit, any mention of Rio+20 in the media, blogosphere, or academic commentary was invariably accompanied by the phrase 'low expectations'. An optimistic minority hoped the international community would recognise the gravity of the ecological crisis and instigate transformational change at the conference. The summit, they argued, should be a 'constitutional moment' (Biermann and Bernstein 2012). The odds of this were low for three reasons. First, economic concerns were paramount in 2012: the Eurozone debt crisis, 'double dip' recessions across Europe, economic slowdown in China and India, slow growth in the US, and stubbornly high unemployment figures in many countries (O'Brien 2012). In this context, any actions that might distract from economic recovery held little appeal. Developing countries have consistently complained about wealthy countries failing to deliver promised financial support for sustainable development (including the pledge to devote 0.7 per cent of gross national wealth to overseas development assistance). If promises were broken when times were good, there was little chance that another summit would help when times were tough.

Second, interest and optimism in Rio+20 were low because 'summit fatigue' had been growing among government delegates and observers since the 2002 Johannesburg summit (VanDeveer 2003). The failure of the highly anticipated 2009 Copenhagen climate summit left many questioning whether inclusive multilateral processes – especially high-profile, high-level events – could deliver effective agreements. Partnerships and small 'minilateral' meetings among the main players were increasingly seen as the only plausible way to coordinate action on environmental problems (e.g., Victor 2009). In the end, some 44,000 people did attend the summit – but only seventy-nine heads of state or government (Bulkeley et al. 2013: 959).

The third reason for doubting that Rio+20 could deliver 'transformational change' was the record on progress since 1992. The extent of global environmental change and degradation was revealed in Chapter 1. This is strong evidence that existing action on sustainable development has been unsatisfactory. Additional evidence came in a report released just before Rio+20. The UN teamed up with the civil society organisation Stakeholder Forum to evaluate how the international community had performed on the goals set at Rio in 1992 (UN DESA 2012). The findings were mixed but generally lamentable. On most Agenda 21 pledges, little progress had been made. The patterns of performance revealed by their evaluation are shown in Table 6.1. Access the evaluation report online and you can see the specific goals that were assessed for each chapter of

Table 6.1: **Evaluating Progress on Agenda 21: 1992–2012**

| Chapter number | Topic | 1st Rating | 2nd Rating |
|---|---|---|---|
| 2 | International cooperation to accelerate SD in developing countries | − | − |
| 3 | Combating poverty | − | − |
| 4 | Changing consumption patterns | ✗ | ✗ |
| 5 | Demographic dynamics | − | − |
| 6 | Protecting/promoting human health conditions | − | − |
| 7 | Promoting sustainable settlements | ✗ | ✗ |
| 8 | Environmental mainstreaming | − | − |
| 9 | Protecting the atmosphere | ✗ | ✗ |
| 10 | Integrated approach to land management | ✗ | − |
| 11 | Combating deforestation | − | − |
| 12 | Combating desertification & drought | − | − |
| 13 | Sustainable mountain development | − | − |
| 14 | Promoting sustainable agriculture & rural development | − | − |
| 15 | Conservation of biodiversity | − | − |
| 16 | Environmentally sound management of biotechnology | − | − |
| 17 | Protection of the oceans | − | − |
| 18 | Protection of freshwater | − | − |
| 19 | Environmentally sound management of toxic chemicals | ↗ | − |
| 20 | Environmentally sound management of hazardous wastes | − | − |
| 21 | Environmentally sound management of solid waste and sewage | − | − |
| 22 | Safe and environmentally sound management of radioactive wastes | − | − |
| 23 | Major groups participation | ↗ | − |
| 24 | Participation of women | − | − |

Table 6.1 (*cont.*)

| Chapter number | Topic | 1st Rating | 2nd Rating |
|---|---|---|---|
| 25 | Participation of children & youth | – | – |
| 26 | Participation of indigenous peoples | – | – |
| 27 | Participation of NGOs | ↗ | ↗ |
| 28 | Participation of local authorities | ✓ | ↗ |
| 29 | Participation of workers & trade unions | ✗ | – |
| 30 | Participation of business & industry | – | – |
| 31 | Participation of science & technology experts | ↗ | – |
| 32 | Participation of farmers | – | – |
| 33 | Financial resources & mechanisms | – | – |
| 34 | Technology transfer & support | – | – |
| 35 | Science for sustainable development | ↗ | ↗ |
| 36 | Promoting education, public awareness, & training | – | – |
| 37 | Support for capacity-building in developing countries | – | – |
| 38 | International institutional arrangements | ✓ | ↗ |
| 39 | International legal instruments & mechanisms | ↗ | ↗ |
| 40 | Information for decision-making | – | – |

Source: Adapted from UN DESA 2012: 22–39
*KEY* ✓ Excellent progress / fully achieved
↗ Good progress / on target
– Limited progress / far from target
✗ No progress or regression

Agenda 21, as well as the justifications for each rating. The summary table (Table 6.1) reveals that states made limited progress on the vast majority of goals. States made no progress or regressed on:

- consumption
- sustainable settlements
- atmospheric protection

- land management
- participation of workers in sustainable development policy and decision-making.

On no chapter do we see full achievement or consistently excellent progress, but areas of good progress are:

- toxic chemicals management
- participation of major groups, especially NGOs and technical experts
- scientific research
- international legal instruments and mechanisms.

The strongest achievements were:

- the inclusion of local authorities in sustainable development governance
- international institutional arrangements.

While participation is highlighted as one of the better-performing commitments of Agenda 21, it is important to remember that participation is uneven and does not necessarily equate to influence. Well-resourced NGOs from the North overwhelmingly dominate civil society participation in environmental negotiations; and within these Northern organisations, white, well educated, and financially secure men are disproportionately represented (Stevenson 2016a: 409). Many voices are not being heard. Similarly, the report also qualified its assessment of institutional arrangements as excellent or fully achieved. These goals were technically achieved, but the substance reveals a different story. The evaluation found that sustainable development units had been created throughout the UN system and new institutions like the Commission on Sustainable Development were created. But in practice, mandates overlap and there is insufficient coherence or coordination to ensure effective international policy on sustainable development. This last point reflects a contentious issue in debates about global environmental governance, which is whether we need a World Environment Organization (akin to the WTO) to provide overarching leadership and authority.

Many observers and seasoned diplomats criticised Rio+20 for lacking focus and purpose. But the summit did have an agenda with two themes: institutional reform and green economy. Let's look at what Rio+20 discussed and achieved on each theme.

By 2012, it was widely acknowledged that the institutional architecture was inadequate for effectively coordinating the hundreds of MEAs and the many international organisations that had some environmental authority (Van Alstine et al. 2013: 335). UNEP's work was mostly limited to partnering up with other

UN agencies to deliver capacity-building programmes in developing countries; it had neither the resources nor mandate to promote transformational change in the international system. As we saw earlier, UNEP wasn't even given responsibility for monitoring implementation of Agenda 21 back in 1992 – this task was given to a new body, the CSD. Maria Ivanova points to this as a sign of states' 'lack of confidence in UNEP's ability to address the issue of sustainable development'. But creating another UN body, Ivanova argues, 'caused further fragmentation of the already cluttered institutional architecture' (Ivanova 2005: 54).

As a subsidiary to ECOSOC, and with a rotating membership of fifty-three states, the Commission on Sustainable Development never had the capacity or status to influence the governance of sustainable development. Meetings were mostly held among mid-level officials, with short sessions for meetings among ministers. One long-term observer describes how the 'moribund' CSD was 'put out its misery after 20 years of underperformance' (Halle 2012: 3), and replaced at Rio+20 with a High-Level Political Forum on sustainable development. Like the CSD, the forum was mandated with reviewing progress on states' sustainable development commitments, as well as providing political leadership and guidance, shaping future sustainable development agendas; improving coordination across the UN system and beyond; and reviewing and disseminating scientific-based reports to inform future policy. Unlike the CSD, all states are members of the High-Level Political Forum. Unlike the CSD, the forum will also facilitate dialogue among heads of state every four years, and among ministers annually (Abbott and Bernstein 2015). This gives the institution more status if not necessarily more influence or resources. But the creation of the High-Level Political Forum was still far less than what some parties had advocated, including the European Union and some African countries. Echoing calls made in Stockholm in 1972, they had called for a UN Environment Organization with the authority to coordinate UN work on the environment, the hundreds of MEAs and their secretariats, as well as international financial institutions like the World Bank and WTO. Yet, continued resistance from the US in particular means that this proposal is unlikely to ever materialise. Without such an overarching organisation, it falls to UNEP and the new High-Level Political Forum to attempt to coordinate global action through leadership and persuasion – a strategy of indirect governance called '**orchestration**' (Abbott and Bernstein 2015). We will return to this topic in the next chapter.

The second theme of Rio+20 was '**green economy**'. This was promoted mostly by UNEP and mostly as a way to revive interest in sustainable development. In the face of continuing environmental degradation, poor performance on Agenda 21, and weak economic conditions in much of the North and South,

UNEP saw 'green economy' as a promising agenda. Out of crisis can come opportunity, so the saying goes. As we saw above, the concept of sustainable development promises that economic growth, social inclusion, and environmental protection are mutually compatible. But by 2012 this promise was looking questionable. According to international organisations like UNEP and the OECD, the logic of sustainable development wasn't flawed but capital wasn't being allocated to the right sectors. The economic crisis presented an opportunity for rectifying this problem in both developed and developing countries, and the solution lay in 'green economy' and 'green growth' strategies. These involved promoting investment in public transport infrastructure; incentivising compact urban planning (rather than urban sprawls); helping workers transition into 'green' sectors; reforming tax systems so that environmentally damaging activities would become more expensive than 'environmentally friendly' ones; removing subsidies on fossil fuels to encourage investment in clean energy; and accounting for the monetary value of nature.

While these policy proposals may be sound, the 'green economy' proposal was criticised from various angles and actors. Some developed countries saw it as too Keynesian and expressed concern at government intervention in the economy. Many developing countries and civil society groups saw it as an attempt to water down existing commitments to sustainable development. Developing countries were wary of attempts to detract attention from the responsibility of developed countries to support them with finance and technology. Some also felt that the green economy idea placed too much emphasis on the environment rather than prioritising their development needs. By contrast, civil society groups were concerned that the 'green economy' idea privileged economic growth at the expense of concerns for social equality and environmental protection. In the Rio+20 **counter-summit**, activists denounced green economy strategies as propping up the unsustainable and unjust capitalist system rather than promoting its transformation.

In the end, the conference outcome document (another soft law text), 'The Future We Want', did refer to the 'green economy', but not as the centrally defining idea that its advocates had hoped (UN 2012). It was mentioned as 'one of the important tools available for achieving sustainable development'; and states were 'encouraged to consider [its] implementation'. But the document devoted more space to clarifying what green economy policies should *avoid* than specifying particular actions that would be undertaken. States insisted that green economy policies respect national sovereignty, avoid imposing conditionalities on foreign aid, and not be used to justify trade restrictions. Any suggested actions were heavily qualified with flexible language such as 'as appropriate' and 'where national circumstances and conditions allow'. In practice, the idea of 'green economy' has not taken hold. Few countries have developed national green economy policies or strategies, and any mention of the green economy is almost always accompanied by 'and sustainable development'.

Even though the promises made for sustainable development in 1992 are mostly unfulfilled, the concept remains salient. 'The Future We Want' reaffirmed its commitment to sustainable development and resolved to begin a process of defining '**Sustainable Development Goals**' (SDGs). This is perhaps the most meaningful – and novel – outcome produced by the Rio+20 summit. Three years later, in 2015, the UN adopted seventeen SDGs with 169 targets to be reached by 2030 (see Box 6.3). The goals are a shopping list of good things – there is little to disagree with. But the scope of these goals and targets is so far beyond the reach

---

### Box 6.3: **Sustainable Development Goals**

1. **No poverty:** End poverty in all its forms everywhere.
2. **Zero hunger:** End hunger, achieve food security and improved nutrition, and promote sustainable agriculture.
3. **Good health and wellbeing:** Ensure healthy lives and promote wellbeing for all at all ages.
4. **Quality education:** Ensure inclusive and equitable quality education and promote lifelong learning opportunities for all.
5. **Gender equality:** Achieve gender equality and empower all women and girls.
6. **Clean water and sanitation:** Ensure availability and sustainable management of water and sanitation for all.
7. **Affordable and clean energy:** Ensure access to affordable, reliable, sustainable, and modern energy for all.
8. **Decent work and economic growth:** Promote sustained, inclusive, and sustainable economic growth, full and productive employment and decent work for all.
9. **Industry, innovation, and infrastructure:** Build resilient infrastructure, promote inclusive and sustainable industrialisation, and foster innovation.
10. **Reduced inequalities:** Reduce inequality within and among countries.
11. **Sustainable cities and communities:** Make cities and human settlements inclusive, safe, resilient, and sustainable.
12. **Responsible consumption:** Ensure sustainable consumption and production patterns.
13. **Climate action:** Take urgent action to combat climate change and its impacts.
14. **Life below water:** Conserve and sustainably use the oceans, seas. and marine resources for sustainable development.
15. **Life on land:** Protect, restore. and promote sustainable use of terrestrial ecosystems, sustainably manage forests, combat desertification, and halt and reverse land degradation, and halt biodiversity loss.
16. **Peace, justice, and strong institutions:** Promote peaceful and inclusive societies for sustainable development, provide access to justice for all, and build effective, accountable, and inclusive institutions at all levels.
17. **Partnerships for the goals:** Strengthen the means of implementation and revitalise the global partnership for sustainable development.

Source: UN DESA 2012

of current political commitment that many observers find it hard to take them seriously. They have been described as 'unactionable', 'unmeasurable', 'unattainable', and 'a high-school wish list on how to save the world' (Easterly 2015). Unlike the Millennium Development Goals, many of the SDG targets are unquantifiable, so it will be impossible to determine whether or not they are achieved. As with every other aspirational and voluntary agreement on sustainable development, civil society groups were quick to point out that the most fundamental flaw in the SDGs is that they ignore power imbalances in the global system (especially multinational corporations' control of natural resources), and they assume technological and market-based approaches will reduce poverty, minimise inequalities, and protect the environment (Dearden 2015).

In sum, Rio+20 delivered some institutional reforms and instigated a process leading to the Sustainable Development Goals. But for many, this wasn't enough, and it certainly didn't justify the investment of large amounts of time and money. One critic described it as 'like setting out to build a high-speed rail link between two distant cities and ending up asking people to be satisfied that the station signs received a fresh coat of paint' (Halle 2012: 4). For the critics, the outcome of Rio+20 justified the growing scepticism in 'mega-summits'. The masses of people, the hundreds of official meetings, the thousands of side events and information stalls all give the impression that sustainability is being taken seriously. But it is hard to avoid the conclusion that these events are not helping to transform the global economy or states' development plans. Carl Death argues that these summits are 'moments of political theatre' through which states signal expectations and shape the conduct of the 'global audience' (Death 2011: 1). It is through these mega-events that states enact the ideals of multilateralism. He writes, 'the dominant message of a successfully performed summit is that political elites have risen to the challenge and are hard at work resolving the differences that stand in the way of effective action on environmental problems' (2011: 7). The problem is that 'audiences' are increasingly un-persuaded by the theatrics; they are not left reassured that states have the problems under control, nor that the multilateral system is working for sustainability.

## Conclusion

For over fifty years the UN has provided a setting for establishing common understandings about sustainability, and pledging collective actions to reduce the human impact on the planet. Differences of opinion and priority between the North and South have been addressed by placing development at the heart of the environment agenda, and placing the onus for leadership and support on developing countries. It would be unfair to overlook the significant diplomatic advances that states have achieved. Since the middle of the twentieth century, hundreds of multilateral environmental agreements have been negotiated, and a complex environmental regime with many institutions and agencies has been constructed. But it would be remiss to ignore the limitations characterising international environmental law.

On the issue of sustainable development, the international community has pursued a soft law approach whereby declarations and plans of action are agreed and revised every ten years. The UN cannot force states to fulfil such promises as changing consumption patterns, reducing deforestation, curbing desertification, improving access to finance and technology in developing countries, and improving urban air quality. We saw in the previous chapter that efforts at cooperation are more common than resorting to conflict. In this chapter we have looked more deeply into international cooperation and discovered that states may be amenable to cooperation but they are also much fonder of words than deeds.

In the next chapter we turn our attention to the issue of climate change where impatience with the slow pace and poor performance of multilateralism has pushed many state and non-state actors to pursue progress in alternative governance mechanisms and processes.

## Discussion Questions

1. What is the difference between hard and soft law? How can the international community ensure that states comply with soft law?
2. What factors explain the proliferation of MEAs in the 1980s and 1990s? Two factors were identified in this chapter, can you identify any others?
3. What are the characteristics of strong sustainability and weak sustainability? What are the prospects of negotiating MEAs that reflect strong sustainability?
4. Table 6.1 reveals general patterns of performance on Agenda 21. Consider those that have the lowest ratings: Why do you think it has

been so difficult to make progress in these areas? To answer this question you will need to access the relevant chapters of Agenda 21 and the 2012 UN DESA report to see what was pledged and the details of the 2012 assessment.

5. Is multilateral diplomacy an effective way of addressing global environmental problems? Why or why not?

# 7 Transnational Governance Experiments

## Climate Change

key points

- Several factors explain the rise of transnational governance. Globalisation has weakened the regulatory capacity of the state and produced more complex threats and challenges. The dominant discourse of neoliberalism depicts the state as inefficient.
- Transnational governance initiatives are particularly prominent in the area of climate change. One of the reasons for the growth of such initiatives is the unsatisfactory progress in UN climate change negotiations.
- Climate change is a 'wicked' policy problem: it is complex, urgent, and there is no international authority to enforce action.
- Non-state actors play an increasingly important role in global climate change governance by developing collective rules, standards, goals, and processes outside the UN system. These are referred to as climate governance 'experiments'.
- Scholars disagree about the merits and limitations of climate governance experiments. But many agree that greater coordination, 'orchestration', or 'meta-governance' would improve coherence, effectiveness, and legitimacy.

## Introduction

The way in which we understand authority in the international system has profoundly changed since the 1990s. Open a textbook on international politics from the twentieth century and you'll quickly form an impression that there is one source of authority: the state. As we saw in Chapter 6, the state can sometimes choose to pool its resources with other states to establish international organisations like the UN. But even when this happens, states retain their sovereignty and remain the primary source of authority in the international system. Sovereignty gives states the power to legally enforce rules, a power that supersedes any rule-making power of sub-national, supra-national, or non-state actors. The UN and other international organisations only function if the state chooses to delegate functions and responsibilities. This is the traditional understanding of international relations. Today most scholars recognise that the state remains a central actor in international relations but that it increasingly vies for power and shares authority with other actors, including business, civil society, regional governments, and cities. These other actors also try to develop collective rules, standards, goals, and processes to bring some order to the international system. This shift from hierarchically organised formal public authority to informal, horizontal connections across actors goes by various names in the academic literature: **networked governance** (e.g., Sørensen and Torfing 2007; Stevenson and Dryzek 2014), transnational governance (e.g., Bulkeley and Newell 2010), and global governance (e.g., Thakur and van Langenhove 2006).

Non-state actors play an increasingly important role in international efforts to address environmental problems. This is particularly the case for climate change, which we examine in this chapter. State efforts to devise collective plans for reducing global greenhouse gas emissions began in the 1980s. But their combined level of ambition has never matched the scale of the problem. Fossil fuels have driven development since the industrial revolution. Decarbonising development is perhaps the greatest challenge the world has ever faced. So it is unsurprising that progress has been slow and disappointing. The lack of effective international action on climate change created a 'regulatory gap' and an opportunity for non-state actors to create alternative processes for reducing GHG emissions.

In this chapter we will first look at the general rise of **transnational governance** and the different types of arrangements that have formed in areas ranging from human rights to trade. We will then focus on the issue of climate change, where transnational activity has been particularly prominent. This section begins with an overview of the scientific basis of climate change, and the complex political factors involved. This helps us to understand why global action has been so difficult and slow. Climate change is depicted as a **'wicked' policy problem** without a simple cause or straightforward solution. Next we examine multilateral efforts to craft agreements on climate change. We look at the norms that have underpinned these negotiations, and the conventions and treaties that states have produced over the past twenty-five years, culminating in the **Paris Agreement** in 2015. We then turn our attention to transnational climate change governance, which is characterised by diverse and fragmented 'experiments' relating to energy, carbon markets, low-carbon technology, and emissions trading. In this section we examine different types of governance experiments, and look at their dominant characteristics (when they emerged, who is involved, where they take place, and what they do). Scholars disagree about the virtues and limitations of transnational climate governance, but many argue that some form of coordination would deliver more effective and equitable outcomes. In the final section of this chapter, we consider these arguments and the potential for the UN system to promote a more coherent climate regime.

## Transnational Governance

Before we identify different types of transnational governance arrangements, let's examine the reasons behind the rise of transnational governance. What explains the diffusion of authority from the state to non-state actors? Globalisation is one answer. Liberalisation and deregulation have led to ever increasing flows of finance, investment, goods, and services across national borders. Production lines are increasingly complex and global. This weakens the regulatory capacity of the state. It also promotes an identity of the 'competition state' whereby states deliberately roll back their regulation to attract foreign investment and grow their economy. This gives private actors – especially corporate ones – more political clout.

Just as economic and financial processes have become globalised, so have the threat and challenges that governments and citizens face. Porous borders make it easier for organised crime and terrorist organisations to move around and expand their operations. Increased travel facilitates the spread of infectious diseases. Droughts or floods in one region can undermine food security in another. Forest fires in one country can create dangerous levels of air pollution in another. Building infrastructure like hydropower dams in one country can disrupt distant ecosystems in other countries. Greenhouse gas emissions accumulate in the atmosphere posing risks to lives and livelihoods across the globe. All of these global and transnational challenges strain the capacity of the state to respond. Whether because of insufficient political will or genuine capacity deficits, there are large regulatory gaps in the international system. Private actors have stepped into this space to create systems of rules and standards, and to deliver transnational public services. Their motives are mixed: genuine benevolent concern, pursuing profit opportunities, and/or a desire to create market-friendly norms to avoid more stringent regulation.

To explain the rise of transnational governance we also need to recognise the ideology of **neoliberalism**, which became dominant in the 1990s. Neoliberalism holds that state institutions are inefficient and stifle innovation unless they play only a minimal regulatory role. At the domestic level this led to privatisation of public infrastructure and service delivery, and the replacement of mandatory regulations with voluntary standards. At the international level, it led to the rise of private and public-private institutions, and a privileging of market mechanisms (like emissions trading) in multilateral agreements created by states.

Kenneth Abbott and Duncan Snidal, two American scholars of transnational regulation, depict transnational governance as a triangle (see Figure 7.1). Their 'governance triangle' helps us to grasp the various ways in which authority is combined to deliver transnational governance.

The seven 'zones' in the triangle each represent a different actor configuration. The State vertex encompasses states and international organisations (as their members are all states); the NGO vertex encompasses all non-state actors (social movements, faith-based organisations, charities, philanthropic foundations, trade unions, and non-governmental organisations); and the Firm vertex encompasses businesses, industry organisations, and corporations (Abbott and Snidal 2010: 320–1):

1. Schemes initiated and dominated by states or IOs *(e.g. the EU's Flower Eco-label)*
2. Schemes initiated and dominated by firms *(e.g. World Diamond Council warranty system for conflict diamonds)*
3. Schemes initiated and dominated by civil society actors *(e.g. Amnesty International Human Rights Guidelines for Companies)*
4. Collaborative schemes among firms and states or IOs *(e.g. United Nations Global Compact)*

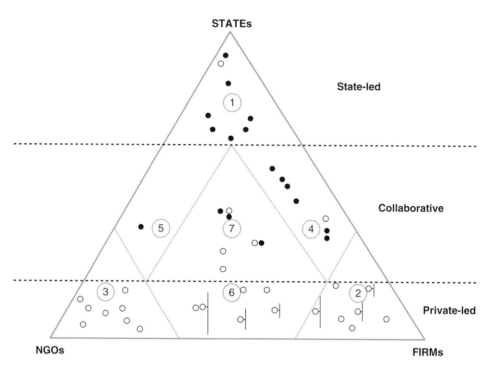

**Figure 7.1:** The governance triangle
Source: Abbott and Snidal 2010: 319

5. Collaborative schemes among civil society and states or IOs *(e.g. Principles for Responsible Investment)*
6. Collaborative schemes among civil society and firms *(e.g. Fairtrade Labeling Organization labelling scheme)*
7. Collaborative schemes among states or IOs, civil society, and firms *(e.g. Extractive Industries Transparency Initiative).*

This proliferation of governance schemes is sometimes referred to as 'fragmentation' (Biermann et al. 2010). As we can see from the examples above, fragmentation is a feature of many areas of global governance, including security, mining, health, finance, agriculture, trade, and the environment. In each of these areas there are many distinct institutions that are not fully interlinked or integrated (Biermann et al. 2010: 17). Some see the fragmentation of governance as a positive development: the greater the scale of activity, the higher the likelihood of successfully confronting common challenges. Others are concerned about the overlaps and lack of coordination in such decentralised arrangements. Frank Biermann and his colleagues warn against making generalisations about fragmented 'governance architectures'. Some arrangements may be *synergistic* (a core institution supported by all relevant actors, coupled with closely integrated secondary institutions that share similar norms), *cooperative* (several core institutions supported by most relevant actors, coupled with loosely integrated and non-contradictory secondary institutions), or *conflictive* (largely unrelated institutions, with conflicting norms, that are aligned with different actors) (Biermann et al. 2010: 19). Coherent governance would be found at the synergistic end of the spectrum.

Scholars concerned about the functional cohesion of fragmented governance call for 'orchestration' by states and international organisations. 'Orchestration', Abbott and Snidal explain, 'entails mobilizing and working with private actors and institutions to achieve regulatory goals, for example, by catalysing voluntary and collaborative programs; convening and facilitating private collaborations; persuading and inducing firms and industries to self-regulate; building private capacities; negotiating regulatory targets with firms; and providing incentives for attaining those targets' (2010: 317).

'Orchestration' is also called 'meta-governance' and is advocated by scholars concerned about the democratic legitimacy of diverse governance schemes. Sørensen and Torfing see **meta-governance** as necessary to democratically 'anchor' diverse governance schemes: 'Governance networks are democratically anchored to the extent that they are properly linked to different political constituencies and to a relevant set of democratic norms that are part of the democratic ethos of society' (Sørensen and Torfing 2005: 201). It is easier to see how this would work in the domestic context (which Sørensen and Torfing had in mind) where we often have elected politicians and national institutions to provide some democratic oversight. At the international level oversight is possible in principle, but without that same enforcement power as the domestic level. Later in this chapter we will see how this might look in the context of fragmented climate change governance.

## Climate Change

The fragmentation of governance is a trend we see across many areas of global politics. But it is perhaps most prominent in the area of climate change where hundreds of public, private, and public-private governance schemes have been launched since the 1990s. Before we look at the rise of transnational climate governance, let's first examine the problem of climate change and consider traditional multilateral arrangements that have attempted – and long failed – to develop a collective response.

## The Science of Climate Change

Scientists have been increasingly concerned about global climate change since the 1980s. But even in the mid-nineteenth century, suspicions were beginning to rise that carbon dioxide and temperature may be related. In the 1850s and 1860s, Irish physicist John Tyndall conducted a series of experiments showing that $CO_2$ absorbed radiation and therefore contributed to regulating the earth's temperature. Swedish chemist Svante Arrhenius took up the issue in about 1906 and calculated that a doubling of $CO_2$ emissions would cause a 5°C rise in the average global temperature (up from 15°C) (Howe 2014: 3–4; Dessler and Parson 2006: 8–9). These arguments remained marginal in the scientific community until scientific tools became sophisticated enough to measure concentrations of $CO_2$ and changes in the absorption of infrared spectra in the atmosphere (Dessler and Parson 2006: 8–9). A breakthrough came when American chemist Charles David Keeling determined that for every million units of atmospheric gases, 315 units were $CO_2$ (Howe 2014: 3). Perhaps you have heard of the climate change campaign network 350.org led by Bill McKibben – this refers to the importance of returning the amount of $CO_2$ in the atmosphere to 350 units (or parts) per million (abbreviated as ppm). In August 2016, atmospheric $CO_2$ was 402 ppm (Earth's $CO_2$ 2016). Over time, scientists have come to understand that carbon dioxide is not the only gas that absorbs radiation and contributes to global warming. Other 'greenhouse gases' (GHGs) are methane, nitrous oxide, hydrofluorocarbons, perfluorocarbons, and sulphur hexafluoride.

Scientists and activists have advocated different numerical targets for global climate change policy. In the late 2000s, 350 ppm was strongly pushed as an aspirational target. But in negotiations, diplomats have generally accepted 400 ppm or even 450 ppm as a more realistic target. This highlights that what is socially desirable is often very different to what is politically viable. Others have suggested that a temperature target is more meaningful than an atmospheric concentration target, and have called on leaders to agree on collective action to limit global temperature increases to 1.5°C or 2°C above pre-industrial levels. While scientists can help us to understand the likely consequences of exceeding, say, 2 degrees warming, or 400 ppm, there is no objectively correct number. These numbers entail different risks, which are unevenly distributed across time and place. So let's look at what these different numbers mean on the ground. What difference would it make if we reached (or failed to reach) a target of 350 ppm, 450 ppm, 1.5°C or 2°C? Thinking in terms of temperature change is perhaps easiest for those of us without a PhD in atmospheric sciences. But the numbers seem deceptively small. After all, it would probably make little impact to your day's plans if your local weather forecast was revised from 15°C to 17°C. But to grasp the significance of global temperature change, an analogy of your body's temperature is more useful than the local weather forecast. A subtle rise from 37 to 39°C would take you from a normal healthy state to a fever, with further subtle rises posing a risk of serious illness or even death.

Scientists have identified 350 ppm or 2°C as defining the 'safe operating space for humanity'. 'Transgressing these boundaries', they write, 'will increase the risk of irreversible climate change, such as the loss of major ice sheets, accelerated sea-level rise and abrupt shifts in forest and agricultural systems' (Rockström et al. 2009). A certain degree of warming is already locked into the climate system, and the effects of this are already being felt. Every five or six years, the Intergovernmental Panel on Climate Change (IPCC) reviews the scientific literature and presents the latest findings on climate change impacts and vulnerabilities. Its most recent report (Intergovernmental Panel on Climate Change 2014) points to evidence of shrinking glaciers, affecting the quantity and quality of water supplies; reduced crop growth (wheat and maize) in many regions; and an increase in heat-related deaths in regions. Poor people and marginalized groups in society are disproportionately exposed to the effects of these changes (IPCC 2014: 4–6). The IPCC models different scenarios based on warming between 1 and 5°C. Eight key risks were identified in the latest report (see Box 7.1). The intensity and severity of these risks rise in conjunction with global temperature rise.

## A 'Wicked' Policy Problem

If you were to ask an environmentalist, politician, CEO, or even your neighbour which environmental problem is most serious, they would very likely name climate change. It attracts so much attention because it implicates so many other environmental issues like water, land degradation, biodiversity, and deforestation. But it also attracts a lot of attention because it is bewildering in its complexity. Attempting to reduce the concentration of greenhouse gases in the atmosphere requires nothing less than the decarbonisation of our global

---

Box 7.1: **Climate Change Risks**

1. Risk of death, injury, ill-health, or disrupted livelihoods in low-lying coastal zones and small island developing states and other small islands, due to storm surges, coastal flooding, and sea-level rise.
2. Risk of severe ill-health and disrupted livelihoods for large urban populations due to inland flooding in some regions.
3. Systemic risks due to extreme weather events leading to breakdown of infrastructure networks and critical services such as electricity, water supply, and health and emergency services.
4. Risk of mortality and morbidity during periods of extreme heat, particularly for vulnerable urban populations and those working outdoors in urban or rural areas.
5. Risk of food insecurity and the breakdown of food systems linked to warming, drought, flooding, and precipitation variability and extremes, particularly for poorer populations in urban and rural settings.
6. Risk of loss of rural livelihoods and income due to insufficient access to drinking and irrigation water and reduced agricultural productivity, particularly for farmers and pastoralists with minimal capital in semi-arid regions.
7. Risk of loss of marine and coastal ecosystems, biodiversity, and the ecosystem goods, functions, and services they provide for coastal livelihoods, especially for fishing communities in the tropics and the Arctic.
8. Risk of loss of terrestrial and inland water ecosystems, biodiversity, and the ecosystem goods, functions, and services they provide for livelihoods.

Source of text: IPCC 2014: 13

---

economy. Since the industrial revolution, we have become dependent on burning fossil fuels to drive economic growth, reduce poverty, build energy infrastructure, and expand agricultural production. Burning fossil fuels supports most modern mobility: from the daily commute to the inter-continental business trip.

Some scholars describe climate change as a 'wicked' policy problem (e.g., Falkner 2016), which is a concept originally mooted by Rittel and Webber (1973). As a wicked problem, it is impossible to simply diagnose and apply a straightforward solution. The fact that burning fossil fuels is entrenched in economic and cultural systems poses a profound challenge. But several other factors amplify the challenge. One is urgency: the longer it takes to reduce GHG emissions, the more intense will be the consequences, and the more costly it will be to adapt. Another factor is the lack of a central authority at the international level to coordinate and enforce action. As we will see in the next section, international negotiations on climate change have been fraught with problems and have ultimately failed to deliver an effective response. This leads some to characterise it is as a 'tragedy of the commons' type of problem (Levin et al. 2012). A further factor is that there is no single way of defining the problem of climate change. The responses we come up with emerge from our definition of the problem. But those with the authority and capacity to respond to climate change have a vested interest in minimising their own costs. As a result, the 'solutions' proposed may be less than adequate to deliver fair and effective outcomes. John Dryzek and I suggest that there are at least four broad ways of understanding the problem of climate change, each pointing to different aims and actions (Stevenson and Dryzek 2014: 31, 41–54):

1. *Mainstream sustainability*, committed to low-carbon capitalism that can be achieved without much disruption to the existing political economy.
2. *Expansive sustainability* that sees a decarbonising capitalist economy as necessarily accompanied by international equity and more in the way of public control.
3. *Limits* and boundaries that stress the impossibility of endless economic and population growth in an ecologically finite world.
4. *Green radicalism* committed to ecological and social justice via the transformation of global capitalist production, and the empowerment of women, indigenous peoples, and local communities.

Different states and civil society actors express these 'climate discourses' in international debates and negotiations. While diplomats are busy discussing how technology transfer and carbon markets can deliver economic growth and climate change **mitigation**, activists outside are frequently denouncing such 'win–win' solutions as fallacy. Their call for 'system change not climate change' directs attention to the deeper transformations needed in our political and economic systems.

## Multilateral Cooperation on Climate Change

Multilateral efforts to protect the climate system began in the late 1980s. Growing confidence in the evidence of global warming pushed many scientists to take on the role of 'knowledge brokers' and advocate for global cooperation on climate change. The role of a scientific knowledge broker is to translate and disseminate scientific knowledge of climate change into public and policy-making circles through conferences, workshops, non-specialist journals, and direct communication with government officials (Bodansky 2001: 27). Governments began to take notice and by the late 1980s there was consensus that the global climate system is a common concern of humankind and requires protection for present and future generations.

A pivotal moment in shaping multilateral negotiations on climate change was the 1988 Toronto Conference on the changing atmosphere. It was not a UN conference, but the tone and substance of its outcome document proved highly influential in subsequent UN negotiations. The Toronto Declaration was unequivocal in defining climate change as an urgent issue warranting immediate action:

Humanity is conducting an unintended, uncontrolled, globally pervasive experiment whose ultimate consequences could be second only to a global nuclear war. The Earth's atmosphere is being changed at an unprecedented rate by pollutants resulting from human activities, inefficient and wasteful fossil fuel use and the effects of rapid population growth in many regions. These changes represent a major threat to international security and are already having harmful consequences over many parts of the globe.

(The Changing Atmosphere 1988)

The declaration recognised that industrialised countries 'have a responsibility to lead the way', and should work towards a global goal of reducing GHG emissions by 20 per cent below 1988 levels by 2005 (The Changing Atmosphere 1988). These two statements came to shape expectations of how the international community should address climate change. They came to define international 'norms' of climate governance, defining *who* should take responsibility for mitigating climate change, and *how* such mitigation should be pursued (Stevenson 2013). The first norm held that international efforts to reduce emissions should be based on universal participation of states but guided by the principle of common but differentiated responsibilities and respective capabilities (CBDR). This norm has an established history in environmental governance and appears in the Conventions on the Law of the Sea, the Vienna Convention on the Protection of the Ozone Layer, and its Montreal Protocol, the Basel Convention on the Control of Transboundary Movements of Hazardous Wastes, and the Rio Declaration on Environment and Development (Rajamani 2000: 121). It puts the leading responsibility on industrialised countries on the basis of their historical contribution to pollution and/or their greater capacity to bear the costs incurred.

The second governance norm held that climate change mitigation should be achieved through domestic emission reduction targets and timetables. Like CBDR, this norm had already been institutionalised in earlier environmental agreements, including the Montreal Protocol and the European Community's Large Combustion Plant Directive. In the late 1980s many rich countries adopted a version of the 'Toronto Target':

- Australia, Austria, and Denmark pledged to reduce emissions to 20 per cent below 1988 levels by 2005;
- Norway committed to stabilising $CO_2$ emissions at 1989 levels by the year 2000;

- Luxembourg, Finland, Switzerland, Canada, and the United Kingdom all pledged to stabilise their $CO_2$ emissions at 1990 levels by the year 2000;
- France and Japan set per capita stabilisation targets;
- The European Community pledged to stabilise emissions at 1990 levels by the year 2000. (Stevenson 2013: 25)

These norms shaped two important multilateral agreements on climate change: the 1992 United Nations Framework Convention on Climate Change (UNFCCC), and the 1997 Kyoto Protocol. But norms are not fixed: they change over time as they are contested or reinterpreted. In fact, over time many scholars and diplomats came to identify the norms of CBDR and domestic targets and timetables as serious problems that were thwarting effective global action. To see why this might be so, let's look more closely at the debates that took place during negotiations on the UNFCCC and the Kyoto Protocol, and what was eventually decided in each of these agreements.

The UNFCCC (known verbally as the 'UNF triple C') was negotiated over sixteen months during 1991 and 1992. The idea that developed countries should assume leadership and responsibility was not disputed. But states (or parties as they are called in negotiations) disagreed over how to define the categories of 'developed' and 'developing'. Some wanted to set a per capita income threshold, while others wanted to simply list the countries belonging to each category. In the end they adopted three categories to acknowledge that not all 'developed' countries are the same: Annex I countries were the wealthiest countries; Annex II countries were 'economies in transition' (namely, Europe's post-communist countries), and all the rest were non-Annex I countries. The principle of common but differentiated responsibilities was enshrined in the convention under Article 3:

The Parties should protect the climate system for the benefit of present and future generations of humankind, on the basis of equity and in accordance with their common but differentiated responsibilities and respective capabilities. Accordingly, the developed country Parties should take the lead in combating climate change and the adverse effects thereof.

(UNFCCC 1992)

Most industrialised countries accepted that 'taking the lead' meant adopting domestic emission reduction targets. But the US strongly resisted this approach, considering it too rigid and unaccommodating of each state's unique circumstances. With the support of oil producing states, the US pushed for a convention based on more general national programmes and strategies. Japan proposed a compromise approach of 'pledge and review' whereby each state would pledge strategies for limiting GHG emissions, which would later be evaluated by an expert panel (Bodansky 1993: 486). In the end, the convention listed mostly *qualitative* commitments (such as compiling national emission inventories, national strategies, and reporting) rather than *quantitative* targets (such as the Toronto-style targets). A fairly loose collective target was agreed in Article 4.2, which instructs industrialised countries to adopt and report on national policies 'with the aim of returning individually or jointly to their 1990 (GHG) levels' (UNFCCC 1992).

The convention was only intended as a first step towards a more detailed multilateral agreement. Soon after it entered into force in 1994, parties began negotiations on what would become the Kyoto Protocol. States continued to debate how CBDR should be interpreted. Germany and the US both pushed the idea of differentiating between developing countries to allow discussions on limiting emissions growth in so-called 'more advanced developing countries', like China, South Korea, and Brazil. Developing countries were united in their rejection of this proposal, arguing that the wealthy countries needed to show genuine leadership in reducing their own emissions given their historical responsibility for creating the threat of climate change. Developing countries were able to resist efforts to differentiate them into groups of more advanced and less advanced developing countries. But pressure for them to increase action was strong during Kyoto Protocol negotiations. Here we see another important compromise emerge that would profoundly affect the future of global climate change governance. By the mid-1990s it was becoming clear to industrialised countries that reducing their GHG emissions was going to be difficult and expensive. The negotiations increasingly focused on the challenge of efficiently reducing global emissions without interrupting economic growth. The idea of 'flexible mechanisms' emerged as way of facilitating action in developing countries while minimizing the cost of meeting emissions targets in developed countries. Flexible mechanisms would allow developed countries to meet their commitments by investing in GHG mitigation in less developed countries, or buying emissions credits through a trading system. Three market-based mechanisms were agreed as part of the Kyoto Protocol:

- *Emissions trading* whereby countries (or businesses within them) could buy and sell emission permits to seek an economically efficient distribution of the burden of reducing overall emissions.
- *Joint Implementation* whereby a country could invest to reduce emissions in another developed country, while claiming the 'credit' towards their own emissions target.

- *Clean Development Mechanism* whereby countries (and businesses within them) could claim emissions credits by investing in emission reduction projects in developing countries. This mechanism had the additional requirement that projects must contribute to sustainable development in the developing country.

Together these mechanisms established what became known as the global 'carbon market'. The rationale for relying on a carbon market to reduce global emissions is that the precise location of reducing emissions is irrelevant; if it is cheaper to reduce emissions in some countries then it makes sense to pursue mitigation there. The argument against this approach is that wealthy fossil fuel-intensive economies need to decarbonise their economies, and carbon markets simply distract from this process. Carbon markets give the false impression that countries are becoming more sustainable. Nevertheless, with these mechanisms in place, developed countries agreed to emissions reduction or limitation targets under the Kyoto Protocol. The parties agreed on a global reduction target of 5 per cent below 1990 levels by 2012. Individual targets were negotiated including -8 per cent for wealthy European countries, -7 per cent for the US, and zero growth for Russia (UNFCCC 1997). Developing countries still did not have quantified targets but they were expected to take action towards managing their emissions, including by participating in the carbon market.

The market mechanisms weren't enough to make the Kyoto Protocol successful. They did help some states fulfil their modest commitments albeit while significantly growing their domestic GHG emissions. But even with the option of market mechanisms, many countries found the task of reducing GHG emissions just too difficult and expensive. The US withdrew support for the agreement in 2001, Canada failed to reach its target, and others including Japan and Russia announced that they would not sign up to new targets under the Kyoto Protocol once the initial commitment period ended in 2012. This cast doubt over the future of the UN's climate change regime, and forced countries to reconsider those fundamental questions about who should take responsibility for mitigating climate change, and how such mitigation should be pursued. Throughout the first decade of the twenty-first century, disagreement over these questions thwarted multilateral efforts to negotiate an agreement that would sustain collective mitigation efforts beyond 2012. As GHG emissions in large industrialising countries like China began to eclipse those of wealthy countries, it became increasingly impractical to exempt them from emission reduction or limitation commitments. But these countries maintained their position that wealthy countries had still failed to limit their own emissions, and had failed to deliver on technological and financial commitments (under the UNFCCC as well as Agenda 21). They also had a strong moral argument on their side: the per capita emissions in developing countries were considerably smaller than in wealthy countries, and poverty reduction would require continued reliance on fossil fuels for some years to come.

Efforts to reach agreement on a complex and intertwined set of issues (mitigation, adaptation, finance, technology) reached a stalemate at the Copenhagen climate summit in 2009. Here the parties stumbled over two more hurdles: the expectation of universal participation in multilateral negotiations, and the rule on consensus. Unable to find compromises and broker deals among 194 parties, the US broke with tradition and gathered in secret with Brazil, Russia, India, China, and South Africa (BRICS) to produce the briefest of documents that would accommodate their interests and preferences. Unsurprisingly, excluded parties were unimpressed by this undemocratic move to 'minilateralism'. Europe was annoyed by the diplomatic snub, especially as the EU had played an important role in saving the Kyoto Protocol after the US withdrew support. Some states were particularly incensed by the 2°C target privately agreed, arguing that this would endanger islands, coastal cities, and the water and food security of millions of people (Stevenson 2014).

Because the parties of the UNFCCC have never managed to agree on formal rules of procedure, consensus remains the default way of making decisions (Yamin and Depledge 2004: 432–3). This means that any party can object to any clause in a negotiated text, and their objection has to be accommodated somehow. While most excluded parties agreed to endorse the text drafted by the US and BRICS in the final hours of the Copenhagen summit, a very small handful of leftist Latin American states (together with Tuvalu and Sudan) objected. As a result, the parties were only able to 'take note' of the text without formally adopting it. The 'Copenhagen Accord' was therefore a very weak piece of soft law universally deemed insufficient for delivering effective action on climate change. For many scholars, diplomats, and professionals, it also sounded the death knell for multilateralism.

After the diplomatic disaster that played out at the 2009 Copenhagen climate summit, states had to rebuild trust and ambition in the UN climate negotiating process. It took a further six years to produce a new climate change treaty. In 2015, states managed to achieve a new UN treaty on climate change: the Paris Agreement. Leadership from the US and China was particularly important in rebuilding political ambition and confidence in the UN process. These two countries alone account for about 40 per cent of global GHG emissions. Through a series of bilateral meetings in 2014, the presidents of China and the US agreed to reduce their emissions as part of a UN agreement. Diplomatically this was significant because the lack of US leadership had long been a stumbling block in climate change negotiations, and the US had long argued that it wouldn't act without comparable commitments from China.

The great strength of the Paris Agreement is that it includes emissions commitments from a larger number of countries than ever before: 188 countries representing 95 per cent of global emissions and 98 per cent of global population pledged action (Ivanova 2016: 414). This was achieved by abandoning the global deal approach that characterised the Kyoto Protocol. Under that approach, a collective emission reduction target of -5 per cent was agreed, and then industrialised states negotiated individual targets within that limit. In Paris this was replaced with a 'pledge and review' model, whereby states independently pledged their own goals (with different types of actions, targets, and timetables), and agreed to have these periodically reviewed by a UN committee. By moving to this flexible model, developing countries were persuaded to pledge their own goals. This was important because the distinction between Annex I and non-Annex I countries had long been a sticking point in negotiations. The agreement still refers to developed and developing countries but does not allocate states to each category. Developed countries are expected to reduce GHG emissions, while developing countries are expected to make mitigation efforts gradually moving towards emission reduction and limitation targets. Once the Paris Agreement entered into force on 4 November 2016, states are legally obliged to submit plans for domestic climate change action, and have these updated and reviewed by an expert panel every five years. But reporting is the only legal element – there is no international legal obligation to fulfil the pledge, and no punishment if the pledge is broken (Falkner 2016).

The Paris Agreement aims to limit global average temperature increase to $2°C$ above pre-industrial levels, and points to the $1.5°$ target as worth pursuing (UNFCCC 2015a). The combined action of all states, business, and civil society is expected to progressively make these goals achievable, but the bottom-up and flexible nature of the agreement makes it impossible to ensure this. This marks a turning point in the global climate regime: the broadening of responsibility to include not only states, but also non-state actors, and the official recognition of action being taken outside the UN system. In fact, transnational 'governance experiments' have been around for many years, as we will now see.

## Transnational Climate Change Governance

Impatience with the slow pace and low ambition of the UN process motivated some non-state actors to look elsewhere for climate change solutions. The market-based mechanisms of the Kyoto Protocol also helped to promote transnational experiments beyond the UNFCCC to flourish. Many businesses saw opportunities to profit from carbon markets and set about creating additional mechanisms that they could control with minimal government intervention. Many private sector and civil society actors also saw the Kyoto Protocol as too weak and limited to drive global 'decarbonisation', and they sought to fill the regulatory gap with their own governance initiatives. What resulted was a proliferation of governance initiatives outside the UN system. As we saw earlier, transnational governance involves states and other public actors (like city mayors, provincial governments, and international organisations), the private sector, and civil society. We glimpse only a small part of global climate governance if we focus on what is happening within the UN.

As public and private actors have sought innovative and additional ways to mitigate and adapt to climate change, the governance space has become very crowded and fragmented. Adding to this fragmentation of governance is a phenomenon known as '**bandwagoning**'. As we saw earlier, climate change is related to many other environmental issues (water, deforestation, food security, and others). Global warming is expected to exacerbate freshwater scarcity; deforestation releases carbon dioxide into the atmosphere; and agricultural yields are affected by changes in rainfall. But climate change attracts much more attention from governments and the public than any of these other environmental issues. People working on other environmental issues often try to attract more attention to those issues by linking their agenda to climate change. Sikina Jinnah and Alexandra Conliffe observe that 'everyone from OPEC to Oxfam is jumping on the proverbial climate change bandwagon' (2012: 199). This means that international coordination on climate change is occurring not only in the UNFCCC and transnational spaces, but also across many multilateral institutions.

## Governance Experiments

Canadian political scientist Matthew Hoffmann argues that since the failed Copenhagen conference in 2009 the 'centre of gravity' in global climate governance has shifted away from the UN and towards what he calls 'experiments in responding to climate change' (Hoffmann 2011: 5). Experimentation is defined as 'a process of making rules outside well-established channels' (2011: 18). Governance experiments shouldn't be understood as scientific experiments whereby hypotheses are tested in controlled settings. Instead, governance experiments are 'tentative procedures' or 'trying anything' to see if it works well (Bulkeley and Castán Broto 2013: 374).

Hoffmann has carried out one of the most comprehensive studies of transnational climate governance. In doing so he identified four types of climate governance experiments, which are summarised here with examples of each.

1. *Networkers*: These experiments bring together government actors (including sub-national actors like city mayors), NGOs, and/or the private sector to build awareness, and share information, experiences, and best practices. These experiments are based on the assumption that a lack of information and experience is holding back action to reduce greenhouse gas emissions. Building networks is therefore a first step towards more effective climate change mitigation.

    a. *Example 1*: The Asia-Pacific Partnership on Clean Development and Climate (APP) was a network created in 2005 by the US, Australia, Republic of Korea, China, India, Japan, and Canada. Many saw this as a deliberate attempt by the US and Australia to undermine the Kyoto Protocol by focusing intergovernmental cooperation on soft action such as exchanging knowledge and experience rather than the hard action of emissions reduction commitments. While it began with some ambition to create benchmarks and performance indicators (e.g., for the energy intensity and recycling of construction materials), by the time it ceased in 2012 the APP had generally only served to promote discussion between the public and private sector about cleaner technologies (Asia-Pacific Partnership 2016).

    b. *Example 2*: Over the years, online community networks have come and gone. Edenbee was one of the first online networks designed to share information about 'carbon neutral' lifestyles and reducing personal carbon footprints, but it closed after just two years. Other citizen initiatives that have emerged in its place often have a petitioning component in addition to sharing information and raising awareness (e.g., Change.org and Care2).

2. *Infrastructure builders*: These experiments move beyond sharing information to building the processes and institutions that can facilitate the reduction of

GHG emissions. Once actors have the essential knowledge to reduce their reliance on fossil fuels, they need access to the tools and resources that can help them to take action. These experiments are based on building such tools and resources.

a. *Example 1*: The Carbon Disclosure Project (CDP) encourages investors to direct their capital to carbon-friendly projects. It facilitates this by providing data on how business, cities, provinces, and regions are reducing their environmental impact. These public and private sector actors are invited to regularly disclose how their operations and supply chains affect climate change, deforestation, and water security. This has been one of the most successful experiments in terms of attracting participation. Over 5,000 companies around the world now disclose their GHG emissions, accounting for about 20 per cent of global emissions. Investors are increasingly using this data to inform decision-making on up to $100 trillion in investment (Carbon Disclosure Project 2016).

b. *Example 2*: The Verified Carbon Standard (VCS) was created in 2006 in response to the private sector's growing interest in carbon offset markets. The intention was to create opportunities for individuals and businesses to buy carbon credits and contribute to climate change mitigation. Many companies were already able to purchase carbon credits through the Kyoto Protocol's **Clean Development Mechanism** (CDM), but many others were not bound to the rules of the Kyoto Protocol (e.g., those in the US, which did not ratify the agreement). VCS doesn't buy and sell carbon credits, but rather facilitates this exchange by establishing criteria for offsets and then accrediting projects. It operates across many sectors including energy production, construction, manufacturing industries, transport, mining and mineral production, waste management, forestry and land use (Stevenson and Dryzek 2014: 110–11). This gives companies greater confidence that the carbon credits they are buying are genuine. Over ten years the VCS has accredited over 1,300 projects that it claims 'have collectively reduced or removed more than 185 million tonnes of GHG emissions from the atmosphere' (Verified Carbon Standard 2016). To put this in perspective, in 2010 global emissions of GHG from human activity were 46 billion metric tons (EPA 2016a).

3. *Voluntary actors*: These experiments take direct action to mitigate climate change by establishing plans to reduce GHG emissions; setting energy efficiency targets; investing in public transport; deploying new technologies in manufacturing, etc. These experiments may also involve the sharing of

information and best practices (like the *Networkers*), and may contribute to building the tools and processes to facilitate action (like the *Infrastructure builders*), but these move beyond those types to experiment to take action that is purely voluntary. Whereas the UNFCCC and Kyoto Protocol require governments to take action, these experiments are not required by any hard or soft international law.

a. *Example 1*: The C40 Climate Leadership Group was established in 2005 to promote climate change mitigation and adaptation within cities. The city was seen as an important focus for action because our societies are increasingly urbanised, and many of these are coastal, making them vulnerable to sea-level rise. Cities account for 70 per cent of global GHG emissions. The C40 now has eighty city members in over fifty countries, accounting for 25 per cent of global GDP (C40 2015). It provides a network for mayors and city officials to share knowledge and ideas about decarbonising city economies and infrastructure. But, importantly, city members are also expected to set 'actionable' and 'measurable' goals on energy, transportation, waste management, and adaptation planning. By 2015, some 10,000 actions had already been taken as part of the C40. If future commitments are met, about 3 gigatons of GHG will be avoided by 2030 (C40 2016).

b. *Example 2*: There are many community-level initiatives that encourage citizens to pledge action to transform their own lives or the towns they live in (such as the Transitions Town movement). FairShare International is one such initiative, launched in Australia in 2001. It defines four goals for members to adopt. Rather than focus exclusively on GHG emissions, the goals provide a formula of 5.10.5.10 for transitioning to more sustainably and socially just societies. Members are encouraged to redistribute 5 per cent of their annual income; reduce resource consumption by 10 per cent; dedicate 5 per cent of their leisure time to collective activities addressing environmental and social challenges; and take 10 democratic actions each year to promote fair and sustainable futures (FairShare International 2016).

4. *Accountable actors*: These experiments include aspects of networking and voluntary action but add the important component of oversight. Although participation in such initiatives is voluntary, once a company, city, or citizen has made the commitment to participate they are held to their word. Monitoring and evaluation processes are put in place to ensure that pledged action is actually delivered. Hoffmann explains that these experiments generally

involve a sub-national or supra-national authority (e.g., the UN), and are mostly emissions trading schemes (Hoffmann 2011: 55).

  a. *Example 1*: The Regional Greenhouse Gas Initiative (RGGI) 'is the first mandatory market-based program in the United States to reduce greenhouse gas emissions' (RGGI 2016). It was created in 2003 by the governors of nine US states (Connecticut, Delaware, Maine, Maryland, Massachusetts, New Hampshire, New York, Rhode Island, and Vermont) with the aim of reducing GHG emissions from electric power plants. Each state created its own $CO_2$ Budget Trading Program, which sets a limit (or 'cap') on emissions and distributes emission permits. Power plants can then buy and sell credits from across the nine states while keeping within the emissions cap (which is lowered each year). Although the RGGI itself does not have authority to regulate and enforce action, the states that participate in the initiative do have this authority. Since trading commenced in 2008, these states have reportedly reduced their emissions from electricity by 37 per cent (Page 2016).

  b. *Example 2*: Climate Savers is an initiative between the environmentalist organisation WWF and global companies. It aims to develop 'climate leadership' at the corporate level. The companies involved are expected to take action within their own operations (using renewable energy, improving energy efficiency, setting GHG emission reduction goals), and act as 'agents of change' by promoting action along their supply chains, and their wider sectors. Its members are mostly well-known companies like Sony, Volvo, and Coca Cola who hope to improve their operations (e.g., cutting costs through efficiency) and improve their reputation among customers and their sector peers. To avoid 'greenwash' (empty gestures or misleading statements), WWF included an oversight component whereby companies' targets are negotiated and reviewed. Companies then have to report, verify, and adjust their actions to align with commitments (Climate Savers 2016).

Hoffmann's categories help us to grasp the diversity of transnational action on climate change. Within this diversity, several key characteristics emerge. Let's look at these characteristics in terms of *when, who, where,* and *what.*

- *When?* Harriet Bulkeley and her colleagues analysed sixty transnational climate governance initiatives spanning over two decades (Bulkeley et al. 2012). Although these are not the only experiments in climate governance (there are probably hundreds), their analysis does allow us to glimpse some important patterns. The overwhelming majority of experiments were established *after* the Kyoto Protocol was agreed in 1997, with many established after the Kyoto Protocol coming into force in 2005. What explains this timing? As we saw earlier, the 'flexible mechanisms' created a role for the private sector to contribute to mitigating climate change. Many saw opportunities to profit from carbon markets; others were concerned about filling a regulatory gap and raising the ambition of action taken under the Kyoto Protocol. Another important temporal aspect of transnational climate governance is that many experiments are short-lived. Initiatives come and go. This makes it hard to know precisely what action is being taken to mitigate and adapt to climate change outside the UN system. This is perhaps an inherent characteristic of governance experimentation – some experiments succeed and some fail.

- *Who and where?* In Bulkeley's study, almost all experiments were initiated by companies, NGOs, or governments in the global North. Local governments and business organisations in the North were the pioneers of transnational climate governance, setting up early initiatives like Cities for Climate Protection and Climate Alliance in the early 1990s. Non-profit organisations followed later and became the leading initiator of climate governance experiments. Nearly half of all initiatives were started by such organisations (e.g., environmental NGOs, business associations, foundations, and community groups) (Bulkeley et al. 2012: 599–600). Governments in the North have also been active in establishing initiatives outside the UNFCCC (especially national governments, but also local and regional governments). The dominance of Northern actors in establishing governance experiments for climate change is perhaps unsurprising: they have greater capacity to take action and some may feel a greater sense of responsibility given historical emissions and/or the higher levels of development (some say 'over-'development) in the global North. They are also more likely to be pressured by citizens, consumers, and social movements. But despite the dominance of Northern actors, actors from the global South do participate in climate governance experiments. In fact about three-quarters of the governance experiments studied by Bulkeley's team involved the participation of at least one Southern actor (including the large developing countries of Brazil, India, China, South Africa, and Mexico, but also smaller and less industrialised countries) (Bulkeley et al. 2012: 601).
- *What?* The overwhelming majority of transnational climate governance experiments are concerned with mitigation. Rightly or wrongly, adaptation is seen less as a concern for transnational governance and more of a local concern for national authorities to integrate into development and planning. But within

climate change mitigation there is great diversity of activity. The most common type of governance experiment focuses on renewable energy, 'clean coal', and energy efficiency; the second most common is carbon markets and investment; followed by land use projects to hold carbon in soil and trees; low-carbon infrastructure; and food security (Bulkeley et al. 2012: 602).

## Virtues of Transnational Climate Governance

Advocates of climate governance experiments highlight many virtues of this way of responding to climate change. Some argue that everyone – states, companies, citizens – is responsible for climate change, and so justice requires that everyone contributes to action to reduce GHG emissions (Dietzel 2015). Since states have failed to take adequate action for so many years, it is perhaps especially important that companies and citizens step up to voluntarily fill the action gap.

Others argue that governance experiments by sub-national and non-state actors have significant *direct* and *indirect* impacts. Direct impacts are the reductions in GHG emissions that are actually achieved (e.g., we saw earlier that the Regional Greenhouse Gas Initiative reportedly reduced emissions from electricity by 37 per cent in member states). Every investment in renewable energy instead of fossil fuels; every technological development that improves energy efficiency; every planning decision that favours public transport over private motorways has a direct impact on the concentration of GHGs in the atmosphere. On their own, these actions may not amount to a lot, but collectively they can have an important impact. Experiments contribute indirectly to raising ambition and expectations; they can develop knowledge and build capacity for decarbonising different sectors of the economy; and they can signal to governments that business and civil society are willing to take action. All of these things can push forward intergovernmental negotiations (Chan et al. 2015: 466–7).

For Hoffmann the value of experiments lies in their potential to promote 'friction' or disruptive change in politics and markets, as well as the technology and institutions that respond to demands for change. Experiments, he explains,

generate friction by pushing the boundaries of traditional notions of which actors are responsible for making rules, creating uneven sets of rules that actors must follow, and generate new coalitions committed to climate action. This friction, in turn, may be able to catalyze broader change as other actors (including national governments) and processes (e.g. multilateral negotiations) and arenas (e.g. global markets) react to the friction.

(2011: 9)

## Limitations of Transnational Climate Governance

Critics identify several problems with the growing role of non-state actors in climate governance, and with the increasing fragmentation of climate governance (e.g., Chan et al. 2015: 1–2). Firstly, while many businesses, cities, and NGOs are taking some kind of climate change action, the vast majority are not. The voluntary nature of most governance experiments means that it is impossible to force non-participants into action. Given that initiatives come and go, and often have a low profile, it is very difficult to discern the scope and scale of action outside the UN system. Even among those that do promote their activities, very few set quantifiable goals for reducing GHG emissions, let alone transparently report on progress towards those goals. There are very few 'accountable actors'. One assessment concludes that 'while transnational climate change governance may be interesting in principle, to date its capacity to make a difference in terms of reducing emissions of GHG may seem limited' (Bulkeley and Newell 2010: 66).

The voluntary and 'spontaneous' character of transnational governance also makes it difficult to coordinate the types of action taken. Without coordination there is no way of ensuring that finance and technology are distributed evenly, or that more effort is directed to adaptation. The Clean Development Mechanism illustrates how problems can arise when governments loosen the regulatory reins. The CDM was designed to promote sustainable development in the global South while helping companies in the global North to reduce their emissions more cost efficiently. From a business perspective it makes sense to invest in a project that is going to produce as many credits as possible. This gives an advantage to places that produce larger volumes of GHGs that can be reduced in exchange for carbon credits. As a result, the geographical distribution of CDM projects was highly skewed: over 90 per cent of credits came from just five countries (China, India, South Korea, Brazil, and Mexico) (Shishlov and Bellassen 2012: 12). There was no way for governments to intervene to ensure that other countries received a share of CDM investments. This inequitable distribution was mirrored within countries, with the wealthiest states and provinces receiving the lion's share of projects (Stevenson 2013: 145).

Most climate governance experiments share a voluntary, market orientation. Actors are free to join and withdraw. If they do join, it is often because they are attracted by economic incentives to engage in carbon markets or emissions trading, or to increase profits through efficiency and technological advances (Hoffmann 2011: 35–6). They reject the idea that growth and environmental protection are incompatible; instead, 'low-carbon development' offers the opportunity for clean and efficient growth. These assumptions reflect '**liberal environmentalism**', a phrase coined by Steven Bernstein to refer to ideas about global environmental governance that became dominant in the 1990s. Bernstein describes liberal environmentalism as a form of international governance that 'predicates environmental protection on the promotion and maintenance of a liberal economic order' (2001: 213). This suggests that to protect the environment we need to protect market norms. Continued economic growth and accumulation become enablers of environmental protection. Some may see liberal environmentalism as an appropriate foundation for governance experimentation because it facilitates action from businesses rather than pushing them into a hostile position. But for those who see capitalism and exponential economic growth as drivers of climate change, liberal environmentalism is part of the problem not the solution.

A final set of concerns relate to the democratic legitimacy of transnational climate governance. Non-state actors are not subject to the same demands for accountability, transparency, and representation as states generally are. UN negotiations on climate change attract considerable attention and participation from civil society groups. Such groups monitor decision-making and push concerns about equity and justice. The fragmented nature of transnational climate governance means that most experiments avoid the scrutiny of civil society. They are not responsive to public demands in the same way that states and the UN are expected to be (Stevenson and Dryzek 2014).

## Coordinating Governance Experiments: NAZCA

Many scholars have converged on the idea that for transnational climate governance to fairly and effectively respond to climate change, some kind of coordinating framework is required (e.g., Stevenson and Dryzek 2014; Chan et al. 2015). Earlier we saw this idea called 'orchestration', defined as efforts by states and international organisations to mobilise and work with private actors and institutions to achieve regulatory goals (Abbott and Snidal 2010: 317). The democratic potential of this is to anchor experiments in norms that 'are part of the democratic ethos of society' (Sørensen and Torfing 2005: 201).

Among the decisions made at the Paris climate summit in 2015 was one that integrates activities by non-state actors into the climate regime in a way that partly reflects what scholars of orchestration have in mind (Hale 2016). The decision 'welcomes the efforts' of non-state actors 'to scale up their climate actions'; and encourages parties to work with non-state actors 'to catalyse efforts to strengthen mitigation and adaptation action'. The decision encourages cities, regions, businesses, and civil society to register their initiatives in an online UN portal called NAZCA (Non-State Actor Zone for Climate Action), and agrees to hold an annual dialogue between high-level officials (such as ministers) and non-state actors to assess voluntary progress (UNFCCC 2015b: 17–18). Two high-level 'champions' will be appointed to facilitate this cooperation. It remains to be seen whether these 'orchestration' efforts will help bring coherence to the fragmented climate governance experiments taking place outside the UN system. But recognition of the importance of such orchestration is a positive step.

# Conclusion

In this chapter we've seen that multilateral efforts to develop collective action on climate change are just one part of global climate governance. Climate change is one of the most complex and challenging problems to address because burning fossil fuels has become central to most states' development strategies. Although states have managed to negotiate several agreements through the UN (both hard and soft law), action to reduce global greenhouse gas emissions has been grossly insufficient. The effects of these failures are already felt in some countries. The year 2016 has been declared the hottest on record. But this is now a familiar announcement: sixteen of the seventeen hottest years on record have been experienced since the turn of the century (Carrington 2016b).

Given the gravity of the problem and the limitations of UN processes, should we welcome the rise of transnational climate governance? One of the lessons from Chapter 2 is that we shouldn't look for one single type of solution for environmental problems. Neither centralised control, nor privatisation, nor voluntary initiatives will necessarily work. Elinor Ostrom's research suggests that experiments in governance are necessary because we don't know what will work where. From this perspective, the rise of climate governance experiments is good news. But we also need to acknowledge that existing climate governance experiments mostly share a single understanding of the problem. We saw that they almost all reflect what Bernstein calls 'liberal environmentalism'. This limits the kind of action that is considered sensible and possible to that which is compatible with the existing liberal economic system. It may well turn out that deeper and more ambitious action is required – action that questions the viability of exponential growth and accumulation. In that case, greater variation in governance experiments should be encouraged.

Even with the Paris Agreement in place, transnational governance experiments are likely to become more important than ever in the years ahead. We saw in this chapter that the positions of China and the US have a significant influence on UN climate negotiations. For much of the twenty-first century, the US was a pariah of the UN climate regime – withdrawing support from the Kyoto Protocol and refusing to commit to domestic emission reductions. The Obama administration worked hard to restore US leadership on climate change, and restore the international community's trust and confidence. With Donald Trump (a climate change denier) now president until at least 2021, the future of the global climate change regime is deeply uncertain. But what is certain is that leadership and ambition from non-state actors will be more important than ever.

## Discussion Questions

1. What factors explain the increasing authority of non-state actors in global politics?
2. What does 'fragmentation' of global governance mean, and is it a positive or negative trend?
3. In what ways is climate change a 'wicked' policy problem?
4. How have understandings of 'responsibility' changed over time in UN climate negotiations?
5. Are transnational governance experiments an effective way of responding to climate change?

# 8 Aid and Finance

## Deforestation

key points

- Finance is central to global environmental governance because there are considerable asymmetries in capacity and responsibility for environmental problems. Developing countries have long pushed for 'environmental aid' to be allocated separately and in addition to general aid.
- Environmental aid is increasingly directed to 'green' projects instead of 'brown' projects. Green projects relate to global or regional problems like climate change and biodiversity, while brown projects relate to local problems like sanitation and soil erosion.
- Since the 1980s, the international community has experimented with financial innovations like debt-for-nature swaps and payments for ecosystem services.
- Global rates of deforestation are declining but remain alarmingly high. The scale of tropical forest clearance is equivalent to about half the size of England every year.
- Financial initiatives to address deforestation generally overlook important drivers of deforestation, which include growing and competing demands for food, feed, fibre, fuel, and forest products.

# Introduction

Global environmental governance is characterised by a set of dilemmas concerning capacity, sovereignty, and responsibility. We can see the effects of these dilemmas in disagreements between the North and South in multilateral negotiations. On the one hand, governments from wealthy developed countries have traditionally been the strongest advocates of international agreements to protect the global environment. These countries have typically contributed most to global GHG emissions; they have cleared their own forests; and they have transitioned to less energy-intensive service-based economies after becoming rich through dirty, poorly regulated, production-based development. In other words, wealthy countries' responsibility for global environmental degradation is great and long-standing. On the other hand, governments from developing countries have long claimed that they cannot afford to protect the environment until levels of poverty are drastically reduced. These countries have contributed least to global GHG emissions, and they claim a sovereign right to exploit their natural resources and pass through dirty phases of development before cleaning up later. What's more, the largest stores of biodiversity and natural resources can be found in the global South. Of course, there are exceptions and not all countries fit into this neat picture. But, generally speaking, these North–South divisions do exist and have had a significant impact on global environmental governance. The global environment cannot be preserved without the South, but the South claims to have many higher priorities.

As we saw in Chapter 3, the narrative of 'development first' was articulated back in 1972 at the first major international environmental conference, the UN Conference on Environment and Development in Stockholm. There India's prime minister, Indira Gandhi, told the international community:

We do not wish to impoverish the environment any further and yet we cannot for a moment forget the grim poverty of large numbers of people. Are not poverty and need the greatest polluters? . . . How can we speak to those who live in villages and in slums about keeping the oceans, the rivers and the air clean when their own lives are contaminated at the source? The environment cannot be improved in conditions of poverty.

(quoted in Rajan 1997: 25–6)

This narrative has proven persuasive and has placed finance at the heart of global environmental governance. This chapter explores different forms of environmental finance, and their effects on deforestation in particular.

We first examine traditional environmental aid and the financial contributions developed countries have pledged (but not always delivered) to developing countries. We then turn to innovative and experimental forms of financial assistance, including 'debt-for-nature swaps' and 'payments for ecosystem services' (PES). Next we turn attention to our case study of deforestation, examining the problem and its causes before looking at the institutions and financial mechanisms that have been developed to address this major problem.

## Aid and Financial Assistance

Public finance has always been and remains the most important source of assistance for environmental protection and sustainable development in the South. As we'll see below, private finance and market-based financial mechanisms have been growing in recent years, but most money still comes from the public purse. **Environmental aid** can be defined as 'a financial transfer from North to South for the purpose of protecting or restoring the environment through the promotion of projects ranging from environmental education to land conservation' (Lewis 2003: 145). This is distinguished from general official development assistance (ODA), which comprises grants and concessional loans provided to developing countries to promote economic development and human welfare. The most comprehensive studies of environmental aid are now somewhat dated, but they do give a good insight into the massive growth in environmental aid throughout the 1980s and 1990s. We can see that between 1980 and 1999, total environmental aid from North to South increased more than three-fold from about $3 billion per year to about $10 billion per year (Figure 8.1).

This rise correlates with two factors. One is the growth in multilateral environmental agreements containing financial commitments for developed countries to support developing countries. The other is growing criticism over the negative impacts of traditional aid on the environment.

### Multilateral Environmental Agreements

Not all of the financial assistance that moves from the North to the South should be put in the 'aid' category. Successive international agreements affirm the need to transfer technical and financial assistance from the North to the South.

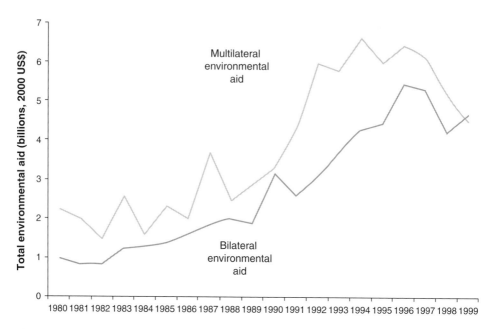

**Figure 8.1:** Growth of environmental aid, 1980–99
Source: Roberts et al. 2009: 12

Developing countries therefore claim that the financial commitments of developed countries are categorically different to ODA. Some countries, like Bolivia, go so far as to claim that the North has an environmental or climate 'debt' that needs to be paid to the South to compensate for exploiting their natural resources over centuries, and for creating global problems like climate change that the South cannot afford to deal with. Others, like the G77 bloc of developing countries, do not always resort to such polemical language but do nevertheless claim that financial commitments are legal obligations not charity or voluntary aid.

The first significant financial commitments were made in the early 1990s, starting with the creation of the **Global Environment Facility (GEF)** in 1991. This was a $1 billion pilot project hosted by the World Bank. The GEF transitioned to a formal and independent organisation in 1994 to facilitate fulfilment of the financial commitments pledged at the 1992 Earth Summit. These pledges were attached to three major agreements signed in Rio. Do you recall these from Chapter 6? There were three: the United Nations Framework Convention on Climate Change (UNFCCC), the United Nations Convention on Biological Diversity (UNCBD), and the United Nations Convention to Combat Desertification (UNCCD). While developed countries didn't put a figure to their individual or collective financial commitments, they did agree to make funds available to cover the full costs incurred by developing countries in pursuing the convention objectives. G77 negotiators have fought long and hard to ensure that finance provided to comply with multilateral agreements like the Rio Conventions is kept separate from existing ODA budgets and pledges. This finance, it is argued, must be 'new and additional'. Wealthy countries must not be allowed to fudge the numbers by lumping their environmental aid with existing commitments such as the 2005 Paris Declaration commitment to increase ODA to 0.7 per cent of national income.

'Double counting' and 'triple counting' are common problems in aid reporting because spending categories overlap and funding flows from one organisation to another. There is also no UN tracking system to monitor pledged and delivered finance. In practice it is very hard to determine the extent to which money promised in MEAs is 'new and additional'. While it may be impossible to precisely measure the distance between pledged and delivered finance, it is clear that the gap is significant. A 2012 UNEP report concluded that 'long-standing commitments from developed countries to improve access to finance for developing countries remain largely unfulfilled, and insufficient and unpredictable financial resources continue to constrain effective environmental governance at all levels' (Baste et al. 2012: 466).

## The Environmental Impact of ODA

The rise in environmental aid also corresponds with the rise of transnational environmental advocacy networks in the 1980s and 1990s. These civil society groups criticised the use of public money for environmentally destructive development projects in the South. While both bilateral and multilateral funds were used to finance 'mega-projects' like roads, mines, dams, and agricultural industrialisation, it was the high-profile World Bank projects that attracted most of the criticism. Two projects were particularly prominent and controversial. One was the Polonoroeste highway project in Brazil, a 1,500-km road through the Amazonian Basin designed to open it up to migrant settlements, industry, and agriculture. The other was the Narmada dam project in India (involving the construction of over 3,000 dams on the north-western river resulting in widespread flooding, displacement, and a host of potential environmental problems). Activist networks persuaded the World Bank to cut millions of dollars in funding for these projects on the grounds of likely environmental destruction and human rights violation (Park 2010: chapter 3). The US Congress also went

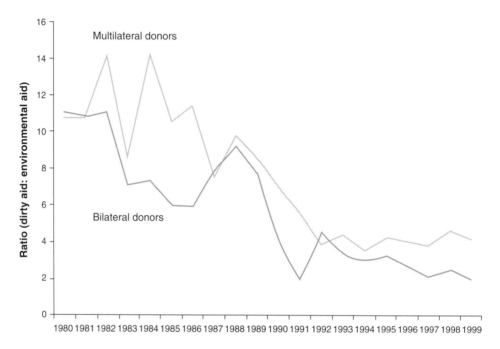

**Figure 8.2**: Falling ratio of dirty aid to environmental aid, 1980–99
Source: Roberts et al. 2009: 14

on to pass an amendment to the 1989 International Development and Finance Act, which required multilateral development banks to carry out environmental impact assessments of proposed projects; failure to do so would result in the withholding of US funds.

There has since been a steady rate of decline in the ratio of 'dirty' aid to environmental aid (from both bilateral and multilateral sources). Research at the College of William and Mary and Brigham Young University (Project-Level Aid – PLAID project) suggests that dirty aid was ten times higher than environmental aid in the 1980s, but had fallen to about three times higher by the end of the century (Roberts et al. 2009). This is shown in Figure 8.2.

Research by the OECD (2012) finds that environmental sustainability became a more significant aim of bilateral aid throughout the 2000s. Funding directed towards environmental protection and 'greening' different sectors of the economy grew more than threefold in that decade, up to more than $25 billion a year by 2010 (OECD 2012: 57).

These figures on aid pledged and delivered only tell part of the story of how environmental aid has evolved over the past few decades. We can also observe important trends in terms of aid *channels* and aid *priorities*. There are strong arguments for channelling environmental aid through multilateral institutions. It can improve coordination and efficiency, and ensure aid is directed to various concerns rather than just the issues that are most visible or fashionable. Developing countries have also been keen to ensure that funds are sent through multilateral institutions because these institutions are typically designed to give them greater representation and a greater say in how money is spent (although it is typically the central government that enjoys greater representation rather than those most affected by environmental change). Working with multilateral institutions also makes developing country governments less vulnerable to the pressure that comes with working in highly asymmetrical power-based partnerships, which is characteristic of bilateral aid relations. Nevertheless, an important trend in global environmental governance has been the 'bilateralisation' of environmental aid (Marcoux et al. 2013: 2). This refers to the fact that environmental funds are being increasingly channelled through bilateral relations rather than multilateral institutions like the World Bank or the GEF. Marcoux and his fellow researchers have calculated that in 1990 to 1994, nearly 60 per cent of all environmental aid was channelled through multilateral institutions, but by 2005 to 2008 the proportion had fallen to 42 per cent (Marcoux et al. 2013: 2).

Multilateral and bilateral environmental aid have both grown since the 1990s, but the rate of growth in bilateral environmental aid has been much more significant than the growth in multilateral aid. This trend is particularly striking when we look at climate finance. Between 2010 and 2012, $33 billion was pledged in 'fast start finance' to support developing countries in reducing their GHG emissions and adapting to climate change. Only 4 per cent of this sum has been channelled through multilateral climate change funds (Marcoux et al. 2013: 2–3). In addition, developed countries pledged to mobilise $100 billion per year up to 2020. The Green Climate Fund was established as the principal mechanism for channelling this finance to countries most in need. In response to demands from developing countries for greater representation and control, Green Climate Fund's governance board is split evenly between developed and developing countries. But the problem is that developed countries like to have greater control over how their financial support is used. Thus we see a tension emerge between legitimacy and effectiveness as the North eschews the GCF. By the end of 2014, only $10 billion had been pledged to the Fund (UNFCCC 2014).

In terms of environmental aid priorities, two trends can be observed. The first is that aid has been increasingly directed to 'green' projects instead of 'brown' projects. This distinction was made in the PLAID project on environmental aid referred to above. The researchers explain that 'green' projects are those 'that address global or regional environmental problems, and encompass projects that positively affect environmental outcomes outside the recipient country. They either enhance or preserve global environmental resources'. These include problems like climate change, ozone depletion, biodiversity, and transnational pollution. 'Brown' projects, by contrast, are those 'that focus primarily on local environmental issues and which improve environmental outcomes or reduce environmental degradation in a specific country or locality'. These projects include sanitation, drinking water treatment, soil erosion, and sewerage (Hicks et al. 2008: 31).

Brown projects have traditionally attracted considerably higher levels of aid than green projects. In the 1980s, just 20 per cent of total environmental aid was directed to green projects. By the late 1990s, this proportion had increased to about 30 per cent (Hicks et al. 2008: 31). Figure 8.3 illustrates how this trend has continued into the twenty-first century. The annual provision of green aid doubled in the 2000s, and by 2008 accounted for about 40 per cent of all environmental aid.

The relative growth in global concerns is also reflected in spending on the Rio Conventions. The impacts of climate change and biodiversity loss have a more global reach than those of desertification. While we've seen considerable growth

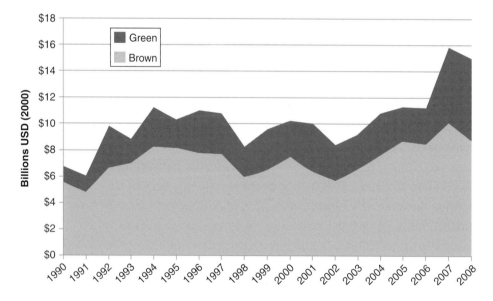

**Figure 8.3:** Comparing 'green' aid and 'brown' aid
Source: Hicks et al. 2008: 10

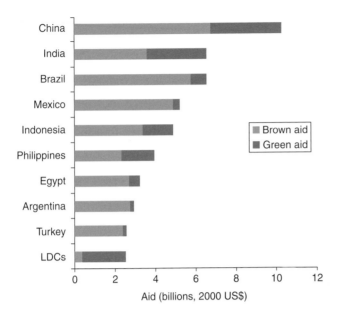

**Figure 8.4:** Top recipients of environmental aid
Source: Roberts et al. 2008: 18

in spending on climate change and biodiversity, funds to prevent further desertification and mitigate the impacts of drought have remained stagnant (OECD 2012: 62).

The second trend in environmental aid priorities concerns the profile of its recipients. Lewis observes that 'environmental aid is biased towards supporting the protection of "pristine" nations (those with high biodiversity and undeveloped areas) rather than nations that are already polluted (those with poor water quality)' (2003: 157). In the 1990s, China, India, Brazil, Mexico, and Indonesia were the top five recipients of environmental aid. These are countries that are important for the global environment because of either their levels of threatened biodiversity or their levels of transnational pollution (including GHG emissions). As shown in Figure 8.4, each of these countries individually received significantly more aid than the forty-eight least developed countries (LDCs) combined. We can see from this figure that these larger countries also managed to attract much more aid for local 'brown' issues than did the LDCs.

What insights should we draw from these figures? In part they reflect a broader trend in prioritising donor interests over recipient needs when allocating environmental aid. Rather than directing aid to where it is most needed (either to protect the environment or assist those people most affected by degradation), aid allocation is strongly affected by the national interests of donor countries. Environmental sociologist Tammy Lewis has analysed this topic and summarises her findings that 'Environmental aid does not target the nations that are most in need of abating local pollution. Instead, environmental aid donors favour nations with whom they have had prior relations (economy and security), nations that are democratic, and nations with unexploited natural resources. In short, donor interests outweigh recipient need' (Lewis 2003: 144). This explains the rather peculiar inclusion of Turkey and Egypt in Figure 8.4. Neither of these has disproportionately high environmental aid needs (especially in terms of global concerns), yet they are significant recipients of aid, and brown aid in particular. This suggests a capacity on their part to negotiate favourable terms with donors, which is commensurable to their historical geostrategic importance (especially to the United States). The PLAID project also supports this trend, finding that economic and political interests are a significantly greater predictor of environmental aid allocation than actual environmental need. But it also finds that bilateral donors are somewhat more responsive to local environmental needs than multilateral donors (Hicks et al. 2008: 93).

In the following section we continue our examination of environmental finance but looking at innovative and experimental forms of international financial assistance.

## Debt-for-Nature Swaps

Public aid has always been the most prominent form of finance for sustainable development. But in the 1980s the international community began to experiment with more innovative forms of finance. One of the earliest experiments was the 'debt-for-nature swap'. These swaps involve 'the purchase of a developing country's debt at a discounted value in the secondary debt market and cancelling the debt in return for environment-related action on the part of the debtor nation' (Hansen 1989: 77). This process is depicted by Pervaze Sheikh in Figure 8.5.

The debt-for-nature mechanism created an important role for NGOs in financing sustainable development. Whereas national governments are the main providers of the aid-based finance discussed earlier, NGOs have played a pivotal role in instigating and financing debt-for-nature swaps. In the 1980s, many developing countries found themselves burdened by significant debts incurred through loans to build infrastructure and industrialise their energy and agricultural sectors. Many of those worst affected were also countries with significant levels of biodiversity. It was not uncommon for countries to unsustainably exploit their natural resources simply to service debt repayments to foreign lenders. This environmental crisis was coupled with an international financial

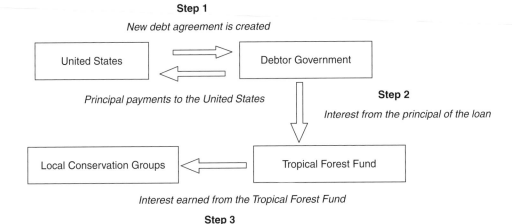

**Step 1**

*New debt agreement is created*

*Principal payments to the United States*

**Step 2**

*Interest from the principal of the loan*

*Interest earned from the Tropical Forest Fund*

**Step 3**

- Step 1 = The current debt agreement is cancelled and a new one is created.

- Step 2 = A Tropical Forest Agreement is created and interest payments to the principal of the loan are deposited in local currency equivalents into a Tropical Forest Fund.

- Step 3 = Interest earned and the principal of the Tropical Forest Fund are generally given in the form of local currency as grants to local conservation groups.

**Figure 8.5:** The process of debt-for-nature swaps
Source: Sheikh 2006: 5

crisis when several countries defaulted on their repayments, citing an inability to pay. This situation was the result of multiple related factors including rising oil prices, depreciating currency values, and high interest rates in wealthier countries. But within this crisis, some saw an opportunity to promote environmental conservation.

The conservation opportunity was first recognised by Thomas Lovejoy in 1984 when he was vice president of the World Wildlife Fund (WWF). Buying debt at a discounted value allowed large NGOs like WWF to secure large-scale conservation for a relatively low investment. Private lenders were happy to come on board because many had resigned themselves to the likelihood that some accumulated debts would never be repaid. Selling off this debt at a discounted rate allowed them to recoup at least some of their money. The original lender need not (and did not) have any interest at all in environmental conservation; the incentive for them was purely a financial one. For the indebted country, the attraction of these swaps lay in the fact that their debts are being reduced or forgiven with only benevolent conditions attached

(Fankhauser and Pearce 2014). The size of 'third world debt' in the 1980s made this a potentially rewarding finance mechanism.

During its heyday there were some notable successes and prominent cases. The first debt-for-nature deal was signed in 1987 between the government of Bolivia and the non-governmental organisation Conservation International. Conservation International paid $100,000 to a private US bank to cancel private debt valued at $650,000, which had accrued to Bolivia. In exchange, the Bolivian government agreed to work with a local NGO in creating a 1.5 million hectare tropical forest reserve, and to provide $250,000 in local currency to finance management of the reserve (Hansen 1989). Similar projects then followed in Brazil, Dominican Republic, Ghana, Guatemala, Peru, Ecuador, Costa Rica, Mexico, Poland, Egypt, and elsewhere. NGOs like WWF, Conservation International, and the Nature Conservancy were the major actors involved in promoting the debt-for-nature model and purchasing developing country debt. Multilateral institutions like the World Bank and individual countries were less involved. The main exception has been the United States, but its motivations have unsurprisingly not been entirely benevolent – or exclusively environmental. Launched by President George H.W. Bush in 1990, the Enterprise for the Americas Initiative linked the debt-for-nature idea to wider plans for a free trade zone with Latin America. It allowed countries engaged in free trade negotiations with the US to redirect interest payments to environmental conservation programmes (USAID 2014). In 1998, coverage was extended to tropical forested countries beyond Latin America when Congress passed the Tropical Forest Conservation Act (Sheikh 2006).

By 2003, about $1 billion in debt had been purchased on secondary debt markets in exchange for environmental conservation projects. Given the significant discounts applied, this translated into about $5 billion in conservation investment (Fankhauser and Pearce 2014). But the debt-for-nature initiative largely ran out of steam towards the end of the twentieth century. The late 1990s saw debt forgiveness campaigns like Jubilee 2000 gather strong momentum, and resulted in programmes like the Heavily Indebted Poor Country Initiative, which cancelled debt in exchange for good financial management (Fankhauser and Pearce 2014).

Other factors also limited the potential for debt swaps to contribute to environmental degradation. Critics pointed out that the amount of debt purchased was typically a very small proportion of the overall debt carried by each developing country. As a result, the incentive for developing countries to engage in debt-for-nature deals was limited. Concerns about compliance were also raised. The risk of non-compliance was greater when debt had been purchased by NGOs because they lacked authority to enforce the deal. If debt was purchased on the basis that a country would protect an area of tropical forest, there was little recourse for action if the developing country government later broke its end of the deal. Compliance was more secure in bilateral deals with the US government simply because it could threaten penalties to ensure agreements were honoured. A final concern and criticism of the debt-for-nature scheme was its potential to infringe on the sovereignty of developing countries. In Bolivia, for example, there was great concern that large swathes of the country were being sold to foreign NGOs, and that the traditional practices of local people would be restricted (Minzi 1993: 58). A former president of Brazil, José Sarney, characterised the deals as a form of colonialism. Expressing his fear that such a deal would be tantamount to foreign possession of national territory, Sarney stated 'We don't want the Amazon to become a green Persian Gulf' (*The New York Times* 1989).

Debt-for-nature swaps largely fell off the international environmental agenda in the 2000s. But a 'second wave' of debt-for-nature swaps began in 2008/9, marked by two significant deals in Madagascar and Indonesia. In the case of Madagascar, the French and Madagascan governments reached a deal that directed $20 million to a conservation trust fund managed by WWF, Conservation International, and the Government of Madagascar. This deal would allow for greater protection of Madagascar's highly unique flora and fauna (WWF 2008). This was followed in 2009 by a deal between the governments of Indonesia and the United States in which $30 billion of bilateral debt repayments would instead be directed to protection of Sumatran tropical forests (Cassimon et al. 2011). The extent to which these will trigger a renewed and widespread interest in debt-for-nature swaps remains to be seen.

## Payment for Ecosystem Services

A further innovation in financing sustainable development emerged in the 1980s, and became known as Payments for Ecosystem Services (PES). Sometimes this initiative is referred to as payments for environmental services. The most commonly cited definition of PES has been crafted by Sven Wunder, who highlights five characteristics: A PES is a *voluntary* transaction in which a *well-defined* ecosystem service is bought by a *buyer* from an ecosystem service *provider*, on the *condition* that the provider actually ensures provision of the service (2005: 3).

So what actually is an ecosystem service? 'Ecosystem service' is a concept that conveys the value of nature to human beings. The landmark 2005 Millennium Ecosystem Assessment (MEA 2005) defined an ecosystem as 'a dynamic complex of plant, animal, and microorganism communities and the nonliving environment interacting as a functional unit'. Ecosystems make various contributions to human welfare. Following the Millennium Ecosystem Assessment, these human benefits are typically categorised as provisioning services (e.g., food, water, timber, fibre); regulating services (affecting climate, waste, water quality, etc.); cultural services (e.g., recreational, aesthetic, and spiritual benefits); and supporting services (e.g., soil formation, photosynthesis, and nutrient cycling).

Richard Norgaard has observed that 'ecosystem services' and the related concept of 'natural capital' were initially crafted as metaphors by ecologists in the 1990s to capture mainstream attention and build popular and political support for conservation (Norgaard 2010). This rhetorical strategy has been fairly successful. Throughout the 1990s and 2000s, international institutions began to link this concept to innovative financial mechanisms that support sustainable development in developing countries. The basic rationale for this was that 'we get what we pay for'. Most people in most places have long paid for the products of nature (e.g., food, fibre, and paper), but not for ecological processes that sustain that production (Kinzig et al. 2011: 603). If we don't factor these natural processes into the cost of the products we buy, we shouldn't be surprised to see them depleted and degraded.

Wunder and his colleagues have further defined the attraction of PES in terms of supply-side innovation and demand-side innovation. On the supply side, paying for conservation responds to the fact that environmental conservation is not inherently win–win: what is good for society in the long term is often not the same as what is good for farmers, fishers, and loggers in the short term. By paying for these long-term social benefits we create a financial incentive for those private actors to provide them. On the demand side, payment for ecosystem services initiatives recognise that people who work close to nature are better placed than governments and bureaucracies to define ecosystem services and ensure that money directed to their conservation is spent efficiently and effectively (Wunder et al. 2008: 850–1). The most common services included in PES schemes concern water (protecting quality and quantity); carbon sequestration (avoiding the release of greenhouse gas emissions); and biodiversity conservation.

PES most commonly takes a non-market form. This involves making a direct payment (usually by a government or public institution) to a landowner (or other provider) to preserve an ecosystem service. There are typically no formal conditions attached to how this payment is spent as long as the service is provided; the provider might invest in housing or transport, or pay for schooling, health care, or leisure activities. While the users may expect the money to be spent on further enhancing 'natural capital', this is not typically enforced (Van Noordwijk et al. 2012: 396). There are numerous emerging cases where PES does take a market form. We saw these in Chapter 7 in the form of carbon markets. Earlier examples can be seen in the United States where tradable permits were issued to large-scale emitters of sulphur dioxide in 1990 to deal with air pollution. Also in the 1990s, the US Clean Water Act created a market-based compensatory scheme for the protection of wetlands. This allowed developers to exploit wetlands in some areas if they purchased permits for protecting wetlands elsewhere (EPA 2016b).

Unlike debt-for-nature swaps, which declined in the 2000s, payments for ecosystem services are growing in popularity. PES initiatives have been introduced in many countries (developed and developing), and these have produced some important successes for environmental protection. The OECD estimates that approximately 300 PES programmes are in place across the world channelling billions of dollars annually to the protection of biodiversity, watershed services, carbon sequestration and landscape beauty (OECD 2010: 1). The case of Costa Rica is particularly notable; the introduction of financial incentives for forest conservation has increased forest cover from 20 per cent of the country in the 1980s to about 50 per cent today (Porras et al. 2013). Given such successes, the international community has been exploring options for further linking of finance and ecosystem services in global environmental governance.

The European Union has been particularly active in promoting institutions for nature valuation. Spurred by Germany's leadership, and with strong support from the European Commission, the international community launched 'The Economics of Ecosystems and Biodiversity' (TEEB) initiative in 2007. This initiative has produced guidelines and methodologies for internalising the value of ecosystems and biodiversity in policy-making, and these are being diffused internationally through national capacity-building programmes. The World Bank's WAVES Partnership (Wealth Accounting and the Valuation of Ecosystem Services) is funded almost entirely by European resources. WAVES is a global partnership of UN agencies, governments, and non-governmental organisations that works with developing countries to implement natural accounting programmes for mainstreaming natural resources in national development planning and economic accounts.

Despite its long-standing and growing popularity, PES has also experienced limitations and setbacks. Muradian and his colleagues observe a pervasive mismatch between the theory and practice of PES: theoretically PES is expected to operate as a voluntary transaction based on a clearly connected land use practice and an ecosystem service. In practice, initiatives are not always voluntary for both buyers and sellers, and are not always monitored to ensure compliance and service provision (Muradian et al. 2010). The typical emphasis on efficiency also subordinates equity concerns, which means that poverty reduction and welfare enhancement do not always accompany PES initiatives. Critics also argue against thinking about nature purely in terms of 'services', or 'stock and flow'. Norgaard (2010) suggests that thinking about natural systems only in terms of 'stock and flow' does not allow us to fully capture the complexity of these systems. A second problem lies in the piecemeal approach to sustainability that the concept of ecosystem services has reinforced. Rather than directing attention to the macro drivers of unsustainability and the political, economic, and social change required for long-term sustainability, the valuing of ecosystem services is typically approached on a project-by-project basis. For some civil society groups and communities, a further problem inherent to the ecosystem services concept is the potential it creates for privatising and commoditising nature. We will explore these concerns in more depth in the following section on deforestation and REDD.

The problems of trying to implement PES on a large scale were demonstrated very clearly with the failed Yasuni initiative in Ecuador. The Yasuni National Park has an extraordinarily high level of biodiversity and is located within territory controlled by indigenous peoples (including uncontacted tribes). However, this land also sits above a 'lake of oil': with an estimated 900 million barrels, it accounts for nearly one-quarter of Ecuador's oil reserves (Kraft 2009). In 2007, President Rafael Correa extended an offer to the international community. In exchange for $350 million per year for ten years, Ecuador would ban oil drilling in Yasuni. Several governments and NGOs supported the plan, but by late 2013 it had been scrapped after only $13 million was delivered. The Ecuadorian government blamed a lack of commitment from foreign governments. Funds were channelled through a UNDP-managed trust fund rather than sent directly to Ecuador, but foreign governments still held concerns about whether the Ecuadorian government could be trusted to keep its promise. Critics say the credibility of the Yasuni plan was in question because it accounted for only a fraction of the total rainforest. What's more, the government was accused of actively exploring a 'Plan B' for oil exploration in case the initiative failed (Zuckerman 2013). Some of the reasons for the initiative's failure are specific to this particular case; other reasons expose the general problems surrounding large-scale payments for ecosystem services. The public benefits would be mostly enjoyed in the long term, whereas the costs would fall on present generations; this became particularly problematic given that it coincided with the global financial crisis when many governments were reducing their public spending. Moreover, given the widespread shift towards market-based conservation mechanisms many governments were reluctant to part with significant sums of money without receiving 'carbon credits' in return. As we will see below, this tension between market- and fund-based conservation measures is a defining characteristic of efforts to control deforestation.

## Finance and Deforestation

We now turn to the case of deforestation. International finance has been central in efforts to reduce deforestation. This is because the world's remaining tropical rainforest lies mainly in developing countries where governments either demand their sovereign right to exploit their natural resources for economic gain, or claim to lack the financial and political capacity to manage their forests sustainably. We first examine the nature and scale of the problem, and then look more closely at the drivers of deforestation. Next we review the institutions and mechanisms that the international community has developed to incentivise sustainable forestry and reduce GHG emissions from deforestation.

### The Nature of the Problem

Over 30 per cent of the planet's land area is covered in forests (Food and Agricultural Organization 2012: 9). Forests provide numerous public goods: they store carbon, protect watersheds, regulate water flows, generate rainfall, contribute to maintaining stable climates and other natural systems. They also provide a range of private goods: sustaining livelihoods, providing jobs and shelter, and generating commodities for trade. The importance of forests for human life cannot be underestimated but we have failed to adequately protect them and this has negative effects from the local level to the global level.

Deforestation is not a new problem; it has existed for thousands of years. For as long as humans have grown food, raised animals, and built settlements, they have cleared forests. What is new is the pace and location of deforestation. Deforestation reflects one of the most significant human impacts on the earth. Over the past 5,000 years, an estimated 1.8 billion hectares of forest have been cleared to promote human and economic development. Prior to the twentieth century, the highest rate of deforestation occurred in the temperate forests of Asia, North America, and Europe. While there has been little deforestation in these areas since the mid-twentieth century, there has been considerable clearing in the world's tropical countries, particularly in Brazil and Indonesia. 'Tropical' countries are those that lie within about 30 degrees north and south of the equator.

The scale of tropical forest clearance is equivalent to about half the size of England every year (Kelly 2010: 64). This has been a cause for concern because much of the world's biodiversity can be found in the tropics, and it is threatened by deforestation.

Although the rate of clearance remains shockingly high, Figure 8.6 reveals that the rate of tropical deforestation has been in constant decline for many years.

This falling rate has been achieved by pressuring tropical countries into action. An important example is Brazil, where moratoria have been placed on

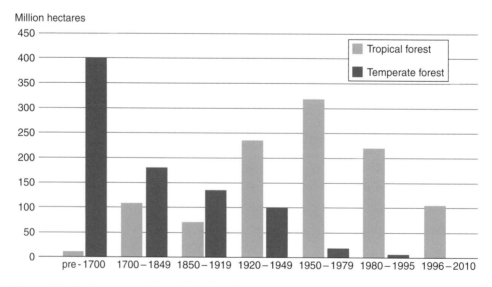

**Figure 8.6:** Declining rate of tropical deforestation
Source: FAO 2012: 9

clearing forests for raising cattle and producing soybeans. While it remains a very serious problem, there is reason to be optimistic. The Union of Concerned Scientists even predicts that we can reduce the rate of forest loss to zero within the next few decades, thereby 'making deforestation history' (Boucher et al. 2011: 9).

## Drivers of Deforestation

Effectively addressing this problem will require a clear understanding of the demographic and economic factors that drive deforestation. There are many different activities we can point to that are implicated in land clearing. Doug Boucher and his colleagues (2011) point to five competing demands for land use: the 'five Fs' of food, feed, fibre, fuel, and forest products. They suggest that food and feed are presently the most prevalent drivers of tropical deforestation, but that fibre, fuel, and forest products play an important and growing role. The neo-Malthusians we encountered in Chapter 3 would attribute the increased demand for food, feed, and forest products to rising populations. They would be right; this is a source of growing demand. But a more significant source is rising global incomes, or affluence.

Although global population is expected to stabilise in the coming decades at about 25–30 per cent higher than present levels, international institutions like FAO and the OECD estimate that 70 per cent more food will be needed by about 2050 (Boucher et al. 2011: 14). This is because as incomes rise, people tend to consume larger quantities of meat and animal-derived products. Producing animal products uses considerably more land than vegetable- and grain-based diets because it requires feeding vast amounts of grain to animals. The diets of the rich are therefore much less efficient than the diets of the poor (Boucher et al. 2011: 14).

While food-based drivers are associated with wealth, fuel-based drivers are associated with poverty. Demand for fuel-wood tends to be associated with lower incomes. Many people around the world (especially in developing countries) continue to rely on wood for their fuel needs (i.e., cooking and heating). Indeed, it is estimated that about half of the timber illegally removed from forests is used as fuel-wood (WWF no date). However, there are concerns that ambitions to substitute fossil fuels for bio-fuels (especially in wealthier countries like those in the EU) will place new and increasing pressures on tropical forests.

When these factors are analysed more closely, we can distinguish direct (or proximate) causes from underlying causes. Helmut Geist and Eric Lambin explain this distinction as follows: 'Proximate causes are human activities or immediate actions at the local level ... that originate from intended land use and directly impact forest cover. Underlying driving forces are fundamental social processes ... that underpin the proximate causes and either operate at the local level or have an indirect impact from the national or global level' (2002: 143).

Proximate causes include infrastructure development (e.g., extending roads and public services, expanding towns and cities); agricultural expansion; and timber extraction. Underlying causes include demographic change (e.g., growing population, increased population density, and migration); economic development (e.g., industrialisation, market growth); technological change (enabling more extensive and intensive clearance); policy and institutions (e.g., economic development priorities, provision of credit, corruption, mismanagement); and culture (e.g., public attitudes and behaviour) (Geist and Lambin 2002: 143).

Proximate and underlying causes are historically and regionally contextual: the factors driving deforestation today are not exactly the same as those driving deforestation 200 years ago. Similarly, the driving factors in the Americas today are not the same as those in Africa. Tropical deforestation in Asia is largely driven by large-scale production of palm oil, coconut, rubber, teak, and pulpwood. In Latin America, logging and large-scale production of beef, soy, and sugar cane are the main drivers. In Africa, small-scale activities such as fuelwood collection and charcoal production are prominent drivers, as is fire (REDD Desk 2015; Boucher et al. 2011: 1).

In recent history, a distinction can be drawn between state-driven deforestation (pre-1990) and enterprise-driven deforestation (post-1990). In the earlier period, governments pursued internal colonisation programmes to open up isolated regions for human settlement and small-scale farming. The cold war had an important impact as the US supported agrarian reform and infrastructure expansion to quell the rural, communist-inspired insurrections that were common in Latin America and Southeast Asia in the 1960s (Rudel et al. 2009: 1398–9). After 1990, indebtedness and a decline in rural insurgencies saw a reduction in government-led expansion and development in forested regions. However, this was replaced by growing support for private enterprise in the forestry and agricultural sectors, which in turn were propelled by growing demand for commodities on the international market (Rudel et al. 2009: 1400).

## Global Forestry Governance

British geographer David Humphreys has provided the most detailed analysis of global forestry governance. He observes that forests have been an issue of international concern since the late nineteenth century, albeit initially only as a scientific issue. In 1892, the International Union of Forest Research Organizations was created, two years after the Congress of Agriculture and Forestry had recommended creating a new scientific body for forest research (Humphreys 2013: 74). The international community's capacity to translate forest science into policy was strengthened in 1945 when the UN's Food and Agriculture Organization (FAO) was established, although with only a minuscule budget for forests.

Throughout the 1960s and 1970s, forests became increasingly politicised in two distinct ways. One reflected intensifying concern among conservationists about rates of tropical deforestation; the other reflected concern among developing countries about the unfair terms of trade for forest products. The institution that emerged in 1985 in response to these concerns, the International Tropical Timber Organization (ITTO), reflected both concerns but with greater emphasis on ensuring fair and transparent trade in tropical timber than conserving tropical forests (Humphreys 2013: 74–5).

Forests have continued to ascend the international political agenda, but what most stands out when we compare this issue to other environmental concerns is the absence of a UN convention. In negotiations leading up to the 1992 Rio Summit, many developed countries pushed hard for a convention on forests and deforestation. But developing countries strongly resisted this, especially large tropical forested countries that feared restrictions on their sovereignty, and negative impacts on their trading and economic development. While resisting the establishment of a convention, developing countries were not entirely opposed to international agreements and mechanisms to address unsustainable deforestation. Indeed, as we saw earlier, they used this as an opportunity to push for greater transfer of financial and technological aid. Humphreys explains these demands as reflecting the concept of 'compensation for opportunity cost forgone'. He explained that 'if tropical countries were to conserve their forests rather than exploit them they would forgo a major revenue stream and should expect to be compensated for this by those countries that wanted tropical forests conserved' (Humphreys 2013: 76).

Instead of an international forest convention, what we have seen is a string of successive institutions creating instruments of 'soft law'. As we saw in

Chapter 6, soft law instruments are non-binding and voluntary. The 1995 Intergovernmental Panel on Forests was succeeded in 1997 by the Intergovernmental Forum on Forests, which in turn was succeeded by the United Nations Forum on Forests in 2000 (Humphreys 2014). The first two institutions produced a set of 270 proposals for action (the IPF/IFF Proposals for Action). These essentially only provided guidance to states on sustainably managing their forests; progress reports were voluntary, and compliance was weak (Maguire 2013: 108–19). Efforts to strengthen global forest governance continued in the United Nations Forum on Forests. This culminated in the 'Non-Legally Binding Instrument on All Types of Forests', an agreement that reaffirmed the primacy of national sovereignty and state responsibility, as well as the importance of financial and technology transfer, and outlined four global objectives on forests (UN 2007b):

1. 'Reverse the loss of forest cover worldwide through sustainable forest management, including protection, restoration, afforestation and reforestation, and increase efforts to prevent forest degradation';
2. 'Enhance forest-based economic, social and environmental benefits, including by improving the livelihoods of forest-dependent people';
3. 'Increase significantly the area of protected forests worldwide and other areas of sustainably managed forests, as well as the proportion of forest products derived from sustainably managed forests';
4. 'Reverse the decline in official development assistance for sustainable forest management and mobilize significantly increased, new and additional financial resources from all sources for the implementation of sustainable forest management'.

Dissatisfaction with the weakness of soft forest law, and the exceedingly slow pace at which it has been made, have prompted conservationists to pursue their aims elsewhere. Two sites of forest governance have become particularly prominent: private market-based institutions and the climate change regime.

The most important private institution in this area is the Forest Stewardship Council (FSC). Under the leadership of the World Wildlife Fund, the FSC was established as a voluntary certification scheme in 1993 following four years of dialogue among timber users, traders, and civil society groups. By designing a global eco-label, it was hoped that customers along the supply chain could be encouraged to purchase products only from sustainably managed forests in which the rights of indigenous people and forest dwellers were respected (Auld and Cashore 2013: 135). The FSC was one of the first institutions to be designed in such a way that sought to counter the power imbalances in the international system. Its General Assembly has a tripartite structure with social, economic, and environmental chambers. Votes are equally distributed among developed and developing countries in each chamber. Membership is open to civil society and the private sector; government-owned forest companies may join but government agencies may not (Auld and Cashore 2013: 135).

Throughout the 2000s, many other forest certification schemes were established. This generated significant competition and overlap in the market. By 2011, there were some thirty schemes in operation covering more than 500 million hectares of forest. While this accounts for about 15 per cent of global forest cover, it includes a mere 1.5 per cent of tropical and subtropical forests, which, you'll recall, are the main source of global concern (Meijaard et al. 2014: 161). One of the main limitations of forest certification schemes is insufficient customer demand and awareness. Another is its broad interpretation of what counts as a forest. The FSC includes plantations in its scheme, and in some countries these account for large areas of certified forest (Marx and Cuypers 2010: 418–19). Partly as a result of the high costs and complex governance arrangements required, participation is also very skewed to countries with high levels of social and economic development (Marx and Cuypers 2010: 420). A further limitation is that certification schemes do not address the underlying drivers of deforestation, only some of the proximate causes.

## Deforestation and the Global Climate Regime

Multilaterally, the 'centre of gravity' has shifted from forest-focused institutions to the UNFCCC (Humphreys 2014: 499). This is perhaps unsurprising when we consider how much deforestation contributes to global warming. The precise contribution has been contested with different organisations citing vastly different figures. In 2006, FAO issued a press release claiming that 25–30 per cent of global GHG emissions came from deforestation (FAO 2006). In 2007, the IPCC concluded that the true figure was actually 17 per cent. In 2012, two leading research teams came together to resolve the dispute. They found that once they selected the same time period (2000–5) and the same methodology (e.g., measuring gross rather than net deforestation, and considering only $CO_2$ rather than other greenhouse gases), they could agree that 10 per cent of global warming is caused by deforestation (Union of Concerned Scientists 2012). This figure is in decline partly due to slowing rates of deforestation, but more importantly due to the fact that fossil fuel-based emissions continued growing while deforestation rates declined. Nevertheless, 10 per cent – or 3 billion tonnes – is not an insignificant contribution. It is the equivalent of all emissions in Western Europe, Scandinavia, and surrounding countries (UCS 2012).

Despite the significant contribution of deforestation to global warming, the climate regime was initially quite slow to take up the issue of forests. It has never been excluded from debates, but for many years its inclusion in agreements was considered too controversial mainly for methodological reasons. While some countries were keen to see forestry activities included in the Kyoto Protocol and its Clean Development Mechanism, the UNFCCC resolved to restrict this to afforestation (creating new forests) and reforestation (restoring destroyed or degraded forests). Methodologies for measuring the emissions associated with deforestation were considered too imprecise to allow for carbon credits and offsetting projects. In the jargon of UNFCCC negotiations, the concerns surrounding deforestation's inclusion relate to additionality, permanence, and leakage (Agrawal et al. 2011: 376–7).

- **Additionality** requires that actions only be rewarded if they generate emissions reduction above and beyond what would have occurred anyway. This addresses the risk that money could be allocated to actions that would have taken place anyway, that is, without any financial incentive. The payment incentive in such cases would be superfluous and inefficient. However, in practice it is very difficult to predict what might occur in the absence of a certain policy or financial incentive.
- **Permanence** concerns the risk of broken promises. Financial rewards may be made on the basis of long-term conservation, but it can be difficult or impossible to guarantee that agreements will be upheld in the future. Rewarding avoided deforestation in the short term only makes sense if that deforestation never takes place in the future, but without a strong system of monitoring and penalties, there is no way of ensuring this. Some risks of 'non-permanence' or 'reversals' are human-induced (deliberately clearing protected forests), but others are natural (such as fires and natural disasters).
- **Leakage** concerns the risk that rewarding the avoidance of deforestation in one place will simply increase deforestation in another place. Unless the underlying drivers of deforestation are addressed, pressures on forests will simply shift rather than disappear. Indeed, deforestation might intensify in other areas as a result of the injection of capital provided by the reward. Leakage may occur within or across countries. The plausibility of this risk can

be illustrated with evidence from narcotics production in Bolivia: the provision of incentives to reduce coca production in the Chapare region simply resulted in significant increases in production in the more weakly controlled Yungas region, as well as in Colombia (Müller 2011: 180).

## REDD+

Concerns about the risks of additionality, permanence, and leakage prevented deforestation from being included in the offsetting mechanisms of the Kyoto Protocol. To deal with these uncertainties, governance experiments have been implemented outside (but with reference to) the UNFCCC. It is expected that these will generate lessons for a future 'REDD+' mechanism within the UNFCCC and gradually build confidence in its viability. These experiments collectively have become known as Reducing greenhouse gas Emissions from Deforestation and forest Degradation, forest stock conservation, sustainable forest management, and the enhancement of forest stock (REDD+). REDD+ is essentially a reward-based system that aims to reduce GHG emissions by offering financial incentives to developing countries to better protect and manage their forests.

One important governance initiative is the UN Collaborative Programme on Reducing Emissions from Deforestation and Forest Degradation in Developing Countries (UN-REDD Programme). It was established in 2008 and is led by FAO, UNEP, and UNDP. The programme works with individual countries in Africa, Asia-Pacific, and Latin America to develop their capacity in designing and implementing REDD+ projects. Its overall goal is to 'assess whether carefully structured payments and capacity support can create the incentives to ensure lasting, reliable and measurable emission reductions while maintaining and improving other ecosystem services as well as the economic and social values that forests provide' (Climate Funds Update 2015). By 2015, contributor countries (EU, Norway, Denmark, Spain, Japan, and Luxembourg) had delivered some $2.5 million to finance projects in over twenty countries (UNDP 2015). The programme does not actually purchase credits from these countries. Instead, UN-REDD is working with them on issues of governance, stakeholder engagement, and financial management to prepare them to engage in forest-based carbon markets.

The other prominent REDD+ initiative is the World Bank Forest Carbon Partnership Facility (FCPF). Also launched in 2008, the FCPF will run until 2020. Like UN-REDD it provides technical and financial assistance to strengthen the capacity of developing countries to participate in a future REDD+

mechanism under the UN climate regime. But this World Bank partnership also makes payments to a small number of pilot countries that are already avoiding GHG emissions through improved forest management. Its 'performance-based payment system' aims to make it more profitable for countries to keep their forests in place than clearing them. Rather than rewarding individual small-scale projects, the Forest Carbon Partnership Facility is targeting large-scale 'jurisdiction or eco-region' approaches that integrate REDD+ into national development strategies and entail significant policies and investments (Forest Carbon Partnership Facility 2013). The 'performance' element ensures that rewards are only issued once emissions reductions or enhancement in forest carbon stocks have been verified. Unlike UN-REDD, the World Bank partnership is financed by contributions from states and the private sector (including BP). By 2015, some $2.5 million had been delivered out of total pledges amounting to some $3.4 million (Climate Funds Update 2015).

These REDD+ initiatives have been particularly concerned with reassuring critics that their concerns are not necessarily justified. Beyond technical concerns around permanence, leakage, and additionality, civil society groups have also raised several moral concerns. These relate to possible impacts on the livelihoods of forest-dwelling communities, as well as issues of equity and participation. Many of these concerns arise from the fact that forest and land tenure is often insecurely defined in developing countries. Schroeder and Okereke explain that it is often the case that '(traditional) customary and (legalized) statutory tenure systems co-exist, making the question of who owns the forest and therefore should rightly receive international payments highly political and contested' (2013: 85). Other scholars point out that fair and successful REDD+ schemes are not dependent on merely clarifying forest tenure rights, but rather on recognising these rights. Customary tenure may provide forest-dwelling communities with rights to use forests for traditional purposes, and to make decisions about using products obtained from forests, but without formal recognition there is no security to this tenure (Kelly 2010: 65–6).

Recognising the rights of forest-dwelling communities (especially indigenous peoples) is considered important to ensure equitable sharing of the benefits of REDD+ projects, and it is considered by some as essential to reducing deforestation more generally. Indian geographer Ashwini Chhatre and his colleagues point out that people who live in and around forests without secure tenure are less likely to invest in its long-term sustainability; they may clear trees to establish rights, and will rarely plant diverse slow-growing tree species (2012: 656). The vast majority of the world's remaining forests are defined as state-owned land; local and indigenous communities have legal tenure over only a very small percentage. Environmental law expert David Kelly suggests that REDD+ programmes need to include procedural rights of participation to protect the interests of forest-dwelling communities (Kelly 2010: 73–5). With very large amounts of money potentially at stake, there is a risk that states will try to centralise all planning, implementation, and management of REDD+ projects. Civil society and indigenous movements have loudly voiced concerns about the risk that REDD+ will promote 'land grabs' whereby local communities are dispossessed of their land by profit-seeking governments and market actors. Even if their land rights are recognised, human rights violations remain a possibility. For example, local people and community leaders may agree to give up land or traditional practices without fully understanding the implications, or they may not be appropriately compensated, or they may not ensure that the financial rewards are equitably distributed (Chhatre et al. 2012: 654–5). This in turn may generate or exacerbate conflict, inequalities, and displacement.

These concerns about participation and the distribution of benefits have led to considerable debate about how to include social 'safeguards' in future REDD+ initiatives. The strongest safeguards would not only prevent harm to indigenous and forest-dwelling communities, but also ensure that they positively benefit from REDD+ projects. These are referred to as 'co-benefits' or 'non-carbon benefits' of REDD+. Civil society groups have been keen to stress that these shouldn't be understood as a benevolent and optional add-on to existing plans. The REDD+ Safeguards Working Group stresses that climate change is a human rights issue not just an environmental or scientific issue:

REDD-plus is more than just forest carbon stocks and on how much monetary value they have. It's also about how it would change the lives of those whose culture, survival and heritage depend on the forests themselves. The safeguards ensure that REDD-plus will be implemented in an inclusive, transparent manner, with respect for the rights of indigenous peoples and local communities and with consideration for the protection of biodiversity.

(REDD Safeguards Working Group 2014)

A range of competing standards have been discussed in the UN and implemented as part of different governance experiments. One promising private (and voluntary) standard is the REDD+ Social and Environmental Standards (REDD+ SES), created by Care International and the Climate, Community and Biodiversity Alliance. REDD+ SES has been adopted in several countries (including Ecuador, Peru, Guatemala, Mexico, and Chile) and sub-state jurisdictions (including Mato Grosso in Brazil, Central and East Kalimantan in Indonesia). It includes provisions for recognising and respecting rights to lands, territories, and resources; equitably sharing benefits; improving the livelihoods of indigenous people and local communities, especially women; contributing to good governance and social justice; and ensuring the participation of all rights holders and stakeholders in a full and effective way (REDD no date). UN-REDD and the World Bank's Forest Carbon Partnership Facility have each adopted similar guidelines to promote social and non-carbon benefits (Moss and Nussbaum 2011). Safeguards for environmental co-benefits have been discussed and implemented in recognition that climate-friendly projects might be detrimental for biodiversity protection. Planting a single species of tree with a high carbon absorption capacity would be very valuable from the perspective of mitigating climate change, but it would undermine biodiversity and potentially promote the conversion of natural forests into plantations.

The agreement of a universal set of social safeguards and the promotion of co-benefits would go some way towards reassuring critical communities and civil society groups. But concerns do remain, especially around the question of how REDD+ will be funded. There are two broad options: a fund-based REDD+ mechanism and a market-based one. The former could involve forest countries making commitments to reduce deforestation (or GHG emissions from forest-based practices) in exchange for international public finance. This could be administered bilaterally or through a multilateral trust fund. A market-based mechanism would tie reductions in deforestation to carbon credits that could be purchased by other countries to meet their international commitments, or by private actors (businesses and individuals) who are voluntarily reducing their carbon footprints.

The possibility of an international market-based REDD+ scheme is highly contentious. Reasons for concern are both economic and philosophical. On the economic side, a market-based scheme would involve fluctuating prices (depending on the international price of carbon); this creates a risk that the price would drop below the level necessary to incentivise conservation. So if the price of a unit of carbon that could be sequestered in a hectare of tropical forest dropped below the price of palm oil that could be obtained from that same hectare of forest, the rational outcome would be to abandon conservation in favour of palm oil production. If left entirely to market forces, there is no way of ensuring that the price of carbon is high enough to compete with alternative land uses; the price will simply be determined by supply and demand for REDD+ credits. Further complicating matters is the fact that sustainability concerns dictate that as much forest as possible should be included in the scheme, but market laws dictate that the price of carbon will fall as the scale of included forest expands (Humphreys 2014: 500–1).

Philosophical objections relate to the ethics of offsetting the carbon-intensive lifestyles of people in wealthy countries in poorer forest countries; from this perspective, REDD+ is nothing more than a cheap and convenient way of avoiding responsibility for global pollution. Market-based approaches are also rejected on the grounds that they reduce nature to a private commodity and deny the multiple inherent values that can be attached to nature. In 2014, social movements convened a symbolic tribunal to bring REDD+ actors to trial for 'crimes against nature'. The International Tribunal for the Rights of Nature took place in Peru and heard from activists and social movements opposed to REDD+. Mary Lou Malig from the Philippines claimed that carbon markets are 'basically a mechanism to cheat. It's about enabling you to pollute. Instead of cutting your emissions, you increase them and pretend to reduce by offsetting'. Ninawa Kaxinawá, an indigenous man from Brazil, shared her concerns arguing that 'Nature has no price. It's our forest, it's our food, it's our spirit.' He claimed that indigenous communities had been threatened with death and loss of social services for objecting to REDD+ projects (Lang 2014). These concerns point to the wider non-carbon value that many people attach to forests. Crucially, they also stress the importance of addressing the underlying – and very complex – drivers of deforestation.

## Conclusion

In this chapter we have examined attempts to prevent environmental degradation through public and private finance initiatives. Governmental aid has long been the dominant source of environmental finance but alongside this aid we have seen experiments such as debt-for-nature swaps and payment for ecosystem services.

We focused on the issue of deforestation in this chapter. Deforestation is a global environmental concern because forests, especially tropical forests, have high levels of biodiversity and are home to many unique species of plants, birds, and other wildlife. Forests also store high levels of carbon dioxide, which makes deforestation an important contributor to climate change. Despite considerable international concern about deforestation, the international community has struggled to establish a strong and effective global regime for protecting forests.

Unlike climate change, biodiversity, desertification, and many other environmental issues, there is no international convention or treaty on forests. What explains this? One reason is that the interests and priorities of different countries and groups diverge: some are more interested in expanding and improving trade in forest products, while others are more concerned about conserving forests. Several pieces of soft international law try to accommodate these competing and perhaps incompatible interests. Just as we saw in climate change governance, impatience and frustration with multilateral processes has pushed private actors to establish parallel governance mechanisms, especially 'eco-labels'. These might help, but they are limited in their capacity to control deforestation.

In recent years, the global governance of forests has been drawn into the climate change regime. Many governments and private sector actors would like to link international carbon markets and forests, but this has been held back due to the concerns about additionality, permanence, and leakage. Social movements and forest-dependent communities raise additional concerns about participation, indigenous rights, and land tenure. They also raise concerns that initiatives like REDD+ that focus on financial incentives for developing countries fail to address the underlying drivers of deforestation. REDD+ initiatives address some of the governance drivers of deforestation (such as capacity, corruption, and mismanagement), but they largely overlook the demographic, economic, and cultural drivers. As long as demands continue to grow for food, feed, fibre, fuel, and forest products, it is difficult to see how tropical deforestation can be curtailed.

## Discussion Questions

1. What factors account for the shifting trends in environmental aid throughout the late twentieth century and early twenty-first century?
2. What principles and assumptions underpin debt-for-nature swaps?
3. What could have been done to prevent the failure of the Yasuni ITT project? Do you see potential for this type of finance initiative in the future?
4. What do you understand by concerns about additionality, permanence, and leakage? Do these reflect inevitable problems or are there ways to overcome them?
5. What sorts of measures could the international community take to address the underlying drivers of deforestation?

# 9 Individualising Responsibility
## Unsustainable Consumption

**key points**

- Consumer culture, or consumerism, rose in the West in the 1960s. This is characterised by high-volume consumption of non-necessary goods. A global 'consumer class' now also includes middle classes in developing countries like China and India.
- The full environmental impact of consumer goods is hard for consumers to detect because different stages of the production process generate different environmental problems.
- The UN has maintained programmes and negotiations on sustainable consumption since 1992, but these have had limited impact.
- The private sector and civil society have developed voluntary tools like eco-labelling and the ecological footprint calculator to support people in reducing the environmental impact of their consumption.
- Some scholars reject the assumption that focusing on individual consumption habits can make a difference to societal-level problems like unsustainable consumption. They reject this as the privatisation or individualisation of responsibility.

# Introduction

For many environmentalists, the defining vision of unsustainability is probably the modern shopping mall: those vast consumerist temples compelling the masses towards mindless and wasteful consumption. If unsustainable consumption is the result of individual actions and behaviour then surely it stands to reason that change needs to start with individual consumers. This is a compelling argument and it is one that underpins the efforts of many green business and civil society initiatives. Given the difficulty of addressing questions of individual lifestyles within intergovernmental institutions like the UN, it is unsurprising that many voluntary initiatives have proliferated within the private sector. This is a pattern of action we increasingly see in global environmental governance: as impatience grows with the slow pace and weak results of government-based action, businesses and civil society organise themselves to fill the governance gap. We saw this in Chapter 7 where 'governance experiments' are growing alongside intergovernmental climate change mitigation efforts, as well as Chapter 8 where private '**eco-labels**' try to control deforestation.

In this chapter we will examine the rise of consumer culture in Western countries in the mid-twentieth century, followed more recently by the emergence of a high-consuming middle class in China, India, and other emerging economies. We will see how the cultural phenomenon of a global consumer class is the result of demographic and socio-economic changes, as well as deliberate efforts to reshape people's desires and preferences. To appreciate the impact that high-volume luxury consumption has on the natural environment, we will then look at two popular items: mobile phones and fashion. Here we see how the environmental effects of consumption are often hidden rather than easily detected. Choices about the design of products and the materials used determine much of their environmental impact before they reach the shop floor. In the following section we examine how the issue of consumption made its way onto the international political agenda in 1992 and how UN programmes on Sustainable Consumption and Production (SCP) have since evolved. While these initiatives aim to coordinate international action on unsustainable consumption, results have so far been very limited. Outside intergovernmental institutions, we have seen many voluntary initiatives developed by the private sector and civil society to encourage change in people's consumption habits and patterns. We will examine the idea of individual responsibility that underpins these initiatives before looking at some prominent examples like the ecological footprint and eco-labelling. The notion that individual-level action is an effective way to target problems like over-consumption is strongly contested by some scholars. We will consider their critiques of the 'individualisation of responsibility' and problems like 'greenwash' that can undermine the capacity of consumers to practice green consumption. A final review of some important counter-critiques helps you reach a critical judgment on the value of addressing environmental problems through appeals to individual responsibility.

# Consumption and Its Environmental Impact

Consumption is a fact of life: the direct or indirect consumption of natural resources is essential to support and enrich human life. However, throughout the twentieth century patterns of consumption began to change in terms of type and volume of consumption. At the individual level, consumption can be categorised as subsistence consumption and luxury consumption. This distinction traces back to the work of Karl Marx for whom it was unsurprisingly rooted in class. The working class was associated with subsistence consumption (namely, the purchasing of basic foods and goods for the home). The capitalist class was associated with luxury consumption (namely, the purchasing of desired goods such as automobiles) (Ritzer 2010: 50). The distinction has also influenced normative theorising about global climate change. Back in 1991, Indian environmentalists Anil Agarwal and Sunita Narain forcefully argued that any international response to climate change must take into account the distinction between greenhouse gas emissions resulting from subsistence-based consumption ('survival emissions') and those resulting from luxury-based consumption ('luxury emissions') (Agarwal and Narain 1991: 3). In Marx's day, luxury consumption was the reserve of a privileged few and only occurred in small volumes. This changed in the twentieth century as more and more people (notably in the industrialised countries) acquired sufficient disposable income to consume for pleasure, convenience, distraction, creativity, and to express their personal identity or signal their status (Fuchs and Boll 2011: 75). This trend resulted in higher volumes of luxury consumption.

High-volume, luxury consumption is associated with the term **consumerism**. Focusing on consumerism instead of consumption allows us to see individual purchases as a collective practice, rather than as based entirely on individual decisions. Luxury consumption is then understood as a cultural system under-pinned by cultural norms that make it appear entirely normal and natural. From this perspective, as Erik Assadourian explains, 'asking people who live in consumer cultures to curb consumption is akin to asking them to stop breathing – they can do it for a moment, but then, gasping, they will inhale again. Driving cars, flying in planes, having large homes, using air conditioning … these are not decadent choices but simply natural parts of life' (2010: 3). While there are different dictionary definitions of consumerism (including consumer rights to certain goods and services, as well as the assump-tion in economic theory that increasing consumption increases social and economic development), the dominant understanding of consumerism refers to the beliefs and behaviours associated with excessive individual consumption (Crocker and Lehmann 2013).

The rise of consumerism in the West is closely associated with the rise of average incomes, but perhaps more importantly with the emergence of new tools to promote, facilitate, and lock in luxury consumption. In Chapter 4 we saw how mass advertising has played a crucial role in spurring desires and needs that either did not exist before or were simply not widely recognised. We saw that in the US alone per capita spending on advertising has risen seventeen-fold since the 1940s. Another important tool in promoting consumption is the popularisation of consumer credit and the invention of the credit card in the 1950s. Critics argue that credit not only facilitates immediate consumption, but also locks people into a continuous cycle of labour and consumption that constrains future individual choices (Ritzer 2010: 24–5). American sociologist Juliet Schor calls this the 'squirrel cage' of capitalism because it keeps people trapped on a fruitless treadmill (2008: 117).

No country has come to symbolise over-consumption more than the United States. Schor estimates that Americans spend three to four times more of their time shopping than Europeans do (2008: 107). 'Once a purely utilitarian chore', she writes, 'shopping has been elevated to the status of a national passion' (2008: 107). Americans – rich, middle class, and poor alike – on average consume about twice as much today as they did in the 1970s. Meanwhile, over the second half of the twentieth century, American houses grew three times, while the average number of dwellers dropped by 35 per cent (2008: 109–10).

Those concerned about the impacts of consumerism have begun expanding their attention beyond the US and the West to take in the burgeoning middle classes in 'emerging economies', especially China and India. The concept that captures this globalisation of luxury consumption is the '**consumer class**', defined as those with annual incomes of over $3,600 PPP (McKinsey Global Institute 2012: 23). PPP refers to 'purchasing power parity' and is a way to equalise incomes for comparative purposes: it adjusts annual income figures to reflect the cost of living in different countries. About 20 per cent of the global consumer class – some 362 million people – now resides in China and India (Worldwatch Institute 2011). McKinsey and Co optimistically see considerable potential for growth in the consumer class of developing countries because it still accounts for less than half their total populations.

Perhaps the most striking symbol of the rise of the consumer class in the global South is the automobile. Today, some 20 million new cars are sold each year in China, reflecting a doubling in demand in just five years (Statistica 2015). The total number of civilian vehicles now travelling China's roads reached nearly 150 million in 2014, up 13 per cent in a single year (National Bureau of Statistics China 2015). As urban roads become more and more congested, private transport becomes less and less convenient. But this also creates its own vicious cycle whereby more people aim to travel by private car to avoid subjecting their lungs to the dangerous levels of air pollution now common in Chinese cities (Watt 2013).

The same forces that shaped Western consumerism in the twentieth century are now shaping the new consumerism in emerging economies. China is already the world's third largest advertising market, with some $70 billion spent on enticing citizens to buy everything from facial tissues to air conditioners and electronics. This money is spent on transforming China from a society of 'pragmatic' consumers to 'emotional' consumers: the former is concerned with the functional attributes of a product, while the latter is concerned with its emotional associations. A Swedish manufacturer of tissues and forest products has set about building a mass market for packaged tissues not by focusing on their banal function, but rather by leaving samples in karaoke bars to develop an association between the fun-loving professional woman and the use of tissues. As with most products, the emotional association may carry no obvious connection to the product's function. Given that the Chinese state takes a light-touch approach to advertisement regulation, advertisements and billboards have proliferated in public space (*The Wall Street Journal* 2014; Magni and Poh 2013). Clearly this phenomenon is not limited to China. Think about the advertisements you have seen in recent days. You can probably identify how companies have tried to establish emotional associations with their products.

Urbanisation is accelerating the growth of the consumer class. Urbanisation has been a universal feature of industrial development, but the scale and speed of urbanisation today makes it very different to historical experiences. The McKinsey Global Institute calls this 'the most significant economic transformation the world has seen' noting that China is urbanising at 100 times the scale and 10 times the speed of Britain in the eighteenth century (Dobbs et al. 2012: 16). The relationship between consumerism and urbanisation comes down to two factors: opportunity and income. Urban settings are more advanced in consumer infrastructure: shopping centres, highways, parking lots, mass advertising. Urban dwellers also have considerably higher levels of disposable income: in China and India today, the average urban citizen's income is three times higher than their rural counterpart (Dobbs et al. 2012: 14). These two factors are closely related: as incomes rise and consumer demands increase, the demands on infrastructure also increase. The capacity of ports in emerging economies will need to expand by 250 per cent to sustain rising consumer demands in the coming decades (Dobbs et al. 2012: 33). Unsurprisingly, all of this carries considerable environmental costs.

To understand the environmental impact of modern consumption, let's look more closely at two popular items: mobile phones and fashion.

## Mobile Phones

The mobile phone has become an indispensable tool of modern life. The International Telecommunications Union estimates that in 2015 the number of mobile phones subscriptions around the world hit 7 billion, almost on par with global population (International Telecommunications Union 2015). Of course this figure does not imply universal access to mobile phone services. Phones are unevenly undistributed; many people now have two or more, and half the world's population has none (Boren 2014). In Russia, for example, there are almost twice as many mobile phone accounts as people (Pramis 2013). Convenient as these devices may be, they leave a heavy imprint on the planet. Much of their environmental impact derives from features inherent to the device: manufacturing a phone requires raw materials and charging a phone requires electricity; other impacts derive from the infrastructure necessary to support the sale and maintenance of phones, including building and maintaining networks, and constructing and running offices, retail stores, and call centres. These impacts are compounded by the **planned obsolescence** that is unnecessarily built into telephones. This is achieved by designing them with intentionally short lifespans, frequently releasing updated versions, and by investing in expensive advertising campaigns to shape the desires of phone users. This planned obsolescence has been remarkably successful: in many countries people now treat mobile phones as disposable products. Americans and Brits, for example, keep their phones for less than two years before upgrading them.

| | 2007 | 2008 | 2009 | 2010 | Prepaid Subscriber | Income in PPP$ |
|---|---|---|---|---|---|---|
| Brazil | 51.5 | 74.2 | 70.4 | 80.8 | 80% | $11,239 |
| Canada | 29.5 | 30.8 | 31.8 | 33.0 | 20% | $39,057 |
| Finland | 41.8 | 58.1 | 74.5 | 74.5 | 14% | $34,696 |
| France | 28.5 | 28.8 | 29.9 | 30.8 | 30% | $34,077 |
| Germany | 43.7 | 55.8 | 49.5 | 45.7 | 55% | $36,033 |
| India | 322.1 | 144.0 | 185.6 | 93.6 | 96% | $3,339 |
| Israel | 67.1 | 56.1 | 67.0 | 76.5 | 53% | $29,631 |
| Italy | 53.3 | 43.1 | 42.9 | 51.5 | 87% | $29,392 |
| Japan | 25.6 | 35.2 | 43.0 | 46.3 | 1% | $33,805 |
| Korea | 27.3 | 25.1 | 24.2 | 26.9 | 0% | $29,836 |
| Mexico | 48.6 | 41.7 | 42.9 | 39.6 | 86% | $14,430 |
| South Africa | 52.3 | 118.6 | 46.3 | 38.2 | 80% | $10,498 |
| United Kingdom | 24.5 | 24.4 | 26.4 | 22.4 | 54% | $34,920 |
| United States | 18.7 | 19.6 | 21.1 | 21.7 | 22% | $47,284 |

**Figure 9.1:** Mobile phone replacement cycle (in months)
Source: Recon Analytics 2011: 2
Income in PPP$ refers to purchasing power parity. This is a method economists use to compare incomes across countries that takes into account differences in the cost of living. Simple comparisons of income are misleading because an hourly wage in one country might buy the same goods as an hourly wage in another country, even if those wages are very different. PPP converts incomes to a common currency for comparative purposes. So in this figure we can see that Brazilians have an average PPP income of $11,329. Phones purchased in Brazil in 2007 were replaced, on average, after 51.5 months; while phones purchased in 2010 were replaced, on average, after 80.8 months.

This is not purely a matter of affluence. For example, the wealthy Finns hold onto their phones for about twice as long as poorer South Africans. In fact, the most influential factor that determines a phone's life expectancy is whether the company subsidises its replacement. Many companies support the premature disposal of mobile phones by subsidising a new device in exchange for the client's extended commitment (Recon Analytics 2011: 3–5). It is thus the business model that dramatically increases the environmental impact of the mobile phone rather than the accumulation of independent individual decisions.

Research by *The Ecologist* magazine calculates the carbon footprint of the Apple Smartphone at 70 kilogrammes of carbon dioxide. The vast majority of this is emitted during the production process, with only about 8 kilogrammes of $CO_2$ being emitted during the actual use of the device (Thomas 2013). The most straightforward option for reducing the environmental impact of mobile phones is obviously to discourage people from buying so many of them.

## Fashion

Globalisation has allowed clothing to be produced at ever lower prices. Meanwhile, strong advertising campaigns promote the idea that clothing styles are only appropriate for a single season. Together these two forces have succeeded in framing clothing as a disposable product. In fact, some high street stores now sell garments with the expectation that they will only be worn ten times – an expectation which likely informs their design processes (McAfee et al., 2004). Most young women, the largest consumers of fashion, are probably unaware of the environmental impact of 'fast fashion' (Claudio 2007: 449). However, an increasing number of corporate-driven campaigns are alerting shoppers to these issues. *Vogue*, for example, talks its readers through the journey of a pair of jeans:

consider denim. It is made from cotton picked from farms all over the world. The cotton is shipped back and forth across the oceans to be made into fabric, sewn, and dyed. Along the way, the average pair of jeans is treated with PFCs, chemicals that make material breathable and stain-resistant, and washed with detergents that contain alkyl-phenol ethoxylates, another hazardous compound. The whole process is incredibly water-intensive, from the farm up, and the carbon load from the shipping of the cotton to mills and the raw denim to factories is astronomical on its own. Then there's the additional impact of the transport, by boat or train or jet, of jeans to stores. They arrive sealed in clear plastic bags, which are promptly trashed.

(Singer 2015).

The contemporary fashion industry is driven by unnecessary consumption (Kozlowski et al. 2012: 20). A genuinely sustainable clothing regime is thereby completely incompatible with the industry's profit expectations. Persuading people to only buy clothing they actually need is not an option, so the industry has turned to technological innovation to reduce the environmental impact of luxury consumption. Typically these focus on just one aspect of a garment's life cycle (such as the textile used or the possibility to recycle the fabric at the end of its life), rather than look at the big picture of fashion's footprint.

The environmental impact of clothing can be measured by analysing the processes it goes through from raw material production to disposal. This is called 'life cycle analysis'. The clothing life cycle entails six key phases: raw material acquisition; material processing and manufacturing; textile processing and manufacturing; apparel production, distribution, and retail; consumer use; and disposal (Kozlowski et al. 2012: 25). Most of the environmental impacts are 'locked in' in the design phase when the company decides which raw materials, textiles, and dyes to use, and how to finish and process the garment. The most widely used fibre – polyester – is a synthetic fibre made from petroleum. During its production, greenhouse gasses are emitted, as well as harmful compounds and particulates that contribute to respiratory disease. In fact, in the United States, many textile manufacturing facilities are classified by the Environment Protection Agency as hazardous waste generators (Claudio 2007: 450). Cotton may be a less toxic option but the production of this fibre relies on very high volumes of water and pesticides (Claudio 2007). In fact, it takes as much as 2,700 litres of water to produce the cotton for a single T-shirt (WWF 2013). Colouring and bleaches use further amounts of water and chemicals that often end up in waterways.

Garments continue to impact the environment long after they have passed their desired-by date. In the UK alone, some 350,000 tonnes of garments are sent to landfill each year (Waste and Resources Action Programme 2015). In the US this figure skyrockets to 11 million tonnes when all textiles are accounted for. As these garments decompose, they emit methane (a potent GHG) into the atmosphere, and release dyes and chemicals into soil and groundwater (Wallander 2012). From an environmental perspective, the most effective action to reduce the impact of fashion would be a reduction in the number of garments produced and purchased. Short of curtailing consumption, the next most effective action would be recycling. Many of the garments that end up in landfill could be resold or reused in the manufacture of insulation and furniture, for example. As long as consumers remain largely unaware of the value of recycling garments and the opportunities to do so, millions of tonnes will continue to go to landfill each year.

Here we have seen how high-volume luxury consumption contributes to environmental problems. Some companies are already responding with consumer education and media campaigns. But below we will review the argument that such campaigns focus too heavily on the individual consumer and ignore the structural factors that drive high-volume, luxury consumption. Before we examine this critique, though, let's first review the ways in which the international community has sought to develop multilateral responses to unsustainable consumption.

## Sustainable Consumption: Intergovernmental Initiatives

The issue of consumption made its way onto the international political agenda in 1992 when states began discussing 'sustainable consumption and production' (SCP) at the Earth Summit in Rio. Until that point, environmental discussions at the intergovernmental level had focused almost exclusively on production. The inclusion of consumption in the Declaration on Environment and Development was the result of campaigners' efforts to rebalance the agenda with attention to the consumption dimension of sustainable development. Principle 8 called on states to 'reduce and eliminate unsustainable patterns of production and consumption and promote appropriate demographic policies' (UN 1992b).

Accompanying the Rio Declaration was the full conference report 'Agenda 21', which elaborated on expectations, and presented an 'action plan' for achieving sustainable development. A full chapter was devoted to 'changing consumption patterns'. The chapter explained that action was justified because although poverty tended to aggravate environmental damage, the main source of global environmental degradation was unsustainable patterns of consumption and production, 'particularly in industrialized countries' (Agenda 21, chapter 4). In wording highly uncharacteristic of a UN document, this chapter pointed to 'excessive demands and unsustainable lifestyles among the richer segments, which place immense stress on the environment', and highlighted the importance of addressing global imbalances (Agenda 21, chapter 4). Developed countries were called in to take the lead in transforming their consumption patterns, while developing countries were instructed to pursue the fulfilment of basic needs while avoiding 'hazardous', 'inefficient', and 'wasteful' consumption patterns characteristic of industrialised countries (Agenda 21, chapter 4).

It was two years later that an accepted working definition of sustainable consumption was agreed, when government ministers gathered in the Norwegian capital of Oslo to advance the SCP agenda. There, they defined sustainable consumption as 'the use of goods and services that respond to basic needs and bring a better quality of life, while minimising the use of natural resources, toxic materials and emissions of waste and pollutants over the life cycle, so as not to jeopardise the needs of future generations' (Oslo Ministerial Roundtable 1994, quoted in Barber 2005: 62).

The Oslo definition provides scope for a broad interpretation of sustainable consumption that might encompass a reduction of consumption that is not necessary for either basic needs or wellbeing. Nevertheless, intergovernmental action subsequently assumed a very narrow interpretation of SCP to focus on energy efficiency and technological innovation. This was already evident in Agenda 21, which outlined actions for reducing the energy intensity of production, disseminating new technologies, minimising waste, encouraging recycling, and educating citizens. What it did not do was point to the strong corporate forces promoting *unsustainable* consumption. Fuchs and Boll refer to these two alternative interpretations as strong sustainable consumption and weak sustainable consumption, noting the dominance of the latter (2011: 74).

In some ways, the tenth anniversary World Summit on Sustainable Development was a moment of *déjà vu*. The 2002 Johannesburg Declaration on Sustainable Development reiterated states' commitment to addressing unsustainable consumption, again recognising that developed countries should take the lead while developing countries should integrate the topic into their poverty reduction strategies (UN 2002a: Chapter 3). As we saw in Chapter 6, an innovative aspect of the Johannesburg declarations was the emphasis on partnerships as a way of promoting international cooperation on sustainable development. Agenda 21 had stressed the importance of a global partnership of states, noting that 'no nation can achieve [sustainable development] on its own; but together we can...' (UN 1992a: 1.1). The 2002 'Joint Programme of Implementation' reconceptualised 'partnership' as an arrangement between governments, but also between governments and 'major groups' (UN 2002b: 1.3). This led to the creation of hundreds of 'public-private partnerships' for sustainable development, including some to address unsustainable consumption. These became known as 'Type II partnerships' to distinguish them from exclusively government-based cooperation, which had previously been the norm. As we saw in Chapter 7, the effectiveness and legitimacy of public-private partnerships have been hotly contested. Nevertheless, the outcomes of the WSSD in Johannesburg strengthened the role of the private sector in global environmental governance, including in the area of sustainable consumption. The Johannesburg summit also saw governments agree to begin working on 'a 10-year framework of programmes in support of regional and national initiatives to accelerate the shift towards sustainable consumption and production' (UN 2002b). In the end, it took governments another seven years to agree on this ten-year framework!

Under the UN's leadership, governments worked with development agencies, the private sector, and NGOs to elaborate and prepare for the ten-year framework of programmes on sustainable consumption and production (10YFP SCP). This came to be known as the Marrakech Process, recognising the host of the first meeting. From 2003 until 2010, dozens of international, regional, and national forums took place. The Marrakech Process was by no means just a drawn out 'talk shop'. Alongside talks to agree on the content of the 10YFP, the UN worked with governments and stakeholders to develop international, national, and local programmes that could build public awareness or tools, strategies, and methodologies for minimising waste and making consumption and production more efficient. This resulted in a set of regional SCP strategies and action plans, including tools and activities such as eco-labelling, green procurement goals, efficiency standards and indicators, and tax reform (UNEP 2012a: 15–16). A set of government-led 'Marrakech Task Forces' were dedicated to seven particular themes for advancing the SCP agenda: sustainable buildings and construction; sustainable tourism; sustainable products; sustainable lifestyles; sustainable public procurement; cooperation with Africa; and education for sustainable development.

The Marrakech Process was completed in time for the 10-Year Framework of Programmes to be adopted at the 2012 Rio+20 summit. This global framework is based on the same 'partnership' model as in Johannesburg and applies to developed and developing countries alike. The idea is that governments, the private sector, and civil society can collaborate on efforts to mainstream sustainable consumption and production into development planning. It is assumed that these actors can promote faster and deeper transformations by pooling resources and expertise. The framework was launched with a set of five programmes dealing with public procurement, consumer awareness, tourism, lifestyles and education, and buildings and construction. In fact, there is little difference between the Marrakech Process and the formally adopted 10YFP. The 10YFP aims to extend, deepen, and replicate the kind of work that was carried out throughout the 2000s but with slightly more financial backing in the form of a UNEP Trust Fund (UNEP 2012b).

## Private Sector and Civil Society Initiatives: Individualising Responsibility

One of the assumptions underpinning the UN's efforts on sustainable consumption is that individuals can make more sustainable consumption choices if they are better informed. This is reflected in four of the five flagship programmes of the 10YFP (consumer information; sustainable tourism; sustainable lifestyles and education; and sustainable buildings and construction). This assumption also underpins a range of other private sector and civil society initiatives that appeal to individual responsibility to promote sustainable consumption. Before we take a closer look at some of these initiatives, let's examine the idea of individual responsibility in more detail. It is an idea supported by normative political theory, social theory, and cultural theory.

Normative political theorists defend the idea of individual responsibility on grounds of justice. An assertion sometimes made is that we all consume so we all have to take our share of the responsibility for bringing about change. This is an idea that certainly has common sense appeal. Avram Hiller argues that we each have an individual moral responsibility to refrain from actions that cumulatively damage the environment or harm other people. In the case of climate change, individuals might be ignorant of the effects of their actions so 'the onus is on those who are aware of the dangers ... to ensure that no one can avoid culpability simply by lacking knowledge' (2011: 353). Even if we concede that individual actions are only one part of system-wide behaviour, we need to acknowledge their causal role (2011: 355). Hiller argues that accepting individual responsibility has practical implications: 'if many individuals become aware of their daily impacts and because of that awareness make changes in their practices, the benefits may add up to a very significant extent' (2011: 365). Alix Dietzel similarly argues that individual actions generally have a significant impact upon climate change, and that individuals often do have the ability to change their behaviour. In light of these two conditions, she argues, individuals have a moral responsibility to make such changes as reducing meat consumption, travel, and luxurious shopping habits (2015: chapter 5).

Some social theorists suggest that we are increasingly a society of individuals. Under conditions of modernity people no longer identify with others in terms of class, status, or gender. Ulrich Beck called these 'zombie categories': dead concepts used by sociologists that have little bearing on reality (1992). Similarly, formerly significant social units like the family and neighbourhood are sometimes now thought to hold little relevance for people's identities and lives (Middlemiss 2014: 942). Some see that social institutions like the labour market and education system are producing and reinforcing individualised societies. The labour market promotes mobility, which distances people from their original homes, while the education system promotes competition and individual achievements (Middlemiss 2014: 933). One implication of this social transformation is that people are more likely to think of their actions as *individual* rather than *collective* actions (such as part of a family, community, or class). This means they are more likely to respond to appeals to change their individual behaviour.

Cultural theorists like Ronald Inglehart (1977) argue that concern for the environment tends to develop only once people have reached a certain level of affluence. This is an idea we saw in Chapter 3 where it was used to suggest that some people are too poor to care about the environment. This is called a 'post-materialist' perspective, and it suggests that an individual will only assume a sense of responsibility for environmental sustainability once their basic material needs have been satisfied (secure housing, nutrition, and employment, for example). Once these needs are secured, people become more concerned about living in a clean environment. The idea that values are connected to needs builds on Maslow's psychological theory of the 'hierarchy of needs', which suggests that people must satisfy their basic 'physiological' needs before becoming concerned for needs for safety, love and belonging, esteem and personal growth (Maslow 1954). Of course, as we saw in Chapter 3, the relationship between affluence, poverty, and environmental concern tends to be more complex than these simple hierarchies would suggest.

## Voluntary Simplicity

Appeals to alter lifestyle and reduce personal impacts on the planet are not new. Precedents can be found in the voluntary simplicity movement that emerged in the 1970s. This movement is based on five values: material simplicity (rejecting consumerism); human scale (small-scale living and working environments); self-determination (less dependence on the formal economy and political process); ecological awareness (recognising the interdependence and interconnectedness of humans and nature); and personal growth (psychological and spiritual) (Elgin and Mitchell 1977: 4–9). Writing in 1977, Elgin and Mitchell imagined that 'voluntary simplicity may prove an increasingly powerful economic, social, and political force over the coming decade and beyond if large numbers of people of diverse backgrounds come to see it as a workable and purposeful response to many of the critical problems that we face' (Elgin and Mitchell 1977: 1). They saw voluntary simplicity as motivated by a sense of urgency over resource scarcity exacerbated by terrorist activity and equity demands of developing countries, and 'a growing social malaise and purposelessness' (1977: 3). Some estimates in the 1990s suggested that 20–28 per cent of Americans had already 'downsized' their lifestyles – living more happily on less income (Maniates 2002: 200).

Today there are many private initiatives that appeal to a sense of personal responsibility to address global environmental problems. They include the 'ecological footprint', carbon neutrality, and eco-labelling.

## Ecological Footprint

The 'ecological footprint' aims to make people aware of the resources they consume directly or indirectly in their everyday lives. This was developed by Mathis Wackernagel and William Rees in the early 1990s 'as an accounting tool that enables us to estimate the resource consumption and waste assimilation requirements of a defined human population or economy in terms of corresponding productive land area' (Wackernagel and Rees 1998: 9). Nowadays a number of sophisticated tools are available online for individuals to calculate their own ecological footprint. These tools take into account our gender, the size of our houses, the types and sources of food we consume, our shopping habits, and our usual mode and frequency of travel. The results then typically tell us how many planets would be required to support humanity if everyone lived like us (Global Footprint Network no date). On a global scale, people are collectively using the equivalent of 1.5 planets to provide the resources we consume and to absorb the waste we generate. What this means in practice is that the earth takes 1.5 years to regenerate what we consume in a single year. This can be sustained in the short term but not in the longer term. Of course, these aggregate global figures hide vast inequalities. The ecological footprint tools therefore allow individuals within wealthy countries to see how much greater their impact is compared to people in other countries (or, similarly, for wealthy people in poor countries to see their disproportionate impact). The five countries with the highest demand on the planet's biosphere are China, United States, India, Brazil, and Russia. Their impact is equal to the rest of the world combined (WWF 2014: 34). Yet by analysing this on an individual level we can see that the average Indian's footprint is less than one hectare, while the average US American uses about 7 hectares (WWF 2014: 36). Determining a sustainable footprint size requires dividing the planet's 'biocapacity' by the world's population. Biocapacity refers to the amount of biologically productive land and sea area that is available to regenerate the resources we consume for food, energy, fibre, land, and to absorb the waste and pollution we generate (WWF 2014: 9). In 2010 the planet's 'biocapacity' was about 12 billion global hectares, which shared out equally would give us each about 1.7 global hectares (WWF 2014: 38).

The footprint calculator tools tend to be incorporated into the campaigns of environmentalist organisations encouraging us to adjust our lifestyles. These campaigns tend to list 'simple' steps individuals can take to reduce their impact on the planet. 'The World Counts' is one initiative that claims that 'every human being on this planet can make simple changes to the way they use energy to reduce their impact on our resources'. It suggests five simple changes to make in our daily lives: avoid excess; buy environmentally friendly products; buy organic and local produce; take your own bags to the shops; and recycle (see Box 9.1).

---

### Box 9.1: **Five Things You Can Do To Help**

1. **Avoid Excess.** This applies to all kinds of excesses. Excess is equal to wastage. If you're not using the light, turn it off. Don't leave your faucet open and unattended. Cook only what you can finish eating. Don't drive when you can walk.
2. **Buy Products That Are Environment Friendly.** Practice your consumer power and buy products that don't harm our environment. Don't patronize products that cause harm. This is to encourage companies from turning to environmentally friendly solutions.
3. **Buy Organic and Local Produce.** Produce that are not treated with pesticides are the best to eat. Buying local produce not only supports your local farmers – it takes less energy for the food to travel from the farm to your table.
4. **Bring Your Own Bag.** Avoid using plastic bags and bring your own when shopping. Plastic is among the most toxic materials on our planet and they do not degrade.
5. **Recycle!** Cardboard, plastic, newspapers, paper materials, glass and electronic devices can be recycled for other uses. Bring them to certified recyclers

Source: www.theworldcounts.com/stories/How-to-Reduce-Our-Ecological-Footprint

Others are more ambitious. The David Suzuki Foundation, for example, appeals to individuals to switch to renewable energy providers, make energy efficiency modifications in the home, reduce meat consumption, avoid air and car travel, reconsider the purchase of luxury electronic goods, choose to live within walking or cycling distance of your workplace, etc. (David Suzuki Foundation 2014).

## Carbon Neutrality

Carbon neutrality is an idea we encountered in Chapter 7. When the Clean Development Mechanism was negotiated in the late 1990s as part of the Kyoto Protocol, the private sector saw an opportunity to create parallel voluntary offset markets. The CDM was designed to help wealthy states achieve their greenhouse gas emission targets by purchasing carbon credits from developing countries. Private schemes, by contrast, were created to allow individuals and businesses to voluntarily offset their activities and contribute to global climate change mitigation. This private offsetting market works by facilitating a transaction between a buyer (e.g., a concerned individual) and a seller (e.g., a project developer). The project developer promises to use this money in a way that will limit GHG emissions or remove existing GHG from the atmosphere. The seller must meet the condition of 'additionality'. As we saw in Chapter 8, additionality means that the project or greenhouse gas measures would not have been possible without the new finance (otherwise they might be just profiting from actions they would have been taken anyway) (Stevenson and Dryzek 2014: 109–10). Imagine that you have decided to attend a summer music festival but you're concerned about the environmental impact: you have to drive to get to the venue, the musicians are flying in with heavy equipment, and large electricity generators will be running to power the sound systems. Before, if you had reflected on the impact of all this you would have had the choice of either forfeiting the event or simply letting it weigh on your conscience. By the turn of the twenty-first century, the environmentally aware individual had a new choice: she could purchase carbon credits from a private company to ensure that her share of the events emissions were being 'offset' by planting trees or investing in a renewable energy project. No regulation would be in place to force her to make this choice; it would be based entirely on her own sense of responsibility for global environmental problems. There are now countless online schemes offering such services. Companies like 'Carbon Footprint$^{TM}$' and charities like the 'World Land Trust' allow individuals to calculate the emissions from flights, car use, and domestic energy use and then make an online payment to offset these. Individuals often have the freedom to choose which projects their money is invested in, such as improved woodstoves in Uganda, water purification in Kenya, avoided deforestation in Brazil, wind farms in the Philippines, and small-scale hydropower generation in Chile (Carbon Footprint no date).

While there is no governmental regulatory oversight of this industry, private standards schemes have been established to bring some structure and stability to the voluntary carbon offsetting market. Of course, offset providers are not forced to comply with any particular standards, but individuals and businesses concerned about the authenticity of their carbon credits can choose to purchase only from a compliant company. The most comprehensive scheme is the Verified Carbon Standard (VCS), whose rules assure buyers that their purchased credits are resulted in genuinely additional mitigation (Stevenson and Dryzek 2014: 110).

## Eco-labelling

It is widely understood that unsustainable consumption results from the mundane choices that millions of individuals make each day. The idea that our shopping habits can help to transform unsustainability underpins the 'eco-consumerist' movement that has developed since the late twentieth century. Böstrom and Klintman explain that 'Eco-consumerism is about leveraging the purchasing power of individual consumers to bring about a transformation toward sustainable consumption and a green economy. The basic idea is for citizens to induce market changes by "voting" for eco-friendly products with their shopping dollars' (2008: 133). Such 'voting' is brought about mainly through eco-labels. Scan the shelves of your local supermarket and you will find hundreds of products with different symbols and logos indicating that they are accredited with one of dozens of private labelling schemes. Coffee, cleaning products, seafood, fruit and vegetables, paper: all of these products are now offered in brands and product lines that promise to be 'environmentally friendly'.

The rationale of eco-labelling is that by selecting responsible varieties, shoppers can send a signal to producers that there is consumer demand, and thereby gradually shift production away from environmentally damaging products to environmentally friendly ones. Early labelling schemes were established for electrical appliances and equipment, and wood products. The 'Energy Star' programme began in the United States and has now spread worldwide to cover business and residential goods such as printers, refrigerators, washing machines, and lighting. An estimated 2 billion energy star labelled products have been purchased since this was launched in 1992.

As we saw in the previous chapter, eco-labelling emerged in the forest products market to address growing public concern over deforestation and biodiversity loss. In 1993, Friends of the Earth, Greenpeace, and the World Wildlife Fund joined forces to establish the 'Forest Stewardship Council' (FSC). Their initial priorities were twofold: first, to create a highly visible and recognisable logo for timber and wood-products (the 'tick tree' logo), and, second, to pressure the major retailers to commit to purchasing wood only from sustainably managed forests. In many ways, FSC has been a great success: in the UK, tens of thousands of products are certified by the FSC, from household furniture to printing paper; and both major retailers and high street stores have committed to stocking these goods (albeit not exclusively). Nevertheless, some scholars have questioned the effectiveness of eco-labelling in general, and forestry labels in particular. Dauvergne and Lister, for example, observe that despite the increase in forest certification in recent years, forest loss is continuing (2010: 132). Of particular concern is the fact that certification is not protecting the most valuable forests. Initiatives like the FSC were designed to protect ancient old-growth forests and prevent tropical deforestation. But by 2009 less than 1 per cent of tropical forests had been certified. Most certified products come from managed plantations rather than vulnerable forests, which continue to be cleared (2010: 139). Dauvergne and Lister conclude that 'forest certification is functioning more effectively as an industrial forest production standard than a forest protection standard' (2010: 140). Moreover, the dominance of large-scale commercial operations pushes out the participation of local forest communities, whose interests will need to be addressed if certification is to genuinely provide social and environmental value.

# The Limits of Individualising Responsibility

A number of criticisms have been directed at schemes like carbon offsetting, eco-labelling, and the individualisation of responsibility more generally. Here we will examine some of these criticisms before looking at counter-arguments that might justify a focus on individual habits and lifestyle changes.

## Over-stating Consumer Sovereignty

Sustainable consumption campaigns rest on an idea we saw in Chapter 4, the idea of 'consumer sovereignty'. This assumes that individuals are autonomous and independent: when they go to the supermarket or plan their shopping they have the freedom to choose from hundreds of products. Moreover, this idea assumes that the desires and preferences of individuals shape the range of products on sale in the first place. Consumer demand is assumed to compel businesses to produce certain types of products and scale back production of others. The voting analogy referred to above makes sense in this context: just as citizens have the democratic capacity to elect their political leaders, consumers have the capacity to determine the products that line supermarket shelves.

The idea of consumer sovereignty is also a value-laden one: it assumes that not only are consumers autonomous and independent, but that governments and businesses should respect this autonomy and independence. The implication, as Christer Sanne explains, is that 'consumers may be informed and educated but not coerced'. Restricting the choices available to consumers would be an act of coercion (Sanne 2002: 275). Critics argue that the idea of consumer sovereignty overlooks the extent to which consumer preferences are constrained by the massive power of marketing, and the impossibility of complete information. Economists call this lack of information 'bounded rationality' (Simon 1955). Under conditions of bounded rationality, people have uncertainties about the future and face costs when they try to acquire information about the present. Each of these factors impedes rational decision-making (Jackson 2005: 35). Tim Jackson explains:

> Not only do I simply not have the time to amass all the information necessary to make a thorough comparison between choices; some of that information is simply not available to me, because it concerns events that lie in the (uncertain) future ... Ordinary people in ordinary situations are simply not capable of processing all the cognitive information required for so-called 'rational' choices.

> (2005: 35–6)

These uncertainties are particularly pronounced in the area of environmental sustainability because a rational calculation of costs and benefits requires an understanding of agricultural, manufacturing, economic and social processes that might be unfolding at a great distance.

It might be argued that eco-labelling simplifies the rational decision-making processes and makes it easy for consumers to purchase sustainable products without collecting their own complete information. Surveys of consumers in eleven emerging and developing markets in 2013 showed that familiarity with the FSC logo was limited to between 9 per cent (in Japan) and 46 per cent (in the UK). Even in a relatively environmentally enlightened country like Germany, only 37 per cent of consumers were at least somewhat familiar with the FSC logo (Forest Stewardship Council 2015: 28). Given that supermarket shelves are displaying an increasing number of logos on products that generally cost more than their logo-free equivalents, there is a significant challenge in convincing consumers to make responsible choices.

## 'Greenwash'

Another limiting factor is the pervasive problem of 'greenwash', defined as 'the act of misleading consumers regarding the environmental practices of a company (firm-level greenwashing) or the environmental benefits of a product or service (product-level greenwashing)' (Delmas and Burbano 2011: 66). Futerra, a sustainability communications group, identify 'ten signs of greenwash' widely found in advertising (Box 9.2).

Even the well-recognised and trusted Energy Star scheme has not been immune to greenwash. LG Electronics was exposed for mislabelling many of its refrigerator models with the Energy Star logo based on erroneous energy usage calculations. Despite bearing the logo, the models did not meet the required standard of energy efficiency (Delmas and Burbano 2011: 66).

---

### Box 9.2: **Ten Signs of Greenwash**

1. **Fluffy language:** words of terms with no clear meaning, e.g. 'eco-friendly'
2. **Green products versus dirty company:** such as efficient light bulbs made in a factory which pollutes rivers
3. **Suggestive pictures:** green images that indicate an (un-justified) green impact, e.g. flowers blooming from exhaust pipes
4. **Irrelevant claims:** emphasising one tiny green attribute when everything else is un-green
5. **Best in class?** declaring you are slightly greener than the rest, even if the rest are pretty terrible
6. **Just not credible:** 'eco friendly' cigarettes anyone? 'Greening' a dangerous product doesn't make it safe
7. **Gobbledygook:** jargon and information that only a scientist could check or understand
8. **Imaginary friends:** a 'label' that looks like third party endorsement except it's made up
9. **No proof:** it could be right, but where's the evidence?
10. **Out-right lying:** Totally fabricated claims or data

Source: Futerra Sustainability Communications no date

---

It would be almost impossible for the average consumer to detect such fraud or errors. Australian writer Guy Pearse documented the prevalence of green-wash by watching thousands of TV commercials, examining thousands more online, billboard, newspaper, and magazine advertisements, and reading nearly 750 company annual reports and sustainability reports (Pearse 2012). Of the large companies presenting themselves as environmentally aware and responsible, the majority were guilty of some degree of misrepresentation.

Such misleading behaviour underscores the limits of so-called 'corporate social responsibility' (CSR). This is a framework that ultimately doesn't challenge corporate rationality: maximising shareholder profits remains the core imperative of corporations, but CSR encourages them to aim to 'do good' at the same time as 'doing well'. While many companies today 'talk the talk' of sustainability, very few are 'walking the walk'. If we listen to the rhetoric of corporations we would be led to believe that it's quite straightforward for companies to increase profits, reduce environmental impact, and respect human rights all at the same time. This is called the 'triple bottom line'. But as management scholar Bobby Banerjee points out, the triple bottom line concept is 'little more than an article of faith' rather than an empirically proven fact (Banerjee 2009: 85–6).

## Attitude–Behaviour Gap

Even if consumer confusion and deception can be overcome, a further limitation to relying on individual responsibility for addressing unsustainability is the attitude–behaviour gap. This refers to the observed discrepancy between stated preferences, values, and concerns and actual behaviour. Dauvergne and Lister lament that 'At the end of the day, even when well-educated and aware consumers say they prefer to buy environmentally friendly products, many do not walk the talk, purchasing traditional (and often cheaper) goods at the point of sale' (2010: 135). Non-environmental concerns like price (or upfront costs), convenience, habit, and style exert a powerful pressure on consumer choices. Consumer research is informed by the assumption that consumers act in ways consistent with their attitudes, and that environmental consumerism can be predicted on the basis of socio-demographic variables, and the geographic, cultural, and personality profiles of consumers. But it turns out that these factors do not neatly map on to either attitudes or behaviour (Gupta and Ogden 2006: 200).

## Depoliticising Unsustainability

The concerns above relate to the limits of people's capacity to change their consumption habits. However, some critics are more concerned about the implications of focusing on individual consumption habits in the first place. Michael Maniates rejects the idea that 'knotty issues of consumption, consumerism, power, and responsibility can be resolved neatly and cleanly through enlightened, uncoordinated consumer choice' (2002: 45). He calls this approach to environmental sustainability the 'individualisation of responsibility'. This approach distracts attention away from political power and institutionalised forms of distributing and consuming resources. It engages people as consumers rather than as citizens. It focuses on individual consumer actions rather than large-scale coordinated change.

Willis and Schor argue that it is naïve to assume that the aggregation of small individual actions can transform the world. It is an assumption that overlooks concentrations of power and sees 'consumer action like a tsunami that can roll over whatever is in its path' (2012: 165). Mulling over the choice between paper and plastic bags, or whether to trade in our old car for a new hybrid-engine model, or dedicating time to carefully sorting the recycling are all examples of individualising responsibility. The point is not that these actions themselves are bad, but rather that they dangerously narrow our 'environmental imagination' (Dowie 1996: 7). An expanded environmental imagination would focus on institutions; it would engage people 'as citizens in a participatory democracy first, working together to change broader policy and larger social institutions, and as consumers second' (Maniates 2002: 46–7). This would shift people's attention from mulling over the pros and cons of buying a Prius, to organising with their fellow citizens to mobilise support for investment in a reliable and affordable public transport system.

Like Maniates, Paul Hawken is concerned about the dangerous effects of 'simple' consumptions changes: 'The problem [is] … the illusion they foster that subtle course corrections can guide us to the good life that will include a "conserved nature" and cozy shopping malls' (quoted in Maniates 2002: 52). By depoliticising and commoditising environmentalism, we are left with the impression that solutions to environmental problems can be found within the capitalist system itself, an impression strongly rejected by many scholars. Feminist scholar Catriona Sandilands argues that the very term 'green consumerism' is an oxymoron: the adjective 'green' becomes meaningless if it loses 'reference to the systemic problems of *over*-production and *over*-consumption;

the point of a "green" politics should be to show how consumerism is, itself, part of the problem'. Far from doing so, 'green' has become a marketing tool and green consumption initiatives like eco-labelling simply reinforce over-production and over-consumption (Sandilands 1993: 45–7). By 'privatising' responsibility for environmental ills, Sandilands argues, we limit the scope for resisting capitalist economic growth and other social relations that have given rise to the environmental crisis (1993: 46).

## Defending Individual Responsibility

While the problems of bounded rationality, 'greenwash', and the attitude–behaviour gap are hard to sidestep, the depoliticisation critique explained above has been counter-critiqued by those who suggest that progressive transform-ation can come about through changes in individual consumption habits. This counter-critique takes aim at the lack of empirical evidence to support the depoliticisation thesis, and suggests that it ultimately rests on a number of erroneous binary oppositions bundled up in a citizen/consumer dichotomy.

Willis and Schor do not want to suggest that consumer-based actions alone are sufficient to overcome major environmental problems, but they do challenge the veracity of the depoliticisation thesis. If appeals to change individual consumption habits really did dissuade people from taking more ambitious and collective action then it might be problematic. But empirical studies from Europe, Canada, and the US contradict the assertion that engaging in consumption-based action 'crowds out' political forms of environmental activ-ism. On the contrary, conscious consumption is found to be significantly and positively related to collective political action (Willis and Schor 2012: 160). There is also evidence to suggest that individuals who engage in environmen-tally responsible consumption (by buying 'green' products) see this action as part of 'a larger repertoire of strategies and actions oriented toward social change' (Willis and Schor 2012: 161). Rather than 'crowding out' political activism, green consumption 'crowds in' such action: the two being integrated into people's lifestyles (Willis and Schor 2012: 180).

By pointing to counter-evidence, the depoliticisation thesis is presented as more of a theoretical argument than an empirically supported theory. Willis and Schor suggest that this theoretical argument has been constructed and maintained on the basis of a set of erroneous binary oppositions that are mapped onto a distinction between citizens and consumers. These oppositions are: collective/individual; politics/market; and public/private. Consumers are represented as individuals operating in the private sphere of the market, as opposed to citizens who are represented as a collective operating in the public sphere of the state. Willis and Schor argue that it is wrong to assume that consumer activity is 'individualized, autonomous, and undertaken in a solitary way', while political activity is collective, solidaristic, and capable of effecting change. The former should not be seen as inherently more effective than the latter. Those warning of depoliticisation and the individualisation of responsibility draw close connections between the *sites* or places of action and the *practices* of action, and Willis and Schor argue that these are actually falsely conflated. People might normally carry out such political actions as voting in the context of the state, and carry out consumption actions like buying in the context of the market. But it doesn't make sense to assume that political actions can only be carried out in the context of the state. People can act in collective, political ways in the market as well as in the state. Indeed, much social transformation comes about when people start to treat the home, workplace or market as sites of political action (Willis and Schor 2012: 164).

Lucy Middlemiss has proposed a middleground position that allows us to harness the transformative potential of political consumption without losing site of the structural factors that can constrain individual action. This allows us to avoid depoliticising unsustainable consumption while recognising that individuals as consumers can contribute to change. In developing this position, Middlemiss constructs a conceptual framework called the 'contextualised ecological footprint' (Middlemiss 2010: 159). This suggests that individuals do have responsibilities to act in sustainable ways, but recognises that these responsibilities are different in different contexts. The 'boundaries of responsibility for practice', Middlemiss argues, are defined by the capacity of a specific individual to act differently, and this capacity is partly a product of the society in which she lives (2010: 159). What factors do you think would define someone's capacity to take on responsibility for environmentally sustainable behaviour? Middlemiss argues that capacity for responsibility is affected by cultural, organisational, and infrastructural factors. Culturally, an individual is more likely to take responsibility for sustainability if this resonates with their existing values and worldview: in some cultures this is more likely than in others. In which cultures do you think environmental values are more and less likely to resonate? Organisational factors concern the institutions and practices that the individual engages with in their day-to-day life: if they are regularly in contact with community organisations and a workplace that promotes sustainability, they have a greater capacity to take on their own responsibility. Infrastructural factors include the services and products made available to the individual but over which they have no direct control (such as mass transit systems or local food markets) (Middlemiss 2010: 162). Thinking about your own town or city, can you see how some citizens have a greater capacity than others to engage in environmentally responsible behaviour because of the way infrastructure is distributed?

## Conclusion

When government action is slow and inadequate, and when multilateral processes prove resistant to tackling tricky issues like over-consumption, it is unsurprising that concerned citizens and the private sector appeal to individuals to 'do their bit' to bring about change. But the focus on individual action has many limitations.

'Voting' at the supermarket check-out reflects an act of faith, a hope that others will also choose the products with the responsible labels and slowly but surely send a message to companies that consumers prefer environmentally sustainably produced goods. But we must acknowledge that this 'vote' is not universal: those with comfortable incomes and some awareness of social and environmental issues are more likely to live in towns and suburbs with people like them, and are more likely to have easy access to responsibly produced goods that they can afford. This is also an issue of justice. Food justice activists have been pointing out for some time that poorer people tend to live in 'food deserts' without farmers' markets and health food stores, or even grocery stores. Instead, poor neighbourhoods have a higher concentration of fast food shops and corner stores selling low-nutritious processed foods. We will examine questions of food, environment and justice in the next chapter. But for now this should serve as a reminder that individual choices are shaped by social and economic forces beyond individuals' direct control. Another limitation of the individual focus is 'greenwashing'. Environmentally aware middle-class shoppers may have a greater capacity to pursue sustainable consumption, but they are not immune to misinformation.

Does this mean that concerned individuals should abandon the idea of modifying their consumption? No. But it does mean that we must remain aware that environmental problems are *political* issues that require collective responses. Fair and effective change won't come from small individual changes. Making 'five simple changes' may make some people feel better, but concerned citizens should make this part of a larger collective project with political aims. Political action takes different forms: joining NGOs, starting campaign groups, joining political parties, voting at local and national elections, meeting with political representatives. In the next chapter we will see how activists have campaigned to ban the dumping of the toxic wastes in developing countries. This response is political because it doesn't simply appeal to consumers to buy fewer goods with toxic elements, but instead tries to change laws and regulations. Then in Chapter 11 we will see how some social movements are collectively organising in response to the globalisation of unsustainable agriculture by building alternative systems.

## Discussion Questions

1. How useful is the distinction between luxury and subsistence consumption? How can this distinction contribute to fair and effective policies on sustainable consumption?
2. To what extent do you think you, your friends, and wider community are aware of the environmental impacts of electronic goods and fashion?
3. What would constitute an effective international policy on sustainable consumption? Is such a policy likely to emerge from an intergovernmental institution like the UN?
4. How significant is the problem of 'greenwash' and how could this be overcome?
5. What are the prospects and limitations of individualising responsibility for unsustainable consumption?

# 10 Problem Displacement
## Hazardous Substances

key points

- Rachel Carson first drew attention to the health and environmental risks of chemicals in the 1960s. Her work had a profound impact on public awareness and regulation in the United States.
- Our reliance on chemicals has grown since the mid-twentieth century – Chemicals a nd metals are central to modern production and industrial development. Most of the items we use have chemical elements that can contribute to toxic waste when disposed.
- The global governance of chemicals is fragmented, with overlaps, gaps, and loopholes that allow large volumes of toxic wastes to be shipped around the world. Poor communities in developing countries are particularly vulnerable to the health and environmental risks of these shipments.
- Activists frame the waste trade as 'environmental injustice'. Green political theorists offer several concepts that help us to understand the nature and consequences of waste trade as injustice. We look at the concepts of displacement, distancing, and remoteness.
- Some people disagree that waste trade reflects environmental injustice. They argue that the waste trade is mostly legal and legitimate, and it supports development and livelihoods in developing countries.

# Introduction

In 1962, Rachel Carson, an American biologist, published *Silent Spring*. This book came to have a profound impact on the American environmentalist movement and environmental regulation. Carson was the first to alert us to the human and environmental damage caused by using chemical pesticides in agriculture. Her opening pages set out a 'fable for tomorrow' in which once fertile farms became barren, and healthy communities fell ill to unknown diseases. She described 'a spring without voices', where silence replaced birdsong. Signs of these maladies were already evident in many American towns. The reason, she argued, was the excessive misuse of chemical pesticides. Less than two years after the book was released, Carson died of breast cancer. The connections between chemical exposure, disease, and pollution are now more widely understood. But at the time Rachel Carson inspired acclaim and disdain in equal measure. The chemical industry went to great lengths to discredit the scientist and her findings. She was depicted as 'hysterical', a 'bird and bunny lover', and a 'spinster' without a PhD (Lear 2002: xvii). Nevertheless, *Silent Spring* remained on *The New York Times* bestseller list for several years. Carson wrote for a public audience, describing complex processes in simple, elegant prose that ordinary citizens understood. This helped galvanise public concern and demands for accountability. In the years following her death, the US Congress banned the domestic production of DDT (dichlorodiphenyltrichloroethane), a potent chemical marketed widely as a pesticide after World War Two. However, exports of the chemical were not banned. Understanding this inconsistency between domestic environmental concerns and international trade practices is one of the core tasks of this chapter.

In earlier chapters we have examined a number of ways in which states, businesses, and citizens try to respond to environmental problems. The kind of response we examine in this chapter might be called 'non-action', NIMBY (Not In My Back Yard), or problem exporting. Each of these terms captures a different element of what we will call 'problem displacement'. Problem displacement allows privileged groups (often, but not exclusively, rich industrialised countries) to enjoy the material benefits of modernity while casting the negative consequences onto less privileged groups (often, but not exclusively, poverty-stricken countries).

In this chapter we will first review the chemicals and metals that are central to modern production and industrial development. We will determine their impacts on the environment and human health, and the ways in which they contribute to hazardous wastes. We will then examine the fragmented ways in which states have sought to control the production, use, and export of hazardous substances. We will see a range of multilateral agreements and hybrid initiatives that, on the whole, have not had the desired effect of protecting human health and the environment. Environmental activists have done the most to raise awareness of the problems associated with hazardous waste. We will analyse their efforts to frame the problems as 'environmental injustice'. Activists criticise governments and international agreements for failing to confront the insidious practice of 'dumping' waste on the poor and vulnerable. We will examine how the notion of dumping can be more deeply understood through concepts including displacement, distancing, and remoteness. Activists' framing of 'waste dumping' has been popularly and politically powerful. The media occasionally features stories of poor communities surrounded by discarded computers, or illegally dumped barrels of toxic residue. But the narrative of the North dumping on the South is challenged by a small but increasingly vocal group of geographers and journalists. In the final section of the chapter we will examine the evidence underpinning their argument that the waste trade is mostly a legal and legitimate form of international trade that supports development and livelihoods in the global South.

## Toxic Elements

The chemical industry has grown dramatically in recent decades. Industry analysts estimate that every person in the world uses an average of $500 worth of chemicals each year. If you live in an industrialised country, your annual estimate is actually $1,200 per person (CIEC 2016). In total, the global industry output is over $4 trillion (UNEP 2013a: xv). Modern society is dependent on thousands of elements that have the potential to become toxic. Almost all modern economic processes and products entail the use of chemicals.

It is difficult to imagine someone getting through the day without relying on many chemical- and metal-based products, and ultimately generating hazardous waste. Let's call our imaginary someone, David. David is woken in the morning by his smartphone's alarm (containing praseodymium and terbium); he lathers up with soap in the shower (perhaps containing triclosan); he puts on his work clothes, perhaps a dry-cleaned suit (using perchloroethylene); he eats a bowl of cereal (perhaps grown with cadmium-based fertilisers); he washes his dishes in detergent (probably containing formaldehyde); he drives a car to work (containing a lead- or cadmium-based battery); he begins work on his laptop (probably containing brominated flame retardants). By midday David has already depended on many chemicals just while carrying out routine activities.

Should we describe David's life as hazardous because he relies on so many chemicals? One day on his way to work, David hears a radio programme on toxicology. He might decide to write up a list of all the toxic elements he wants to avoid. Hopefully he has a lot of time on his hands, because there are many factors to consider. What level of risk is he prepared to take? Is he going to value other people's lives in the same way as he values his own? What about workers and people living in faraway places? What about future generations? Is all the information he needs publicly accessible, or does he need to embark on a chemistry degree? Determining which elements are toxic is difficult because their toxicity can change throughout their life cycle. We see in Chapter 9 that 'greenwashing' or misinformation makes it hard for people to make informed decisions. Here we can see that hidden and complex information makes this even harder.

The chemical life cycle begins when raw materials like coal, gas, and biomass are extracted from the earth. Organic and inorganic chemicals are then derived from these materials. The distinction comes down to carbon: organic chemicals contain carbon compounds (and are sometimes called petrochemicals); inorganic chemicals do not. Can you bring to mind the names of any of these chemicals? Some, like methanol and ammonia, will be familiar; others, like ethylene and toluene, probably less so. Just a dozen organic and inorganic chemicals provide the 'building blocks' of the many thousands of chemical products used by industry and in the home (Massey and Jacobs 2013: 17–22).[1] These form the basis of products like paints, insulation, PVC (polyvinyl chloride) window frames, fibres, cosmetics, dyes, pesticides, building products, fertilisers, etc. These products generally contain a mixture of chemical compounds that may be toxic, and elements that on their own are considered toxic. Once they reach the end of their life, all of these products eventually become waste. *Hazardous* waste is waste that is corrosive, explosive, or contains toxic elements or compounds.

Many countries have management systems in place to minimise the use of toxic elements and to safely handle hazardous waste. But effective regulation is challenging even for developed countries with a high capacity for testing chemicals. This is because there are thousands of chemicals. Effective regulation requires a high level of understanding of these chemicals and the effects of their interactions with other chemicals. But we are still a long way from having such a complete understanding. Pooling knowledge and efforts at the international level is not just desirable; it is essential for improving the effectiveness of chemical regulation. As we'll see in the next section, a set of multilateral agreements is in place to facilitate international cooperation on the control of chemicals and hazardous wastes. But before we take a closer look at these agreements and their impacts, it is important to have a clear understanding of the effects that toxic elements can have on our bodies and the natural environment. The WHO's Programme on Chemical Safety focuses on 'Ten chemicals of major public health concern'. Let's take a look at four of these to understand what is at stake.

## Mercury

Stocks of mercury have been present in the earth's crust since well before the time of humans. However, it is only with increased extractive and industrial processes since the 1800s that significant levels of this element have been released into the atmosphere. Once in the atmosphere, traces of mercury find their way into soils, freshwater, oceans, and ultimately into the food chain. Estimates of the amount of mercury emitted into the atmosphere each year range from about 5,000 to 8,000 tonnes. Human activity accounts for about 30 per cent of these emissions. Mercury is present in fossil fuels and raw materials. When these are extracted, burned, and transformed into metals and cement, the mercury is emitted into the atmosphere. These are the 'anthropogenic sources' of mercury emissions associated with industry. But mining also takes place on a small scale. The international community is increasingly concerned about 'artisanal and small-scale gold mining' because of its significant human and environmental impact. Small-scale gold miners use mercury intentionally to extract gold from rocks and soils. Another key anthropogenic source of mercury emissions is industrial production involving chlorine (e.g., for synthetic rubber, solar cells, vinyl plastics like floor coverings and pipes, polymers, and many others). Finally, many consumer goods contain mercury, and this seeps into the earth when these products are discarded.

Mercury is being phased out of many products, but progress is slow, especially in developing countries. Depending on where you are reading this book, you may be surrounded by products containing mercury: batteries, paints, energy-saving lamps, cosmetics, electronic devices, etc. Apart from anthropogenic sources of mercury emissions, natural processes like volcano eruptions and geothermal activity emit mercury. By far the greatest source of today's mercury emissions is what is called 're-emission'. When mercury is first emitted through human or natural activity it settles into water, soils, and vegetation. Disruptions like forest fires can re-emit this mercury, or move it from soil to the sea. Depending on the direction of movement, humans may be exposed (UNEP 2013b: 4–8). In fact, the main way in which people are exposed to mercury is through eating fish. In water bodies and beds (like the sediment at the bottom of a river), mercury converts to a more poisonous form called methylmercury, which then seeps into aquatic food systems. Fish become increasingly toxic, and the effects ripple through ecosystems as predators (like eagles, otters, seals, and whales) absorb mercury into their body tissue (UNEP 2013b: 26–7). Exposure to mercury poses considerable risks to human health. The World Health Organization considers this one of the top ten chemicals of public health concern (WHO 2016a). Infants and unborn babies are most vulnerable to mercury poisoning. They may experience stunted neurological, nerve, and cognitive development, or impaired movement, spatial, and language skills. The most infamous public health disaster involving mercury poisoning occurred in Minamata, Japan in the mid-twentieth century. Over several decades, high levels of methylmercury were spilled into the Minamata Bay by a local acetic acid factory. Tens of thousands of people were affected by brain damage, slurred speech, paralysis, and delirium. This became known as Minamata disease (WHO 2016a).

## Lead

Lead is a naturally occurring substance but human activities have increased environmental concentrations of lead to levels that are harmful to humans and the environment. Today lead is typically found in ore, and is extracted at the same time as other metals such as zinc, silver, and copper. Since Roman times lead has been used to make pipes, paints, and glazes. Women even painted their faces with white lead until at least the early twentieth century (and perhaps later in some countries). In the process of beautifying themselves, they were slowly poisoning themselves, as well as their suckling infants (Warren 2001: 20–1).

Probably the most disastrous innovation was the addition of tetraethyl lead to fuel (gasoline) in the twentieth century – what *Time* magazine names one of the '50 Worst Inventions' ever (Gentilviso 2010). The negative impact of lead exposure on human health was suspected as early as the 1920s. Workers developing leaded fuel in the United States presented with symptoms we now know to be lead poisoning. But in the pursuit of profit, gas companies turned a blind eye. By the 1960s, all cars ran on leaded petrol and it wasn't until the mid-1980s that it was banned and fully phased out in the US, and later in most of Europe (Gentilviso 2010; Emsley 2011: 287). Industry actors fought against this phasing out; they cast doubt over scientific studies in much the same way that climate change denialists have done (Dauvergne 2010: 79–88). It remains in use (albeit in smaller quantities) in some other parts of the world.

Demand for lead hasn't diminished or disappeared; instead it has simply changed. Industry bodies claim that global demand for lead doubled between the early 1990s and 2012 (International Lead Association 2012). Much of this demand comes from China and other fast-growing economies. It is no longer used in fuel, cosmetics, or insecticides, but it still has various uses in the construction industry and miscellaneous production (e.g., pigments, television and computer screens, weights for lifting, ammunition, protective clothing). Lead batteries account for more than 80 per cent of all lead used (mostly for cars, boats, submarines, and other vehicles) (Emsley 2011: 285–6).

The earth naturally emits small amounts of lead through volcanic eruptions and rock erosion. But due to human activity, concentrations of lead in soil and water are significantly higher than natural levels. Once lead is emitted into the air it may travel long distances before settling into soil, and then seeping down into groundwater. These emissions occur during the mining, smelting, and refining stages (i.e., before the lead is actually used), as well as in the production, use, recycling, and disposal of products that contain lead.[2] All of these processes can inflict considerable damage on human health long after the element was initially released into the air. People are exposed to lead through:

- Industrial processes – e.g., producing batteries and heavy lead glass, applying and removing leaded paints, working on construction and demolition.
- Food – e.g., eating foods that have been grown in contaminated soils (especially around mines and smelters), consuming foods and beverages from lead-soldered cans.
- Water – e.g., drinking water that has passed through lead pipes or fittings;
- Dust in the home – e.g., from inhaling dust from workers' clothes; playing with toys containing lead; or touching leaded paint that is peeling off the walls. (WHO 2010a)

This exposure can affect people's neurological, haematological, gastrointestinal, cardiovascular, and renal systems. Extended periods of exposure can lead to chronic health problems like anaemia, headaches, lethargy, convulsions, and paralysis. Children are most at risk because they absorb up to five times as much lead as adults, and this can significantly affect their brain development. Pregnant women exposed to lead are also more susceptible to miscarriage and birth complications (WHO 2010a).

## Cadmium

Cadmium is produced in two ways. Primarily, it is extracted from the earth as a by-product of zinc mining. About 14,000 tonnes are extracted globally each year, and further amounts are recovered from used batteries (i.e., nickel-cadmium batteries) and other scrap materials (U.S. Geological Survey 2016). Like mercury and lead, cadmium is naturally emitted into the atmosphere through volcanic eruptions and rock erosion. But at least half of all emissions are anthropogenic (from mining, smelting, burning of fossil fuels, leaking batteries in landfill, burning of waste, and use in fertilisers) (European Chemical Agency 2014: 10). Cadmium was originally used in the nineteenth century as a pigment for producing brilliant yellows, oranges, and reds, and indeed made a splash in the art world (perhaps you can bring to mind the strong colours in Matisse's *The Red Studio* or Monet's *Autumn effect, Argenteuil*). Today, it is still sometimes used as pigment, but more typically used in the industrial production of rechargeable batteries, alloys (mixed metals), coating, and in plastics. Solar cells are mostly manufactured from silicone but a cadmium-based product offers a thinner alternative for solar power (USGS 2016). If these become commercially viable in the future, consumption of cadmium will increase. However, future demand may dampen as the risks associated with cadmium become better understood.

In 2014, the European Chemical Agency added cadmium fluoride and cadmium sulphate to its candidate list of 'Substances of Very High Concern'. This chemical poses a persistent health risk because concentrations of cadmium are held in the environment for long periods of time. The risk is particularly high near mines and smelters because there are high concentrations of cadmium in the soil, and this can leak into the food chain (ECHA 2014: 10–11). But because cadmium emissions can travel long distances in the air, concentrations may be high even in unexpected places. Plant-based foods like rice, wheat, potatoes, and green leafy vegetables take up high levels of cadmium from the soil and these toxins are then passed on to people who eat these crops. Workers in mining, smelting, construction, recycling, landfill, and waste incineration are among the most vulnerable to cadmium exposure. Some 300,000 workers are exposed to cadmium in the United States alone (Occupational Safety and Health Administration no date).

When humans ingest cadmium they risk developing multiple health problems, particularly affecting their kidneys. Long periods of exposure (even at low levels) may only be revealed in renal damage after ten years, but some cases of immediate kidney damage occur after high-level exposure. Findings are still inconclusive on the 'safe level' of cadmium exposure for avoiding kidney disease. Other studies tentatively connect cadmium exposure to lung disease and emphysema, hypertension, peripheral artery disease, and osteoporosis (Centre for Disease Control and Prevention 2011). Humans aren't the only ones at risk of cadmium exposure. When even low levels of the chemical are absorbed into the soil, soil organisms like earthworms can suffer poisoning and die. This has knock-on effects for ecosystems and soil quality (in turn affecting food production). Animals can also have high levels of cadmium in their bodies as a result of consuming toxic food and water, leading to liver, nerve, and brain damage (Lenntech 2016).

The European Chemical Agency acknowledges that action has been slow in response to concerns about cadmium: 'Already 25 years ago it was acknow-ledged within the EU that cadmium exposure constitutes a problem for human health and the environment' (ECHA 2014: 5). It recommends accelerated action to limit the use of cadmium and to invest in research to find alternatives where they don't already exist (ECHA 2014).

## Dioxins and Dioxin-like Substances

The term 'dioxins and dioxin-like substances' is used as an easy way to refer to three highly unmemorable names: polychlorinated dibenzodioxins (PCDDs), polychlorinated dibenzofurans (PCDFs), and polychlorinated biphenyls (PCBs).[3] PCDDs and PCDFs are naturally emitted into the atmosphere when volcanoes erupt and forests burn. More often, however, they are released as by-products in the manufacture of chlorinated herbicides and pesticides, when paper pulp is bleached with chlorine, when wood, coal, or oil is burned, when waste is inciner-ated (including when people burn rubbish in their backyards), and during the smelting processes described earlier. It is important to understand that these types of dioxins serve no useful function: they are not intentionally produced for any purpose. Instead, they are emitted as a by-product of other activities. This means that there is no dioxin industry with an interest in protecting their production, but efforts to control their emission may indeed be costly, so industry groups have at times criticised studies and proposed regulation (Cappiello 2012).

Unlike their close relatives just described, PCBs have no natural source; they are a human-made substance only (WHO 2010b: 1; European Commission 2015). Originally this chemical was intentionally used in a variety of industrial processes, including as dielectric fluids (i.e., insulators) in electrical products, and in industrial oils and lubricants. But its production has been banned in most countries since the mid-2000s. Nevertheless, PCBs are still released into the atmosphere when products in which they are present are discarded as waste (WHO 2010b: 1).

Dioxins and dioxin-like substances are called 'persistent organic pollutants' because they linger in the atmosphere and human body for long periods of time, and can travel vast distances (including across national borders). Human exposure to dioxins mostly occurs by eating contaminated food. Backyard burning is particularly dangerous because most people don't take measures to protect against inhalation or to protect the soil from becoming toxic (EPA 2016c). Dioxins stick to plants, and once consumed by animals and fish they persist in fat tissue. This is then passed on to humans (especially those with diets high in animal fats and full-fat dairy products), and further passed on to breast-fed babies. The WHO identifies three main risks to human health posed by dioxin exposure. Short-term exposure can cause persistent skin irritations resembling extreme acne (called 'chloracne'). Longer-term exposure can have negative effects on hormones and reproduction, and affect development of the brain and functioning of the immune system. Finally, dioxin exposure is suspected to cause cancer (and has shown to do so in studies on animals) (WHO 2010b: 3).

# Global Governance of Chemicals and Hazardous Waste

Effectively governing the use of toxic elements is a significant international challenge. This challenge arises because our knowledge of chemicals and their interactions is incomplete; because chemicals are used extensively; and because chemicals are transported around the world, including into countries with limited capacity to manage them safely. As we will see in the next section, civil

Box 10.1: **Global Chemical Agreements**

| MEA | SIGNED | INTO FORCE | PARTIES[1] |
|---|---|---|---|
| Basel Convention | 1989 | 1992 | 183 |
| Rotterdam Convention | 1998 | 2004 | 155 |
| Stockholm Convention | 2001 | 2004 | 180 |
| Minamata Convention | 2013 | 90 days after 50th ratification | 28 |

1. As of 24 June 2016. Note that parties are those countries that have *ratified* the agreement (see Chapter 6). A country can become a party to a convention in one of two ways: (1) by *ratification* – by which the country first signs the agreement (becoming a signatory), and then later ratifies the agreement; or (2) by *accession*, by which the country skips the signature stage and accede to the agreement at a later stage.

society was fundamental in bringing the production and trade of hazardous substances to the attention of governments. Largely as a result of their campaigning, multilateral agreements have proliferated since the 1980s. Like climate change, this area of governance is highly fragmented, but an institutional core is provided by four multilateral environmental agreements (Box 10.1).

Let's look at the key details of each agreement.

1. *Basel Convention on the Control of Transboundary Movements of Hazardous Wastes and their Disposal*: The **Basel Convention** aims to control shipments of hazardous waste between countries. Its overall objective is 'to protect human health and the environment against the adverse effects of hazardous wastes' (Basel Convention 2011). It covers many hazardous substances including used oil, biomedical and pharmaceutical waste, used lead acid batteries, pesticides, polychlorinated biphenyls (PCBs), and waste from paint and dye production. The convention makes several demands on parties (i.e., states). They are only allowed to ship wastes to other parties; and consent must be obtained from the receiving country before a shipment is sent. Shipments of waste that do not comply with these rules are deemed illegal. In addition, parties are expected to pass domestic laws to prevent illegal shipments of hazardous waste, and to prosecute those who break these laws.

Overall, parties should make an effort to reduce the amount of hazardous waste that leaves their borders. An amendment to the convention was agreed in 1995, which would prohibit all exports in hazardous substances from the global North to the global South. This amendment, known as the **Basel Ban,** was strongly pushed by civil society groups and some developing countries as essential for promoting environmental justice. But this amendment will not come into force until it has been ratified by three-quarters of the Basel parties. After more than two decades, we are still a long way off this required number. Below we will examine the environmental justice demands and critiques that relate to this agreement.

2. *Rotterdam Convention on the Prior Informed Consent Procedure for Certain Hazardous Chemicals and Pesticides in International Trade*: The **Rotterdam Convention** builds on the rules of the Basel Convention by adding additional responsibilities to share knowledge and build capacity for making informed decisions about accepting hazardous waste imports. Like Basel, the Rotterdam Convention has the ultimate aim of protecting human health and the environment from potential harm. A central procedure of this agreement is **Prior Informed Consent** (PIC). This had previously been used voluntarily by some international organisations but is a legal requirement under the Rotterdam Convention. This requires chemical *importing* parties to make known their position on all named hazardous chemicals (see Table 10.1). Based on knowledge made available about each chemical's toxicity, incidents and adverse effects, hazardous qualities, and available substitutes, parties have the option to consent to import of a chemical; not consent to import; or consent to import only under certain conditions (Article 10). The PIC procedure requires chemical *exporting* countries to assist importing parties to obtain all the information they require to make a decision about importing certain chemicals, and to contribute to building importing parties' capacity to manage chemicals safely (Article 11). It is illegal for an exporting party to contravene the decision taken by an importing Party (Rotterdam Convention 1998/2013).

3. *Stockholm Convention on Persistent Organic Pollutants*: The **Stockholm Convention** shares the aim of protecting human health and the environment from hazardous chemicals. This agreement focuses on a particular type of chemical: that which remains in the environment for prolonged periods of time, can travel over a large distance, and accumulates in human and animal bodies. The potential for 'persistent organic pollutants' (or POPs) to cross national borders requires governments to cooperate in reducing or

Table 10.1: **Chemicals and Chemical Compounds Controlled by the Main Multilateral Agreements**

| | BASEL | ROTTERDAM | STOCKHOLM | MINAMATA |
|---|---|---|---|---|
| Metal carbonyls | ✓ | | | |
| Beryllium | ✓ | | | |
| Hexavalent chromium | ✓ | | | |
| Copper | ✓ | | | |
| Zinc | ✓ | | | |
| Arsenic | ✓ | | | |
| Selenium | ✓ | | | |
| Cadmium | ✓ | | | |
| Antimony | ✓ | | | |
| Tellurium | ✓ | | | |
| Mercury | ✓ | ✓ | | ✓ |
| Thallium | ✓ | | | |
| Lead | ✓ | ✓ | | |
| Inorganic fluorine compounds | ✓ | | | |
| Inorganic cyanides | ✓ | | | |
| Acidic solutions or solids | ✓ | | | |
| Basic solutions or solids | ✓ | | | |
| Asbestos | ✓ | ✓ | | |
| Organic phosphorus | ✓ | | | |
| Organic cyanides | ✓ | | | |
| Phenols | ✓ | | | |
| Ethers | ✓ | | | |
| Halogenated organic solvents | ✓ | | | |

Table 10.1 (*cont.*)

| | BASEL | ROTTERDAM | STOCKHOLM | MINAMATA |
|---|---|---|---|---|
| Organic solvents | ✓ | | | |
| Polychlorinated dibenzodioxins | ✓ | | | |
| Polychlorinated dibenzofurans | ✓ | | | |
| Polychlorinated biphenyls | ✓ | ✓ | ✓ | |
| Polybrominated biphenyls | ✓ | ✓ | | |
| Polychlorinated terphenyls | ✓ | ✓ | | |
| Polychlorinated naphthalenes | | | ✓ | |
| Organohalogen | ✓ | | | |
| 2,4,5-Trichlorophenoxyacetic acid | | ✓ | | |
| Alachlor | | ✓ | | |
| Aldicarb | | ✓ | | |
| Aldrin | | ✓ | ✓ | |
| Azinphos-methyl | | ✓ | | |
| Binapacryl | | ✓ | | |
| Captafol | | ✓ | | |
| Chlordane | | ✓ | ✓ | |
| Chlordimeform | | ✓ | | |
| Chlorobenzilate | | ✓ | | |
| DDT | | ✓ | ✓ | |
| Dieldrin | | ✓ | ✓ | |
| Dinitro-ortho-cresol | | ✓ | | |
| Dinoseb | | ✓ | | |
| 1,2-dibromoethane | | ✓ | ✓ | |
| Endosulfan | | ✓ | | |
| Ethylene dichloride | | ✓ | | |

Table 10.1 (*cont.*)

|  | BASEL | ROTTERDAM | STOCKHOLM | MINAMATA |
|---|---|---|---|---|
| Ethylene oxide |  | ✓ |  |  |
| Fluoroacetamide |  | ✓ |  |  |
| HCH (mixed isomers) |  | ✓ |  |  |
| Heptaclor |  | ✓ | ✓ |  |
| Hexachlorobenzene |  | ✓ | ✓ |  |
| Lindane |  | ✓ | ✓ |  |
| Monocrotophos |  | ✓ |  |  |
| Parathion |  | ✓ |  |  |
| Pentachlorophenol |  | ✓ | ✓ |  |
| Toxaphene |  | ✓ | ✓ |  |
| Tributyltin |  | ✓ |  |  |
| Benomyl |  | ✓ |  |  |
| Carbofuran |  | ✓ |  |  |
| Methamidophos |  | ✓ |  |  |
| Phosphamidon |  | ✓ |  |  |
| Methyl-parathion |  | ✓ |  |  |
| Octabromodiphenyl ether |  | ✓ |  |  |
| Pentabromodiphenyl ether |  | ✓ | ✓ |  |
| Perfluorooctanes |  | ✓ | ✓ |  |
| Tris (2,3-dibromopropyl) phosphate |  | ✓ |  |  |
| Alpha & beta hexachlorocyclohexane |  |  | ✓ |  |
| Chlordecone |  |  | ✓ |  |
| Hexabromobiphenyl |  |  | ✓ |  |

Table 10.1 (*cont.*)

|  | BASEL | ROTTERDAM | STOCKHOLM | MINAMATA |
|---|---|---|---|---|
| Hexabromodiphenyl |  |  | ✓ |  |
| Mirex |  |  | ✓ |  |
| Pentachlorobenzene |  |  | ✓ |  |
| Tetrabromodiphenyl ether |  |  | ✓ |  |
| Heptabromodiphenyl ether |  |  | ✓ |  |
| Hexabromocyclododecane |  |  | ✓ |  |
| Hexachlorobutadiene |  |  | ✓ |  |

eliminating their emission into the atmosphere. The Stockholm Convention initially focused on twelve harmful substances (dubbed 'the dirty dozen' by civil society groups). But over several rounds of negotiations governments have slowly doubled the number of chemicals and compounds that apply to the convention. The agreement creates different rules for different categories (Annex A and Annex B chemicals) (Stockholm Convention 2001/2009). States pledge to pass domestic laws to *prohibit* production, use and trade of the most harmful chemicals (Annex A), and *restrict* production and use of other listed chemicals (Annex B). Exceptions are made for certain acceptable purposes (e.g., disease control and fire fighting equipment) and to permit the import of POPs if the purpose is to dispose of them in an environmentally sound way. Recognising that some chemicals are emitted unintentionally, Article 5 of the Convention softens the expectations for regulating these chemicals (Annex 3 chemicals). For these chemicals, states are required to monitor and evaluate emissions, and promote development of substitute substances. Rules are also established to promote awareness, and sharing of public information on the health and environmental hazards of POPs.

4. *Minamata Convention on Mercury*: The most recent multilateral agreement to protect human health and the environment from hazardous substances is the mercury convention signed in the Japanese city of Minamata. Agreements are usually named after the locations in which they are signed. This one, however, had a different symbolic significance. In the mid-twentieth century, residents of fishing villages along Minamata Bay were exposed to hazardous mercury

waste from a chemicals plant. This lasted for well over ten years. The chemical company, Chisso, used mercury compounds in chemical production and discharged wastewater into the Minamata Bay. Mercury then accumulated in the bodies of local people who ate fish from the bay. The effects of this exposure were first observed and attributed to the chemical waste in 1956. It was later referred to as 'Minamata disease' (and characterised by many of the mercury effects we saw earlier: pp. 228–9). Chisso was forced to change its practices in 1968. Tens of thousands of Japanese people are thought to be victims of Minamata disease. This was the first large-scale incident of mercury poisoning and it served to draw widespread attention to the hazards of mercury exposure (International POPs Elimination Network 2014: 24–6). The **Minamata Convention** requires parties to prohibit new mercury mining; phase out existing mercury mining and manufacturing of many mercury-containing products; and dispose of existing stocks of the chemical in safe ways. Mercury exports are only permitted with the consent of importing countries, and only for special purposes and safe storage and disposal (Minamata Convention 2013).

## Fragmented Global Chemical Governance: Overlaps and Gaps

There are overlaps in the aims, coverage, and oversight of these four multilateral agreements. UNEP acts as the Secretariat of the Basel, Rotterdam, and Stockholm Conventions, and of the Minamata Convention on an interim basis. But there are also gaps in this chemicals regime: many chemicals are not addressed; there is no process or authority for addressing illegal chemicals trafficking; and no concerted effort to promote substitutes and safer chemicals in products (Geiser 2015: 76–7). In recognition of the governance gaps and overlaps, in 2006 states agreed on a Strategic Approach to International Chemicals Management (SAICM). This is designed to promote synergies in efforts to regulate and phase out harmful chemicals (Geiser and Edwards 2013: 183). Its overall objective is named as achieving 'the sound management of chemicals throughout their life-cycle so that, by 2020, chemicals are used and produced in ways that lead to the minimization of significant adverse effects on human health and the environment' (UNEP 2006: 14). Chemicals management expert Ken Geiser describes the Strategic Approach as 'a nonbinding strategy rather than a regulatory treaty' (Geiser 2015: 78). It does, however, provide a range of additional initiatives that states are expected to cooperate with, including on heavy metals, nanotechnology, and e-waste.

Part of the challenge of promoting synergies within the governance of hazardous substances is that the four multilateral agreements outlined above are not the only relevant institutions and mechanisms. Although these provide the 'institutional core' of a chemicals regime, there are many other initiatives. The governance of hazardous substances is highly fragmented. In recent years, dozens of state, corporate, and civil society initiatives have been designed to support responsible and rational decision-making about the use of chemicals. All of these initiatives potentially advance the aims of the four main multilateral agreements, albeit to varying degrees. Figure 10.1 shows over forty of these initiatives, and more could probably be found. These initiatives perform different functions from classifying chemicals by their type of hazard; providing tools for assessing the toxicity of a product, supply chain, or company; providing guidance on reporting of toxicity and efforts to reduce the use of harmful substances; providing information about the toxicity of different elements and products, and raising awareness about the impacts of hazardous substances on human health and the environment; providing databases and tools for

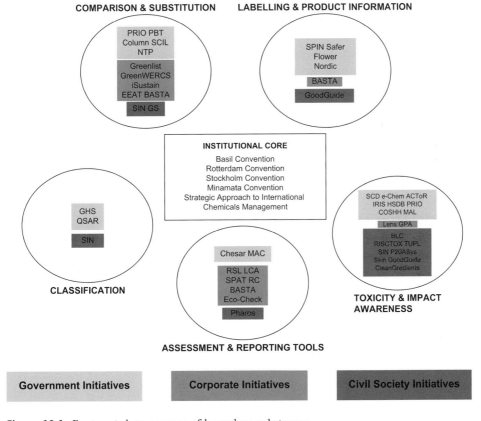

**Figure 10.1:** Fragmented governance of hazardous substances
Source: Classified based on information provided in Geiser and Edwards 2013: 184–97

comparing the toxicity of different chemicals and identifying less harmful substitutes; to providing labels, certification, and product information to help consumers select the least harmful products.

As we saw in Chapter 7, scholars disagree about the merits and problems associated with fragmented governance. On balance, would you expect that more is better when it comes to chemical management initiatives? Certainly the proliferation of tools, guidance, labels, etc. provides a wealth of information, but is this necessarily useful? UNEP has raised doubts:

> The range of these tools is so broad that the challenge is not whether to adopt such mechanisms, but how to select among them. Indeed, the proliferation of these mechanisms is so diverse and varied that it tends to add confusion for government policy makers rather than assist them … There is a clear need for a comprehensive assessment of the efficacy and value of these measures that compares them in terms of potential goals and identifies strategies where some or a combination of these tools might be most effective.
>
> (Geiser and Edwards 2013: 198)

Ambiguity, confusion, and regulatory options can undermine the responsible management of hazardous substances. Clear expectations and strong standards are necessary to ensure states and corporations cannot avoid responsibility for the use of toxic chemicals. This is a major concern of many NGOs, and it is what drove campaigns to put chemicals on the political agenda in the 1980s. The most serious manifestation of averting responsibility is 'hazardous waste dumping', and this is what we will examine in the next section.

## Displacing the Problem

Civil society organisations have played the most important role in drawing attention to the human and environmental impacts of exposure to hazardous substances. The problem has been framed as one of 'environmental justice'. NGOs like Greenpeace, BAN (Basel Action Network), and IPEN (International POPS Elimination Network) argue that wealthy countries have responded to problems of chemicals largely by avoiding responsibility. Weaknesses and loopholes in international agreements allow the North to 'dump' its waste on the 'South' and in this way shift the burden to distant people and places. In this section we will look at an example of waste dumping, and then see how it has been framed as 'environmental injustice'. Concepts of displacement, distancing, and remoteness permit a deeper understanding of dumping and injustice. We then examine how international agreements fail to curb this activity, before finally considering the argument that international agreements shouldn't ban this activity because it contributes to economic development.

## The *Khian Sea*

The case of the cargo vessel **Khian Sea** became emblematic of a wider problem of waste dumping. In 1986, this ship set off from the city of Philadelphia carrying some 14,000 tonnes of incinerator ash produced by the burning of municipal waste. Such waste is highly toxic given the presence of dioxins, lead, and cadmium. This particular load also showed traces of arsenic and cyanide. Even when disposed of in designated landfills the hazardous elements of incinerator ash can leach into the soil and make their way into food chains and water sources. The network of people involved in loading the *Khian Sea* with tonnes of ash had no intention of responsibly disposing of the waste so as to minimise harm to humans and the environment. Philadelphia had until that point buried its ash in neighbouring New Jersey. But as awareness of the toxicity of the waste increased, local resistance grew and the state of New Jersey refused to accept any more of Philadelphia's ash. With growing consumption and growing volumes of municipal waste, the city's authorities had a dilemma. Their solution was to contract out to a private company to handle it: a move that set in motion a two-year voyage across the world.

The first company to receive the waste handed it over to a second company, which loaded it onto the *Khian Sea* ship before setting sail for the Bahamas. Alerted to its toxicity, country after country refused to accept the waste. Eventually, the ship docked in Haiti, the poorest country in the Americas. The Haitian government (then under military rule) accepted the waste as 'soil fertiliser'. As the ship's crew offloaded the ash onto the Haitian beach, local citizens and environmental authorities grew suspicious that the waste was falsely labelled as fertiliser. Orders by the Haitian government to reload the waste were ignored. The *Khian Sea* left over 3,000 tonnes of toxic waste on the beach, and set sail during the night to resume its search for an obliging dumping ground. The final destination of the waste was never determined; it is believed to have been dumped at sea somewhere in the Indian Ocean during 1988. It took a decade for the US to assume responsibility for the ash and have it removed from the Haitian beach. The US owners of the vessel were convicted of ocean dumping and sentenced to prison, but never faced charges relating to the ash left on Haiti's beach (Pellow 2007: 107–10; Detjen and Jaffe 1993). This case generated considerable publicity, and environmentalist groups campaigned hard to show that it was not an isolated incident but part of a pervasive problem of toxic dumping that required a coordinated response from governments.

## Environmental Injustice

For many environmentalists, the spectre of 'garbage barges' and 'poison ships' (McFadden 1987; *Herald Journal* 1988) represents a problem of environmental injustice. Environmental justice movements emerged in the US in the 1980s as people became aware that poor people and racial minorities are disproportionately exposed to environmental risks and degradation relative to the rest of the population. This awareness led communities, particularly African-Americans, to begin demanding equitable environmental protection. In practice, environmental injustice still occurs – within the United States and elsewhere. Studies of pollution in London and Delhi show that low-income residents are far more exposed to fine particulate air pollution than average and high-income residents (Garg 2011; Moore 2012). This means they are more vulnerable to respiratory and cardiovascular disease and shortened lives. Studies of other cities are likely to show similar patterns of environmental harm.

Politically, activists have had success in institutionalising principles of justice in domestic and international environmental law. The US was the first country to recognise the principle of environmental justice. In 1994, President Clinton issued a legally binding order (Executive Order 12898), which directs federal agencies to take action on environmental injustice. It requires agencies (principally the Environmental Protection Agency) to 'identify and address the disproportionately high and adverse human health or environmental effects of their actions on minority and low-income populations ... [;] develop a strategy for implementing environmental justice ... [;] promote nondiscrimination in federal programs that affect human health and the environment ... [and] provide minority and low-income communities access to public information and public participation' (EPA 2015a). An Environmental Justice Office was later established, which defined the principle as 'the fair treatment and meaningful involvement of all people, particularly minority, low-income and indigenous populations, in the environmental decision-making process' (EPA 2016b). As we will see below, the international community has taken up this principle in multilateral agreements like the Basel Convention. Before we examine this agreement from an environmental justice perspective, let's take a closer look at the theoretical and conceptual tools available for understanding environmental injustice.

## Understanding Environmental Injustice

Green political theorists have developed several concepts that help us to understand environmental injustice. John Dryzek's concept of 'displacement' reminds us to be alert to the 'illusion' of problem solving: sometimes a problem that has apparently been solved has merely become 'somebody else's problem' (Dryzek 1987: 16). This, he suggests, is not an occasional lapse in responsibility, but a common trend: 'we tend to export or displace ecological problems, rather than truly solve them' (1987: 19). Dryzek identifies three types of displacement: spatial displacement, temporal displacement, and cross-medium displacement.

- *Spatial displacement*: this occurs when a problem is resolved in such a way that its effects are no longer felt locally, but are indeed felt in some distant place. For example, the problem of air pollution might be 'solved' by building tall smokestacks that send sulphur dioxide emissions high into the atmosphere. They no longer pollute the local air but the emissions cause acid rain to fall in distant places (1987: 16).
- *Temporal displacement*: this occurs when the effects of current actions are knowingly deferred to the future. This may mean that negative effects are felt only or predominantly in the future. For example, by applying more and more pesticides to her crops, a farmer may enhance yields in the short term, but in the future soil fertility will be greatly reduced. Temporal displacement may also mean denying future generations access to the environmental benefits we enjoy today (such as diverse species and a relatively stable climate) (1987: 19).
- *Cross-medium displacement*: this occurs when we generate new problems in the process of trying to respond to existing ones. For example, many countries are turning to nuclear energy to reduce greenhouse gas emissions and mitigate global temperature rises. In the process, these countries are generating greater amounts of radioactive waste, for which we have no safe and permanent disposal method. Nuclear power plants also pose a risk of leaking radionuclides in the atmosphere, which at high levels (such as following the Chernobyl disaster in 1986) can disrupt ecosystems and find their way into food sources.

In the early twenty-first century, environmental philosopher Val Plumwood offered a deeper theorisation of the conditions that allow displacement to occur. Plumwood used the term 'remoteness', which she defined as the disruption of 'connections and balances between decisions and their consequences' (Plumwood 2002: 72). Like Dryzek, she observed that this disruption takes various forms: spatial, temporal, consequential, communicative, epistemic, and technological. At around the same time, Thomas Princen developed the concept of 'distancing', which he explained as 'the severing of ecological and social feedback as decision points along the chain are increasingly separated along the dimensions of geography, culture, agency, and power' (Princen et al 2002b: 16).

Various factors contribute to displacement, distancing, or remoteness. Inequality is a predominant cause. Plumwood explains that inequality is 'a major sponsor' of remoteness. National and international inequalities in power and wealth provide 'systematic opportunities and motivations to shift ecological ills onto others rather than to prevent their generation in the first place' (Plumwood 2002: 81). Indeed, studies show that higher levels of inequality are associated with greater levels of pollution and environmental degradation, and more inequitable distributions of environmental harm (e.g., Boyce 2008; Holland et al. 2009; Dorling 2010). When people find themselves in a disempowered or marginalised position, they are often unable to adapt to environmental change or move to a healthier environment. They may also be willing to accept a higher level of environmental and health risk in an effort to improve their contemporary living conditions. When things go wrong and they bear a disproportionate burden of environmental damage, disempowered groups are also often unable to demand justice and compensation. After all, the main perpetrators of the environmental problem may be very far away – in time or in space.

Globalisation is another important factor in allowing us to displace our problems rather than genuinely solve them. Why would this be so? Globalisation has undoubtedly delivered many cultural, economic, and social benefits. But these benefits are not evenly distributed. People are disadvantaged and potentially harmed by many aspects of globalisation. The most relevant aspect here is that the liberalisation of international trade policies has made it easier for countries to export waste (legally and illegally), and for hazardous industries to relocate to countries with lower environmental standards.

Jennifer Clapp uses the concept of 'distancing' to explain the causes and consequences of trading toxic waste across borders. The causes, she argues, are 'the growing scale of economic life, economic globalization, and economic inequality' (Clapp 2002). As a consequence of being able to distance ourselves from the waste we produce, we produce excessive amounts of it and place excessive demands on 'waste-sink capacity'. Waste-sink capacity refers to the biophysical and social capacity of the planet to absorb our waste. This capacity might be constrained by physical space. Several counties in the UK and states in the US are running out of landfill space and transporting their waste to other counties and states (Kellett 2014; West 2015; Zimlich 2015). Capacity might also be constrained by social tolerance levels: your community might tolerate a small waste dump on the outskirts of town, but as landfill increases there you might decide that the smell is too offensive, or the risk of soil contamination is too great. Waste-sink capacity might also be constrained by biophysical factors: for example, a waste dump built on clayey soils has a lower capacity to oxidise methane (a powerful greenhouse gas) than a waste dump built on sandy soil (American Society of Agronomy 2009). The more waste we produce, the greater the likelihood of exceeding these limits and resorting to a strategy of problem displacement. Clapp explains that distancing occurs when consumers are separated from their waste. This separation has geographical, cultural, power, and agency dimensions:

Part of the separation occurs along a geographical dimension. With economic globalization, especially, the physical distances between producers and consumers as well as between consumers and wastes, expand. But part of distancing occurs along other dimensions as well. These include a cultural dimension, that is, the way consumers lack information about the specific environmental impacts of wastes; a bargaining power dimension, that is, asymmetries among decision-makers and other stakeholders over the siting of waste disposal; and an agency dimension, that is, the role of middle agents between consumption and waste disposal decisions. All of these dimensions of 'distance' create not just a geographical distance, but also a mental distance, what I will call an 'understanding gap' – a gulf of information, awareness and responsibility between consumers and wastes.

(Clapp 2002: 157–8)

We saw earlier that states have negotiated several international agreements to manage international flows of hazardous waste. But many critics argue that these agreements are inadequate for preventing environmental injustices. Drawing on the conceptual tools we have just encountered, we might say that these agreements are insufficient for addressing problem displacement, remoteness, or distancing. It has been a political victory for activists to get the issue of hazardous waste trade on the international political agenda. But if the evidence on waste dumping is correct, there is still a long way to go to reach conditions of justice. Let's now take a closer look at the specific criticisms of the most important agreement on trading waste: the Basel Convention.

## The Basel Convention: Weaknesses and Limitations

Earlier in this chapter we saw that the main objective of the Basel Convention is 'to protect human health and the environment against the adverse effects of hazardous wastes' (Basel Convention 2011). It does so by defining rules that restrict trade in hazardous wastes. Under the auspices of the UN, states began negotiating an agreement on this issue in 1987. They completed negotiations in 1989, and the agreement came into force three years later once ratified by twenty parties.

A division emerged in the early days of negotiations. One side took a pro-trade position and aimed to regulate and perhaps limit the movement of hazardous wastes across countries. Japan, the United States, Canada, Australia, and New Zealand (collectively known as JUSCANZ) all aligned with this pro-trade position. Some countries took a more ambitious and hard line, advocating not a limit on toxic trade, but an outright ban. Developing countries and the EU (with the support of civil society groups) aligned with this pro-ban position. The division was resolved in favour of the pro-trade group and the Basel Convention only imposed *restrictions* on trade. For the state and non-state actors who had fought to get this issue on the political agenda, the result was weak and disappointing. They argued that the Basel Convention legitimised and legalised the trade in hazardous waste, which allowed wealthy countries in the North to continue evading responsibility for a problem of their creation. States later agreed to discuss a ban on the movement of hazardous wastes across borders. As we saw above, an amendment to the Basel Convention was agreed in 1995, but without support from enough states it has not entered into force.

There is certainly evidence to suggest that the convention's trade restrictions have been inadequate for addressing the problem. In 1992, when the convention came into force, some 45 million tonnes of waste were transferred between countries each year. By 2008, this amount had grown by 500 per cent to reach 221 million tonnes (Kellenberg and Levinson 2013: 6). Part of the reason for this dramatic increase is that the Basel Convention does not restrict the movement of material for recycling. This is particularly a problem for discarded electronic goods, or 'e-waste'. Activist groups are deeply sceptical about how many electronic goods are genuinely recycled, and about the negative impacts involved in the recycling process when goods are genuinely recycled (Gutierrez 2014: 407–8; Electronics Take Back Coalition no date). The Basel Action Network suggests that between 50 and 80 per cent of the electronic products collected for recycling in the United States are shipped abroad. Once an importing country receives a shipment, there is no way of verifying that the products are indeed recycled (and, of course, no products are 100 per cent recyclable; there will always be some elements that have to be discarded). Critics call this the 'recycling loophole'. It refers to Article 4(9)(b) of the convention, which permits the transboundary movement of waste if it is 'required as a raw material for recycling or recovery industries in the State of import' (Basel Convention 1989). But even if the products are recycled, the problem is not necessarily resolved but rather displaced to a distant future and distant place. Recycling and reuse may prolong the lifespan of an electronic product like a computer or telephone. But eventually (perhaps after only six months or a couple of years) it will become unusable and will pose environmental and health risks in the importing country. The problem of planned obsolescence (deliberately limiting the durability of a product) exacerbates this.

The risks are particularly acute when the importing country does not have the facilities to manage recycling in a safe and controlled environment. When the plastics from e-waste are recycled, highly toxic chemicals are released into the atmosphere. The EU prohibits member states from recycling these parts. But such controls are not in place in developing countries, and workers including children are exposed to dangerous levels of dioxins, furans, and other dangerous chemicals (Greenpeace 2009). Even in the United States where the recycling industry is regulated (albeit to a lower standard than the EU), dangerous levels of lead and cadmium have been detected in the bodies of recycling workers (and even their families) (Alecci 2016; Ceballos and Page 2014).

Another weakness that critics point to in the Basel Convention is its failure to control the illegal waste trade. Since Basel came into effect, the black market for hazardous substance disposal has grown. There are push and pull factors involved. The main factor pushing actors to pursue illicit trade channels is the cost differential: it is more expensive to dispose of hazardous materials in the global North than in the global South. Pulling the shipments 'southward' are weak regulations, corruption, and structural disadvantage. Countries in a weaker financial position are more likely to accept the higher levels of risk that hazardous shipments carry. Furthermore, the individuals involved in illicit trade networks are unlikely to bear the main brunt of the impact. This is true whether the individuals are in wealthy countries sending the waste, or in poorer countries accepting the waste. The case of the **Probo Koala** illustrates this grim situation. This ironically named vessel (*probo* comes from the Latin *probus*, meaning virtuous or good) was Korean-built, Greek-owned, Panamanian-registered, and crewed by Russians. In 2006, it was chartered by a Dutch subsidiary of the global oil company Trafigura to dispose of 500–600 tonnes of mixed chemical wastes, including caustic soda and petroleum residues. Dutch authorities initially assumed the waste was relatively benign and accepted to dispose it for $15,000. Once they determined it to be highly toxic, it was directed to a special facility where disposal would cost $650,000. Seeking a better deal, the *Probo Koala* sailed onto Estonia, where it was offered disposal for $260,000. Trafigura again rejected the offer and sailed down to West Africa. After failing to strike a deal in Nigeria, a recipient was found in the Ivory Coast. The recipient was a nascent company called Tommy Ltd., which was likely established with the sole purpose of receiving the shipment. It had no facilities for treating toxic waste and simply dumped it untreated in urban outskirts under the cover of darkness. Fifteen local residents subsequently died from exposure, dozens were hospitalised, and over 100,000 sought medical attention for nausea, vomiting, skin reactions, and a range of other problems affecting their eyes, ears, noses, and throats. Criminal charges were eventually brought against the ship's captain, Dutch port authorities, and Trafigura executives and local subsidiaries. Most of these charges were dropped in exchange for settlements payments. This is a case of environmental injustice and the vast majority of victims never received due compensation (Environmental Justice Organisations, Liabilities and Trade 2015; White 2008).

This wasn't an isolated incident; it is part of a wider problem. A year before the *Probo Koala* odyssey began, inspections at European ports found that nearly half of all waste destined for export was illegal. Recent estimates suggest that only between 10–40 per cent of e-waste is properly recycled and disposed of. Much of it is simply dumped or illegally traded (UNEP 2015). The United States has never ratified the Basel Convention so it is not legally bound to its rules. Export practices that would be deemed illegal in Europe and elsewhere are widespread in the US (Greenpeace 2009). Much of the illegal trade goes undetected because the hazardous substances are either mislabelled or mixed with non-hazardous substances. Moreover, there is no precise definition of what constitutes hazardous waste, which creates ambiguity. Where there is ambiguity, there is space for displacing problems onto distant people and places.

## E-waste Dumping or Much Needed Trade?

A small number of scholars and investigative journals challenge the dominant environmental justice lens through which this issue is understood. Focusing on electronic waste, they dispute the characterisation of this trade as immoral and unjust, and a case of avoided responsibility. They also dispute the North–South 'geographical imaginary' that underpins the Basel Convention as well as critiques of this convention. Let's first examine the reasons for rejecting the idea that this is a North–South problem. We'll then consider whether there is justification for accepting e-waste trade as a legitimate part of development.

Canadian geographer Josh Lepawsky argues that the Basel Convention is inconsistent with contemporary political economic conditions. The Basel Convention divides the world neatly into Annex VI countries (OECD members, the European Community, and Liechtenstein) and non-Annex VI countries (all the rest). The convention rules restrict (with the aim of eventually banning) trade in hazardous waste, including e-waste, from the former to the latter. But it is simplistic, Lepawsky argues, to treat waste trade as a problem of wealthy developed countries shipping their unwanted waste to poor developing countries. It is simplistic because it assumes that 'all non-Annex VII territories are equally vulnerable to hazardous waste dumping from Annex VII territories, but not vulnerable to such dumping amongst themselves' (Lepawsky 2015a: 7). In fact, non-Annex VII countries are incredibly diverse in their economic profiles, consumption patterns, and technological capacities. If that is the case, can there be any justification for treating countries like India, Israel, Botswana, Benin, Haiti, and Honduras in the same way? Critics like Lepawsky argue that there is not.

Critics consider the North–South 'geographic imaginary' problematic because most waste is not traded between these groups of countries. We can see this clearly in the statistics on e-waste trade. In the mid-1990s, e-waste trade from Annex VII countries to non-Annex VII countries represented about 35 per cent of total e-waste trade. By 2012, the figure was less than 1 per cent. Annex VII countries (developed countries) are mostly moving waste among themselves, and mostly on a regional basis. Non-Annex VII countries (developing countries) are trading e-waste among themselves, and even exporting it to Annex VII countries (Lepawsky 2015b: 147). Japan (a wealthy Annex VII country) receives the largest share of China's e-waste, followed by South Korea and India. India sends most of its e-waste to Belgium, followed by countries in Africa and the Arabian Peninsula (Lepawsky 2015a: 12). This is partly explained by the fact that wealthy countries like Belgium have sophisticated technology for extracting precious metals from electronic goods. They are therefore able to offer a higher price for the used goods than a poorer country.

Critics argue that we need to rethink our assumptions about electronic waste not only because the directions of trade are more nuanced than we thought, but also because the nature of traded goods is different to what we thought. Research by Shinkuma and Huong (2009) suggests that most e-waste shipments contain products for reuse not disposal. This is supported by another study showing that over 90 per cent of the electronic goods that Nigeria imports from Europe are either immediately functional or usable after repair (Manhart et al. 2011). Given that many Nigerians cannot afford to buy new computers, televisions, and mobile phones, the trade in used goods gives them access to communications equipment that they otherwise wouldn't have. The refurbishment of used goods supports livelihoods and promotes innovation and technological capacity (Lepawsky 2015b: 151–2). This is the positive story told of e-waste trade. It is not limited to Nigeria but arguably is true of other developing countries too. E-waste trade is thereby recast as a story of development rather than dumping.

Activist groups like the Basel Action Network respond by pointing out that used electronic goods have a short lifespan. When they are no longer functional, they will be dismantled under dangerous conditions, and toxic chemicals will pose a threat to local people's health and the local environment. Unlike the sophisticated technology used in countries like Belgium, workers resort to using acid to strip valuable metals from used electronic equipment. Jim Puckett of the Basel Action Network not only questions the interpretation of critics like Josh Lepawsky. He also questions their motives. He likens efforts to cast doubt on the dumping of e-waste to efforts to cast doubt on the science of climate change or tobacco and cancer (Puckett 2015). He calls it 'waste trade denial', and suggests that it is used to protect the powerful electronics industry. He calls into question the validity of studies purporting to show the development benefits of the waste trade. While some of Puckett's arguments are spurious,[4] he is certainly right to point out that we lack adequate data to accurately determine the precise flows in trade. We simply don't know precisely what volume of used electronics is reused or recycled domestically, how much flows illegally to developing countries, and how long it stays in use before being discarded in those countries. Nevertheless, Puckett warns that we can safely assume that the volume of hazardous materials exported from developed to developing countries is much higher than official data suggests. This is because criminals have opportunities to mislabel cargo, or mix in hazardous waste with relatively benign cargo (Basel Action Network 2016).

A place called Agbogbloshie presents a useful context for observing how e-waste trade can be interpreted in two very different ways. This suburb of Accra in Ghana has become infamous as the world's digital dumping ground. In BAN's assessment, much of the electronic equipment that ends up here is imported illegally, albeit with the stated intent to repair or reuse it. Cargo therefore does not travel directly from the port to the dumpsites, but rather passes through small roadside shops, and sometimes then onto local consumers (Puckett 2015: 44). Google the name Agbogbloshie and you'll most likely see grim images of burning trash, and children sifting through waste with their bare hands. Science journalist Adam Minter is one person who challenges this depiction (Minter 2016). Visiting the suburb, what stands out to him is the flourishing computer refurbishment industry. Investigative reporter Jon Spaull also disputes the depiction of Agbogbloshie as a digital dump. He characterises it as a 'well-organised scrapyard' with no more e-waste 'than you might expect for a dump in a city of more than two million people, with a growing middle class' (Spaull 2015). He reports on interviews with local entrepreneurs who stress the benefits of access to affordable electronic equipment: imports of used goods largely explain why the number of computers per person in Africa rose tenfold between 2001 and 2011, the number of telephone subscribers rose 100 times. From this perspective, waste trade promotes economic development and opportunities, and efforts to restrict this will have a negative impact on importing countries.

## Conclusion

We've seen in this chapter that chemicals are central to modern life. Most of the things we use on a day-to-day basis contain chemicals that have the potential to damage human health and the environment. While it can be difficult for the average person to determine the precise risks of using any particular product, at a general level the risks of chemical exposure have been known for over fifty years. Concern about chemical use has pushed governments in many wealthy countries to create regulations and monitoring systems to minimise the risks to human health and the environment. Internationally we've seen states cooperate to create several multilateral agreements to control chemicals. But loopholes and non-compliance mean that serious problems remain.

We've seen that not everyone agrees with the framing of this issue as 'environmental injustice'. Some point to the economic benefits offered by the trade in wastes. This remains a contentious debate. But whether we understand the trade in waste as promoting development or displacing responsibility, there are clearly environmental justice concerns to be addressed. The benefits of production and the costs of disposal are distributed unevenly. Environmental and health risks are distributed unevenly: socially, spatially, and temporally. Depending on where they live, people face different degrees of exposure and vulnerability to illness. Some people have options for minimising their exposure, or for distancing themselves from the effects of their consumption. Others have few such options. These are all issues of environmental justice that deserve concern. How we channel concern into action is an important question. One important insight from this chapter is that civil society groups haven't relied on appealing to consumers to buy, say, fewer televisions. Instead they have been politically engaged and maintained pressure on states and international organisations over several decades to push for more just rules. This is important for environmental justice.

## Discussion Questions

1. Revisit the description of David's morning on page 226–7. Thinking now about your own daily routines, how might it be possible to reduce your indirect use of harmful chemicals?
2. See Table 10.1 and select two unfamiliar chemicals that are regulated by the Rotterdam Convention. Investigate the hazards these pose to human health and the environment. Imagine you are a national regulator who has received a request from another country to accept a shipment of this chemical for use or disposal. Decide whether you would consent to the import; consent only if specific conditions are met; or reject the import under all circumstances.
3. The international community has taken steps to address the gaps and overlaps in global chemical governance. What are the factors that make it difficult to improve the effectiveness and cohesion of the chemicals regime?
4. We have seen how waste trade can be understood as a case of 'problem displacement'. What other environmental problems tend to be displaced? How and to whom are they displaced?
5. Does the Basel Convention need to be revised to suit contemporary political economic conditions? If so, what changes would you advocate?

# Notes

1. They are methanol, ethylene, propylene, butadiene, xylenes, benzene, toluene, lime/limestone, sulphuric acid, ammonia, sulphur, and phosphoric acid.
2. *Mining* refers to the extraction of ore from the earth; *smelting* refers to heating processes by which the metal is separated from the ore; and *refining* refers to the stage of removing non-lead elements from the mixture so that it is ready for production.
3. To further complicate matters, PCDDs are sometimes called CDDs (chlorinated dibenzo-p-dioxins), and PCDFs are sometimes called CDFs (Chlorinated dibenzofurans).
4. For example, he suggests that research funded by national research councils like Canada's Social Science and Humanities Council is government research. This is a misrepresentation of what is actually intellectually independent scholarship. Lepawsky responded by questioning the independence of BAN and implying that they have a vested interest in peddling the trade dump storyline (Lepawsky 2015c). Unfortunately, this contest between Puckett and Lepawsky does little to advance our understanding of this important issue.

# 11 Resistance and Localisation
## Unsustainable Agriculture

**key points**

- Social movements have played an important role in challenging neoliberal globalisation, which they see as socially and environmentally destructive.
- Social movements challenge the idea that a sustainable and just agricultural system is compatible with the international liberal economic system.
- Modern agriculture is highly dependent on fossil fuels. Heavy use of energy and chemicals in agriculture has an environmental impact. Agriculture is also affected by environmental change, especially by climate change.
- Resistance to existing systems of economic development and agriculture take various forms including protest, confrontation, and building alternative systems.
- Social movements like La Via Campesina promote alternative systems of agriculture based on food sovereignty and agroecology. These are smaller in scale and oriented to local markets.

# Introduction

Most of the chapters in this book focus on how states, multilateral institutions, and corporate actors have responded to global environmental problems. We have seen that civil society groups often play an important role in shaping the decisions and actions of these state and corporate actors. But in this chapter, civil society – and social movements in particular – moves to centre stage. Social movements are defined as 'collective challenges, based on common purposes and social solidarity, and sustained interaction with a common opponent and authorities' (Tarrow 2011: 9). Social movements are often not central to studies of global governance or domestic politics, but to ignore them risks overlooking the central role they have played in bringing about progressive change since the late eighteenth century (Fominaya 2014: 4). In Chapters 6 and 7 we saw how contemporary global environmental governance is characterised by a commitment to the liberal economic system; this predicates environmental protection on existing systems of international trade, capitalist accumulation, and economic growth. Social movements from the North and South have fiercely resisted this approach. Through repertoires of protest and experimental practices, social movements have challenged the principles and assumptions that underpin unsustainable practices and 'liberal environmentalist' policies. In this chapter we explore how this resistance has manifested in the context of unsustainable agriculture.

The chapter begins with an overview of resistance, touching on questions of definition and strategy before briefly reviewing how movements have resisted neoliberal economic globalisation and neoliberal environmental projects. We then pick up the case study of unsustainable agriculture by first charting the rise of the modern industrialised agricultural system, and then unpacking the relationship between environmental change and modern agriculture. Here we examine the various ways in which industrialised agriculture is both implicated in and vulnerable to climate change and environmental degradation. Concerns about the environmental and social impacts of the modern agricultural system have motivated social movements to demand far-reaching reforms to agricultural and trade policies, and to develop alternative practices of sustainable agriculture based on agroecology and the localisation of food production and trade. We examine this demand-based resistance and action-based resistance and explore a set of prominent case studies to more deeply understand what resistance to unsustainable agriculture looks like in practice. Critics have raised doubts about the viability of agroecology and the desirability of localisation, and we will briefly consider these criticisms, as well as how the movement has defended its positions against these criticisms.

## Social Movements and Resistance

What does it mean to 'resist'? The simplest way of understanding resistance is as organised opposition to power and domination. It is generally understood that resistance is collective and intentional. But scholars like James Scott remind us to also tune into 'everyday forms of resistance': the day-to-day struggles that may be uncoordinated, unplanned, and low profile (Scott 1985). Political geographer Louise Amoore sees a common trend in the literature of using organic and animate metaphors to depict resistance: social movements are presented as mosquitoes irritating those with power and disturbing their claims of legitimacy, and as termites eating away at powerful structures (2005: 2–3).

There are various analytical distinctions available to help us make sense of resistance. Saturnino Borras Jr. and his colleagues distinguish between cooperative and confrontational tactics (2008: 188). Cooperative action allows for collaboration and alliances between civil society and state-based institutions or the private sector. Confrontation is a tactic that rejects cooperation as a way of avoiding either co-optation or the legitimation of institutions that reinforce neoliberal globalisation. When institutions or decision-making bodies co-opt dissenters they push them to moderate their demands in exchange for inclusion. But for many social movements it is more important to be sincere and consistent, even if this means being excluded from decision-making processes. Often the price of inclusion is compromise, and for some social movements this defeats the purpose of their struggle. Groups engaged in confrontation may also wish to avoid cooperation or engagement because this would recognise – and reinforce – the authority and power of state-based or corporate actors.

Groups who choose to cooperate with powerful actors have decided – either uncritically or upon reflection – that this is the best way to advance their goals even if this requires moderating their demands to make them more 'realistic'. An effective strategy in the long term may be one that uses tactics of cooperation and tactics of confrontation at different times to secure their independence and avoid being pigeonholed. As Borras Jr. and colleagues explain,

Assessing which strategies and forms of actions are more effective depends largely on the goals and targets of a particular campaign. If the goal is to delegitimise specific institutions, then public shaming through confrontational actions may indeed be an appropriate approach. In campaigns where the goal is to secure concessions, as for example, expanding 'invited spaces' (Gaventa 2002) for civil society participation, then a more critical collaborative interaction would likely be more effective.

(Borras Jr. et al. 2008: 188–9)

An alternative distinction is Day's 'politics of demand' and 'politics of the act' (2004: 733). The politics of demand involves protest and other pressure tactics to influence state-based institutions and corporations, the aim here is to mitigate the negative impact of powerful actors' behaviour. Protest and pressure can take a moderate or progressive tone, or something more radical. Each has the aim of forcing the more powerful actor to alter their policies and practices. The most iconic example of protest-based resistance to neoliberal globalisation is the 1999 'Battle of Seattle' blockade at the free trade negotiations of the WTO. The blockade, street rallies, and protest performances served multiple purposes: they prevented delegates from entering the opening ceremony; they highlighted the strength of opposition to neoliberal economic globalisation; they raised awareness of the social impacts of WTO rules; and reframed free trade as anti-democratic and oppressive. Some protesters wanted the WTO to be abolished; others demanded reforms. But the protesters were united in a vision of democratised economic decision-making that responded to values beyond just maximising profits (Smith 2001).

In contrast to the politics of demand, the politics of the act involves autonomous action on the part of citizens 'to block, resist and render redundant both corporate and state power in local, national and transnational contexts' (Day 2004). In John Holloway's memorable terms, autonomous action seeks to 'change the world without taking power' (2002). This involves experimenting with alternative ways of living that do not conform to the rules and procedures imposed by state and corporate actors. It involves acting in a way that is consistent with their aspirations for society. Sometimes scholars call this behaviour 'prefigurative politics' (Fominaya 2014: 10). We can observe action-based resistance to neoliberal globalisation following the 1994 Zapatista uprising in Mexico. On 1 January 1994, the North American Free Trade Agreement (NAFTA) came into effect. On this day the Ejército Zapatista de Liberación Nacional

(EZLN – Zapatista Army of National Liberation) took up arms in the indigenous region of Chiapas to resist the agreement. It was widely feared that NAFTA would flood Mexico with cheap, industrially produced corn from the United States, and that this would threaten indigenous culture, land, and livelihoods. The movement was not a traditional revolutionary movement; it did not aim to seize power from the state. It was a resistance movement that sought to change state policies without taking power. Guerrilla tactics failed to produce the changes the EZLN wanted and this eventually led the group to cut itself off from the state and create autonomous zones of control (Mattiace 2012: 401–2). Throughout the uprising and the ensuing periods of low-intensity warfare, negotiation, and autonomous organisation, the EZLN practised non-hierarchical forms of governance that reflected their aspirations. Dialogue and public consultation featured prominently (Fominaya 2014: 64).

## Globalisation and the Environment

For more than two decades, social movements have played an important role in challenging particular forms of globalisation that they see as socially and environmentally destructive. By refusing to accept power imbalances and injustices as inevitable, these groups aim to disrupt the actions of powerful international actors and push for transformative change. These movements have been branded as 'anti-globalisation' but the groups themselves tend to reject this label preferring to identify as 'alternative globalisation' movements. This emphasises that they do not reject globalisation per se, but rather a neoliberal kind of globalisation.

One scholar who has analysed the resistance of social movements is Barry Gills. He identifies the 'main historical thrust' of economic neoliberal globalisation as

bring[ing] about a situation in which private capital and 'the market' alone determine the restructuring of economic, political and cultural life, making alternative values or institutions subordinate. Rather than capital and 'the economy' being embedded in society and harnessed to serve social ends, 'the economy' becomes the master of society and of all within it, and society exists to serve the ends of capital and its need for self-expansion.

(2000: 4–5)

A rejection of neoliberal economic globalisation is often at the heart of many environmental movements. This can be seen in the 'mega-protests' that have accompanied the 'mega-events' for sustainable development that we saw in Chapter 6 (Death 2010). Writing about the 2002 Johannesburg Summit, Carl Death observes that

> for many of those who protested … the marches were a defiant statement of resistance against the South African state, the UN, global governance and neo-liberal capitalism … The forms of resistance and representation adopted by the protesters explicitly contested the means, scope and ends of the advanced liberal government of sustainable development, yet they also relied upon the theatrical stage of the Summit, and in many cases urged governments to govern sustainable development more intensely.
>
> (2010: 120)

Just as the Battle for Seattle brought together those demanding the abolition of the WTO and those demanding reforms, environmental summitry protests tend to bring together those who thoroughly reject multilateral environmental institutions as well as those who wish to see those institutions reformed. This division was also on display at the World People's Conference on Climate Change and the Rights of Mother Earth, held in the Bolivian city of Cochabamba in 2010. Some participants there aimed to transfer their declaration to the UNFCCC, while others demanded that the UN representative to the conference be thrown out (Stevenson 2014: 199–200).

For social movements, environmental and social concerns are often entwined. The case of food and agriculture exposes how concerns about equity and livelihoods are wrapped up with evolving unsustainable practices.

## Agriculture and the Environment

In this section we examine how agriculture has evolved in modern times from mechanisation, specialisation, and 'chemicalisation', to corporatisation, liberalisation, and globalisation. We also unpack the relationship between agriculture and the environment. Understanding these conditions is essential to appreciate how and why social movements for sustainable agriculture emerged, which we will analyse in the following section.

## The Rise of Modern Agriculture

The industrialisation of agriculture marks one of the most prominent socio-ecological shifts of the twentieth century. The production, distribution, and consumption of food have all been transformed by a combination of science and technology and the gradual adoption of a 'logic of industrialism' (Fitzgerald 2003). The scale and character of farms began to change in the United States in the early 1900s as tractors and other machinery (as well as cheap fossil fuels) became available. Supported by a growing network of rural banks and insurance companies, together with the increasing demands of a growing domestic population and consumers in warring Europe, American farmers were able to purchase machinery and farm vaster areas of land. At a time when labour was in short supply, there was considerable interest in developing mechanised techniques for planting, cultivating, and harvesting. The government provided guaranteed prices, which gave farmers additional confidence to mechanise and expand. This proved profitable during World War One, but when the bubble burst at the end of the war, millions of farms failed together with many of the financial institutions that had backed their expansion (Fitzgerald 2003). Multiple factors drove this crisis, including the reimposition of restrictions on food imports to Europe at the end of the war.

Politicians blamed the farmers themselves for the farming crisis. They were cast as ignorant immigrants with neither the means nor ethic to run successful farms. Or politicians reasoned that there were simply too many farmers to ensure an efficient sector (Fitzgerald 2003: 20). And so, as historian Deborah Fitzgerald documents, the 'logic of industrialism' began to permeate the agricultural sector. Farmers were to become less like peasants and labourers and more like 'businessmen', and their business model would be that of the factory. The characteristics of a successful factory could, it was believed, be mimicked on the land: 'large-scale production, specialized machines, standardization of processes and products, reliance on managerial (rather than artisanal) expertise, and a continual evocation of "efficiency" as a production mandate' (2003: 23). This logic literally changed the landscape of the United States. By the end of the century the number of farms had dropped by over 70 per cent and the vast majority of these were now over 500 acres (or about 2 square kilometres) (Giménez and Shattuck 2011: 110–11).

The pattern of agricultural specialisation had already been established in much of the world through colonisation. To compensate for their own production deficiencies, European powers transformed many of their colonies into specialised producers of one or two products: Malaysia became a rubber exporter, Egypt and India cotton exporters, Ghana a cocoa exporter, Cuba a sugar exporter, and Argentina a wheat and beef exporter (Gonzalez 2004: 433–4). The global South was drawn further into an industrial agriculture regime in the 1960s and 1970s through what became known as the **Green Revolution**. The aim was to address the problem of hunger and the escalating demands of growing populations. This saw international private foundations (like the Ford Foundation and Rockefeller) cooperate with aid agencies (like USAID) to supply farmers in Asia and Latin America with hybrid (crossbred) high-yielding varieties of wheat and rice, replacing the variety of local seeds in use. At the same time they promoted the modernisation of agriculture in these countries, in particular through replacing labour-intensive techniques with mechanised ones, and natural fertilisers with the synthetic ones designed to be used in conjunction with the patented hybrid seeds. The modern seeds were incompatible with traditional farming techniques because they relied on intensive irrigation and chemical fertilisers. Whether the impact of this process on food security was, on balance, positive or negative is highly contested. The fact that production levels increased dramatically is beyond question: production of rice in India doubled in the first six years and had quadrupled by the early twenty-first century. Overall it is estimated that crop production across the developing countries would have been 16–19 per cent lower in 2000 if the modern varieties had not been introduced in the 1960s and 1970s (Paarlberg 2013: 64–5). What is contested is whether the environmental costs outweighed this benefit, and whether in fact higher yields translate directly into greater food security. Critics of the Green Revolution argue that modern agricultural techniques have degraded soils, depleted water resources, diminished diversity, and damaged ecosystems (e.g., Ehrenreich and Lyon 2011). These arguments are examined in more detail below. Proponents of the Green Revolution respond that if the modern varieties were not introduced in the developing countries harvests would have been less stable, farm incomes would have been lower, and environmental degradation would have been worse (e.g. Borlaug 2000). Robert Paarlberg, for example, argues that 'If India had been forced to rely on its pre-green revolution, low-yield farming techniques to secure the production gains it needed during these decades of rapid population growth, there would have been no option but to expand the area under cultivation by cutting more trees, destroying more wildlife habitat, and plowing up more fragile sloping on dryland soils' (2013: 73). The use of these hybrid seeds is now widespread; farmers in the global North rely almost exclusively on hybrid seeds, and they are heavily used in Asia and Latin America.

The commercialisation of hybrid seeds and synthetic fertilisers is part of what has been called the 'chemicalisation' of agriculture, a post-war process pushed in large part by the private chemical industry (Mazoyer and Roudart 2006: 375–6). This industry expanded during World Wars One and Two to supply first the Germans and later the Allies with bombs, poisonous gases, and insecticides (McKenney 2002: 123; Langston 2014: 267). At the end of World War Two the industry sought to capitalise on its technology and scientific knowledge by moving into new markets. In North America it found a receptive consumer base and rapidly established a stronghold in the seed production market. Environmental historian Nancy Langston explains that World War Two 'led to intense advertising and marketing campaigns for new chemicals, linking victory in war with victory over insects, cementing synthetic chemicals' reputations as miracle workers, and submerging concerns over toxicity. Wartime publicity campaigns created civilian expectations that the new chemical wonders could solve all insect problems – on the farm, in the suburban landscape, and in the house' (2014: 268). Before long chemical companies were selling large volumes of seeds and chemical treatments (pesticides and fertilisers) (Gonzalez 2004: 438–9). According to one estimate, the use of chemical pesticides in the United States subsequently increased fifty-fold from the late 1940s to 1990 (Gonzalez 2004: 439). Concerns about the environmental and health dangers of the widespread use of chemicals like DDT were not entirely absent – even during the war ecologists and epidemiologists had urged caution in the face of uncertainty about long-term effects. But the urgency of building a post-war economy took precedence over precaution and long-term interests (Langston 2014: 269).

The industrialisation of agriculture took a giant leap forward in the 1970s when scientists mastered the genetic manipulation of seeds in a process that came to be known as genetic engineering. Earlier forms of crossbreeding involved the deliberate pollination of a similar or related plant species to combine the naturally occurring characteristics of the two species. This relatively rudimentary technique was what produced the higher-yielding varieties that were disseminated through the Green Revolution. Genetic engineering or manipulation (GM), by contrast, transgresses the genetic boundaries of plants. Rather than crossbreeding similar or related plant species it involves combining the genes of biologically distinct products such as plants and bacteria. This produces 'transgenic' crops with characteristics such as tolerance to herbicides, disease, insects, and biological stresses (drought, poor and acidic soil, etc.). Corporate actors have used the technique to protect their intellectual property by ensuring that the seeds saved from their patented crops are sterile, or requiring the application of a chemical fertiliser to activate fertility (Nelson 2001: 8). Bt corn, potatoes, and cotton, for example, are engineered from strains of *Bacillus thuringiensis* to generate a toxic substance upon contact with an insect's digestive enzymes, the result being that pests are repelled from eating crops – or killed if they persist. The substance is designed to have no effect on mammals or benign insects (Nelson 2001: 9).

Proponents of GM see the technology as merely an extension of naturally occurring processes and argue that there are no grounds for being concerned about the impact of transgenic crops on human health or the environment. Nobel Prize winning biologist Norman Borlaug, a leading scientist of cross-breeding and 'father of the green revolution', was one such advocate. Borlaug was emphatic that GM 'is not some kind of witchcraft; rather, it is the progressive harnessing of the forces of nature to the benefit of feeding the human race' (2000: 489). Proponents often see potential for a 'second green revolution' or 'Gene Revolution' by making transgenic varieties of rice and wheat much more commercially available around the world (*The Economist* 2014). Indeed, such a revolution is often seen as essential given global population growth projections.

Opponents of GM argue that the social and environmental costs of this technology are substantial. Traditionally farmers would not purchase new seeds each season; instead they would harvest seeds at the end of each season. Forcing farmers to purchase new seeds annually (either through sterilisation techniques or intellectual property laws) substantially increases the costs of farming. This has a particular impact on farmers in developing countries. Packaging the seeds up with essential fertilisers adds to these costs. Additional concerns relate to the diminishing diversity associated with GM crops. This is a concern with both social and environmental dimensions. It is not just a matter of pretty and colourful corn (Ehrenreich and Lyon 2011: 12). Environmentally, diversity is important for resilient ecosystems. Agronomist Henk Hobbelink explains that 'Diversity of genetic resources is a basic cornerstone for any effort to sustain or improve the performance of agricultural crops and animals. It is also a crucial prerequisite for natural ecosystems to respond to changing circumstances, now and in the future' (1991: 3). Socially, genetic diversity serves as an 'insurance policy' for farmers: if disaster or disease strikes a diverse farm will probably only be partially affected; if a single variety of crop is planted the entire harvest may be lost (1991: 3).

Even strong GM advocates like Borlaug have recognised the social challenges associated with GM, especially the high financial costs that are imposed on farmers in developing countries. Proponents see these challenges as surmountable through regulatory frameworks and closer cooperation between governments and the private sector (2000: 488). Critics of GM agree that governmental regulation is needed not simply to make biotechnology more widely available but rather to promote food security and alternative forms of sustainable agriculture. Some express concern that an emphasis on increasing food production will fail to address global food insecurity, now or in the future. Holt-Giménez and Altieri, for instance, observe that 'A new Green Revolution could conceivably concentrate food production on some 50,000 industrial farms worldwide. Given the best land, subsidized inputs, and favorable market access, these farms could produce the world's food (although not very sustainably). But how would 2.5 billion displaced smallholders buy this food?' (2013: 94). Even today, hunger is not the result of lack of food, but rather of lack of access to food. More than enough food is produced to satisfy the calorie needs of the world's 7 billion people. But large numbers remain under-nourished because global markets distribute food on an inequitable basis. 'Those who can afford food have a diet far in excess of their needs, while those who cannot afford food go hungry' (Pfeiffer 2006: 10).

As we will see below, many social movements see the solution as lying beyond conventional industrial agriculture in more localised and small-scale agricultural systems. A strong feature of these alternative visions is their rejection of corporate dominance in the production, processing, distribution, and marketing of food. Since the mid-twentieth century, control of these processes has become increasingly concentrated within a small number of multinational corporations. The corporations that sell seeds and fertilisers are typically the same ones that purchase the produce. Farmers generally do not sell their crops on an open market these days; instead contract farming is becoming the global norm. This means that farmers are paid an agreed rate for their produce, and may be required to follow the methods and procedures preferred by the purchaser (corporation).

This dominant practice has come about through the liberalisation of agriculture, a process that has unfolded unevenly across the world since the 1980s. In a reform process that became known as the Washington Consensus, indebted developing countries found themselves under pressure to reduce tariffs and subsidies in agriculture and other sectors. Led by the Washington-based (and US-dominated) International Monetary Fund (IMF) and the World Bank, the order of the day was 'stabilise, liberalise, privatise'. Generally, the level of public support for agriculture in developing countries was already low compared to developed countries, which were largely immune to the influence of the IMF and World Bank. The result was a more unequal international market for agriculture, and increasingly open borders in the global South for agricultural investment from multinational corporations. In theory the reduction of tariffs and subsidies was intended to make markets more efficient, increase trade, and make food cheaper for consumers. But with currencies devaluing, citizens did not find themselves with increased purchasing power at the supermarket; instead they were often paying higher prices for imported food that had been produced in subsidised conditions in the North. Jennifer Clapp estimates that OECD farmers received about 40 per cent of their income from subsidies in the 1980s (Clapp 2012: 65). Local producers in developing countries often could not compete with their imports. This precipitated a further wave of rural exodus and urban migration.

This pattern of uneven liberalisation was further consolidated through negotiations in the World Trade Organization (WTO) in the 1990s. Although developing countries managed to secure differentiated commitments on reducing tariffs and subsidies, the outcome of the 1994 Agreement on Agriculture still placed them at a disadvantage vis-à-vis developed countries. This is because developing countries had already undergone the Washington Consensus treatment; they had far less to reduce than the wealthier countries. Moreover, the WTO agreement allowed for *average* reductions in tariffs and subsidies, which meant that the US and Europe were able to maintain higher tariffs on goods that are also produced and exported from developing countries. The result was that rich countries' markets were still hard for developing countries' farmers to access, but developing country markets were even more open. Another outcome was the further consolidation of corporate power in both the North and the South, because it is these larger and more powerful actors that can best survive on lower subsidies and tariffs. These are the conditions under which social movements have emerged and strengthened, in both the North and the South.

## The Relationship Between the Environment and Agriculture

Having outlined the main characteristics of modern agriculture we can now more closely examine the relationship between agriculture and the environment. This is a dynamic relationship: agriculture impacts the environment but it is also impacted by environmental change. There has been growing attention to the relationship between the environment and agriculture among scientists and policy-makers. The issue that tends to capture the most attention is climate change. This concern is understandable because the world's capacity to nourish current and future generations is threatened by warming that has already been locked in. Capacity will be further undermined if the international community does not manage to deliver ambitious mitigation action in the future. Scientists estimate that each 1°C of warming during local growing seasons will reduce yields of major crops like corn, wheat, and rice by an average of 10 per cent (Brown 2005: 10–11). Future impacts will be felt unevenly across the world with some regions (notably North America) expected to see increases in crop yields as a result of longer growing seasons at upper latitudes, more rainfall, and higher levels of carbon in the soil (Paarlberg 2013: 129–30). European farmers are also expected to fare quite well due to a combination of higher adaptive capacity and the improved cultivation conditions that are anticipated (FAO 2015: 130). On balance, though, the news is not good for global food security. The Intergovernmental Panel on Climate Change (IPCC) concluded in its most recent assessment that failure to keep global temperature increases below 4°C 'would pose large risks to food security globally and regionally' (IPCC 2014: 489).

However, it is important to recognise that climate change is not a problem that will have only future impacts on global food systems. The most recent IPCC report documents the significant impacts that are already occurring. Scientists are already observing lower yields of corn and wheat on a global scale. Fisheries have also been affected with key species migrating away from tropical areas and towards the poles. This impacts food security because fish are an important food source for many people, and it also impacts the livelihoods of fishing communities in tropical countries (Vermeulen 2014: 2). Extreme climatic events (e.g., droughts, floods) are also already increasing, and these tend to lead to immediate price hikes in basic foods. Given that people in developing countries spend a higher proportion of their incomes on food, they tend to be the worst affected, with the least capacity to absorb higher prices. The social effects of these crises were on display throughout the 2000s. In 2007–8 when the price of key crops soared, food riots took place in several countries. The environmental triggers of price rises were compounded by food-exporting countries hoarding food and banning exports. When wheat crops failed in the Black Sea region in 2010–11, Russia restricted exports, which lead to panic buying in distant import-dependent countries (Terazono 2014).

Agriculture is not only affected by climate change, it is also a major contributor to climate change. Carbon dioxide is released into the atmosphere when land is cleared of trees and when soil is prepared for cultivation through mechanical processes of digging and overturning (i.e., tillage). The reliance of modern agriculture on fossil fuels adds to the sector's carbon footprint: manufacturing of chemical fertilisers, powering farm machinery, transporting produce by trucks and airplanes across vast distances, processing foods, and refrigerating products in supermarkets – all of these activities depend on fossil fuels and therefore emit greenhouse gases. Making agriculture more sustainable will require addressing this excessive reliance on fossil fuels.

We can see how inefficient the current system is when we recognise that agriculture is a process of energy conversion. Agriculture converts solar energy, fossil fuel energy, and chemical products into food that provides human energy (Heller and Keoleian 2000: 39). Enormous amounts of energy are lost in this conversion process. One study estimates that the modern food system uses an average of three calories of energy to produce a single calorie of edible food. Some foods use much more, especially meat. Thirty-five calories of energy are used to produce a calorie of grain-fed beef (Ehrenreich and Lyon 2011: 22). Large amounts of crops are produced to feed livestock and meet growing demands for meat-based diets. These animals in turn will emit methane in the process of digesting these crops, and methane is a highly potent greenhouse gas. Taking all of these aspects into account leads to estimates that the food and farming sector contributes between one-third and one-fifth of global anthropogenic GHG emissions (Paarlberg 2013: 131). This proportion is in relative decline not because food systems are becoming more sustainable (although deforestation is decreasing, and afforestation increasing), but because emissions in the energy sector continue to grow (IPCC 2014: 816).

Climate change poses a significant threat to global food security, but it would be a mistake to subsume all sustainability concerns under climate change. Environmental degradation associated with modern agriculture can also be observed in relation to water availability, biodiversity, and soil quality. Agriculture has an enormous water footprint, accounting for an extraordinary 92 per cent of all freshwater used around the world (Gerbens-Leenes et al. 2013: 25). About 1,000 litres of water are used to produce a kilo of wheat, while a kilo of rice requires about 2,000 litres (Paarlberg 2013: 133). Meat has a particularly large water footprint, requiring about twenty times as much water per calorie than cereals and root vegetables (Mekonnen and Hoekstra 2012: 401). This is largely due to the amount of pasture and crops consumed by livestock. With rising consumption of meat and animal products, the challenge of using water sustainably will be immense. The global production of meat doubled between 1980 and 2004, and is expected to double again up to the year 2050 (Mekonnen and Hoekstra 2012: 401). Like many environmental problems, the unsustainable level of water consumed in agricultural activities is largely invisible. Lester

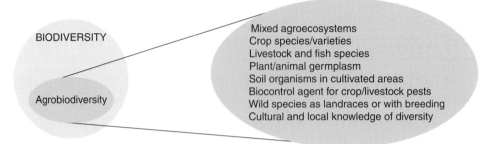

AGROBIODIVERSITY IS CENTRAL TO OVERALL BIODIVERSITY

BIODIVERSITY

Agrobiodiversity

Mixed agroecosystems
Crop species/varieties
Livestock and fish species
Plant/animal germplasm
Soil organisms in cultivated areas
Biocontrol agent for crop/livestock pests
Wild species as landraces or with breeding
Cultural and local knowledge of diversity

**Figure 11.1:** Elements of agricultural biodiversity
Source: FAO 2004

Brown explains that the global water deficit occurs through aquifer over-pumping and falling water tables; the warning signs are generally not observable in the pursuit of extensive irrigation (2005: 9–10). Our capacity to over-use water to this extent is a feature of modern agriculture; it is the result of modern technology such as electric and diesel-powered pumps. These technologies waste a lot of water because they are generally imprecise (using flooding techniques as opposed to spray-and-drip techniques), and because access to water is often under-regulated or subsidised (Paarlberg 2013: 134–5).

We saw above that the Green Revolution produced impressive increases in crop yields. But this came at an environmental cost. **Agricultural biodiversity** (or 'agrobiodiversity') has been one of the big losers. The various elements of agrobiodiversity are shown in Figure 11.1, including crop and animal species, soil organisms, and farming knowledge.

FAO estimates that some 75 per cent of plant genetic diversity was lost during the twentieth century when local varieties were replaced with genetically uniform high-yielding varieties (FAO 2004: 3). Most of the world's food is produced today from just a handful of plant and animal species. Despite the existence of hundreds of thousands of edible plant species, humans consume only about 150–200 species, and tend to rely mainly on just three species: rice, maize, and wheat (FAO 2004: 3). Carmen Gonzalez points to the 1840s Irish potato famine to illustrate the dangers of genetic uniformity in food production:

Native to the Andes, the potato was introduced into Spain in 1570 and into England and Ireland in approximately 1590. For over two centuries, all of the potatoes cultivated in Europe descended from these two introductions. The Irish potato famine was caused by a fungus known as *phytophthora infestans*. Due to the genetic uniformity of the Irish potato crop, a single infestation was sufficient to produce widespread devastation. The Irish potato famine lasted for five years, and resulted in the death of as many as 2,000,000 people and the migration to the United States of a comparable number. Eventually, potato varieties resistant to *phytophthora infestans* were discovered among the thousands of distinct potato varieties in the Andes and in Mexico, thus enabling potato cultivation to recover in Ireland. If some of these resistant potato varieties had originally been planted in Ireland along with the more vulnerable varieties, then the Irish potato famine might have been averted.

(2011: 497)

The impacts of agrobiodiversity loss can also be seen in the declining fertility of soils. As we saw in Chapter 4, the growing distance between the production of food and its consumption disrupts the natural processes of soil renewal. The crops and natural wastage that would once have been returned to the land instead often now end up as urban waste. This robs soil of nitrogen, phosphorus, and potassium and reduces its fertility. The long-term impacts of agriculture on soil quality can be witnessed in the Great Plains region of North America, described by one author as an 'agricultural factory of immense proportion' (Wishart 2004: 27). This region has become one of the world's largest wheat producers, a crop that requires significantly more water than the native grasses that covered the land in pre-agricultural times. American geologist Dale Pfeiffer explains that 'soil is eroding 30 times faster than the natural formation rate … As a result, the remaining topsoil is increasingly depleted of nutrients … Much of the soil in the Great Plains is now little more than a sponge into which we must pour hydrocarbon-based fertilizers in order to produce crops' (2006: 12). Not only is the health of the soil depleted in this process, but also the health of surrounding ecosystems. The nitrification of groundwater supplies is one such problem. As more and more fertilisers, pesticides, and herbicides are added to the soil to support continued intensive crop production, increasing levels of nitrate contaminate groundwater sources (Wishart 2004: 27–8). This in turn has knock-on effects for human health when the water is used domestically, and also harms amphibian species by depleting the water of oxygen (a process known as eutrophication). This problem is not isolated to the Great Plains. The Gulf of Mexico, for example, contains a 6,000-square-kilometre 'dead zone' that is unable to support aquatic life due to excessive use of nitrogen fertiliser on farms along the Mississippi River (Paarlberg 2013: 117–18).

Awareness of the environmental problems created by modern agriculture is growing. In 2005, a group of multilateral institutions led by the World Bank and the United Nations launched a three-year scientific review into the state of global agriculture. The International Assessment of Agricultural Knowledge, Science and Technology for Development (IAASTD) brought together hundreds of scientists from across the world to answer the following question: 'How can we reduce hunger and poverty, improve rural livelihoods, and facilitate equitable, environmentally, socially and economically sustainable development through the generation, access to, and use of agricultural knowledge, science and technology?' (McIntyre et al. 2009). The final report was highly critical of the modern food system, concluding that 'chemical-intensive industrial agriculture has degraded the natural resource base on which human survival depends and now threatens water, energy and climate security' (Ishii-Eiteman 2009). The review process involved the participation of civil society and industry groups. The final report reflected many of the demands that social movements have been making for several years. The recommendations were sufficiently radical to upset those with a significant stake in the status quo; the United States, Australia, and Canada participated in the governmental plenary review of the report but refused to approve it; while the agrochemical company Syngenta withdrew their participation in the final days (Ishii-Eiteman 2009).

## Resisting Unsustainable Agriculture

The most ambitious actions to address the environmental and social problems of the modern agricultural system come from social movements. We will examine their efforts in this section of the chapter. Social movements have sought to resist unsustainable agriculture in multiple ways. Earlier in this chapter we explored a set of analytical distinctions that aid in understanding resistance. We can now see these distinctions at work in the ways in which social movements resist unsustainable agriculture.

Protest, or the 'politics of demand', is pervasive. The most extreme act of protest performed in response to the neoliberal agricultural model was the suicide of South Korean farmer Lee Kyang Hae, who set himself on fire outside the Cancun WTO negotiations. Other radical protests have involved destroying a McDonald's outlet in France, burning down a Kentucky Fried Chicken in India, and destroying experimental GM crops in Australia. More moderate acts include the frequent peaceful protests held outside meetings of the WTO or FAO. Action-based resistance is also pervasive. As we will see below this can take the form of organic farms and local markets, and self-organised training and education. Rather than just demanding changes in policy and regulation and waiting for these to come into effect, autonomous actions create alternative systems where people can put their values into practice irrespective of what is happening elsewhere in the country or world.

It's important to keep in mind that the distinction between demanding and acting is purely analytical. In practice, social movements and civil society groups may often resist on both of these fronts at the same time. In his study of the rise of the global organic farming movement, Matthew Reed observes that much social movement activity occurs out of sight. To those not involved in the movement it may appear that it is inactive when protests and marches are not taking place. But these periods may well be the most creative and constructive for a social movement seeking to transform unsustainable agriculture (Reed 2010: 17). But the distinction between demanding change and enacting change is a useful one to see how resistance occurs, so let's look more closely at each of these.

## Demanding Sustainable Agriculture

Protests against the modern industrialised system of agriculture increasingly coalesce around demands for 'food sovereignty'. These demands are articulated in opposition to mainstream goals of 'food security'. Whereas food security seeks to reduce hunger and increase food production within the confines of the existing model of agriculture, food sovereignty demands a transformation of this existing model. **Food sovereignty** has been defined as 'the right of peoples to healthy and culturally appropriate food, produced through ecologically sound and sustainable methods, and their right to define their own food and agricultural systems' (Holt-Giménez and Altieri 2013: 95). To demand food sovereignty is to demand that states and international institutions recognise this right and change their policies and practices to respect and protect this right. This poses a considerable challenge to the status quo because it would require recognising food and farming as culturally important rather than just commodities to be produced in industrially rational ways for export and import. In many cases, this would also require significant public support for agricultural and rural communities, to restrict permissible farm sizes, and ensure equitable access to land, water, and seeds (Rosset 2006: 34–5).

Demands for food sovereignty are made in various ways. The group that has done most to advance demands for food sovereignty is **La Via Campesina**, a

Box 11.1: **The Six Pillars of Food Sovereignty**

1. **Focuses on food for people:** people's right to sufficient, healthy, and culturally appropriate food is at the centre of policies; food is recognised as more than just a commodity.
2. **Values food providers:** the livelihoods of all producers is supported, respected, valued.
3. **Localises food systems:** the distance between food providers and consumers is reduced; local food providers are protected from food aid dumping; consumers are protected from poor-quality food and GM organisms; the power of remote and unaccountable corporations is resisted.
4. **Puts control locally:** control over land and resources is placed in the hands of local food providers; geopolitical borders do not erode the rights of local communities to inhabit their territories; the privatisation of 'natural resources' is rejected.
5. **Builds knowledge and skills:** food systems are conserved on the basis of local skills and knowledge; research systems are developed to build knowledge and skills and pass these on to future generations.
6. **Works with nature:** the contributions of ecosystem services are maximised to improve resilience and adaptation to climate change; energy-intensive, monocultural, industrialised production methods are rejected.

Source: Nyéléni Declaration 2007

transnational network of farming and peasant organisations in sixty-eight countries. Since 1996, La Via Campesina has been gathering in counter-summits alongside governmental meetings, where they carry out their own talks and prepare parallel declarations on sustainable agriculture. Their declarations often call for a rollback of international trade rules that push farmers off the land and flood local markets with generic commodities from abroad. Taking food out of the WTO remains the most important goal of the food sovereignty movement because until this happens few other progressive reforms can take place. Beyond this aim, six pillars of the food sovereignty paradigm have been developed (Box 11.1).

The food sovereignty movement has had some small but important victories. In 2007, French farmer José Bové embarked on a 100-day hunger strike to highlight the threats posed by the GM industry to French rural life and food cultures more broadly. After eight days the French government agreed to one of his demands and banned a GM form of maize in the country (Ayres and Bosia 2014: 319–20). This incident is celebrated by the food sovereignty movement as a victory against the GM industry, and in particular against one of the world's largest agribiotechnology corporations, Monsanto. The following year Ecuador's government responded to social movement concerns by redrafting the constitution to include food sovereignty. The Ecuadorian constitution now obligates the state to promote food sovereignty, and pledges that people will have secure and permanent access to sufficient, healthy, and nutritious food preferably produced locally in accordance with cultural customs (Article 13).

## Practising Sustainable Agriculture

The sustainable agriculture and food sovereignty movement is not sitting back and waiting for governments to establish sustainable food systems. Instead, communities in the global North and South are actively working to transform their visions into reality. Optimistic advocates suggest that the transition to a sustainable food system could be achieved through grassroots action alone, but could be greatly advanced with the involvement and support of governments (Pfeiffer 2006: 53). Given the diversity of farming communities around the world it is no surprise that experiments in sustainable agriculture vary from place to place. But many of these experiments share an approach that has been called 'agroecology'.

Agroecology has been defined in two ways: narrowly and broadly. Narrowly it is defined as a scientific discipline that applies ecological concepts to the management of agrifood systems. Broadly it is defined as a holistic approach to managing agrifood systems that combines Western science, traditional and indigenous knowledge, and economic, political, and social values (Tomich et al. 2011; Kremen et al. 2012: 45). Agroecology is underpinned by principles of ecology. These hold that humans are embedded in the natural environment; and that humans are dependent on and shape ecological processes and landscapes (Tomich et al. 2011: 196). The emphasis on the 'agrifood system' takes in more than just the production of food and instead considers the interaction of factors that affect food access; quantities and qualities of food; and food production, processing, marketing, and distribution (Tomich et al. 2011: 195). Unlike industrial food systems that focus on producing crops for export over long distances, agroecological systems focus on producing food for local, regional, or national markets. Chemical fertilisers are replaced with plant- and animal-derived organic matter; and external corporate-influenced scientific techniques are rejected in favour of local innovation and cooperative learning (Altieri and Toledo 2011: 592). Agroecological systems are also inherently small scale because they require farmers to closely observe natural processes and respond to changes: 'the farmer must be intimately familiar with every patch of soil, knowing exactly where to add fertilizer, and where pests are being harboured or are entering the field' (Pfeiffer 2006: 58–9).

Agroecology has been particularly strong in Latin America. In fact, Miguel Altieri and Victor Manuel Toledo suggest that an 'agroecological revolution' is taking place there and identify six common features of Latin American agroecosystems (see Box 11.2).

Box 11.2: **Features of Agroecosystems**

1. High levels of biodiversity.
2. Ingenious systems and technologies of landscape, land and water resource management and conservation.
3. Diversified agricultural systems that contribute to local and national food and livelihood security.
4. Systems that exhibit resiliency and robustness in coping with disturbance and change, minimising risk in the midst of variability.
5. Agriculture nurtured by traditional knowledge systems and farmers' innovations and technologies.
6. Socio-cultural institutions regulated by strong cultural values and collective forms of social organisation including normative arrangements for resource access and benefit sharing, value systems, rituals, etc.

Source: Altieri and Toledo 2011: 591

We can develop a clearer picture of what agroecology looks like in practice by examining prominent cases from South and Central America.

## Brazil and the Landless Rural Workers Movement

The Movimento dos Trabalhadores Rurais Sem Terra (MST) is one of the largest and most active member organisations of La Via Campesina. The history of the MST very explicitly shows how the 'politics of the act' differs from the 'politics of demand'. Rather than just demanding land reform, the MST has actively resisted what it sees as unjust land laws in Brazil. Over several decades the MST has organised thousands of non-violent occupations on unproductive land owned by large landowners. These occupations have succeeded in legally settling 370,000 families on about 7.5 million hectares of land. This settlement reversed the massive rural exodus that took place in the country in the 1960s to 1980s when agriculture was mechanised and industrialised under the military dictatorship regime. Large landowners came to dominate food production and Brazil became an agricultural superpower, but the social costs were significant as agrarian workers and their families moved into urban slums. The return to democracy produced a new constitution in 1988 with clauses requiring that land serve a social function and allowing for expropriation for public use (Article 5: XXIII, XXIV). Despite these constitutional provisions, social movements like the MST have had to push hard to have their rights recognised via agrarian reform.

Members of MST include land occupiers as well as those who have been successfully settled. Both groups of people actively push for extended reforms, social services, and recognition of cultural, economic, and environmental rights (Friends of the MST 2015; Holt-Giménez and Patel 2012). Agroecology was not initially central to the MST mission but it eventually became MST policy as awareness grew of the limitations of industrial agriculture. Here we can see that the social and political values of the movement pushed them towards agroecology, an approach that resonates with the small-scale, livelihood-centric, and anti-corporate position of the MST. Since the year 2000, the MST has established several schools and training courses to promote agroecology and train youth in sustainable farming techniques (Holt-Giménez and Patel 2012: 95–6).

## Campesino a Campesino, Central America

The agroecology movement points to the experience of Central America to support claims that agroecology offers a more resistant model of agriculture than the conventional industrial model. As a social movement, agroecology had limited success in this region. Conventional agriculture remains dominant; the general picture of farming in Central America is one of large-scale plantations and export-oriented cattle ranches alongside small, subsistence farms on ecologically fragile lands (Holt-Giménez 2002). Conventional farming organisations also dominate unions and decision-making bodies. But over 10,000 farmers are now practising agroecology in Central America and are united in a movement called Campesino a Campesino (Farmer to Farmer). The movement focuses on small-scale experimentation and innovation, and exchanging knowledge and experience from farmer to farmer in a spirit of solidarity. This has allowed farm systems to be redesigned to reduce reliance on external inputs (e.g., fertilisers, pesticides, irrigation) and instead strengthen habitats, restore watersheds, and enhance biodiversity to allow nature to perform these functions. The merits of this approach were proven when Hurricane Mitch hit the region in 1998. The hurricane was the strongest for 200 years and left thousands of people dead and millions homeless, and destroyed vast areas of crops. Research carried out in 360 communities in Nicaragua, Honduras, and Guatemala found that, overall, conventional farms suffered greater losses of topsoil, higher levels of soil damage, more erosion, and more crop losses than those based on agroecology. Farmers practising agroecology also suffered fewer economic losses than conventional farmers, particularly because they grew a diverse variety of crops rather than a single crop (Holt-Giménez 2006: 189).

## Cuba and Organic Agriculture

The Cuban experience shows what is possible on a national level when a government is committed to large-scale reform. It is widely viewed as a symbolically important case that demonstrates the viability of alternatives to the conventional model of industrial agriculture. Agrarian reform in Cuba dates back to the 1959 communist revolution. At the time of the revolution, land ownership was highly concentrated: about 8 per cent of the country's farmers controlled about 70 per cent of the land. The rural workforce was largely impoverished, with precarious seasonal employment. The revolution saw the land expropriated and converted to large state-owned farms and thousands of small labourer-owned farms. A series of reforms then imposed restrictions on the size of private land ownership (first to 1,000 acres and later to 165 acres per person). Foreign ownership of land was banned, and local farmers were supported with low-interest credit, technological assistance, insurance, transport, free education and health care (Pfeiffer 2006: 54–5).

The model of agriculture that developed in Cuba throughout the 1960s, 1970s, and 1980s may have achieved many of the social goals of the communist regime, but it was certainly not environmentally or economically sustainable: it was centralised, specialised, inefficient, chemical intensive, and export oriented. The Achilles' heel of the system was its reliance on the Soviet Union. Cuba specialised in producing sugar, tobacco, and citrus fruits for the Soviet market, and the country imported most of its food, oil, feedstock, pesticides, fertiliser, and fuel from the Soviet Union. The collapse of the Soviet Union seriously undermined Cuba's food security. Food imports halved; per capita daily calorie intake dropped by 36 per cent; and protein intake dropped by 40 per cent. Cuba's capacity to rebound and reorient its markets was severely limited by US-imposed diplomatic restrictions, which excluded Cuba from major international institutions and forbid trade with US trade partners.

Following the collapse of the Soviet Union, Cuba found itself economically isolated. Carmen Gonzalez observes a paradox here: 'while Cuba's economic isolation produced enormous hardship, it also gave Cuba free rein to respond to the crisis … in ways that diverged radically from the prevailing neoliberal model' (2004: 482). Fortunately for the Cubans, the country had established one of the most sophisticated scientific research sectors in Latin America after the revolution, and research into sustainable agriculture was quite advanced by the end of the cold war. The government rapidly drew on this body of knowledge to begin transitioning to a self-sufficient, decentralised, low-input model of farming. Large state farms were converted into small cooperatised farms. Dale Pfeiffer explains that ancestral techniques of inter-cropping and manuring were soon reinstated; organic, non-chemical pesticides and fertilisers were manufactured from worms, compost, natural rock phosphate, and manures, and these replaced fossil fuel based inputs; weed-suppressant crops were incorporated into farms, and diverse crops were rotated as seasons changed; and animal traction was reintroduced to replace tractors. Organic urban agriculture took off later and this now produces the majority of the vegetables consumed (Pfeiffer 2006: 58). Restrictions on private trade were relaxed so that once farmers had met their state-imposed production quotas they could sell their surplus at market rates. The result of these reforms has been increased yields of staple and export crops (Gonzalez 2004: 480).

## Questioning Agroecology

Champions of agroecology present it as socially and environmentally superior to conventional agriculture, but critics have raised doubts. For some, organic farming is just 'muck and magic' (Reed 2010: 9). Ecological science underpins many alternative farming practices, but it is true that some practitioners look beyond the science and find inspiration in cosmology and non-scientific teachings, employing such techniques as homeopathy and aura readings of plants (Reed 2010: 9). But it would be incorrect and unfair to cast all sustainable farming in this light.

Other critics question the efficiency of organic farming and defend conventional farming as the only viable model for achieving food security. Paarlberg, for example, sees merit in combining some techniques of agroecology with conventional farming. One example of this is to use no-till planting techniques on conventional farms. 'No-till' means that the land is not cleared and ploughed prior to planting; the seeds are inserted directly into the soil through the residue of the previous season's harvest. But he rejects the idea that agroecology alone can support livelihoods and provide sufficient food for growing populations (2013: 77). This combination of techniques is consistent with an approach that has recently been called 'sustainable intensification', which aims to increase yields with few units of land, water, and fertiliser. Sustainable intensification was proposed by FAO in 2008, and its advocates say that it will be necessary to double food production by 2050 to feed 9 billion people. For La Via Campesina this represents nothing more than an attempt to co-opt agroecology 'to fine-tune the industrial food system'. They resist the selective use of agroecology that strips it of its social and political dimensions (La Via Campesina 2015). It is worth recalling that hunger and food shortages are not the result of under-production but rather inequitable distribution and food waste. Today the world wastes between 30 per cent and 50 per cent of all food that is produced, which raises questions about assumptions that food production must double to meet the needs of growing populations (This is Rubbish 2014).

Others have critiqued an unreflective celebration of localism that underpins the demands and practices of the sustainable agriculture movement. Brandon Born and Mark Purcell argue that food systems research and advocacy are characterised by 'the local trap'. This refers to 'the tendency ... to assume something inherently good about the local scale. The local is assumed to be desirable, and it is preferred a priori over larger scales ... the local trap assumes that a local-scale food system will be inherently more socially just than a national-scale or global-scale food system' (2009: 117). Born and Purcell do not argue that the local scale is necessarily problematic but rather that it is not inherently good; local-scale food systems are just as likely to be unjust and undemocratic as global-scale systems. Local food systems are also equally likely to be ecologically unsustainable if the goal is simply to eliminate distance between the production and consumption of food. In a place like Arizona people would either go hungry or rely on significant amounts of water to eat locally produced food (2009: 126). Critics also see the risk of cultivating or strengthening xenophobic sentiments by presenting local producers and locally produced food as superior. Local food advocates have recognised the possibility of this, but respond that localisation can also be highly reflexive. Localisation does not have to be only a reactionary, defensive, and unreflective celebration of the local scale. 'Reflexive localisation' offers the possibility for sustainable agriculture movements to experiment with localisation while acknowledging its limitations and tensions and maintaining an open mind about the boundaries of the 'local' (DuPuis et al. 2011: 297; Hinrichs 2003: 38).

## Conclusion

In this chapter social movements have moved to centre stage. We have already seen in earlier chapters that civil society plays important roles in advocating that governments take action, monitoring promises and performance, and working with public and private actors to advance the goals of global environmental agreements. This chapter shows that social movements play a key part in expanding our 'environmental imagination' (Dowie 1996: 7) by demonstrating that alternative systems are possible.

The modern agricultural system is beset with social and environmental limitations. Productive capacity has expanded enormously since the end of World War Two, and many argue that it will need to continue to expand to feed 9 billion people in 2050. Critical voices point out that we already produce more than enough to feed the world's 7 billion people, yet many remain undernourished or starving. This suggests that the main problem is not underproduction but mal-distribution. Existing production methods are also energy and chemical intensive, which means they contribute to climate change and other environmental problems. For social movements like La Via Campesina, these social and environmental problems justify transformational change. We have seen that experiments in agroecology and food sovereignty have delivered positive results in some Latin American communities. But the potential for globalising these alternative systems remains to be seen.

## Discussion Questions

1. Which forms of resistance do you think are mostly likely to bring about changes in unsustainable practices and policies?
2. In what ways is industrialised agriculture implicated in and vulnerable to climate change and environmental degradation?
3. Does agroecology offer a viable alternative to conventional farming?
4. What potential problems have been identified in the project of localisation? Are these insurmountable?
5. What are the prospects for feeding 9 billion people in 2050 in an environmentally sustainable and socially just way?

# 12 Appraising Global Environmental Governance

**key points**

- The distinction between local environmental problems and global environmental problems is increasingly blurred, and problems are increasingly interconnected.
- While some progress has been made, overall political responses to global environmental problems remain inadequate and poorly aligned with the scale and severity of problems.
- Environmental problems are political problems that affect different people in different ways. The responses to environmental problems can distribute costs and benefits unevenly.
- Environmental inequalities can be analysed in temporal, social, and geographic terms.
- The weaknesses of environmental policies may not be immediately apparent. Moving towards more fair and effective global environmental governance requires committed critical observation.

## Introduction

At the beginning of this book we encountered the concept of the Anthropocene. What this concept captures is the scale of environmental change brought about by human activity, so great that we have provoked an epochal shift. Humans have left a footprint on the planet since our ancient ancestors began foraging for plants and hunting animals at least 2 million years ago. The advent of agriculture and then industrialisation established modes of development that would have profound impacts on the earth. But an acceleration of human activities since about the middle of the twentieth century is responsible for the most serious impacts on the earth. As our collective understanding of environmental problems has grown, attempts at agreeing on collective action have also grown. But an unfortunate reality of global environmental politics is that *problems*, *policy*, and *practice* are rarely aligned. Even when problems are recognised and policy responses are designed, performance is frequently far weaker than promises.

In this final chapter we will revisit some of the key themes of the book. We begin by recalling the causes of environmental change and degradation, and reflect on their key characteristics. The distinction between local environmental problems and global environmental problems is increasingly blurred, and problems are increasingly interconnected. This has important implications for the effectiveness of global environmental governance. In the following section we examine the various forms of policy and practice that we have seen throughout the book, and consider how effective these are for improving environmental conditions. Environmental problems are political problems that affect different people in different ways. The responses to environmental problems can distribute costs and benefits unevenly. It is therefore important to follow our examination of policy effectiveness with an assessment of the environmental inequalities that emerge in global environmental politics. This is done by drawing out insights from the chapters about how the costs of environmental harm are inequitably distributed in temporal, social, and geographic terms. Finally, the chapter and book concludes with a look to the future. What are the prospects for more effective and equitable responses to global environmental problems in the years ahead?

# The Nature of Environmental Problems

The causes of global environmental change form a complex web. We risk overlooking important factors if we focus exclusively on one type of cause. Scientists put the shift from the Holocene to the Anthropocene down to a series of converging socio-economic trends: growth in population, GDP, energy use, water use, fertiliser consumption, and others. But if we recall some of the explanations we found in Part 1 of this book, we can understand these trends as the proximate causes of environmental change, but not the actual drivers. In those chapters we saw that the underlying causes of environmental problems can be identified in different ways. For some the underlying causes are short-sighted and selfish human nature; poorly managed resources; or the absence of national or international regulation or markets. For others it's the endurance of poverty that leaves many countries too poor to prioritise a clean environment; global capitalism that depends on competition and exponential economic growth; or people's alienation from the natural world.

When scientists talk of the Anthropocene they draw attention to the immense scale of human-induced environmental change. Unsurprisingly, this raises significant concerns about how governments and communities can adapt to or deal with the problems generated by such large-scale change. While we tend to focus on questions about action, we should be careful to avoid losing sight of those underlying drivers of environmental change.

One useful distinction we encountered in this book was between 'green' and 'brown' environmental issues (see Chapter 8). This distinction helps us appreciate that environmental priorities differ across the world. Asymmetrical priorities have often been a source of tension in international environmental politics. Wealthy industrialised countries have traditionally been more concerned about global-scale, slow-developing problems that emerge from growth-based, energy-intensive, industrial development. These green environmental problems include climate change, biodiversity loss, and ozone depletion. Countries with widespread poverty have traditionally been more concerned about problems arising at local and regional scales that undermine people's immediate quality of life. These 'brown' environmental issues include inadequate access to clean water and sanitation, soil erosion that reduces crop yields, and local exposure to air pollution causing premature death and disease.

But the distinction between **green and brown** issues is becoming limited in helping us to understand the different nature of environmental problems and the different concerns they raise. Global environmental problems increasingly manifest as local environmental problems with immediate and short-term impacts. 'Climate refugees' are no longer a distant prospect. There remains some dispute about using 'refugee' terminology because this is usually reserved for those facing persecution and those seeking refuge beyond their national borders.

But the United Nations is nevertheless concerned about the numbers of people already forced to flee their homes as a result of climate change. Over 20 million people have been displaced by climate- and weather-related events since 2009 (UNHCR 2015). Coastal and delta-based communities are most vulnerable to rising sea levels. Even relatively slight increases in sea levels cause problems by contaminating freshwater sources and arable land, exacerbating erosion, and disrupting terrestrial and marine ecosystems. All of these problems in turn lead to biodiversity loss and greater food insecurity. Deforestation and wetland destruction (often carried out for agricultural expansion) make natural environments less resilient to flooding. These brief examples show that environmental problems cannot be placed in neat boxes with discrete labels such as deforestation, climate change, biodiversity, and water scarcity. These problems are interconnected in various ways, both in terms of their **direct and indirect causes** and their consequences.

We have no World Environment Organization to respond to overlapping and interconnected problems in a coordinated and coherent fashion. Instead we often see that individual environmental problems are addressed in their own discrete ways. The concept of sustainable development comes closest to overcoming this reductionism. As we saw in Chapter 6, the sustainable development concept was coined in the late twentieth century to facilitate environmental cooperation between the global North and the global South. It made poverty reduction and economic development central to environmental protection. It reflected a marriage of green and brown environmental problems by recognising that development must overcome immediate threats to human wellbeing, while keeping distant and slow-developing problems in view.

The most recent policy incarnation of sustainable development are the Sustainable Development Goals. A generous interpretation of these goals would be to label them as ambitious given they cover over a dozen issues and provide 169 targets. On a more pessimistic reading they are deliberately vague. The absence of quantifiable targets will make it hard to distinguish between pure rhetoric and actual performance in the future.

One clear lesson that we can take from the past few decades of global environmental governance is that strong words do not easily translate into effective and equitable action. Indeed, one of the starkest patterns we have seen in this book is a mismatch between problem recognition, political promises, and actual performance. Let's turn now to look more closely at the forms of policy and practice we have seen throughout the book, and consider how they measure up in terms of effectiveness.

# Evaluating Policy and Practice

Despite Garrett Hardin's warning that shared environments are destined for destruction we saw considerable efforts at cooperation throughout this book. We saw cooperation among states; among private sector actors; among civil society groups; as well as various attempts at cooperation across these types of actors. In Chapter 2 we learnt from the Nobel Prize winning political scientist Elinor Ostrom that there is no 'one size fits all' approach to managing common resources and shared environments (1999: 497). Political hubris should be abandoned in the pursuit of effective environmental governance. This is true for local and national environmental problems, but it is even more significant for global environmental problems where complexity is magnified. We have seen attempts at cooperation that take the forms of markets, multilateral agreements, and voluntary schemes. Following Ostrom's wisdom, we should treat these as policy experiments. We should refrain from ruling out any particular political response to environmental problems, but we certainly ought to scrutinise the performance of different experiments with the aim of deepening our understanding of what is and is not working well. An evident pattern is that political responses to global environmental problems have so far been inadequate and poorly aligned with their scale and severity. But to draw out a more nuanced picture of the effectiveness of policy and practice, let's take lessons from each of the contexts analysed in this book.

A lesson we can take from the experience of water politics is that cooperative-type behaviour is more common than conflictive-type behaviour, at least at the level of international interactions (i.e., between states). This insight runs counter to common wisdom: it is widely assumed that violent conflict is likely under conditions of shrinking shared resources. This assumption leaves scarce resources and environmental problems open to securitisation, which is unlikely to lead to the types of action that are in the interests of vulnerable groups. We also saw in Chapter 5 that even when international institutions effectively avoid violent conflict between states there are still winners and losers from cooperative arrangements. International agreements can consolidate inequitable access to water and other resources. They can also give a façade of cooperation while keeping sensitive political questions off the agenda, such as debates about how water should be used and distributed. As we saw in Chapter 1, environmental problems are political problems; they cannot be solved once and for all because different groups disagree about what the real problems are and what should be done in response.

In Chapter 6 we examined the case of sustainable development. We saw that the United Nations can provide a setting for states to gradually develop shared understandings about the nature of environmental problems and how they can be addressed. Diplomacy can produce different types of multilateral agreements among states. Some of these are 'soft' law (e.g., resolutions, guidelines, declarations, action plans, and roadmaps) that allow states to recognise an issue as serious without committing themselves to strong action. Other agreements are 'hard' law (e.g., international treaties), which legally bind states to specific actions. Soft law shouldn't be dismissed as mere rhetoric or inconsequential: states often make an effort to comply with their stated commitments. Compliance may be in states' own national interest, but governments may also perceive the broader benefits of international cooperation and good international citizenship. In the context of sustainable development, however, performance has consistently lagged behind pledges and promises. Every ten years the international community meets in a large summit to reflect on the persistent problem of unsustainable development, but these gatherings have so far delivered limited results.

The case of climate change shows how non-state actors can move into the regulatory gap generated by inadequate multilateral cooperation. States have been working on international agreements to reduce greenhouse gas emissions for about three decades, but the scale of the problem still exceeds their combined ambition. The private sector and civil society have developed various alternative governance arrangements with the aim of decarbonising the global economy. Voluntary action outside the UN is an important way of experimenting with policy, but in Chapter 7 several weaknesses became apparent. These factors limit the potential for voluntary initiatives to effectively address climate change. In some cases, transnational governance efforts serve mainly to displace carbon emissions rather than genuinely change production and consumption patterns. This is the main criticism of markets for carbon 'offsets'. We saw that climate governance experiments tend to take a market-friendly approach that doesn't question the viability of exponential economic growth. Effective climate change policies are likely to require more diverse policy experimentation. By its very nature, voluntary action cannot be directed or closely monitored by central actors (like states or the UN), but without any form of coordination we have no way of knowing how voluntary initiatives are genuinely performing and whether they are effectively contributing to climate change mitigation and adaptation.

The case of deforestation discussed in Chapter 8 shows that innovative financial mechanisms have existed alongside traditional 'environmental aid' for many years. Debt-for-nature swaps, payments for ecosystem services, and other environmental markets aim to make it financially viable for developing countries to preserve their natural environments rather than sell off natural resources as commodities on international markets. The private sector has assumed an important role in global forestry governance. As in the context of climate change this is partly explained by the failure of states to establish and maintain effective multilateral institutions. In the case of deforestation, states' inability to agree on the nature of the problem has prevented negotiation of an international convention. Instead we have only soft law instruments that have largely failed to bring deforestation under control. Market-based schemes have helped to limit deforestation in some areas. But these initiatives suffer from the fundamental weakness that they neglect the underlying drivers of deforestation, which are found in growing demands for food, feed, fibre, fuel, and forest products. Without addressing unsustainable consumption, deforestation will continue on a large scale.

Chapter 9 revealed the wider failings of the international community to curb unsustainable consumption. UN efforts to make consumption patterns more sustainable have been underway since the early 1990s, but member states have consistently resisted ambitious action. In this context we see the familiar pattern of voluntary initiatives emerging to fill the governance gap. The private sector and civil society have cooperated to raise public awareness and create tools to help people reduce the environmental impact of their consumption. Developing public understanding of unsustainability is clearly a crucial element of effective global environmental governance. But as we saw in Chapter 9, initiatives that promote change through individual voluntary action have limitations that we need to recognise. Responsibly produced goods often come with a premium price tag, which limits their availability to certain classes. But those with the purchasing power to buy 'green' products still confront the problem of 'greenwash', which makes it hard to purchase genuinely sustainable goods. A focus on individual consumption can also give the misleading impression that problems of unsustainability can be resolved through simple lifestyle changes. The most effective initiatives for promoting sustainable consumption would encourage citizens to adjust their individual habits at the same time as engaging in political action to demand better laws and regulation.

Chapter 10 revealed the importance of activism for promoting international political action. The case of hazardous wastes confirms one of our lessons from Chapter 9 on unsustainable consumption. If activists had focused on encouraging consumers to buy fewer goods with toxic elements, it is unlikely that they would have effected much change. In part this is because it is very difficult for the average consumer to determine the full chemical composition of the goods they buy. Most of the items we use in everyday life have chemical elements that can contribute to toxic waste when disposed of. States have responded to civil society concerns with a patchwork of agreements to control the production, trade, and disposal of hazardous substances. These agreements are among the most ambitious of any environmental issue. They create rules that prohibit the use of certain chemicals, restrict shipments of hazardous wastes, and promote capacity-building in developing countries' waste management systems. One of the factors that weaken the effectiveness of these UN rules is that they are only one part of global chemical governance. Dozens of other state, corporate, and civil society initiatives also exist to control hazardous substances. This fragmentation risks ambiguity and confusion, which in turn creates opportunities for states and corporations to avoid responsibility for their use of toxic chemicals.

The case of unsustainable agriculture explored in Chapter 11 reveals the role that civil society can play in creating alternative systems of production outside the confines of the liberal international economy. This alerts us to the possibility that the most ambitious, innovative, and progressive change may be led from below rather than above. Many social movements see neoliberal globalisation as inherently unsustainable and have little faith in environmental policies that are crafted within the parameters of that system. Modern agriculture imposes a heavy impact on the planet. It relies on large amounts of fossil fuel-based energy and chemicals to power equipment, maintain soil fertility under intensive conditions, and transport food across the world as a global commodity. Social movements like La Via Campesina have responded with political demands to make agricultural systems more just and sustainable. But importantly they have also built alternative agricultural systems based on food sovereignty and agroecology. These alternative systems are small scale and focus on supplying local markets. These alternative systems are limited in scope and do not pose any real threat to the dominance of the globalised and corporate agricultural system. But they do make an important contribution to global environmental governance by expanding our 'environmental imagination' (Dowie 1996: 7) and demonstrating that alternative systems are possible.

## Distributing Environmental Harm

Environmental problems are political problems that create winners and losers. Environmental problems do not affect all people equally. Environmental harm is not distributed equally across time, place, and social class. The actions taken by states, the private sector, and civil society benefit or harm some people more than others. We can find many cases of environmental inequality and injustice within the pages of this book. Let's distil these insights into three categories to see how environmental harm is distributed temporally, socially, and geographically. In practice these categories tend to overlap, but they are analytically useful.

### Temporal Inequality

In Chapter 3 we encountered the Environmental Kuznets Curve that suggests that environmental quality deteriorates as a country's economy grows but starts to improve when the country reaches a certain level of development (Grossman and Krueger 1991, 1996). While there is inconsistent evidence about the relationship between economic growth and environmental improvement, the EKC appears to only exist when problems are immediately perceptible and relatively affordable to address. Responsibility for addressing an environmental problem is pushed into the future when the effects are not immediately visible, it has limited impact on the people's lives in the short term, and is costly to reduce. Which environmental problems fall into this category? Examples include biodiversity loss, ozone depletion, and soil degradation. Perhaps the classic case is climate change, which we saw in Chapter 7. Even though states and non-state actors have recognised the problem of $CO_2$ pollution, their combined action is far below what is required to limit global temperature increases to $1.5°C$ or $2°C$ above pre-industrial levels. The consequence of inadequate ambition is that future climate change risks are magnified.

### Social Inequality

The poor and socially marginalised tend to bear the brunt of environmental problems. In Chapter 2 we saw that environmental injustice extends back as far as the thirteenth century. While Garrett Hardin blamed selfish and short-sighted human nature for degradation of the commons, there is evidence that wealthy landowners kept the most fertile land in private hands while making poorer-quality land available for collective grazing and cultivation. Poorer farmers were therefore more exposed to environmental degradation than wealthy landowners. We saw a related phenomenon in Chapter 5 in the context of water. It is possible to find carefully constructed lists and maps showing water insecure cities and countries around the world. But we should not assume that water scarcity is a purely environmental problem that can be objectively determined based on measurements of water supply. Freshwater is unequally distributed. This means that some people may experience water scarcity even if they live in cities and countries that have adequate water supplies to meet their populations' needs. Poorer and marginalised groups of society are most likely to experience freshwater scarcity.

In Chapter 3 we began to see how environmental policies can be socially unjust unless people's human rights are taken into account. Concerns about population growth led governments, private foundations, and multilateral agencies to promote birth control in developing countries. Some women welcomed this because birth control gave them new opportunities to plan their families and consider alternative life choices. Other women found themselves subjected to draconian programmes that focused exclusively on their fertility while ignoring their wellbeing and the disempowered conditions in which they lived. In Chapters 7 and 8 we saw other ways in which the social dimensions of environmental problems can be overlooked. Climate change policies are often designed on the basis of efficiency rather than equity. One of the consequences of this is that carbon offset markets have directed most mitigation investment to more advanced developing countries. Countries like South Korea and China (and their wealthier provinces, in particular) are more attractive than less developed countries because they have higher volumes of emissions to offer companies in the market for carbon credits. Another consequence of favouring efficiency over equity is that adaptation needs of vulnerable communities are overlooked in favour of mitigation efforts. Unlike mitigation, adaptation policies do not fit well with the market rationality that guides transnational climate governance. Similar trends were seen in Chapter 8 where innovative financial mechanisms for environmental protection risk exacerbating inequalities when they focus primarily on efficiency. Environmental protection policies could sometimes help to reduce poverty and promote social development, but only if such social objectives are deliberately included in policy design. The example of REDD+ (which offers financial incentives to developing countries to better protect and manage their forests) also reveals that environmental policies can risk exacerbating conflict, inequalities, and displacement if human rights and procedural justice are overlooked.

## Geographic Inequality

Globalisation presents many opportunities for displacing the environmental costs of economic development. As we saw in Chapter 3, critics of the Environmental Kuznets Curve argue that apparent improvements in efficiency and pollution often only reflect 'an illusion of sustainability' (Rothman 1998: 186). As countries move towards service-based economies, they 'outsource' the production of the resource-intensive goods that their citizens continue to consume. Environmental impact is therefore not minimised just displaced. This concern drives some of the criticisms about carbon offsetting schemes and market-based REDD+ proposals, which we saw in Chapters 7 and 8. Critics question the ethics of offsetting the carbon-intensive lifestyles of people in wealthy countries by paying people in poorer countries to limit their own carbon emissions. They also question whether REDD+ is merely a cheap and convenient way to focus attention on action in tropical countries instead of addressing unsustainable demands for food, feed, fibre, fuel, and forest products in other countries. Chapter 10 shone a spotlight on the international trade in hazardous wastes. This phenomenon represents the geographical displacement of environmental harm. Historically hazardous waste was predominantly shipped from wealthy countries to poorer countries. In recent years the directions of trade have become more complicated. Wealthy European countries often have sophisticated technologies for extracting valuable elements from waste before treating it in the safest way possible. As a result, smaller volumes of hazardous material are shipped to countries with dangerously weak disposal capacities. Nevertheless, the issue of hazardous waste continues to raise serious concerns about environmental injustice. The illegal waste trade continues, as does the shipment of materials for recycling. This trade presents environmental and health risks to which poorer communities are disproportionately exposed.

## Towards Effective and Equitable Governance

More than forty-five years have passed since astronauts aboard the *Apollo 17* spacecraft captured the first full images of earth from space. Commander Eugene Cernan hoped that these photographs would trigger a new era of cooperation in which states and citizens would recognise that 'the planet we share unites us in a way far more basic and far more important than the differences in skin colour or religion or economic system' (quoted in White 1998: 37). Our understanding of global environmental problems has increased enormously since this time. Societal interdependence is no longer a mystery. The pursuit of economic development in one country can affect social and environmental conditions in near and distant places. Processes of resource extraction, production, consumption, and disposal have effects that are not contained within national borders. Awareness of this fact has generated important experiments in global environmental governance. Often these political efforts create their own social and environmental problems, or benefit some more than others.

The environment is now firmly established as an issue of political concern. While we shouldn't lose sight of progress that has been made, it is equally important not to become complacent once issues are integrated into international and national institutions. Political responses to environmental problems always suffer from some kind of weakness. A response might be insufficiently ambitious, or it may somehow shift environmental harm onto other people or places, now or in the future. The precise weaknesses of a political response may not be immediately apparent, but they are usually revealed when we dig beneath the surface of policies and agreements, and start looking at their substance. The lesson here is not to become cynical about global environmental governance. Incremental and progressive change requires the critical gaze of close observers. Observation, of course, is not sufficient but merely necessary. We've seen throughout this book how environmentally aware citizens take different forms of action to push for positive change. Sometimes they focus on consumer campaigns, encouraging individuals to make lifestyle or consumption changes; other times they focus on regulatory campaigns, encouraging policy makers to develop new laws and regulations; and other times they focus on building alternative systems. Elinor Ostrom taught us that no single approach to resource governance would be suitable and effective in all contexts. Extracting insights from experience and pushing for fairer and more effective environmental governance is clearly a task for us all.

## Discussion Questions

1. Is the Anthropocene a useful way to understand the human impact on the planet?
2. We have encountered various explanations of the causes of environmental degradation in this book. What do you identify as the most significant causes?

3. In what ways are the costs of environmental problems and policies distributed unevenly? Can you identify additional environmental inequalities and injustices beyond those outlined in this book?
4. Why is it so challenging for the international community to develop fair and effective responses to global environmental politics?
5. What roles can concerned citizens play to improve global environmental governance?

# Glossary

**Acid rain:** sulphur dioxide ($SO_2$) and nitrogen oxides ($NO_X$) are emitted into the atmosphere from cars, industrial processes, and burning fossil fuels. These chemicals convert to acid in the air and mix with rain, snow, and hail, which then pollute the land.

**Additionality** is a requirement attached to many environmental finance initiatives. It requires that actions only be financially supported or rewarded if they generate environmental improvements beyond what would have occurred anyway. For example, a GHG emissions offset project will only receive money if it can be shown that emissions will be reduced more than already anticipated reductions.

**Agenda 21** is one of the main documents to come out of the 1992 Earth Summit. It is a non-binding, voluntary action plan for pursuing sustainable development. It defines actions for states, local governments, business and industry, and civil society.

**Agricultural biodiversity** is sometimes shortened to agrobiodiversity. It refers to the biological elements that support agriculture and food production, including crop and animal species, plant varieties, soil organisms, and farming knowledge.

**Agroecology** is narrowly defined as a scientific discipline that applies ecological concepts to the management of agricultural systems. Broadly it is defined as a holistic approach to managing agricultural systems that combines Western science, traditional and indigenous knowledge, and economic, political, and social values.

**Alienation** refers to an artificial separation of naturally related elements. It signifies the breakdown of a harmonious order or relationship. Marx believed the class system alienated people from their true selves. Ecological Marxists believe that capitalism alienates people from the natural (non-human) world.

**Anthropocene:** many scientists claim that an epochal shift took place in the twenty-first century for the first time in 11,000 years. The Holocene was replaced by the Anthropocene, the 'era of the human'.

**Asia–Pacific Partnership on Clean Development and Climate** was a network created in 2005 by Australia, the United States, Republic of Korea, China, India, Japan, and Canada. It aimed to promote technological innovation and cooperation to reduce GHG emissions, until it ceased operating in 2012.

**BAN** is the Basel Action Network, an activist group established in 1997 to raise awareness about the social and environmental impacts of hazardous waste, and to push governments to ban international trade of hazardous waste.

**Bandwagoning** refers to a strategy of negotiators and campaigners to attract attention to other environmental agendas by linking them to climate change. The rationale for this strategy is that climate change attracts more attention and finance than most other environmental issues.

**Basel Ban** is an amendment to the Basel Convention to prohibit all exports in hazardous substances from the global North to the global South. It was agreed in 1995 but it will not enter into force until three-quarters of signatory states also ratify the amendment.

**Basel Convention** on the Control of Transboundary Movements of Hazardous Wastes and their Disposal aims to control shipments of hazardous waste between countries. Its overall objective is 'to protect human health and the environment against the adverse effects of hazardous wastes' (Basel Convention 2011). It was adopted in 1989 and came into force in 1992.

**Biodiversity** is the shortened form of biological diversity. The UN Convention on Biological Diversity defines it as 'the variability among living organisms from all sources including, inter alia, terrestrial, marine and other aquatic ecosystems and the ecological complexes of which they are part' (UNCBD 1992: Article 2).

**Brundtland Commission** is the commonly used name for the UN's World Commission on Environment and Development. It takes its name from the former prime minister of Norway, Gro Harlem Brundtland, who chaired the commission. The Brundtland Commission's 1987 report *Our Common Future* popularised the concept of sustainable development.

**Carbon markets** provide a system for buying and selling permits for emitting greenhouse gases. They are widely seen as the most cost-efficient way of reducing global emissions but critics argue that they can distract from the task of making economies less reliant on fossil fuels. Carbon markets take various forms including emissions trading and carbon offset initiatives.

**CBDR** is a shortened acronym for 'common but differentiated responsibilities and respective capabilities'. It is an international norm of climate governance that holds that all states should participate in international efforts to reduce GHG emissions, but that obligations should be differentiated to recognise different levels of responsibility and capacity.

**Certification schemes** indicate to consumers that goods have been produced in line with certain environmental and social standards. A well-known forest certification scheme is the Forest Stewardship Council's 'tick tree' logo, which indicates that wood-based products originated in sustainably managed forests.

**Circular economy** is an idea for transforming the dominant production model of take–make–use–dispose into a sustainable system whereby resources are reused to derive their maximum value, waste is recovered and used as a resource, and pollution is minimised. The circular economy requires innovation in all phases of the production cycle from design, to retail, household use, and recycling.

**Civil society** refers to the voluntary associations that exist outside the state and market. The United Nations organises civil society into nine 'major groups', which are intended to reflect all sectors of society: women, children and youth, indigenous peoples, non-governmental organisations, local authorities, workers and trade unions, business and industry organisations, scientific and research organisations, and farmers.

**Clean Development Mechanism is** one of the market-based mechanisms agreed as part of the Kyoto Protocol, whereby countries (and businesses within them) could claim emissions credits by investing in emission reduction projects in developing countries. This mechanism had the additional requirement that projects must contribute to sustainable development in the developing country.

**Climate change** is defined by the United Nations as 'a change of climate which is attributed directly or indirectly to human activity that alters the composition of the global atmosphere and which is in addition to natural climate variability observed over comparable time periods' (UNFCCC 1992).

**Climate governance 'experiments'** are the collective rules, standards, goals, and processes developed by non-state actors outside the UN system with the intention of mitigating climate change. They include carbon markets, emissions trading schemes, information-sharing networks, and voluntary GHG reduction programmes. Few experiments focus on adapting to climate change.

**Club of Rome:** an international group of economists, industrialists, and scientists whose aim was to promote understanding of the economic, political, natural, and social dimensions of the global system. They produced an important report in 1972 called *The Limits to Growth*, which generated debate about whether growth in population, food production, and resource use could be sustained in the long term.

**Commission on Sustainable Development** is a UN body established to monitor implementation of Agenda 21 across national, regional, and international levels, and to promote further multilateral cooperation on sustainable development. It was replaced in 2013 with the High-Level Political Forum on Sustainable Development.

**Common pool resources** are sometimes referred to simply as 'commons'. They are resources that are not exclusively owned by any person(s), sharing two characteristics:

- excludability: meaning it is difficult or costly to control access to the resource;
- subtractability: meaning that when one person uses the resource it reduces the quantity or quality for others.

**Commons** (see common pool resources)

**Conflict** emerges whenever two or more actors confront one another over diverging values or interests at stake in a particular issue. Conflict takes many forms depending on the actors involved, the measures they take, and the intensity of the events that unfold. It can be violent or non-violent.

**Consumer class** refers to those with the capacity to engage in some forms of luxury consumption (purchasing food and goods beyond what is required for subsistence). The global management consultants, McKinsey, define this class as comprising individuals with annual incomes of over $3,600 PPP (McKinsey Global Institute 2012: 23).

**Consumer sovereignty** is the idea that consumers can make free and independent consumption choices, and their individual desires and preferences shape the range of products on sale and the quantity of goods sold. Consumers therefore have the responsibility and capacity to promote sustainable consumption. Critics argue that this idea ignores the enormous amounts of money invested in advertising, and the various factors that constrain consumption choices.

**Consumerism** can refer to several distinct ideas about people's rights to certain goods and services, and the assumed relationship between consumption and development. However, it is generally used to refer to the beliefs and behaviours associated with excessive individual consumption.

**Core and periphery** are central concepts in Marxist theory, including ecological Marxism. European colonisation created a global core (Europe) and periphery (colonised territories). Resources in the colonies were exploited and depleted to generate profit in Europe. The global capitalist system depends on similar unequal relations whereby prosperity is generated in one place at the expense of environmental degradation in distant places.

**Counter-summit** is a forum set up by civil society in parallel to official UN conferences. Counter-summits provide a venue for activists and citizens to debate issues of global concern, develop alternative agendas, and prepare alternative declarations.

**Debt-for-nature swaps** involve 'the purchase of a developing country's debt at a discounted value in the secondary debt market and cancelling the debt in return for environment-related action on the part of the debtor nation' (Hansen 1989: 77).

**Deforestation** occurs when trees are cleared to allow land to be used for another purpose, typically agriculture or infrastructure development.

**Degrowth** is an idea for equitably downsizing production and consumption to ensure that societies are sustainable and just. It is a citizen-led movement based primarily in Europe but with growing support in other regions.

**Dematerialisation** refers to a reduction in the amount of energy and resources required to produce a good or service. Scholars refer to the dematerialisation of an economy when this trend can be observed across multiple sectors.

**Direct causes** of environmental problems are the actions that have an immediate and often visible impact. Sometimes they are called proximate causes. They include infrastructure development, agricultural expansion, and timber extraction.

**Displacement** occurs when an environmental problem is resolved in one place by exporting it to another place, or to the future. This allows privileged groups to enjoy the material benefits of modernity and high-consumption lifestyles while casting the negative consequences onto less privileged groups or future generations.

**Distancing** refers to 'the severing of ecological and social feedback as decision points along the (commodity) chain are increasingly separated along the dimensions of geography, culture, agency, and power' (Princen et al. 2002b: 16).

**Doubling time** is the time it takes for a population to double in size.

**Earth Summit** is the commonly used name for the UN Conference on Environment and Development (UNCED). It was an important multilateral event held in Rio de Janeiro in 1992. Several multilateral agreements were signed at the Earth Summit, including the UN Framework Convention on Climate Change (UNFCCC) and Agenda 21.

**Eco-development** is a concept first defined in the 1970s as a style of development that takes into account the growth needs of current generations as well as the natural resource needs of future generations. Later, the concept developed a more radical tone, calling for a new equitable international economic order that provided for the needs of the poorest while restraining over-consumption.

**Eco-labels** are different symbols and logos on consumer product packaging indicating that the product is accredited with a private certification scheme, promising the product to be 'environmentally friendly'.

**Ecological contradiction** is an important concept in ecological Marxism. Many scholars argue that capitalism suffers from an inherent ecological contradiction because the earth is a closed system that cannot support infinite growth, but capitalism cannot survive without continual growth.

**Ecological footprint** is 'an accounting tool that enables us to estimate the resource consumption and waste assimilation requirements of a defined human population or economy in terms of corresponding productive land area' (Wackernagel and Rees 1998: 9). Digital tools make it possible to understand the environmental impact of consumption by calculating the resources consumed directly or indirectly in our everyday lives.

**Ecological imperialism** is a central concept in ecological Marxism. Scholars argue that environmental degradation needs to be understood in the context of relations between the 'core' and 'periphery'. Since colonisation, the resources of non-European territories have been exploited to generate wealth and profit in distant countries. Colonial and post-colonial countries have become locked into unequal relations whereby they incur most of the costs of environmental degradation and resource depletion in order to supply raw materials to industrialised countries.

**Ecological rift** is related to the concept of alienation. It refers to the 'artificial divisions' that have opened up between humanity and the natural world (Foster et al. 2010: 7). Global capitalism has disrupted the natural processes by which natural materials support human wellbeing, and are in turn returned to nature in productive ways. Food production is a key example: whereas crop residue and waste would have previously been returned to the soil as natural fertiliser, it is now more profitable in the short term to dispose of food waste in landfill and apply chemical-based fertilisers to the depleted soil. In the long term this undermines our capacity to sustain food production.

**Economic Malthusianism:** Traditional Malthusians are concerned that the planet can support only a limited number of people; they call for different measures to control population growth. Economic Malthusians shift focus from the overall number of people to their consumption habits and call for restraints on consumption.

**Economism** refers to the fact that GDP is the primary measure of progress in almost all countries, and exponential economic growth is the overarching goal of nearly all governments.

**Eco-socialism:** For many anti-capitalist ecological thinkers, the solution to our environmental crises lies in some form of socialism. In a socialist society, the forces of production would be publicly owned, and the relations of production would be based on cooperation. Eco-socialists infuse this idea with ecological principles. Some take an instrumentalist view of nature and argue that nature should service the needs of the working class; others argue that a socialist system must respect the natural world and promote solidarity across species.

**Ecosystem:** The landmark 2005 Millennium Ecosystem Assessment (MEA 2005) defined an ecosystem as 'a dynamic complex of plant, animal, and micro-organism communities and the nonliving environment interacting as a functional unit'. An ecosystem is composed of living (biotic) and non-living (abiotic) elements: e.g., organisms, animals, soil, sunlight, air, humidity, and temperature. An ecosystem can be as small as a tidal pool or as large as the earth's biosphere.

**Ecosystem services is** a concept that conveys the value of nature to human beings. One of the most influential books in popularising the concept of ecosystem services was *Nature's Services* (Daily 1997). Daily defined ecosystem services as

> the conditions and processes through which natural ecosystems, and the species that make them up, sustain and fulfil human life. They maintain biodiversity and the production of *ecosystem goods*, such as seafood, forage, timber, biomass fuels, natural fibre, and many pharmaceuticals, industrial products, and their precursors . . . In addition to the production of goods, ecosystem services are the actual life-support functions, such as cleansing, recycling, and renewal, and they confer many intangible aesthetic and cultural benefits as well.
>
> (Daily 1997: 3)

**Emissions trading** whereby countries (or businesses within them) could buy and sell emission permits to seek an economically efficient distribution of the burden of reducing overall emissions.

**Environmental aid:** 'a financial transfer from North to South for the purpose of protecting or restoring the environment through the promotion of projects ranging from environmental education to land conservation' (Lewis 2003: 145).

**Environmental injustice** is the concept that poor people and racial minorities are disproportionately exposed to environmental risks and degradation relative to the rest of the population.

**Environmental Kuznets Curve:** Many resource economists claim that the relationship between environmental pollution and economic growth takes the shape of an inverted U curve. This suggests that environmental quality deteriorates as a country's economy grows but starts to improve when the country reaches a certain level of development.

**Environmental refugees** are people who are forced to leave their homes due to environmental degradation or change. In international law, those seeking refuge elsewhere within their own countries are termed 'internally displaced people', but scholars often use the term environmental refugees to refer to people who have or will be internally or internationally displaced.

**Eutrophication** is an over-accumulation of nutrients in the environment. In marine environments this can lead to algae blooms, which disrupt ecosystems and photosynthesis, and kill marine life. The use of fertilisers on farms is one of the main causes of eutrophication.

**E-waste** is discarded electronic goods.

**Food security** is defined by the UN's Food and Agriculture Organization as a condition in which 'all people, at all times, have physical, social and economic access to sufficient, safe and nutritious food which meets their dietary needs and food preferences for an active and healthy life' (FAO 2003). International food security policies aim to reduce hunger and increase access to nutritious food by increasing food production.

**Food sovereignty** demands a transformation of the existing 'food security' model, and can be defined as 'the right of peoples to healthy and culturally appropriate food, produced through ecologically sound and sustainable methods, and their right to define their own food and agricultural systems' (Holt-Giménez and Altieri 2013: 95).

**Forest Stewardship Council** is a voluntary certification scheme established in 1993 by timber users, traders, and civil society groups. By designing a global eco-label, it aims to encourage consumers and buyers along the supply chain to purchase products only from sustainably managed forests in which the rights of indigenous people and forest dwellers are respected.

**Fragmentation** of global environmental governance occurs when states, non-state actors and sub-national actors establish alternative governance mechanisms and processes to address global environmental problems. These may complement, compete with, or undermine UN processes.

**GEF** is the Global Environment Facility. It is a partnership of UN agencies, multilateral development banks, governments, and non-government organisations, which was established in 1992 to channel financial support from the global North to the global South for environmental sustainability projects.

**Global commons** refers to common pool resources that are global in scope, including oceans, atmosphere, outer space, and the solar system. International law distinguishes between *res nullius* and *res communis*. *Res nullius* (nobody's property) refers to parts of nature over which no state has recognised ownership, and all are legally free to use as they wish. *Res communis* (common property) refers to parts of nature over which no state can claim ownership but for which rules have been agreed to regulate all states' use of the resource, and to ensure that their use does not undermine the ability of other states to also use it. *Res communis* therefore refers to resources that are governed in common.

**Global governance** encompasses the 'formal and informal institutions, mechanisms, relationships, and processes between and among states, markets, citizens, and organizations – both intergovernmental and nongovernmental – through which collective interests are articulated, rights and obligations are established, and differences are mediated' (Thakur and Van Langenhove 2006: 233).

**GM:** Genetic engineering or manipulation involves combining the genes of biologically distinct products such as plants and bacteria. This produces 'transgenic' crops with characteristics such as tolerance to herbicides, disease, insects, and biological stresses (drought, poor and acidic soil, etc.).

**Governance** refers to 'the various ways through which social life is co-ordinated, including governmental regulation, bureaucratic rules, market mechanisms, and voluntary networks (Heywood 2015: 84).

Governments are just one actor involved in governance; corporate actors and non-governmental organisations are also involved.

**Green and brown aid** is a distinction based on the types of projects funded. 'Green' projects are those 'that address global or regional environmental problems, and encompass projects that positively affect environmental outcomes outside the recipient country'. Brown projects are those 'that focus primarily on local environmental issues and which improve environmental outcomes or reduce environmental degradation in a specific country or locality' (Hicks et al. 2008: 31).

**Green economy** refers to a set of policies for promoting economic growth while mitigating greenhouse gas emissions. This typically involves promoting investment in public transport infrastructure; incentivising compact urban planning; helping workers transition into 'green' sectors; reforming tax systems so that environmentally damaging activities would become more expensive than 'environmentally friendly' ones; removing subsidies on fossil fuels to encourage investment in clean energy; and accounting for the monetary value of nature.

**Green Revolution** was an industrial agriculture regime in the 1960s and 1970s, aiming to address the problem of hunger and the escalating demands of growing populations in the global South. This saw international private foundations cooperate with aid agencies to supply farmers in Asia and Latin America with hybrid (crossbred) high-yielding varieties of wheat and rice, replacing the variety of local seeds in use. At the same time they promoted the modernisation of agriculture through replacing labour-intensive techniques with mechanised ones, and natural fertilisers with the synthetic ones designed to be used in conjunction with the patented hybrid seeds.

**Greenwash** refers to empty gestures or misleading statements; it can be defined as 'the act of misleading consumers regarding the environmental practices of a company (firm-level greenwashing) or the environmental benefits of a product or service (product-level greenwashing)' (Delmas and Burbano 2011: 66).

**Hard and soft law** is a distinction based on whether an agreement is legally binding. Soft law agreements are not legally binding, whereas hard law agreements are. Soft law includes intergovernmental resolutions, guidelines, declarations, action plans, and roadmaps. Hard law includes treaties and protocols with legally binding obligations.

**Hazardous waste** refers to industrial residue and discarded goods containing chemicals and metals that are harmful to human health and the environment.

**IPCC** is the Intergovernmental Panel on Climate Change, the United Nations' main scientific body on climate change.

**Jevons Paradox** is also known as the rebound effect. It challenges the idea that gains in efficiency reduce resource consumption. In the nineteenth century, Stanley Jevons observed that increased efficiency actually leads to higher use of a resource in the long term because it is cheaper to consume.

*Khian Sea* was a cargo vessel that became emblematic of the global problem of waste dumping. In 1986, the ship was loaded with 14,000 tonnes of incinerator ash in Philadelphia. Haiti was misled into accepting 3,000 tonnes under the belief that it was soil fertiliser. The ship sailed the world for two years unable to find a country that would accept the waste. The remaining 11,000 tonnes of toxic waste is believed to have been dumped somewhere in the Indian Ocean.

**Kyoto Protocol** is an international treaty on climate change that was negotiated by states in 1997, and came into force in 2005. It was the first agreement to set legally binding, quantified GHG emission reduction targets for member states. Its first commitment period ran from 2008 to 2012; and a smaller number of states signed a second commitment period for 2013 to 2020.

**La Via Campesina** is a transnational network of farming and peasant organisations in sixty-eight countries. It is a social movement promoting alternative systems of agriculture based on food sovereignty and agroecology.

**Land grabs** whereby local communities are dispossessed of their land by profit-seeking governments and market actors.

**Leakage** is the risk that rewarding the avoidance of deforestation in one place will simply increase deforestation in another place.

**Liberal environmentalism** is the dominant form of international governance that 'predicates environmental protection on the promotion and maintenance of a liberal economic order' (Bernstein 2001: 213). This suggests that to protect the environment we need to protect market norms. Continued economic growth and accumulation become enablers of environmental protection.

**Life cycle analysis** measures the total environmental impact of a product by capturing all the processes it goes through from raw material production to disposal. Between these two end points lie many processes, each of which has an environmental impact, including the various stages of processing and manufacturing, transportation, retailing, and consumer use.

**Localisation** is a vision and movement for scaling down the scope of economic development such that people predominantly rely on goods and services produced in their own town, city, or region. Many environmentalists argue that this would be more sustainable, especially if diets shift towards seasonal and climate-appropriate foods.

**Luxury consumption** is distinguished from subsistence consumption. It refers to the purchase of desired but non-essential goods.

**Major groups** (see civil society)

**Metabolic rift:** Karl Marx observed that capitalism interrupted the natural dynamic processes that connected humans with the earth. He called this disruption a 'metabolic rift'.

**Meta-governance** refers to efforts to loosely coordinate or link up governance networks and experiments.

**Millennium Development Goals** were a set of eight goals agreed by the UN in 2000 to improve living conditions in developing countries. They included aims to reduce poverty and hunger, illiteracy, morbidity and mortality rates from communicable diseases, and gender inequality.

**Minamata Convention:** The most recent multilateral agreement to protect human health and the environment from hazardous substances is the mercury convention signed in the Japanese city of Minamata. The Minamata Convention requires parties to prohibit new mercury mining; phase out existing mercury mining and manufacturing of many mercury-containing products; and dispose of existing stocks of the chemical in safe ways.

**Minilateralism** refers to the use of small, exclusive institutions for international policy-making and cooperation outside the larger and inclusive institutions (especially the UN). Participation is limited to a small number of powerful or like-minded states. The effectiveness and legitimacy of minilateral institutions (compared to the UN) is contested.

**Mitigation** is typically used in the context of climate change. It refers to efforts to reduce greenhouse gas emissions to limit the extent of global warming, and minimise the impacts of climate change.

**Montreal Protocol** along with the Vienna Convention created mutually agreed rules to phase out the production and use of CFCs, for ozone protection. The Vienna Convention came into force in 1988, and the Montreal Convention in 1989.

**Multilateralism** refers to cooperation among states to respond to issues of shared concern. Despite differences in power, states formally participate as equals in multilateral institutions. The UN is the most important multilateral institution.

**Natural capital** is a term that many governments, scholars, and private sector actors use to refer to renewable and non-renewable resources, seas, and forests that act as pollution 'sinks', and natural systems that regulate the climate.

**Neoliberalism** holds that state institutions are inefficient and stifle innovation unless they play only a minimal regulatory role.

**Neo-Malthusianism** refers to the position that population growth is the main cause of environmental problems. Concern about the sustainability of a growing population dates back centuries and is commonly associated with the eighteenth-century cleric, Thomas Malthus.

**Networked governance** is another term for transnational governance. It refers to the horizontal and non-hierarchical efforts by state and non-state actors to respond to international concerns.

**Non-state actors** are businesses, NGOs, philanthropic foundations, community groups.

**North** or global North is a term frequently used instead of 'developed' or 'industrialised' countries. Also see South.

**Ocean acidification** refers to the increasing acidity of oceans, which is caused by the absorption of high levels of carbon dioxide from the atmosphere. The main cause of high levels of carbon dioxide in the atmosphere is the burning of fossil fuels. This is harmful for marine organisms and coral.

**Open access** refers to the condition whereby neither access nor use of a resource is controlled.

**Orchestration** is defined as 'mobilizing and working with private actors and institutions to achieve regulatory goals, for example, by catalysing voluntary and collaborative programs; convening and facilitating private collaborations; persuading and inducing firms and industries to self-regulate; building private capacities; negotiating regulatory targets with firms; and providing incentives for attaining those targets' (Abbott and Snidal 2010: 317).

*Our Common Future* is the first high-profile international report to promote the vision of 'sustainable development', which acknowledges the importance of clean and efficient economic development, particularly in developing countries. It was published in 1987 by a group of policy elites and economists who formed the Brundtland Commission.

**Ozone depletion** refers to the depletion of stratospheric ozone, which protects the earth's surface from excessive amounts of ultraviolet radiation. It is caused by the accumulation in the atmosphere of chlorofluorocarbon compounds (CFCs), which were widely used in refrigerators and air conditioners before multilateral agreements to phase them out were negotiated in the 1980s.

**Paris Agreement** is the 2015 UN treaty on climate change, which includes emissions commitments from a larger number of countries than any previous international climate change agreement. It aims to limit global average temperature increase to 2°C above pre-industrial levels.

**Payments for ecosystem services** are *voluntary* transactions in which a *well-defined* ecosystem service is bought by a *buyer* from an ecosystem service *provider*, on the *condition* that the provider actually ensures provision of the service (Wunder 2005).

**Permanence** is usually used in the context of deforestation. It refers to the concern that financial rewards and incentives will be paid in the short term without any guarantee that states will keep their promises to avoid deforestation in the long term. Rewarding avoided deforestation in the short term only makes sense if that deforestation never takes place in the future, but this is difficult to ensure.

**Persistent organic pollutants** refers to dioxins and dioxin-like substances that linger in the atmosphere and human body for long periods of time, and can travel vast distances (including across national borders).

**Planetary boundaries** are thresholds in the earth system. Scientists have identified nine planetary boundaries (stratospheric ozone depletion; loss of biosphere integrity; chemical pollution; climate change; ocean acidification; freshwater consumption and the global hydrological cycle; land system change; nitrogen and phosphorus flows to the biosphere and oceans; and atmospheric aerosol loading). Large-scale and irreversible environmental change is likely if these thresholds are crossed, and this would significantly undermine the wellbeing of future and current generations.

**Planned obsolescence** refers to designing technology with intentionally short lifespans, frequently releasing updated versions, and investing in expensive advertising campaigns to shape the desires of users.

**Pollution haven hypothesis** holds that the weaker environmental regulation of developing countries makes them an attractive investment option for dirty industries.

**Polycentric governance systems** is an approach to addressing environmental problems that relies on dispersed experimentation in regulation, market mechanisms, and communal or voluntary management. In different contexts and for different problems, some types of rules may be better than others at changing incentives, or providing information and feedback, or monitoring and ensuring compliance.

**Prior Informed Consent** is a rule whereby those potentially exposed to risks must be fully informed about the nature and scope of those risks before giving consent. It is most commonly used in the trade of chemicals, and in development projects on indigenous land.

**Problem displacement** occurs when privileged groups enjoy the material benefits of modernity while casting the negative consequences onto less privileged groups.

*Probo Koala* was a vessel that symbolises environmental injustice in the toxic waste industry. To avoid the high costs of waste treatment in Europe, in 2006 a Dutch subsidiary of the global oil company Trafigura dumped 500–600 tonnes of mixed chemical wastes in the Ivory Coast. There were over 100,000 victims, and most never received due compensation.

**Protocol** refers to an international agreement that establishes specific obligations for states, and instruments for meeting those obligations. Protocols are usually legally binding, and they are usually negotiated after states have negotiated and signed a more general agreement (convention or framework).

**REDD+** stands for Reducing greenhouse gas Emissions from Deforestation and forest Degradation, forest stock conservation, sustainable forest management, and enhancement of forest stock (REDD+). It is a reward-based system that aims to reduce GHG emissions by offering financial incentives to developing countries to better protect and manage their forests.

**Remoteness** is a concept developed by Australian environmental philosopher Val Plumwood to refer to the disruption of 'connections and balances between decisions and their consequences' (2002: 72).

*Res communis* (common property) refers to parts of nature over which no state can claim ownership but for which rules have been agreed to regulate all states' use of the resource, and to ensure that their use does not undermine the ability of other states to also use it. *Res communis* therefore refers to resources that are governed in common (Milun 2011: 57–8).

*Res nullius* (nobody's property) refers to parts of nature over which no state has recognised ownership, and all are legally free to use as they wish.

**Resistance** is organised opposition to power and domination. Resistance is usually collective and intentional, but some scholars include day-to-day struggles that may be uncoordinated, unplanned, and low profile.

**Resource curse:** Resource abundant countries are said to have a 'resource curse' because citizens are vulnerable to the violence, human rights abuse, and environmental degradation that accompany struggles among rebel groups and oppressive governments for the control of valuable resources.

**Rio+20** is the 2012 UN Conference on Sustainable Development (UNCSD).

**River basins** are sometimes called drainage basins. They are the areas of land drained by rivers and their tributaries (the small rivers that connect to a large river). Often these land areas cross national borders, which creates international river basins.

**Rotterdam Convention** on the Prior Informed Consent Procedure for Certain Hazardous Chemicals and Pesticides in International Trade: This convention builds on the rules of the Basel Convention by adding additional responsibilities to share knowledge, and build capacity for making informed decisions about accepting hazardous waste imports. It has the ultimate aim of protecting human health and the environment from potential harm.

**Securitisation** refers to the framing of environmental problems as security threats.

**Social movements** are collective efforts to challenge the authority or domination of states and other powerful actors like corporations through protest and creating alternative systems.

**South** or global South is a term frequently used instead of 'developing countries'. Over the years different classifications have been used to distinguish countries along socio-economic and geopolitical lines (others include developed/developing countries; first/second/third worlds; and majority/minority worlds).

**Steady-state economy** is one that maintains a stable size in terms of both population and material consumption.

**Stockholm Conference** refers to the 1972 Stockholm Conference on environment that marked the birth of environmental multilateralism.

**Stockholm Convention** is the short name of the Stockholm Convention on Persistent Organic Pollutants. It is a multilateral agreement that aims to control the use of chemicals that remain in the environment for prolonged periods of time, can travel over a large distance, and accumulate in human and animal bodies.

**Summits** are events at which high-level state representatives gather to establish principles, set goals, pledge action, and review progress on sustainable development.

**Sustainable agriculture** refers to ideas and practices for reducing the resource intensity and environmental impact of food production.

**Sustainable capitalism** is the belief that ecological sustainability and business profitability can be compatible if the right regulations or market-based mechanisms are in place.

**Sustainable consumption** is often defined as 'the use of goods and services that respond to basic needs and bring a better quality of life, while minimising the use of natural resources, toxic materials and emissions of waste and pollutants over the life cycle, so as not to jeopardise the needs of future generations' (Oslo Ministerial Roundtable 1994, quoted in Barber 2005: 62).

**Sustainable development** is typically defined as 'development that meets the needs of the present without compromising the ability of future generations to meet their own needs' (WCED 1987: chapter 2.1).

**Sustainable Development Goals** (SDGs) are the most recent policy incarnation of sustainable development, covering over a dozen issues and providing 169 targets to be reached by 2013. They were adopted by the UN in 2015.

**Tragedy of the commons**: Garrett Hardin's 1968 parable of environmental degradation under conditions of human freedom. Hardin's 'tragedy' is the unhappy inevitability that so long as human freedom is respected, and land and natural resources are freely available for anyone to use, they will slowly but inevitably be destroyed.

**Transnational governance** refers to initiatives by business, civil society, regional governments, and cities to respond to international problems through collective rules, standards, goals, and processes. Transnational governance initiatives sometimes but not always include the involvement of states. When states do participate they tend to do so as equal partners, rather than superior authorities.

**Treaties** are internationally negotiated agreements that have legally binding obligations for the states that sign and ratify them. Also referred to as hard law.

**UN Conference on Environment and Development** (UNCED): the first major international environmental conference in Stockholm in 1972.

**Underlying causes** of environmental problems are social forces that lead to certain human actions, including demographic change, economic development, technological change, cultural change, and institutional change.

**UNEP** is the United Nations Environment Programme, the UN's main environmental agency.

**UNFCCC** is the United Nations Framework Convention on Climate Change, the UN's main body for negotiating climate change agreements.

**Vienna Convention** is one of the main international agreements for phasing out the production and use of synthetic chemicals called chlorofluorocarbon compounds (CFCs), which deplete the ozone layer and expose people to dangerous levels of ultraviolet radiation.

**Wicked policy problems** are those that are complex and urgent, have no single cause or straightforward solution, and cannot be managed by a single central authority.

**World Summit on Sustainable Development**: ten years after Rio, the international community reconvened to assess progress and discuss new ways of advancing sustainable development. Over 20,000 participants, including 191 governments (and 104 heads of state) gathered in Johannesburg in August 2002 for the World Summit on Sustainable Development.

# References

Abbott, K.W. and Bernstein, S. 2015. 'The High-Level Political Forum on Sustainable Development: Orchestration by Default and Design', *Global Policy* 6(3): 222–33.

Abbott, K.W. and Snidal, D. 2010. 'International Regulation Without International Government: Improving IO Performance Through Orchestration', *Review of International Organizations* 5: 315–44.

Agarwal, A. and Narain, S. 1991. *Global Warming in an Unequal World*. New Delhi: Centre for Science and Environment.

Agrawal, A., Nepstad, D., and Chhatre, A. 2011. 'Reducing Deforestation from Deforestation and Forest Degradation', *Annual Review of Environmental Resources* 36: 373–96.

Alecci, S. 2016. 'How Lead In Recycled Electronics Can Poison Workers' Families', *Huffington Post*, http://www.huffingtonpost.com/entry/lead-poisoning-recycled-electronics_us_56abb437e4b077d4fe8dee5b. Last accessed 12 December 2016.

Altieri, M.A. and Toledo, V.M. 2011. 'The Agroecological Revolution in Latin America: Rescuing Nature, Ensuring Food Sovereignty and Empowering Peasants', *The Journal of Peasant Studies* 38(3): 587–612.

American Society of Agronomy. 2009. 'Landfill Cover Soil Methane Oxidation Underestimated', ScienceDaily www.sciencedaily.com/releases/2009/04/090427121637.htm. Last accessed 12 December 2016.

Amoore, L. 2005. 'Introduction: Global Resistance – Global Politics'. In Amoore, L. (ed.) *The Global Resistance Reader*. New York: Routledge, pp. 1–11.

Anderson, D. 2012. 'Law of the Sea'. In Anheier, H.K. and Juergensmeyer, M. (eds.) *Encyclopedia of Global Studies*. Los Angeles: Sage.

Anderson, T.L. and Leal, D.R. 1996. 'Free Market Environmentalism'. In Cahn, M.A. and O'Brien, R. (eds.) *Thinking about the Environment: Readings on Politics, Property and the Physical World*. Armonk: M.E. Sharpe, pp. 242–9.

Andresen, S. 2012. 'Do We Need More Global Sustainability Conferences?' In Dauvergne, P. (ed.) *Handbook of Global Environmental Politics*, 2nd edition. Cheltenham: Edward Elgar, pp. 87–96.

Angus, I. and Butler, S. 2011. *Too Many People?: Population, Immigration, and the Environmental Crisis*. Chicago: Haymarket Books.

Aristotle. 1998. *Politics*. Oxford University Press.

Asia-Pacific Partnership (APP). 2016. 'Asia-Pacific Partnership on Clean Development and Climate', www.asiapacificpartnership.org/english/Default.aspx. Last accessed 12 December 2016.

Assadourian, E. 2010. 'The Rise and Fall of Consumer Cultures'. In Starke, L. and Mastny, L. (eds.) *State of the World 2010: Transforming Cultures, From Consumerism to Sustainability.* Washington DC: Worldwatch Institute.

Auld, G. and Cashore, B. 2013. 'The Forest Stewardship Council'. In Reed, D., Utting, P., and Mukherjee Reed, A. (eds.) *Business Regulation and Non-State Actors: Whose Standards? Whose Development?* London: Routledge, pp. 134–47.

Ayres, J. and Bosia, M.J. 2014. 'Food Sovereignty as Localized Resistance to Globalization in France and the United States'. In Andrée, P., Ayres, J., Bosia, M.J., and Massiocotte, M.J. (eds.) *Globalization and Food Sovereignty: Global and Local Change in the New Politics of Food.* University of Toronto Press, pp. 319–44.

Baker, A. 2015. 'How Climate Change is Behind the Surge of Migrants to Europe', *Time*, time.com/4024210/climate-change-migrants. Last accessed 22 December 2015.

Banerjee, S.B. 2009. *Corporate Social Responsibility: The Good, the Bad and the Ugly.* Cheltenham: Edward Elgar.

Barber, J. 2005. 'Production, Consumption and the World Summit on Sustainable Development'. In Hens, L. and Nath, B. (eds.) *The World Summit on Sustainable Development: The Johannesburg Conference.* Dordrecht: Springer, pp. 57–88.

Barnett, J., Matthew, R.A., and O'Brien, K.L. 2010. 'Global Environmental Change and Human Security: An Introduction'. In Mathew, R.A., Barnett, J., McDonald, B., and O'Brien, K.L. (eds.) *Global Environmental Change and Human Security.* Cambridge, MA: MIT Press, pp. 1–31.

Basel Action Network (BAN). 2016. 'Exporting Deception, Continued', www.ban.org/news/2016/1/26/exporting-deception-continued. Last accessed 16 December 2016.

Basel Convention. 1989. 'Text of the Convention', www.basel.int/TheConvention/Overview/TextoftheConvention/tabid/1275/Default.aspx. Last accessed 16 December 2016.

Basel Convention. 2011. 'Overview', www.basel.int/TheConvention/Overview/tabid/1271/Default.aspx. Last accessed 16 December 2016.

Baste, I., Ivanova, M., and Lee, B. 2012. 'Global Responses'. In *Global Environment Outlook-5: Environment for the Future We Want.* Nairobi: UNEP.

Beck, U. 1992. *Risk Society: Towards a New Modernity.* London: Sage.

Beckerman, W. 1992. *Economic Development and the Environment.* Washington DC: World Bank.

Beinart, W. 2000. 'African History and Environmental History', *African Affairs* 99: 269–302.

Benton, T. 1996. 'Introduction to Part III'. In Benton, T. (ed.) *The Greening of Marxism.* New York: Guilford Press, pp. 187–96.

Berkes, F., Feeny, D., McCay, B., and Acheson, J.M. 1989. 'The Benefits of the Commons', *Nature* 340: 91–3.

Bernauer, T. and Kalbhenn, A. 2010. 'The Politics of International Freshwater Resources'. In Denemark, R. (ed.) *The International Studies Encyclopedia.* Hoboken, NJ: Wiley-Blackwell, pp. 5800–21.

Bernstein, S. 2000. 'Ideas, Social Structure and the Compromise of Liberal Environmentalism', *European Journal of International Relations* 6(4): 464–512.

Bernstein, S. 2001. *The Compromise of Liberal Environmentalism.* New York: Columbia University Press.

Biermann, F. and Bernstein, S. 2012. 'How Rio+20 Can Herald a Constitutional Moment', *The Guardian*, www.theguardian.com/environment/2012/mar/15/rio20-constitutional-moment. Last accessed 7 December 2016.

Biermann, F., Zelli, F., Pattberg, P., and van Asselt, H. 2010. 'The Architecture of Global Climate Governance: Setting the Stage.' In Biermann, F., Pattberg, P., and Zelli, F. (eds.) *Global Climate Governance Beyond 2012: Architecture, Agency, and Adaptation.* Cambridge University Press, pp. 15–24.

Bodansky, D. 1993. 'The United Nations Framework Convention on Climate Change: A Commentary', *Yale Journal of International Law* 18: 453–558.

Bodansky, D. 2001. 'The History of the Global Climate Change Regime'. In Luterbacher, U. and Sprinz, D.F. (eds.) *International Relations and Global Climate Change.* Cambridge, MA: MIT Press.

Bodansky, D. 2010. *The Art and Craft of International Environmental Law.* Harvard University Press.

Boren, Z.D. 2014. 'There are Officially More Mobile Devices Than People in the World', *The Independent*, www.independent.co.uk/life-style/gadgets-and-tech/news/there-are-officially-more-mobile-devices-than-people-in-the-world-9780518.html. Last accessed 19 December 2016.

Borlaug, N.E. 2000. 'Ending World Hunger: The Promise of Biotechnology and the Threat of Antiscience Zealotry', *Plant Physiology* 124: 487–90.

Born, B. and Purcell, M. 2009. 'Food Systems and the Local Trap'. In Inglis, D. and Gimlin, D. (eds.) *The Globalization of Food.* Oxford: Berg Publishers, pp. 117–38.

Borras Jr., S.M., Edelman, M., and Kay, C. 2008. 'Transnational Agrarian Movements: Origins and Politics, Campaigns and Impact', *Journal of Agrarian Change* 8(2/3): 169–204.

Boström, M. and Klintman, M. 2008. *Eco-Standards, Product Labelling and Green Consumerism.* Houndmills: Palgrave Macmillan.

Boucher, D., Elias, P., Lininger, K., Tobin, C.M., Roquemore, S., and Saxon, E. 2011. 'The Root of the Problem: What's Driving Deforestation Today?', Union of Concerned Scientists, www.ucsusa.org/.../UCS_RootoftheProblem_DriversofDeforestation_FullReport.pdf. Last accessed 22 February 2015.

Boyce, J.K. 2008. 'Is Inequality Bad for the Environment?' In Wilkinson, R.C. and Freudenburg, W.R. (eds.) *Equity and the Environment.* Amsterdam: Elsevier.

Boyce, J.K. and Shrivastava, A. 2016. 'Delhi's Air Pollution is a Classic Case of Environmental Injustice', *The Guardian*, www.theguardian.com/sustainable-business/2016/mar/09/delhi-india-air-pollution-environmental-injustice-car-tax. Last accessed 21 November 2016.

Bradshaw, C.J.A. and Brook, B.W. 2014. 'Human Population Reduction is not a Quick Fix for Environmental Problems', *Proceedings of the National Academy of Sciences of the United States of America* 111(46): 16610–15.

Brochmann, M. and Gleditsch, N.P. 2012. 'Shared Rivers and Conflict: A Reconsideration', *Political Geography* 31: 519–27.

Broder, J.M. 2008. 'Obama Affirms Climate Change Goals', *The New York Times*, www.nytimes.com/2008/11/19/us/politics/19climate.html?_r=0. Last accessed 7 December 2016.

Brower, D. 1968. 'Foreword'. In Ehrlich, P.R., *The Population Bomb*. New York: Ballantine Books, pp. 13–14.

Brown, L.R. 2005. *Outgrowing the Earth*. Abingdon: Earthscan.

Buck, S.J. 1985. 'No Tragedy of the Commons', *Environmental Ethics* 7: 49–61.

Bulkeley, H. and Castán Broto, V. 2013. 'Government by Experiment? Global Cities and the Governing of Climate Change', *Transactions of the Institute of British Geographers* 38: 361–75.

Bulkeley, H. and Newell, P. 2010. *Governing Climate Change*. London: Routledge.

Bulkeley, H., Jordan, A., Perkins, R. and Selin, H. 2013. 'Governing Sustainability: Rio+20 and the Road Beyond', *Environment and Planning C: Government and Policy* 31: 958–70.

Bulkeley, H., Andonova, L., Backstrand, K., Betsill, M., Compagnon, D., Duffy, R., Kolk, A., Hoffmann, M., Levy, D., Newell, P., Milledge, T., Paterson, M., Pattberg, P., and VanDeveer, S. 2012. 'Governing Climate Change Transnationally: Assessing the Evidence from a Database of Sixty Initiatives', *Environment and Planning C: Government and Policy* 30: 591–612.

Burgiel, S.W. and Wood, P. 2012. 'Witness, Architect, Detractor: The Evolving Role of NGOs in International Environmental Negotiations'. In Chasek, P. and Wagner, L.M. (eds.) *The Roads from Rio: Lessons Learned from Twenty Years of Multilateral Environmental Negotiations*. New York: RFF Press, pp. 127–48.

Bush, G.H.W. 1992. 'The Earth Summit', *The New York Times*, www.nytimes.com/1992/06/13/world/the-earth-summit-excerpts-from-speech-by-bush-on-action-plan.html. Last accessed 7 December 2016.

Buzan, B., Wæver, O., and Wilde, J. 1998. *Security: A New Framework for Analysis* Boulder, CO: Lynne Rienner Publishers.

C40. 2015. 'Why Cities?', www.c40.org/why_cities. Last accessed 12 December 2016.

C40. 2016. 'About C40 Cities', www.c40.org/about. Last accessed 12 December 2016.

Cappiello, D. 2012. 'Food Industry Frets About Federal Dioxin-Risk Report', *The Washington Times*, www.washingtontimes.com/news/2012/feb/19/food-industry-frets-about-federal-dioxin-risk-repo. Last accessed 12 December 2016.

Capstick, S., Whitmarsh, L., Poortinga, W., Pidgeon, N., and Upham, P. 2015. 'International Trends in Public Perceptions of Climate Change Over the Past Quarter Century', *WIREs Climate Change* 6(1): 35–61.

Carbon Disclosure Project (CDP). 2016. 'Why Disclose?', www.cdp.net/en/companies-discloser. Last accessed 12 December 2016.

Carbon Footprint. No date. 'Carbon Offset Projects', www.carbonfootprint.com/carbonoffsetprojects.html. Last accessed 5 November 2015.

Carrington, D. 2016a. 'The Anthropocene Epoch: Scientists Declare Dawn of Human-Influenced Age', *The Guardian*, www.theguardian.com/environment/2016/aug/29/declare-anthropocene-epoch-experts-urge-geological-congress-human-impact-earth. Last accessed 21 November 2016.

Carrington, D. 2016b. '2016 Will be the Hottest Year on Record, UN Says', *The Guardian*, www.theguardian.com/environment/2016/nov/14/2016-will-be-the-hottest-year-on-record-un-says?CMP=share_btn_tw. Last accessed 19 December 2016.

Carson, R.T. 2010. 'The Environmental Kuznets Curve: Seeking Empirical Regularity and Theoretical Structure', *Review of Environmental Economics and Policy* 4(1): 3–23.

Carter, N. 2001. *The Politics of the Environment: Ideas, Activism, Policy.* Cambridge University Press.

Cassimon, D., Prowse, M., and Essers, D. 2011. 'The Pitfalls and Potential of Debt-for-Nature Swaps: A US–Indonesian Case Study', *Global Environmental Change* 21: 93–102.

Ceballos, D. and Page, E. 2014. 'Occupational Exposures at Electronic Scrap Recycling Facilities', blogs.cdc.gov/niosh-science-blog/2014/09/30/escrap/. Last accessed 12 December 2016.

Centre for Disease Control and Prevention. 2011. 'Cadmium Toxicity', www.atsdr.cdc.gov/csem/csem.asp?csem=6&po=12. Last accessed 16 December 2016.

Chan, S. 2015. 'Mega-Conferences'. In Pattberg, P.H. and Zelli, F. (eds.) *Encyclopedia of Global Environmental Governance and Politics.* Cheltenham: Edward Elgar, pp. 275–81.

Chan, S., van Asselt, H., Hale, T., Abbott, K.W., Beisheim, M., Hoffmann, M., Guy, B., Höhne, N., Hsu, A., Pattberg, P., Pauw, P., Ramstein, C., and Widerberg, O. 2015. 'Reinvigorating International Climate Policy: A Comprehensive Framework for Effective Nonstate Action', *Global Policy.* 6(4): 466–73.

Chase, A. 1977. *The Legacy of Malthus.* Chicago: University of Illinois Press.

Chatterjee, P. and Finger, M. 1994. *The Earth Brokers: Power, Politics and World Development.* London: Routledge.

Chhatre, A., Lakhanpal, S., Larson, A.M., Nelson, F., Ojha, H., and Rao, J. 2012. 'Social Safeguards and Co-Benefits in REDD+: A Review of the Adjacent Possible', *Current Opinion in Environmental Sustainability* 4: 654–60.

CIEC (Centre for Industry Education Collaboration). 2016. *The Essential Chemical Industry.* York: University of York, http://www.essentialchemicalindustry.org/the-chemical-industry/the-chemical-industry.html. Last accessed 22 May 2017.

Clapp, J. 2002. 'The Distancing of Waste: Overconsumption in a Global Economy'. In Princen, T., Maniates, M., and Conca, K. (eds.) *Confronting Consumption.* Cambridge, MA: MIT Press, pp. 155–76.

Clapp, J. 2012. *Food.* Cambridge: Polity Press.

Claudio, L. 2007. 'Waste Couture: Environmental Impact of the Clothing Industry', *Environmental Health Perspectives* 115(9): 448–54.

Climate Funds Update. 2015. 'UN-REDD Programme', www.climatefundsupdate.org/listing/un-redd-programme. Last accessed 3 March 2015.

Climate Savers. 2016. 'Overview of Climate Savers', http://climatesavers.org/about-us-2-7/. Last accessed 23 October 2016.

Cocoyoc Declaration. 1974. 'The Cocoyoc Declaration Adopted by the Participants in the UNEP/UNCTAD Symposium on Patterns of Resource Use, Environment and Development Strategies', *International Organisation* 29(3): 893–901.

Cohen, J. 1995. *How Many People can the Earth Support?* New York: Norton.

Collier, P. and Hoeffler, A. 2012. 'High-Value Natural Resources, Development, and Conflict: Channels of Causation. In Lujala, P. and Rustad, S.A. (eds.) *High-Value Natural Resources and Peacebuilding.* London: Earthscan, pp. 297–312.

Commoner, B. 1971. *The Closing Circle: Nature, Man, and Technology.* New York: Alfred A. Knopf.

Corporate Europe Observatory. 2002. 'WSSD: A Little More Conversation, A Little Less Action', www.globalpolicy.org/component/content/article/225/32235.html. Last accessed 29 August 2016.

Crocker, R. and Lehmann, S. 2013. *Motivating Change: Sustainable Design and Behaviour in the Built Environment.* Abingdon: Routledge.

Daily, G.C. 1997. 'Introduction: What are Ecosystem Services?' In Daily, G.C. (ed.) *Nature's Services: Societal Dependence on Natural Ecosystems.* Washington DC: Island Press, pp. 1–10.

Daily, G.C., Ehrlich, A.H., and Ehrlich, P.R. 1994. 'Optimum Human Population Size', *Population and Environment* 15(6): 469–75.

Dalton, R. and Rohrschneider, R. 2015. 'Environmental Concerns During a Time of Duress: An Introduction', *Environmental Politics* 24(4): 523–9.

Daly, H. 2014. *From Uneconomic Growth to a Steady-State Economy.* Cheltenham: Edward Elgar.

Dauvergne, P. 2010. *The Shadows of Consumption: Consequences for the Global Environment.* Cambridge, MA: MIT Press.

Dauvergne, P. and Lister, J. 2010. 'The Prospects and Limits of Eco-Consumerism: Shopping Our Way to Less Deforestation?', *Organization & Environment* 23(2): 132–54.

David Suzuki Foundation. 2014. 'Reduce Your Carbon Footprint', www.davidsuzuki.org/what-you-can-do/reduce-your-carbon-footprint. Last accessed 4 November 2015.

Day, R.J.F. 2004. 'From Hegemony to Affinity: The Political Logic of the Newest Social Movements', *Cultural Studies* 18(5): 716–48.

Dearden, N. 2015. 'The UN Development Goals Miss the Point – It's All About Power', Global Justice Now, www.globaljustice.org.uk/blog/2015/sep/25/un-development-goals-miss-point-%E2%80%93-it%E2%80%99s-all-about-power. Last accessed 9 December 2016.

Death, C. 2010. *Governing Sustainable Development: Partnerships, Protests and Power at the World Summit.* Abingdon: Routledge.

Death, C. 2011. 'Summit Theatre: Exemplary Governmentality and Environmental Diplomacy in Johannesburg and Copenhagen', *Environmental Politics* 20(1): 1–19.

Delmas, M. and Burbano, V.C. 2011. 'The Drivers of Greenwashing', *California Management Review* 54(1): 65–87.

Dessler, A.E. and Parson, E.A. 2006. *The Science and Politics of Global Climate Change.* Cambridge University Press.

Detjen, J. and Jaffe, M. 1993. 'Ship's Operators Get Jail Time The *Khian Sea* Dumped Its Cargo Of Incinerator Ash Into The Ocean. Two Men Will Bear The Penalty',

Philadelphia Media Network, articles.philly.com/1993-10-05/news/25935658_1_coastal-carriers-khian-sea-william-p-reilly. Last accessed 30 June 2016.

Dickens, P. 1992. *Society and Nature: Towards a Green Social Theory*. Philadelphia: Temple University Press.

Dietrich, J.W. 2015. *The George W. Bush Foreign Policy Reader: Presidential Speeches with Commentary*. Abingdon: Routledge.

Dietz, T., Dolšak, N., Ostrom, E., and Stern, P.C. 2009a. 'The Drama of the Commons'. In Ostrom, E., Dietz, T., Dolšak, N., Stern, P.C., Stonich, S., and Weber, E.U. (eds.) *The Drama of the Commons*. Washington DC: National Academy Press, pp. 3–35.

Dietz, T., Ostrom, E., and Stern, P.C. 2009b. 'The Struggle to Govern the Commons', *Science* 302(12 December): 1907–12.

Dietzel, A. 2015. 'Global Justice and Climate Change: Bridging the Gap Between Theory and Practice'. PhD thesis. University of Sheffield.

Dobbs, R., Remes, J., Manyika, J., Roxburgh, C., Smit, S., and Schaer, F. 2012. 'Urban World: Cities and the Rise of the Consuming Class', www.mckinsey.com/global-themes/urbanization/urban-world-cities-and-the-rise-of-the-consuming-class. Last accessed 19 December 2016.

Dodds, F. 1997. *The Way Forward: Beyond Agenda 21*. London: Earthscan.

Dorling, D. 2010. 'Social Inequality and Environmental Justice', *Environmental Scientist* (December): 9–13.

Dowie, M. 1996. *Losing Ground*. Cambridge, MA: MIT Press.

Doyle, T. 1998. 'Sustainable Development and Agenda 21: The Secular Bible of Global Free Markets and Pluralist Democracy', *Third World Quarterly* 19(4): 771–86.

Dryzek, J.S. 1987. *Rational Ecology: Environment and Political Economy*. Oxford: Basil Blackwell.

DuPuis, E.M., Harrison, J.L., and Goodman, D. 2011. 'Just Food?'. In Alkon, A.H. and Agyeman, J. (eds.) *Cultivating Food Justice: Race, Class, and Sustainability*. Cambridge, MA: MIT Press, pp. 283–307.

Eager, P.W. 2004. 'From Population Control to Reproductive Rights: Understanding Normative Change in Global Population Policy (1965–1994)', *Global Society* 18(2): 145–73.

Earth's $CO_2$. 2016. www.co2.earth. Last accessed 12 December 2016.

Easterly, W. 2015. 'The SDGs Should Stand for Senseless, Dreamy, Garbled', *Foreign Policy*, 28 September, http://foreignpolicy.com/2015/09/28/the-sdgs-are-utopian-and-worthless-mdgs-development-rise-of-the-rest/ . Last accessed 24 May 2017.

Eckersley, R. 1992. *Environmentalism and Political Theory: Toward an Ecocentric Approach*. New York: SUNY Press.

Ehrenreich, N. and Lyon, B. 2011. 'The Global Politics of Food: A Critical Overview', *The University of Miami Inter-American Law Review* 43(1): 1–43.

Ehrlich, PR. 1968. *The Population Bomb*. New York: Ballantine Books.

Ehrlich, P.R. and Ehrlich, A.H. 2009. 'The Population Bomb Revisited', *The Electronic Journal of Sustainable Development* 1(3): 63–71.

Ehrlich, P.R., Ehrlich, A.H., and Daily, G. 1995. *The Stork and the Plow: The Equity Answer to the Human Dilemma*. New Haven: Yale University Press.

Eurostat. 2014. 'Waste Generation by Economic Activities and Households, EU-28, 2014', http://ec.europa.eu/eurostat/statistics-explained/index.php/File:Waste_gen eration_by_economic_activities_and_households,_EU-28,_2014_(%25)_YB16.png. Last accessed 24 May 2017.

Electronics Take Back Coalition. No date. 'Where's the Harm – Recycling or Disposal?', www.electronicstakeback.com/toxics-in-electronics/wheres-the-harm-disposal. Last accessed 6 July 2016.

Elgin, D. and Mitchell, A. 1977. 'Voluntary Simplicity', *Co-Evolution Quarterly*. Summer. http://duaneelgin.com/wp-content/uploads/2010/11/voluntary_simplicity.pdf. Last accessed 21 May 2017.

Elmer-DeWitt, P. 1992. 'Summit to Save the Earth: Rich vs. Poor', *Time*, http://content .time.com/time/magazine/article/0,9171,975656-3,00.html. Last accessed 9 December 2016.

Emsley, J. 2011. *Nature's Building Blocks: An A–Z Guide to the Elements*. Oxford University Press.

Environmental Justice Organisations, Liabilities and Trade. 2015. 'The Trafigura Case', EJOLT Fact Sheet 045, www.ejolt.org/2015/08/trafigura-case. Last accessed 16 December 2016.

EPA (Environmental Protection Agency). 2015a. 'Summary of Executive Order 12898 – Federal Actions to Address Environmental Justice in Minority Populations and Low-Income Populations', www.epa.gov/laws-regulations/summary-executive-order-12898-federal-actions-address-environmental-justice. Last accessed 21 June 2016.

EPA. 2015b. 'Office of Environmental Justice', www.epa.gov/aboutepa/about-office-enforcement-and-compliance-assurance-oeca#oej. Last accessed 21 June 2016.

EPA. 2016a. 'Climate Change Indicators: Global Greenhouse Gas Emissions', www.epa.gov/climate-indicators/climate-change-indicators-global-greenhouse-gas-emissions. Last accessed 12 December 2016.

EPA. 2016b. 'Mitigation Banking Factsheet', www.epa.gov/cwa-404/mitigation-banking-factsheet. Last accessed 19 December 2016.

EPA. 2016c. 'Dioxins Produced by Backyard Burning', www.epa.gov/dioxin/dioxins-produced-backyard-burning. Last accessed 21 June 2016.

European Chemical Agency (ECHA). 2014. 'Cadmium Fluoride', echa.europa.eu/docu ments/10162/6eb02b71-b691-4b53-b0f1-c8c68b2b3083. Last accessed 19 June 2016.

European Commission. 2015. 'What are the Sources of Dioxins?', ec.europa.eu/environ ment/archives/dioxin/sources.htm. Last accessed 21 June 2016.

FairShare International. 2016. 'About FairShare International', www.fairshare international.org/about. Last accessed 23 October 2016.

Falk, R.A. 1971. *This Endangered Planet*. New York: Random.

Falkner, R. 2016. 'The Paris Agreement and the New Logic of International Climate Politics', *International Affairs* 92(5): 1107–25.

Fankhauser, S. and Pearce, D. 2014. 'Financing for Sustainable Development'. In Atkinson, G., Dietz, S., Neumayer, E., and Agarwala, M. (eds.) *Handbook of Sustainable Development*, 2nd edition. Cheltenham: Edward Elgar, pp. 399–417.

FAO (Food and Agriculture Organization). 2003. 'Trade Reforms and Food Security: Conceptualising the Linkages', ftp://ftp.fao.org/docrep/fao/005/y4671e/y4671e00.pdf. Last accessed 3 February 2017.

FAO. 2004. 'What is Agrobiodiversity?', www.fao.org/docrep/007/y5609e/y5609e00.htm#Contents. Last accessed 19 December 2016.

FAO. 2006. 'Deforestation Causes Global Warming', www.fao.org/NEWSROOM/en/news/2006/1000385/index.html. Last accessed 19 December 2016.

FAO. 2012. *State of the World's Forests 2012*. Rome: FAO.

FAO. 2015. *Climate Change and Food Systems: Global Assessments and Implications for Food Security and Trade*. Rome: Food Agriculture Organization of the United Nations.

Farley, H.M. and Smith, Z.A. 2014. *Sustainability: If It's Everything, Is It Nothing?* London: Routledge.

Feeny, D., Berkes, F., McCay, B.J., and Acheson, J.M. 1990. 'The Tragedy of the Commons: Twenty-Two Years Later', *Human Ecology* 18(1): 1–19.

Fitzgerald, D. 2003. *Every Farm a Factory: The Industrial Ideal in American Agriculture*. New Haven: Yale University Press.

Floyd, R. and Matthew, R.A. 2013. 'Environmental Security Studies: An Introduction'. In Floyd, R. and Matthew, R.A. (eds.) *Environmental Security*. Abingdon: Routledge, pp. 1–20.

Fluehr-Lobban, C. 2006. *Race and Racism: An Introduction*. Lanham: AltaMira Press.

Fominaya, C.F. 2014. *Social Movements and Globalization*. New York: Palgrave Macmillan.

Forest Carbon Partnership Facility. 2013. *Carbon Fund Brochure*, http://www.forestcarbonpartnership.org/sites/fcp/files/2013/june2013/Carbon%20Fund-web_1.pdf. Last accessed 12 December 2016.

Foster, J.B. 1998. 'Malthus' Essay on Population at Age 200: A Marxian View', *Monthly Review* 50(7): 1–18.

Foster, J.B. 2000. *Marx's Ecology*. New York: Monthly Review Press.

Foster, J.B., Clark, B., and York, R. 2010. *The Ecological Rift: Capitalism's War on the Earth*. New York: Monthly Review Press.

Founex. 1971. 'The Founex Report on Development and Environment', www.stakeholderforum.org/fileadmin/files/.../founex%20report%201972.pdf. Last accessed 13 May 2017.

Fremlin, J.H. 1964. 'How Many People Can the World Support?', *New Scientist* 415: 285–7.

Friends of the MST. 2015. 'What is the MST?', www.mstbrazil.org/content/what-mst. Last accessed 19 December 2016.

FSC (Forest Stewardship Council). 2015. *Market Info Pack 2015*, https://ic.fsc.org/pre-download.2015-fsc-market-info-pack.2437.htm. Last accessed 17 May 2017.

Fuchs, D. and Boll, F. 2011. 'Sustainable Consumption'. In Kutting, G. (ed.) *Global Environmental Politics*. London: Routledge, pp. 72–87.

Futerra Sustainability Communications. No date. 'The Greenwash Guide', https://www.2degreesnetwork.com/groups/2degrees-community/resources/futerras-greenwash-guide/attachments/7834/. Last accessed 17 May 2017.

Galbraith, J.K. 1958. *The Affluent Society*. Boston: Houghton Mifflin Company.

Garg, A. 2011. 'Pro-equity Effects of Ancillary Benefits of Climate Change Policies: A Case Study of Human Health Impacts of Outdoor Air Pollution in New Delhi', *World Development* 39(6): 1002–25.

Gaventa, J. 2002. 'Exploring Citizenship, Participation and Accountability', *IDS Bulletin* 33(2): 1–14.

Geiser, K. 2015. *Chemicals without Harm: Policies for a Sustainable World*. Cambridge, MA: MIT Press.

Geiser, K. and Edwards, S. 2013. 'Instruments and Approaches for the Sound Management of Chemicals', in *Global Chemicals Outlook – Towards Sound Management of Chemicals*, www.turi.org/TURI_Publications/Presentations/General/Instruments_and_Approaches_for_the_Sound_Management_of_Chemicals. Last accessed 12 December 2016.

Geist, H. and Lambin, E. 2002. 'Proximate Causes and Underlying Driving Forces of Tropical Deforestation', *BioScience* 52(2): 143–50.

Gentilviso, C. 2010. 'Leaded Gasoline' *Time*, http://content.time.com/time/specials/pack ages/article/0,28804,1991915_1991909_1991817,00.html. Last accessed 12 December 2016.

Gerbens-Leenes, P.W., Mekonnen, M.M., and Hoekstra, A.Y. 2013. 'The Water Footprint of Poultry, Pork and Beef: A Comparative Study in Different Countries and Production Systems', *Water Resources and Industry* 1–2: 25–36.

Gills, B.K. 2000. 'Introduction: Globalization and the Politics of Resistance'. In Gills, B.K. (ed.) *Globalization and the Politics of Resistance*. Basingstoke: Macmillan, pp. 3–11.

Giménez, E.H. and Shattuck, A. 2011. 'Food Crises, Food Regimes and Food Movements: Rumblings of Reform or Tides of Transformation?', *The Journal of Peasant Studies* 38(1): 109–44.

Gleditsch, N.P., Furlong, K., Hegre, H., Lacina, B., and Owen, T. 2006. 'Conflicts Over Shared Rivers: Resource Scarcity or Fuzzy Boundaries?', *Political Geography* 25: 361–82.

Gleick, P.H. 1993. 'Water and Conflict: Fresh Water Resources and International Security', *International Security* 18(1): 79–112.

Global Footprint Network. No date. www.footprintnetwork.org/en/index.php/GFN. Last accessed 19 December 2016.

Gómez-Baggethun, E. and Naredo, J.M. 2015. 'In Search of Lost Time: The Rise and Fall of Limits to Growth in International Sustainability Policy', *Sustainability Science* 10(3): 385–95.

Gonzalez, C.G. 2004. 'Trade Liberalization, Food Security and the Environment: The Neoliberal Threat to Sustainable Rural Development', *Transnational Law & Contemporary Problems* 14: 19–98.

Gonzalez, C.G. 2011. 'Climate Change, Food Security, and Agrobiodiversity: Toward a Just, Resilient, and Sustainable Food System', *Fordham Environmental Law Review* 22: 419–98.

Grammaticas, D. 2012. 'Chinese Colonialism?', *BBC News*, www.bbc.co.uk/news/world-asia-18901656. Last accessed 8 December 2016.

Greenpeace. 2009. 'Where Does E-waste End Up?', www.greenpeace.org/international/en/campaigns/detox/electronics/the-e-waste-problem/where-does-e-waste-end-up. Last accessed 12 December 2016.

Greer, G. 1985. *Sex and Destiny: The Politics of Human Fertility*. New York: Harper & Row.

Grinspoon, D. 2016. 'Welcome to Terra Sapiens', *Aeon*, 20 December, https://aeon.co/essays/enter-the-sapiezoic-a-new-aeon-of-self-aware-global-change. Last accessed 21 December 2016.

Grossman, G.M. and Krueger, A.B. 1991. 'Environmental impacts of the North American Free Trade Agreement'. NBER Working Paper 3914. Cambridge, MA: National Bureau of Economic Research.

Grossman, G.M. and Krueger, A.B. 1996. 'The Inverted-U: What Does It Mean?', *Environment and Development Economics* 1(1): 119–22.

Guha, R. and Martinez-Alier, J. 1997. *Varieties of Environmentalism: Essays North and South*. Abingdon: Earthscan.

Gupta, S. and Ogden, D.T. 2006. 'The Attitude–Behavior Gap in Environmental Consumerism'. Proceedings of the Association of Pennsylvania University Business & Economics Faculty (APUBEF), 5–6 October, Clarion University of Pennsylvania pp. 199–205, www.nabet.us/Archives/2006/f%2006/APUBEF%20f2006.pdf. Last accessed 24 May 2017.

Gutierrez, R. 2014. 'International Environmental Justice on Hold: Revisiting The Basel Ban From A Philippine Perspective', *Duke Environmental Law and Policy Forum* 24: 399–426.

Hale, T. 2016. 'All Hands on Deck: The Paris Agreement and Nonstate Climate Action', *Global Environmental Politics* 16(3): 12–22.

Halle, M. 2012. 'Life After Rio: A Commentary', International Institute for Sustainable Development, www.iisd.org/library/life-after-rio-commentary-mark-halle-iisd. Last accessed 9 December 2016.

Hance, J. 2015. 'How Humans are Driving the Sixth Mass Extinction', *The Guardian*, 20 October, https://www.theguardian.com/environment/radical-conservation/2015/oct/20/the-four-horsemen-of-the-sixth-mass-extinction. Last accessed 26 December 2016.

Hansen, S. 1989. 'Debt for Nature Swaps: Overview and Discussion of Key Issues', *Ecological Economics* 1(1): 77–93.

Hardin, G. 1968. 'The Tragedy of the Commons', *Science* 162(3859): 1243–8.

Hardin, G. 1977. 'Denial and Disguise'. In Hardin, G. and Baden, J. (eds.) *Managing the Commons*, 1st edition. New York: W.H. Freeman, pp. 45–52.

Hardin, G. 1994. 'The Tragedy of the Unmanaged Commons', *Trends in Ecology and Evolution* 9(5). Reprinted in (2007) Penn, D.J. and Mysterud, I. (eds.) *Evolutionary Perspectives on Environmental Problems*. New Brunswick: Transaction Publishers, pp. 105–8.

Hardin, G. 1998. 'Extensions of "The Tragedy of the Commons"', *Science* 280(5364): 682–3.

Hartmann, B. 1995. *Reproductive Rights and Wrongs: The Global Politics of Population Control*, 2nd edition. Boston: South End Press.

Hartmann, B., Hendrixson, A., and Sasser, J. 2015. 'Population, Sustainable Development and Gender Equality'. In Leach, M. (ed.) *Gender Equality and Sustainable Development*. Abingdon: Routledge, pp. 56–82.

Harvey, D. 2014. *Seventeen Contradictions and the End of Capitalism*. Oxford University Press.

Hawken, P., Lovins, A.B., and Lovins, L.H. 1999. *Natural Capitalism: The Next Industrial Revolution*. London: Earthscan.

Heidelberg Institute for International Conflict Research. 2014. Conflict Barometer 2013, hiik.de/de/downloads/data/downloads_2013/ConflictBarometer2013.pdf. Last accessed 11 December 2015.

Heller, M.C. and Keoleian, G.A. 2000. 'Life Cycle-Based Sustainability Indicators for Assessment of the U.S. Food System', The Center for Sustainable Systems, Report no. CSS00-04, http://css.snre.umich.edu/publication/life-cycle-based-sustainabil ity-indicators-assessment-us-food-system. Last accessed 24 May 2017.

*Herald Journal.* 1988. 'Poison Ship to Unload Toxic Cargo', news.google.com/ newspapers?nid=1876&dat=19880526&id=81IgAAAAIBAJ&sjid=js4EAAAAIBAJ& pg=5852,5856267&hl=en. Last accessed 12 December 2016.

Heywood, A. 2015. *Key Concepts in Politics and International Relations*. Houndmills: Palgrave Macmillan.

Hicks, R.L., Parks, B.C., Roberts, J.T., and Tierney, M.J. 2008. *Greening Aid? Understanding the Environmental Impact of Development Assistance*. Oxford University Press.

Hiller, A. 2011. 'Climate Change and Individual Responsibility', *The Monist* 94(3): 349–68.

Hinrichs, C.C. 2003. 'The Practice and Politics of Food System Localization', *Journal of Rural Studies* 19: 33–45.

Hobbelink, H. 1991. *Biotechnology and the Future of World Agriculture: The Fourth Resource*. London: Zed Books.

Hoffmann, M.J. 2011. *Climate Governance at the Crossroads*. Oxford University Press.

Holland, T.G., Peterson, G.D., and Gonzalez, A. 2009. 'A Cross-National Analysis of How Economic Inequality Predicts Biodiversity Loss', *Conservation Biology* 23(5): 1304–13.

Holloway, J. 2002. *Change the World Without Taking Power: The Meaning of Revolution Today*. London: Pluto Press.

Holt-Giménez, E. 2002. 'Measuring Farmers Agroecological Resistance to Hurricane Mitch in Nicaragua: A Case Study in Participatory, Sustainable Land Management Impact Monitoring', *Agriculture, Ecosystems & Environment* 93(1): 87–105.

Holt-Giménez, E. 2006. *Campesino a Campesino: Voices from Latin America's Farmer to Farmer Movement for Sustainable Agriculture*. Oakland: Food First.

Holt-Giménez, E. and Patel, R. 2012. *Food Rebellions: Crisis and the Hunger for Justice*. London: Zed Books.

Holt-Giménez, E. and Altieri, M.A. 2013. 'Agroecology, Food Sovereignty, and the New Green Revolution', *Agroecology and Sustainable Food Systems* 37(1): 90–102.

Homer-Dixon, T. 1999. *Environment, Scarcity, and Violence.* Princeton University Press.

Hough, P. 2014. *Environmental Security: An Introduction.* Abingdon: Routledge.

Howe, J.P. 2014. *Behind the Curve: Science and the Politics of Global Warming.* Seattle: University of Washington Press.

Humphreys, D. 2013. 'Deforestation'. In Falkner, R. (ed.) *The Handbook of Global Climate and Environmental Policy.* Cambridge: Polity Press, pp. 72–88.

Humphreys, D. 2014. 'Forests'. In Harris, P.G. (ed.) *Routledge Handbook of Global Environmental Politics.* London: Routledge, pp. 494–505.

Hunter, D.B. 2014. 'International Environmental Law: Sources, Principles, and Innovations'. In Harris, P.G. (ed.) *Routledge Handbook of Global Environmental Politics.* London: Routledge, pp. 124–37.

Inglehart, R. 1977. *The Silent Revolution.* Princeton University Press.

Intergovernmental Panel on Climate Change (IPCC). 2014. *Climate Change 2014 – Impacts, Adaptation and Vulnerability: Global and Sectoral Aspects.* Cambridge University Press.

International Energy Agency. 2016. *Energy Efficiency Market Report 2016,* www.iea.org/eemr16/files/medium-term-energy-efficiency-2016_WEB.PDF. Last accessed 8 December 2016.

International Institute for Sustainable Development. 2002. 'Summary of the World Summit on Sustainable Development: 26 August–4 September 2002', *Earth Negotiations Bulletin* 22(51), www.iisd.ca/vol22/enb2251e.html. Last accessed 9 December 2016.

International Lead Association (ILA). 2012. 'Significant Growth in Lead Usage Underlines its Importance to the Global Economy', http://www.ila-lead.org/news/lead-in-the-news/2012-11-30/significant-growth-in-lead-usage-underlines-its–importance-to-the-global-economy-. Last accessed 18 June 2016.

International POPs Elimination Network (IPEN). 2014. 'An NGO Introduction to Mercury Pollution and the Minamata Convention on Mercury', www.ipen.org/documents/ngo-introduction-mercury-pollution-and-minamata-convention-mercury. Last accessed 25 June 2016.

International Telecommunications Union (ITU). 2015. 'ICT Facts and Figures', www.itu.int/en/ITU-D/Statistics/Documents/facts/ICTFactsFigures2015.pdf. Last accessed 12 October 2015.

Ishii-Eiteman, M. 2009. 'Feeding the World, Greening the Planet. Summary of Findings of the International Assessment of Agriculture Knowledge, Science and Technology for Development', https://www.globalonenessproject.org/sites/default/.../IAASTD%20Fact%20Sheet.pdf. Last accessed 18 November 2016.

Ivanova, M. 2005. 'Environment: The Path of Global Environmental Governance – Form and Function in Historical Perspective'. In Ayre, G. and Callway, R. (eds.) *Governance for Sustainable Development: A Foundation for the Future.* London: Earthscan, pp. 45–72.

Ivanova, M. 2010. 'UNEP in Global Environmental Governance: Design, Leadership, Location', *Global Environmental Politics* 10(1): 30–59.

Ivanova, M. 2016. 'Good COP, Bad COP: Climate Reality after Paris', *Global Policy* 7(3): 411–19.

Jackson, T. 2005. 'Motivating Sustainable Consumption: A Review of Evidence on Consumer Behaviour and Behavioural Change'. *A Report to the Sustainable Development Research Network*. University of Surrey: Centre for Environmental Strategy.

Jackson, T. 2009. *Prosperity without Growth? The Transition to a Sustainable Economy. Sustainable Development Commission*, http://www.sd-commission.org.uk/publications.php?id=914. Last accessed 24 June 2015.

Jägerskog, A. 2005. 'Water Sharing Between Israel, Jordan, and the Palestinians'. In Starke, L. (ed.) *State of the World 2005: Redefining Global Security*. Washington DC: Worldwatch Institute, p. 86.

James, B. 2002. 'Johannesburg Summit: Big Agenda, Little Action on World's Problems', *The New York Times*, www.nytimes.com/2002/09/07/news/johannesburg-summit-big-agenda-little-action-on-worlds-problems.html. Last accessed 9 December 2016.

Jevons, W.S. 1866. *The Coal Question: An Inquiry Concerning the Progress of the Nation, and the Probable Exhaustion of Our Coal-mines*. London: Macmillan.

Jinnah, S. and Conliffe, A. 2012. 'Climate Change and Bandwagoning: Climate Change Impacts on Global Environmental Governance.' In Chasek, P. and Wagner, L.M. (eds.) *The Roads from Rio: Lessons Learned from Twenty Years of Multilateral Environmental Negotiations*. New York: RFF Press, pp. 199–217.

Kaika, D. and Zervas, E. 2013. 'The Environmental Kuznets Curve (EKC) Theory. Part B: Critical issues', *Energy Policy* 62: 1403–11.

Kalbhenn, A. 2011. 'Liberal Peace and Shared Resources – A Fair-Weather Phenomenon?', *Journal of Peace Research* 48(6): 715–35.

Kaplan, R.D. 1994. 'The Coming Anarchy', *The Atlantic*, www.theatlantic.com/magazine/archive/1994/02/the-coming-anarchy/304670. Last accessed 24 December 2015.

Kellenberg, D. and Levinson, A. 2013. 'Waste of Effort? International Environmental Agreements'. NBER Working Paper No. 19533. Cambridge, MA: National Bureau of Economic Research, www.nber.org/papers/w19533. Last accessed 16 December 2016.

Kellett, L. 2014. 'How Long Will Our Landfills Last?', *Direct365*, www.direct365.co.uk/blog/how-long-will-landfills-last. Last accessed 16 December 2016.

Kelley, C.P., Mohtadi, S., Cane, M.A., Seager, R., and Kushnir, Y. 2015. 'Climate Change in the Fertile Crescent and Implications of the Recent Syrian Drought', *Proceedings of the National Academy of Sciences* 112(11): 3241–6.

Kelly, D.J. 2010. 'The Case for Social Safeguards in a Post-2012 Agreement on REDD Law', *Environment and Development Journal* 6(1): 61–81.

Kennan, G. 1985. 'Morality and Foreign Policy', *Foreign Affairs* 64(2): 205–18.

Keohane, R.O. 1990. 'Multilateralism: An Agenda for Research', *International Journal* 45: 731–64.

Keohane, R.O. and Ostrom, E. 1995. 'Introduction'. In Keohane, R.O. and Ostrom, E. (eds.) *Local Commons and Global Interdependence.* London: SAGE Publications, pp. 1–26.

Kinzig, A.P., Perrings, C., Chapin, F.S., Polasky, S., Smith, V.K., Tilman, D., and Turner, B.L. 2011. 'Paying for Ecosystem Services – Promise and Peril', *Science* 334: 603–5.

Klare, M.T. 2001. 'The New Geography of Conflict', *Foreign Affairs* 80(3): 49–61.

Kotasova, I. 2016. 'More Plastic than Fish in Oceans by 2050', 19 January, http://money.cnn.com/2016/01/19/news/economy/davos-plastic-ocean-fish. Accessed 26 December 2016.

Kozlowski, A., Bardecki, M., and Searcy, C. 2012. 'Environmental Impacts in the Fashion Industry: A Life-Cycle and Stakeholder Framework', *Journal of Corporate Citizenship* 45(1): 16–36.

Kraft, R. 2009. 'Pondering Ecuador's Yasuni Proposal', http://www.ecosystemmarketplace.com/articles/pondering-ecuador-s-yasuni-proposal. Last accessed 16 May 2017.

Kremen, C., Iles, A., and Bacon, C. 2012. 'Diversified Farming Systems: An Agroecological, Systems-based Alternative to Modern Industrial Agriculture', *Ecology and Society* 17(4): 44–63.

Kuznets, S. 1955. 'Economic Growth and Income Inequality', *The American Economic Review* 45(1): 1–28.

La Via Campesina. 2015. 'Declaration of the International Forum for Agroecology', viacampesina.org/en/index.php/main-issues-mainmenu-27/sustainable-peasants-agriculture-mainmenu-42/1749-declaration-of-the-international-forum-for-agroecology. Last accessed 19 December 2016.

Lang, C. 2014. 'REDD on Trial: "As Long as Nature is Seen as Property in Law, There Can Be No Justice for Communities, the Climate or Nature"', www.redd-monitor.org/2014/12/11/redd-on-trial-as-long-as-nature-is-seen-as-property-in-law-there-can-be-no-justice-for-communities-the-climate-or-nature. Last accessed 9 March 2015.

Langston, N. 2014. 'New Chemical Bodies: Synthetic Chemicals, Regulation, and Human Health'. In Isenberg, A.C. (ed.) *The Oxford Handbook of Environmental History.* Oxford University Press, pp. 259–81.

Lavaux, S. 2006/2007. 'Natural Resources and Conflict in Colombia: Complex Dynamics', *Narrow Relationships' International Journal* 62(1): 19–30.

Le Billon, P. 2001. 'The Political Ecology of War: Natural Resources and Armed Conflicts' *Political Geography* 20: 561–84.

Lear, L. 2002. 'Introduction'. In Carson, R. *Silent Spring.* New York: First Mariner Books, pp. x–xix.

Lenntech. 2016. 'Cadmium', www.lenntech.com/periodic/elements/cd.htm. Last accessed 12 December 2016.

Lepawsky, J. 2015a. 'Are We Living in a Post-Basel World?', *Area* 47(1): 7–15.

Lepawsky, J. 2015b. 'The Changing Geography of Global Trade in Electronic Discards: Time to Rethink the E-Waste Problem', *The Geographical Journal* 181(2): 147–59.

Lepawsky, J. 2015c. 'Trading on Distortion', *E-Scrap News*, December, https://resource-recycling.com/e-scrap/2016/03/10/trading-on-distortion/ Last accessed on 24 May 2017.

Levin, K., Cashore, B., Bernstein, S., and Auld, G. 2012. 'Overcoming the Tragedy of Super Wicked Problems: Constraining our Future Selves to Ameliorate Global Climate Change', *Policy Science* 45: 123–52.

Lewis, T.L. 2003. 'Environmental Aid: Driven by Recipient Need or Donor Interests', *Social Science Quarterly* 84(1): 144–61.

Lipp, R.L. 2001. 'Tragic, Truly Tragic: The Commons in Modern Life'. In Machan, T.R. (ed.) *The Commons: Its Tragedies and Other Follies*. Stanford: Hoover Institution Press, pp. 89–119.

Lippit, V.D. 2005. *Capitalism*. London: Routledge.

Lloyd, W.F. 1832. *Two Lectures on the Checks to Population*. Oxford: University of Oxford.

Lohmann, L. 2005. 'Malthusianism and the Terror of Scarcity'. In Hartmann, B., Subramaniam, B., and Zerner, C. (eds.) *Making Threats: Biofears and Environmental Anxieties*. Lanham: Rowman and Littlefield, pp. 81–98.

Lovelock, J. 2006. *The Revenge of Gaia*. London: Penguin Books.

MacQuarrie, P. and Wolf, A.T. 2013. 'Understanding Water Security'. In Floyd, R. and Matthew, R.A. (eds.) *Environmental Security*. Abingdon: Routledge, pp. 169–96.

Magni, M. and Poh, F. 2013. 'Winning the Battle for China's New Middle Class', McKinsey and Company, www.mckinsey.com/industries/consumer-packaged-goods/our-insights/winning-the-battle-for-chinas-new-middle-class. Last accessed 19 December 2016.

Maguire, R. 2013. *Global Forest Governance: Legal Concepts and Policy Trends*. Cheltenham: Edward Elgar.

Malthus, T.R. 1798. *An Essay on the Principle of Population*. London: J. Johnson.

Manahan, S.E. 2008. *Fundamentals of Environmental Chemistry*. Boca Raton: CRC Press.

Manhart, A., Osibanjo, O., Aderinto, A., and Prakash, S. 2011. 'Informal E-Waste Management in Lagos, Nigeria – Socioeconomic Impacts and Feasibility of International Recycling Co-operations Secretariat of the Basel Convention', www.basel.int/Portals/4/Basel%20Convention/docs/eWaste/E-waste_Africa_Project_Nigeria.pdf. Last accessed 19 December 2016.

Maniates, M. 2002. 'In Search of Consumptive Resistance: The Voluntary Simplicity Movement'. In Princen, T., Maniates, M., and Conca, K. (eds.) *Confronting Consumption*. Cambridge, MA: MIT Press.

Marcoux, C., Parks, B.C., Peratsakis, C.M., Roberts, J.T., and Tierney, M.J. 2013. 'Environmental and Climate Finance in a New World: How Past Environmental Aid Allocation Impacts Future Climate Aid', *WIDER Working Paper No. 2013/128*. Helsinki: UNU-WIDER.

Markey, D. 2011. 'Pakistan'. In Moran, D. (ed.) *Climate Change and National Security: A Country-Level Analysis*. Washington DC: Georgetown University Press, pp. 85–102.

Marx, A. and Cuypers, D. 2010. 'Forest Certification as a Global Environmental Governance Tool: What is the Macro-Effectiveness of the Forest Stewardship Council?', *Regulation and Governance* 4: 408–34.

Maslow, A.H. 1954. *Motivation and Personality*. New York: Harper and Row.

Mason, S.A., Hagmann, T., Bichsel, C., Ludi, E., and Arsano, Y. 2009. 'Linkages Between Sub-national and International Water Conflicts: the Eastern Nile Basin'. In Brauch, H.G., Behera, N.C., Kameri-Mbote, P., Grin, P., Spring, U.O., Chourou, B., Mesjasz, C., and Krummenacher, H. (eds.) *Facing Global Environmental Change*. Berlin: Springer-Verlag, pp. 325–34.

Massey, R. and Jacobs, M. 2013. 'Trends and Indicators'. In *Global Chemicals Outlook – Towards Sound Management of Chemicals*, www.turi.org/TURI_Publications/Presenta tions/General/Instruments_and_Approaches_for_the_Sound_Management_of_Chem icals. Last accessed 12 December 2016.

Mathews, J. 1989. 'Redefining Security', *Foreign Affairs* 68(2): 162–77.

Mattiace, S. 2012. 'Social and Indigenous Movements in Mexico's Transition to Democracy'. In Camp, R.A. (ed.) *The Oxford Handbook of Mexican Politics*. Oxford University Press, pp. 398–422.

Mazoyer, M. and Roudart, L. 2006. *A History of World Agriculture*. New York University Press.

McAfee, A., Dessain, V., and Sjoeman, A. 2004. *Zara: IT for Fast Fashion*. Cambridge, MA: Harvard Business School Publishing.

McCormick, J. 1989. *Reclaiming Paradise: The Global Environmental Movement*. Bloomington: Indiana University Press.

McFadden, R.D. 1987. 'Garbage Barge Returns in Search of a Dump', *The New York Times*, www.nytimes.com/1987/05/18/nyregion/garbage-barge-returns-in-search-of-a-dump.html. Last accessed 30 June 2016.

McIntyre, B.D., Herren, H.R., Wakhungu, J., and Watson, R.T. (eds.). 2009. *International Assessment of Agricultural Knowledge, Science and Technology for Development: Synthesis Report*. http://apps.unep.org/redirect.php?file=/publications/pmtdocu ments/-Agriculture%20at%20a%20crossroads%20-%20Synthesis%20report-2009 Agriculture_at_Crossroads_Synthesis_Report.pdf. Last accessed 24 May 2017.

McKenney, J. 2002. 'Artificial Fertility: The Environmental Costs of Industrial Fertilizers'. In Kimbrell, A. (ed.) *The Fatal Harvest: The Tragedy of Industrial Agriculture*. Sausalito: Deep Ecology Press, pp. 121–9.

McKinney, M.L., Schoch, R.M., and Yonavjak, L. 2012. *Environmental Science: Systems and Solutions*. Burlington: Jones and Bartlett Learning.

McKinsey Global Institute. 2012. 'Urban World: Cities and the Rise of the Consuming Class', www.mckinsey.com/~/media/mckinsey/global%20themes/urbanization/urban %20world%20cities%20and%20the%20rise%20of%20the%20consuming%20class/mgi_ urban_world_rise_of_the_consuming_class_full_report.ashx. Last accessed 8 November 2016.

Meadows, D.H., Meadows, D., Randers, J., and Behrens III, W.W. 1972. *The Limits To Growth; a Report for the Club of Rome's Project on the Predicament of Mankind*. New York: Universe Books.

Meijaard, E., Wunder, S., Guariguata, M.R., and Sheik, D. 2014. 'What Scope for Certifying Forest Ecosystem Services?', *Ecosystem Services* 7: 160–6.

Mekonnen, M.M. and Hoekstra, A.Y. 2012. 'A Global Assessment of the Water Footprint of Farm Animal Products', *Ecosystems* 15: 401–15.

Middlemiss, L. 2010. 'Reframing Individual Responsibility for Sustainable Consumption: Lessons from Environmental Justice and Ecological Citizenship', *Environmental Values* 19: 147–67.

Middlemiss, L. 2014. 'Individualised or Participatory? Exploring Late-modern Identity and Sustainable Development', *Environmental Politics* 23(6): 929–46.

Millennium Ecosystem Assessment. 2005. www.millenniumassessment.org/en/Reports.html#. Last accessed 16 May 2017.

Milun, K. 2011. *The Political Uncommons: The Cross-cultural Logic of the Global Commons*. Farnham: Ashgate.

Minamata Convention. 2013. 'Minamata Convention on Mercury: Text and Annexes', www.mercuryconvention.org/Convention/tabid/3426/Default.aspx. Last accessed 25 June 2016.

Minter, A. 2016. 'The Burning Truth Behind an E-Waste Dump in Africa', 13 January, www.smithsonianmag.com/science-nature/burning-truth-behind-e-waste-dump-africa-180957597/?no-ist. Last accessed 18 May 2017.

Minzi, M.L. 1993. 'The Pied Piper of Debt-for-Nature Swaps', *University of Pennsylvania Journal of International Law* 14(1), scholarship.law.upenn.edu/jil/vol14/iss1/2. Last accessed 12 December 2016.

Mitchell, R.B. 2002–16. International Environmental Agreements Database Project, iea.uoregon.edu/environmental-agreements-date. Last accessed 9 December 2016.

Monbiot, G. 1994. 'The Tragedy of Enclosure', *Scientific American* 270(1): 159.

Moore, J.W. 2003. 'The Modern World-System as Environmental History? Ecology and the Rise of Capitalism', *Theory and Society* XXXII(3): 307–77.

Moore, S. 2012. 'Something in the Air: The Forgotten Crisis of Britain's Poor Air Quality', London: Policy Exchange, www.policyexchange.org.uk/images/publications/something%20in%20the%20air.pdf. Last accessed 12 December 2016.

Moss, N. and Nussbaum, R. 2011. 'A Review of Three REDD+ Safeguard Initiatives', Forest Carbon Partnership Facility and UN-REDD, www.cbd.int/forest/doc/analysis-redd-plus-safeguard-initiatives-2011-en.pdf. Last accessed 9 March 2015.

Müller, R. 2011. 'Possibilities to Reduce Tropical Deforestation by Carbon Funding: General Reflections and Examples from Bolivia'. In Hansjürgens, B., Antes, R., and Strunz, M. (eds.) *Permit Trading in Different Applications*. Abingdon: Routledge, pp. 174–93.

Muradian, R., Corbera, E., Pascual, U., Kosoy, N., and May, P.H. 2010. 'Reconciling Theory and Practice: An Alternative Conceptual Framework for Understanding Payments for Environmental Services', *Ecological Economics* 69(6): 1202–8.

Najam, A. 1996. 'A Developing Countries' Perspective on Population, Environment, and Development', *Population Research and Policy Review* 15: 1–19.

National Bureau of Statistics China. 2015. 'Statistical Communiqué of the People's Republic of China on the 2014 National Economic and Social Development', www.stats.gov.cn/english/PressRelease/201502/t20150228_687439.html. Last accessed 11 October 2015.

Nelson, G.C. 2001. 'Traits and Techniques of GMOs'. In Nelson, G.C. (ed.) *Genetically Modified Organisms in Agriculture: Economics and Politics*. London: Academic Press, pp. 7–14.

Newman, E., Thakur, R., and Triman, J. 2006. 'Introduction'. In Newman, E., Thakur, R., and Triman, J. (eds.) *Multilateralism Under Challenge: Power, International Order, And Structural Change.* Tokyo: United Nations University Press, pp. 1–17.

Norgaard, R.B. 2010. 'Ecosystem Services: From Eye-Opening Metaphor to Complexity Blinder', *Ecological Economics* 69: 1219–27.

Nyéléni Declaration. 2007. 'Forum for Food Sovereignty: Synthesis Report', nyeleni.org/ IMG/pdf/31Mar2007NyeleniSynthesisReport-en.pdf. Last accessed 19 December 2016.

O'Brien, M. 2012. 'Everything You Need To Know About the Economy in 2012, in 34 Charts', *The Atlantic*, www.theatlantic.com/business/archive/2012/12/everything-you-need-to-know-about-the-economy-in-2012-in-34-charts/266467. Last accessed 9 December 2016.

Occupational Safety and Health Administration (OSHA). No date. 'Safety and Health Topics: Cadmium', United States Department of Labor, www.osha.gov/SLTC/cad mium. Last accessed 16 December 2016.

O'Connor, J. 1998. *Natural Causes: Essays in Ecological Marxism.* New York: Guilford Press.

O'Connor, M. 1994. 'Introduction: Liberate, Accumulate and Bust?'. In O'Connor, M. (ed.) *Is Capitalism Sustainable? Political Economy and the Politics of Ecology.* New York: Guilford Press, pp. 1–21.

OECD. 2010. *Paying for Biodiversity: Enhancing the Cost-Effectiveness of Payments for Ecosystem Services. Executive Summary.* Paris: OECD.

OECD. 2012. 'Trends in Aid to Environment, a Component of Sustainable Development Finance (1991–2011)'. In *Development Co-operation Report 2012: Lessons in Linking Sustainability and Development.* OECD Publishing. dx.doi.org/10.1787/ dcr-2012-10-en. Last accessed 12 December 2016.

Ostrom, E. 1999. 'Coping with Tragedies of the Commons', *Annual Review of Political Science* 2: 493–535.

Ostrom, E. 2015. *Governing the Commons.* Canto Classics edition. Cambridge University Press.

Ostrom, E., Burger, J., Field, C.B., Norgaard, R.B., and Policansky, D. 1999. 'Revisiting the Commons: Local Lessons, Global Challenges', *Science* 284: 278–82.

Paarlberg, R. 2013. *Food Politics: What Everyone Needs to Know.* Oxford University Press.

Page, S. 2016. 'The Northeast Is Considering a Major Extension To Its Emissions Program', Think Progress, thinkprogress.org/the-northeast-is-considering-a-major-extension-to-its-emissions-program. Last accessed 23 October 2016.

Pallermaerts, M. 2005. 'Is Multilateralism the Future?' In Hens, L. and Nath, B. (eds.) *The World Summit on Sustainable Development: The Johannesburg Conference.* Dordrecht: Springer, pp. 373–94.

Park, J., Finger, M. and Conca, K. 2008. 'The Death of Rio Environmentalism'. In Park, J., Finger, M., and Conca, K. (eds.) *The Crisis of Global Environmental Governance: Towards a New Political Economy of Sustainability.* London: Routledge, pp. 1–12.

Park, S. 2010. *World Bank Group Interactions with Environmentalists*. Manchester University Press.

Pearse, G. 2012. *Greenwash: Big Brands and Carbon Scams*. Collingwood: Black Inc.

Pellow, D.N. 2007. *Resisting Global Toxics: Transnational Movements for Environmental Justice*. Cambridge, MA: MIT Press.

Pfeiffer, D.A. 2006. *Eating Fossil Fuels: Oil, Food and the Coming Crisis in Agriculture*. Gabriola Island, BC: New Society Publishers.

Plumwood, V. 2002. *Environmental Culture: The Ecological Crisis of Reason*. London: Routledge.

Porras, I., Barton, D.N., Miranda, M., and Chacón-Cascante, A. 2013. *Learning from 20 Years of Payments for Ecosystem Services in Costa Rica*. London: International Institute for Environment and Development.

Porritt, J. 2007. *Capitalism as if the World Matters*. New York: Earthscan.

Postel, S. and Wolf, A.T. 2009. 'Dehydrating Conflict', *Foreign Affairs* (September/October Issue): 60–7.

Pramis, J. 2013. 'Number of Mobile Phones to Exceed World Population by 2014', www.digitaltrends.com/mobile/mobile-phone-world-population-2014. Last accessed 8 November 2016.

Princen, T., Maniates, M., and Conca, K. 2002a. 'Conclusion: To Confront Consumption'. In Princen, T., Maniates, M., and Conca, K (eds.) *Confronting Consumption*. Cambridge, MA: MIT Press, pp. 317–28.

Princen, T., Maniates, M., and Conca, K. 2002b. 'Confronting Consumption'. In Princen, T., Maniates, M., and Conca, K. (eds.) *Confronting Consumption*. Cambridge, MA: MIT Press, pp. 1–20.

Puckett, J. 2015. 'Exporting Deception: The Disturbing Trend of Waste Trade Denial', *E-Scrap News*, August, https://resource-recycling.com/e-scrap/2015/11/10/exporting-deception-disturbing-trend-waste-trade-denial/ pp. 38–46. Last accessed 24 May 2017, pp. 38–46.

Rajamani, L. 2000. 'The Principle of Common but Differentiated Responsibility and the Balance of Commitments under the Climate Regime', *Review of European Community and International Environmental Law* 9(2): 120–31.

Rajan, M.G. 1997. *Global Environmental Politics: India and the North–South Politics of Global Environmental Issues*. Delhi: Oxford University Press.

Ramsbotham, O., Miall, H., and Woodhouse, T. 2011. *Contemporary Conflict Resolution*. Cambridge: Polity Press.

Recon Analytics. 2011. 'International Comparisons: The Handset Replacement Cycle', mobilefuture.org/resources/international-comparisons-the-handset-replacement-cycle-2. Last accessed 12 October 2015.

REDD. No date. 'Standards', www.redd-standards.org. Last accessed 19 December 2016.

REDD Desk. 2015. 'What is REDD+?', theredddesk.org/what-is-redd. Last accessed 22 February 2015.

REDD Safeguards Working Group. 2014. 'What are REDD+ Safeguards?', http://reddplussafeguards.com. Last accessed 10 July 2015.

Reed, M. 2010. *Rebels for the Soil: The Rise of the Global Organic Food and Farming Movement*. London: Earthscan.

Regional Greenhouse Gas Initiative (RGGI). 2016. www.rggi.org. Last accessed 23 October 2016.

Renner, M. 2005. 'Resource Wealth and Conflict'. In Starke, L. (ed.) *State of the World 2005: Redefining Global Security*. Washington DC: Worldwatch Institute, pp. 96–7.

Revkin, A., Carter, S., Ellis, J., Hossa, F., and McLean, A. 2008. 'On the Issues: Climate Change', *The New York Times* elections.nytimes.com/2008/president/issues/climate.html. Last accessed 9 December 2016.

Richerson, P.J., Boyd, R., and Paciotti, B. 2009. 'An Evolutionary Theory of Commons Management'. In Ostrom, E., Dietz, T., Dolšak, N., Stern, P.C., Stonich, S., and Weber, E.U. (eds.) *The Drama of the Commons*. Washington DC: National Academy Press, pp. 403–42.

Ricks, T.E. 2011. 'The Future of Water Wars', *Foreign Policy* https://foreignpolicy.com/2011/05/05/the-future-of-water-wars. Last accessed 9 December 2016.

Rittberger, V., Zangl, B., and Kruck, A. 2012. *International Organization*. Houndmills: Palgrave Macmillan.

Rittel, H.W.J. and Webber, M.M. 1973. 'Dilemmas in a General Theory of Planning', *Policy Sciences* 4: 155–69.

Ritzer, G. 2010. *Enchanting a Disenchanted World: Continuity and Change in the Cathedrals of Consumption*. London: Sage.

Roberts, J.T., Parks, B.C., Tierney, M.J., and Hicks, R.L. 2009. 'Has Foreign Aid Been Greened?', *Environment: Science and Policy for Sustainable Development* 51(1): 8–21.

Robertson, T. 2012. *The Malthusian Moment: Global Population Growth and the Birth of American Environmentalism*. New Brunswick: Rutgers University Press.

Rockström, J., Steffen, W., Noone, K., Persson, A., Chapin, F.S., Lambin, E.F., Lenton, T.M., Scheffer, M., Folke, C., Schellnhuber, J.H., Nykvist, B., de Wit, C.A., Hughes, T., van der Leeuw, S., Rodhe, H., Sörlin, S., Snyder, P.K., Costanza, R., Svedin, U., Falkenmark, M., Karlberg, L., Corell, R.W., Fabry, V.J., Hansen, J., Walker, B., Liverman, D., Richardson, K., Crutzen, P., and Foley, J.A. 2009. 'A Safe Operating Space for Humanity', *Nature* 461: 472–5.

Ross, M.L. 2004. 'How Do Natural Resources Influence Civil War? Evidence from Thirteen Cases', *International Organization* 58(1): 35–67.

Rosset, P. 2006. *Food is Different: Why We Must Get the WTO out of Agriculture*. London: Zed Books.

Rothman, D.S. 1998. 'Environmental Kuznets Curves – Real Progress or Passing the Buck? A Case for Consumption-based Approaches', *Ecological Economics* 25: 177–94.

Rotterdam Convention. 1998/2013. 'Rotterdam Convention on the Prior Informed Consent Procedure for Certain Hazardous Chemicals and Pesticides in International Trade: Texts and Annexes', www.pic.int/TheConvention/Overview/TextoftheConvention/tabid/1048/language/en-US/Default.aspx. Last accessed 24 June 2016.

Rudel, T,K., Defries, R., Asner, G.P., and Laurance, W.F. 2009. 'Changing Drivers of Deforestation and New Opportunities for Conservation', *Conservation Biology* 23(6): 1396–1405.

Ruggie, J.G. 1993. *Multilateralism Matters: The Theory and Praxis of an Institutional Form*. New York: Columbia University Press.

Russi, D., ten Brink, P., Farmer, A., Badura, T., Coates, D., Förster, J., Kumar, R., and Davidson, N. 2013. *The Economics of Ecosystems and Biodiversity for Water and Wetlands*. IEEP, London and Brussels: Ramsar Secretariat, Gland.

Sandilands, C. 1993. 'On "Green" Consumerism: Environmental Privatization and "Family Values"', *Canadian Woman Studies* 13(3): 45–7.

Sanne, C. 2002. 'Willing Consumers – or Locked-in? Policies for a Sustainable Consumption', *Ecological Economics* 42: 273–87.

Schneider, F., Kallis, G., and Martinez-Alier, J. 2010. 'Crisis or Opportunity? Economic Degrowth for Social Equity and Ecological Sustainability. Introduction to this Special Issue', *Journal of Cleaner Production* 18: 511–18.

Schneider, K. 1992. 'Campaign: Issues – The Environment; Clinton and Bush Show Contradictions in Balancing Jobs and Conservation', *The New York Times*, www.nytimes.com/1992/10/13/us/1992-campaign-issues-environment-clinton-bush-show-contradictions-balancing-jobs.html?pagewanted=all. Last accessed 9 December 2016.

Schor, J. 2008. *The Overworked American: The Unexpected Decline of Leisure*. New York: Basic Books.

Schroeder, H. and Okereke, C. 2013. 'REDD+ and Social Justice: Adaptation by Way of Mitigation?'. In Moser, S.C. and Boykoff, M.T. (eds.) *Successful Adaptation to Climate Change: Linking Science and Policy in a Rapidly Changing World*. Abingdon: Routledge, pp. 81–94.

Scott, J.C. 1985. *Weapons of the Weak: Everyday Forms of Peasant Resistance*. New Haven: Yale University Press.

Selby, J. 2003. 'Dressing up Domination as "Cooperation": The Case of Israeli–Palestinian Water Relations', *Review of International Studies* 29(1): 121–38.

Seoul Metropolitan Government. 2014. 'Ordinance on the Promotion of Sharing No. 5619', legal.seoul.go.kr/legal/english/front/page/law.html?pAct=lawView&pPromNo=1191. Last accessed 8 December 2016.

Seoul Metropolitan Government. 2016. 'Mayor Park Won Soon Introduced by NHK as "4 World's Innovative Mayors"', Seoul Government Press Release, english.seoul.go.kr/mayor-park-won-soon-introduced-nhk-4-worlds-innovative-mayors/. Last accessed 8 December 2016.

Shafık, N. 1994. 'Economic Development and Environmental Quality: An Econometric Analysis', *Oxford Economic Papers* 46: 757–73.

Sheikh, P.A. 2006. 'Debt-for-Nature Initiatives and the Tropical Forest Conservation Act: Status and Implementation', *CRS Report for Congress*. Washington DC: US Library of Congress.

Shinkuma, T. and Huong, N.T.M. 2009. 'The Flow of E-Waste Material in the Asian Region and a Reconsideration of International Trade Policies on E-Waste', *Environmental Impact Assessment Review* 29: 25–31.

Shishlov, I. and Bellassen, V. 2012. '10 Lessons from 10 Years of the CDM', *Climate Report* 37, www.cdcclimat.com/IMG/pdf/12-10-05_climate_report_37_-_10_lessons_from_10_years_of_cdm.pdf. Last accessed 25 October 2016.

Simon, H.A. 1955. 'A Behavioral Model of Rational Choice', *The Quarterly Journal of Economics*, 69(1): 99–118.

Singer, M. 2015. 'The Clothing Insurrection: It's Time to Take on the Fashion Supply Chain', www.vogue.com/13268385/fashion-supply-chain-environmental-impact. Last accessed 11 October 2015.

Smith, J. 2001. 'Globalizing Resistance: The Battle of Seattle and the Future of Social Movements', *Mobilization: An International Quarterly* 6(1): 1–19.

Smith, T.W. 2013. 'Public Attitudes towards Climate Change & Other Environmental Issues Across Time and Countries, 1993–2010', www.norc.org/PDFs/Public_Atti tudes_Climate_Change.pdf. Last accessed 3 November 2016.

Soper, K. 1996. 'Greening Prometheus: Marxism and Ecology'. In Benton, T. (ed.) *The Greening of Marxism*. New York: Guilford Press, pp. 81–99.

Sørensen, E. and Torfing, J. 2005. 'The Democratic Anchorage of Governance Networks', *Scandinavian Political Studies* 28(3): 195–218.

Sørensen, E. and Torfing, J. (eds.) 2007. *Theories of Democratic Network Governance*. Houndmills: Palgrave Macmillan.

Soroos, M.S. 2005. 'Garrett Hardin and Tragedies of Global Commons'. In Dauvergne, P. (ed.) *Handbook of Global Environmental Politics*. Cheltenham: Edward Elgar, pp. 35–51.

Spaull, J. 2015. 'World's Biggest E-dump, or Vital Supplies for Ghana?', 5 October, SciDevNet, http://www.scidev.net/global/digital-divide/multimedia/electronic-waste-dump-supplies-ghana.html. Last accessed 22 May 2017.

St. Fleur, N. 2015. 'Deforestation May Threaten Majority of Amazon Tree Species, Study Finds', *The New York Times*, 20 November, www.nytimes.com/2015/11/21/science/deforestation-may-threaten-majority-of-amazon-tree-species-study-finds.html. Last accessed 26 December 2016.

Statistica. 2015. 'Car Sales (Passenger and Commercial Vehicles) in China from 2008 to 2016 (in Million Units)', www.statista.com/statistics/233743/vehicle-sales-in-china. Last accessed 19 December 2016.

Statistica. 2016. 'Global Advertising Spending from 2011 to 2018', www.statista.com/statistics/273288/advertising-spending-worldwide. Last accessed 10 November 2016.

Steffen, W., Broadgate, W., Deutsch, L., Gaffney, O., and Ludwig, C. 2015. 'The Trajectory of the Anthropocene: The Great Acceleration', *The Anthropocene Review* 2(1): 81–98.

Stern, D. 2006. 'Reversal of the Trend in Global Anthropogenic Sulphur Emissions', *Global Environmental Change* 16: 207–20.

Stern, D., Common, M.S., and Barbier, E. 1996. 'Economic Growth and Environmental Degradation: The Environmental Kuznets Curve and Sustainable Development', *World Development* 24(7): 1151–60.

Stern, D.I. 2015. The Environmental Kuznets Curve after 25 Years', CCEP Working Paper 1514. Crawford School of Public Policy, The Australian National University.

Stevenson, H. 2013. *Institutionalizing Unsustainability: The Paradox of Global Climate Governance*. Berkeley: University of California Press.

Stevenson, H. 2014. 'Representing Green Radicalism: The Limits of State-based Representation in Global Climate Governance', *Review of International Studies* 40: 177–201.

Stevenson, H. 2016a. 'The Wisdom of the Many in Global Governance: An Epistemic-Democratic Defence of Diversity and Inclusion', *International Studies Quarterly* 60(1): 400–12.

Stevenson, H. 2016b. 'Sustainable Societies: Designing Sustainable Economies: Translating Ideas and Research into Policy and Practice', *ESRC-SPERI Workshop Report, 28–29 July*, http://speri.dept.shef.ac.uk/wp-content/uploads/2016/11/Sustainable-Societies-report.pdf. Last accessed 9 December 2016.

Stevenson, H. and Dryzek, J.S. 2014. *Democratizing Global Climate Governance.* Cambridge University Press.

Stockholm Convention. 2001/2009. 'Stockholm Convention on Persistent Organic Pollutants (POPs): Texts and Annexes', chm.pops.int/TheConvention/Overview/TextoftheConvention/tabid/2232/Default.aspx. Last accessed 12 December 2016.

Tainter, J.A. 2008. 'Foreword'. In Polimeni, J.M., Mayumi, K., Giampietro, M., and Alcott, B. *The Myth of Resource Efficiency Improvements: The Jevons Paradox.* London: Earthscan, pp. i–vii.

Tarrow, S. 2011. *Power in Movement: Social Movements and Contentious Politics*, 3rd edition. Cambridge University Press.

Terazono, E. 2014. 'Climate Extremes Inflate Food Prices', *The Financial Times*, www.ft.com/content/5c4500fc-a518-11e3-8988-00144feab7de#axzz3fzUJTBFH. Last accessed 19 December 2016.

Thakur, R. and van Langenhove, L. 2006. 'Enhancing Global Governance Through Regional Integration', *Global Governance* 12(3): 233–40.

The Changing Atmosphere. 1988. 'The Changing Atmosphere: Implications for Global Security'. 1988 Conference statement. Toronto, Canada, 27–30 June. Reprinted in American University *Journal of International Law and Policy* 5 (1990): 515.

*The Economist.* 2013. 'Famine Mortality', www.economist.com/blogs/graphicdetail/2013/05/daily-chart-10. Last accessed 19 December 2016.

*The Economist.* 2014. 'A Bigger Rice Bowl', www.economist.com/news/briefing/21601815-another-green-revolution-stirring-worlds-paddy-fields-bigger-rice-bowl. Last accessed 19 December 2016.

*The New York Times.* 1989. 'Brazil's Debt Can Save the Amazon', www.nytimes.com/1989/02/03/opinion/brazil-s-debt-can-save-the-amazon.html. Last accessed 12 December 2016.

*The New York Times.* 2016. 'The Climate Refugees of the Arctic', *The New York Times*, 20 December, www.nytimes.com/2016/12/20/opinion/the-climate-refugees-of-the-arctic.html. Last accessed 26 December 2016.

*The Wall Street Journal.* 2014. 'China Soon to Have Almost as Many Drivers as U.S. Has People', blogs.wsj.com/chinarealtime/2014/11/28/china-soon-to-have-almost-as-many-drivers-as-u-s-has-people. Last accessed 19 December 2016.

This is Rubbish. 2014. '10 Flooring Food Waste Facts', www.thisisrubbish.org.uk/resources/10-flooring-food-waste-facts. Last accessed 19 December 2016.

Thomas, D. 2013. 'The Carbon Credentials of Smartphones', *The Ecologist*, www.theeco logist.org/green_green_living/2084407/the_carbon_credentials_of_smartphones.html. Last accessed 12 December 2016.

Tomich, T.P., Brodt, S., Ferris, H., Galt, R., Horwath, W.R., Kebreab, E., Leveau, J.H.J., Liptzin, D., Lubell, M., Merel, P., Michelmore, R., Rosenstock, T., Scow, K., Six, J., Williams, N., and Yang, L. 2011. 'Agroecology: A Review from a Global-Change Perspective', *Annual Review of Environmental Resources* 36: 193–222.

Toppa, S. 2016. 'Breathing in Poison – Lahore's Growing Air Pollution Problem', *The Guardian*, 8 December, www.theguardian.com/global-development-profession als-network/2016/dec/08/breathing-in-poison-lahores-growing-air-pollution-prob lem. Last accessed 26 December 2016.

Toset, H.P.W., Gleditsch, N.P., and Hegre, H. 2000. 'Shared Rivers and Interstate Conflict', *Political Geography* 19(8): 971–96.

UN. 1968. 'ECOSOC Resolution 1356', 30 July, www.un.org/en/ga/search/view_doc.asp? symbol=e/res/1346(XLV). Last accessed 26 December 2016.

UN. 1992a. *Agenda 21*. United Nations Conference on Environment and Development Rio de Janeiro, Brazil, 3–14 June, sustainabledevelopment.un.org/content/docu ments/Agenda21.pdf. Last accessed 17 May 2017.

UN. 1992b. 'Rio Declaration on Environment and Development', 12 August, A/CONF.151/26, http://www.un.org/documents/ga/conf151/aconf15126-1annex1.htm. Last accessed 21 May 2017.

UN. 1992c. 'UN Conference on Environment and Development', www.un.org/geninfo/ bp/enviro.html. Last accessed 9 December 2016.

UN. 1996. 'ECOSOC Resolution 1996/31', http://www.un.org/documents/ecosoc/res/ 1996/eres1996-31.htm. Last accessed 9 December 2016.

UN. 2002a. 'Johannesburg Declaration on Sustainable Development', www.un-documents.net/jburgdec.htm. Last accessed 9 December 2016.

UN. 2002b. 'Plan of Implementation of the World Summit on Sustainable Development', www.un.org/esa/sustdev/documents/WSSD_POI_PD/English/WSSD_PlanImpl.pdf. Last accessed 9 December 2016.

UN. 2004. 'Map No.3584 Rev. 2', Department of Peacekeeping Operations, Geospatial Information Section, www.un.org/Depts/Cartographic/map/profile/israel.pdf. Last accessed 12 November 2016.

UN. 2007a. 'Security Council Holds First-Ever Debate On Impact Of Climate Change On Peace, Security, Hearing Over 50 Speakers', http://www.un.org/press/en/2007/ sc9000.doc.htm. Last accessed 22 December 2015.

UN. 2007b. 'ECOSOC Resolution 2007/40', www.un.org/esa/forests/pdf/ERes2007_ 40E.pdf. Last accessed 26 December 2016.

UN. 2012. *The Future We Want*. Outcome document of the United Nations Conference on Sustainable Development, Rio de Janeiro, Brazil, 20–2 June 2012, sustainable development.un.org/content/documents/733FutureWeWant.pdf. Last accessed 13 May 2017.

UN. 2015. 'World Population Projected to Reach 9.7 Billion by 2050 with Most Growth in Developing Regions, Especially Africa – says UN', United Nations Press Release,

July 29th, www.un.org/en/development/desa/population/events/pdf/other/10/World_Population_Projections_Press_Release.pdf. Last accessed 26 December 2016.

UN DESA. 2012. 'Review of Implementation of Agenda 21 and the Rio Principles', sustainabledevelopment.un.org/content/documents/641Synthesis_report_Web.pdf. Last accessed 9 December 2016.

UN Panel of Experts. 2000. 'Report of the Panel of Experts Appointed Pursuant to UN Security Council Resolution 1306', mondediplo.com/IMG/pdf/un-report.pdf. Last accessed 14 December 2015.

UN-Water. 2006. *Coping with Water Scarcity: A Strategic Issue and Priority for System-wide Action*, www.unwater.org/downloads/waterscarcity.pdf. Last accessed 13 May 2017.

UNCBD (United Nations Convention on Biological Diversity). 1992. www.cbd.int/convention/text/default.shtml. Last accessed 3 February 2017.

UNCHE. 1972. 'Report of the United Nations Conference on the Human Environment', www.un-documents.net/aconf48-14r1.pdf. Last accessed 9 December 2016.

UNDP. 2015. 'UN REDD Programme Fund: Trust Fund Fact Sheet', mptf.undp.org/factsheet/fund/CCF00. Last accessed 10 June 2015.

UNEP. 2006. 'Strategic Approach to International Chemicals Management: SAICM Texts and Resolutions of the International Conference on Chemicals Management', https://sustainabledevelopment.un.org/content/.../SAICM_publication_ENG.pdf. Last accessed 31 May 2017.

UNEP. 2011. 'How Many Species on Earth? 8.7 Million, Says New Study', http://old.unep-wcmc.org/how-many-species-on-earth-87-million-says-new-study-_704.html. Last accessed 24 May 2017.

UNEP. 2012a. *Global Outlook on SCP Policies: Taking Action Together*, https://wedocs.unep.org/rest/bitstreams/12945/retrieve. Last accessed 21 May 2017.

UNEP. 2012b. 'The 10-Year Framework of Programmes on Sustainable Consumption and Production', http://www.unep.org/10yfp. Last accessed 24 May 2017.

UNEP. 2013a. *Global Chemicals Outlook – Towards Sound Management of Chemicals*. Geneva, Switzerland: UNEP Chemicals Branch.

UNEP. 2013b. *Global Mercury Assessment 2013: Sources, Emissions, Releases and Environmental Transport*. Geneva: UNEP Chemicals Branch, https://wedocs.unep.org/bitstream/handle/20.500.11822/11401/GlobalMercuryAssessment2013.pdf?sequence=1&isAllowed=y. Last accessed 24 May 2017.

UNEP. 2015. 'Waste Crime – Waste Risks: Gaps in Meeting the Global Waste Challenge', http://apps.unep.org/publications/index.php?option=com_pub&task=download&file=011703_en. Last accessed 24 May 2017.

UNEP-DHI and UNEP. 2016. *Transboundary River Basins: Status and Trends*. Nairobi: United Nations Environment Programme, www.geftwap.org/water-systems/river-basins Last accessed 24 May 2017.

UNESCO. 1968. 'Use and Conservation of the Biosphere: Proceedings of the Intergovernmental Conference of Experts on the Scientific Basis for Rational Use and Conservation of the Resources of the Biosphere'. Paris, 4–13 September.

UNESCO. 2016. 'Introducing UNESCO', en.unesco.org/about-us/introducing-unesco. Last accessed 9 December 2016.

UNFCCC. 1992. 'United Nations Framework Convention on Climate Change', unfccc.int/files/essential_background/background_publications_htmlpdf/applica tion/pdf/conveng.pdf. Last accessed 9 December 2016.

UNFCCC. 1997. 'Kyoto Protocol to the United Nations Framework Convention on Climate Change', unfccc.int/essential_background/kyoto_protocol/items/1678.php. Last accessed 26 October 2016.

UNFCCC. 2014. 'Green Climate Fund Exceeds $10 Billion', newsroom.unfccc.int/finan cial-flows/green-climate-fund-exceeds-10billion. Last accessed 8 November 2016.

UNFCCC. 2015a. 'The Paris Agreement', unfccc.int/paris_agreement/items/9444.php. Last accessed 26 October 2016.

UNFCCC. 2015b. 'Report of the Conference of the Parties on its Twenty-first Session', unfccc.int/resource/docs/2015/cop21/eng/10a01.pdf#page=2. Last accessed 26 October 2016.

UNGA. 1968. 'Resolution 2398', www.un.org/en/ga/search/view_doc.asp?symbol=a/res/2398(XXIII). Last accessed 24 May 2017.

UNGA. 1972. 'Institutional and Financial Arrangements for International Environmental Cooperation', www.un-documents.net/a27r2997.htm. Last accessed 9 December 2016.

UNGA. 1983. 'Process of Preparation of the Environmental Perspective to the Year 2000 and Beyond', www.un.org/documents/ga/res/38/a38r161.htm. Last accessed 9 December 2016.

UNGA. 2001. 'Towards Global Partnerships', www.unglobalcompact.org/docs/about_the_gc/government_support/A-RES-56-76.pdf. Last accessed 9 December 2016.

UNHCR. 2015. 'Climate Change, Disasters and Displacement', www.unhcr.org/uk/cli mate-change-and-disasters.html. Last accessed 21 December 2016.

Union of Concerned Scientists (UCS). 2012. 'Deforestation and Global Warming', www.ucsusa.org/global_warming/solutions/stop-deforestation/deforestation-global-warming-carbon-emissions.html. Last accessed 2 March 2015.

Union of International Associations. 2016. 'Yearbook of International Organizations', www.uia.org/yearbook. Last accessed 9 December 2016.

University of Leicester. 2016. 'Media Note: Anthropocene Working Group (AWG)', www2.le.ac.uk/offices/press/press-releases/2016/august/media-note-anthropocene-working-group-awg. Last accessed 21 November 2016.

US Census Bureau. 2016a. 'World Population Growth Rates: 1950–2050', www.census.gov/population/international/data/idb/worldgrgraph.php. Last accessed 28 December 2016.

US Census Bureau. 2016b. 'World Population: 1950–2050', www.census.gov/popula tion/international/data/idb/worldpopgraph.php. Last accessed 28 December 2016.

USAID. 2014. 'Enterprise for the Americas Initiative', www.usaid.gov/biodiversity/TFCA/enterprise-for-the-americas-initiative. Last accessed 8 November 2016.

U.S. Geological Survey (USGS). 2015. 'How Much Water is There on, in, and Above the Earth?', water.usgs.gov/edu/earthhowmuch.html. Last accessed 9 December 2015.

U.S. Geological Survey. 2016. 'Cadmium: Statistics and Information', minerals.usgs.gov/minerals/pubs/commodity/cadmium. Last accessed 19 June 2016.

Van Alstine, J., Afionis, S., and Doran, P. 2013. 'The UN Conference on Sustainable Development (Rio+20): A Sign of the Times or "Ecology as Spectacle"?', *Environmental Politics* 22(2): 333–8.

VanDeveer, S.D. 2003. 'Green Fatigue', *Wilson Quarterly* (Autumn): 55–9.

Van Noordwijk, M., Leimona, B., Jindal, R., Villamor, G.B., Vardhan, M., Namirembe, S., Catacutan, D., Kerr, J., Minang, P.A., and Tomich, T.P. 2012. 'Payments for Environmental Services: Evolution Toward Efficient and Fair Incentives for Multifunctional Landscapes', *Annual Review of Environment and Resources* 37: 389–420.

Vaughan, A. 2016. 'Biodiversity is Below Safe Levels Across More Than Half of World's Land – Study', *The Guardian*, www.theguardian.com/environment/2016/jul/14/biodiversity-below-safe-levels-across-over-half-of-worlds-land-study. Last accessed 21 November 2016.

Verified Carbon Standard (VCS). 2016. www.v-c-s.org/project/vcs-program/. Last accessed 16 May 2017.

Vermeulen, S.J. 2014. 'Climate Change, Food Security and Small-Scale Producers', CCAFS Info Brief. CGIAR Research Program on Climate Change, Agriculture and Food Security (CCAFS). Copenhagen, Denmark, www.ccafs.cgiar.org. Last accessed 19 December 2016.

Victor, D.G. 2009. 'Plan B for Copenhagen', *Nature* 461(17): 342–4.

Vlacho, A. 1996. 'The Contradictory Interaction of Capitalism and Nature'. In Benton, T. (ed.) *The Greening of Marxism*. New York: Guilford Press, pp. 229–34.

Von Mises, L. 1949. *Human Action: A Treatise on Economics*. Auburn: The Ludwig Von Mises Institute.

Wackernagel, M. and Rees, W. 1998. *Our Ecological Footprint: Reducing Human Impact on the Earth*. Gabriola Island, BC: New Society Publishers.

Wall, D. 2014. *The Commons in History: Culture, Conflict, and Ecology*. Cambridge, MA: MIT Press.

Wallander, M. 2012. 'Why Textile Waste Should be Banned From Landfill', www.triplepundit.com/2012/01/textile-waste-be-banned-landfills. Last accessed 19 December 2016.

Warren, C. 2001. *Brush with Death: A Social History of Lead Poisoning*. Baltimore: Johns Hopkins University Press.

Waste and Resources Action Programme. 2015. 'Fast Facts for Textiles', www.wrap.org.uk/content/fast-facts-textiles. Last accessed 11 October 2015.

Watt, L. 2013. 'China Pollution: Cars Cause Major Air Problems In Chinese Cities', www.huffingtonpost.com/2013/01/31/china-pollution-cars-air-problems-cities_n_2589294.html?ir=India&adsSiteOverride=in. Last accessed 12 December 2016.

West, K. 2015. 'Waste Not, Want Not: How the Rubbish Industry Learned to Look Beyond Landfill', *The Guardian*, www.theguardian.com/environment/2015/feb/27/waste-rubbish-industry-landfill-recycling-dumps-incineration. Last accessed 16 December 2016.

White, F. 1998. *The Overview Effect: Space Exploration and Human Evolution*. Reston: American Institute of Aeronautics and Astronautics.

White, R. 2008. 'Toxic Cities: Globalizing the Problem of Waste', *Social Justice* 35(3): 107–19.

Whitfield, R. 2005. 'Partnerships'. In Hens, L. and Nath, B. (eds.) *The World Summit on Sustainable Development: The Johannesburg Conference*. Dordrecht: Springer, pp. 347–72.

WHO. 2010a. 'Exposure to Lead: A Major Public Health Concern', www.who.int/entity/ipcs/features/lead..pdf?ua=1. Last accessed 18 June 2016.

WHO. 2010b. 'Exposure to Dioxins and Dioxin-Like Substances: A Major Public Health Concern', www.who.int/ipcs/features/dioxins.pdf. Last accessed 18 May 2017.

WHO. 2016a. 'Mercury and Health', www.who.int/mediacentre/factsheets/fs361/en. Last accessed 16 December 2016.

WHO. 2016b. 'Ten Chemicals of Major Public Health Concern', www.who.int/ipcs/assessment/public_health/chemicals_phc/en. Last accessed 16 December 2016.

WHO. 2016c. 'Air Pollution Levels Rising in Many of the World's Poorest Cities', www.who.int/mediacentre/news/releases/2016/air-pollution-rising/en/. Last accessed 21 November 2016.

Wishart, D.J. 2004. *Encyclopedia of the Great Plains*. Lincoln: University of Nebraska Press.

Willis, M.M. and Schor, J.B. 2012. 'Does Changing a Light Bulb Lead to Changing the World? Political Action and the Conscious Consumer', *The Annals of the American Academy of Political and Social Science* 644(1): 160–90.

Winslow, M. 2005. 'The Environmental Kuznets Curve Revisited Once Again', *Forum for Social Economics* 35(1): 1–18.

Wolf, A.T. 1998. 'Conflict and Cooperation Along International Waterways', *Water Policy* 1: 251–65.

Wolf, A.T., Yoffe, S.B., and Giordano, M. 2003. 'International Waters: Identifying Basins at Risk', *Water Policy* 5: 29–60.

Wolf, A.T., Kramer, A., Carius, A., and Dabelko, G.D. 2005. 'Managing Water Conflict and Cooperation'. In Starke, L. (ed.) *State of the World 2005: Redefining Global Security*. Washington DC: Worldwatch Institute, pp. 80–95.

Workman, K. 2016. 'August Ties July for Hottest Month on Record', *The New York Times*, 12 September, www.nytimes.com/2016/09/13/science/august-hot-record-temperature.html?_r=0. Last accessed 26 December 2016.

World Bank. 1992. *Development and the Environment. World Development Report 1992*. Oxford University Press.

World Commission on Environment and Development (WCED). 1987. 'Report of the World Commission on Environment and Development: Our Common Future', www.un-documents.net/our-common-future.pdf. Last accessed 9 December 2016.

Worldwatch Institute. 2011. *The State of Consumption Today*, http://www.worldwatch.org/node/810. Last accessed 21 May 2017.

Wunder, S. 2005. 'Payments for Environmental Services: Some Nuts and Bolts', *CIFOR Occasional Paper No. 42*. Jakarta: Center for International Forestry Research.

Wunder, S., Engel, S., and Pagiola, S. 2008. 'Taking Stock: A Comparative Analysis of Payments for Environmental Services Programs in Developed and Developing Countries', *Ecological Economics* 65: 834–52.

WWF. 2008. 'Monumental Debt-for-Nature Swap Provides $20 Million to Protect Biodiversity in Madagascar, WWF Announces', www.worldwildlife.org/press-releases/monumental-debt-for-nature-swap-provides-20-million-to-protect-bio diversity-in-madagascar-wwf-announces. Last accessed 19 December 2016.

WWF. 2013. 'The Impact of a Cotton T-Shirt', www.worldwildlife.org/stories/the-impact-of-a-cotton-t-shirt. Last accessed 12 October 2015.

WWF. 2014. *Living Planet Report 2014*. Switzerland: World Wildlife Fund.

WWF. 2016. *Living Planet Report 2016*, wwf.panda.org/about_our_earth/all_publica tions/lpr_2016/. Last accessed 21 November 2016.

WWF. No date. 'Deforestation', www.worldwildlife.org/threats/deforestation. Last accessed 10 February 2016.

Yamin, F. and Depledge, J. 2004. *The International Climate Change Regime: A Guide to Rules, Institutions, and Procedures*. Cambridge University Press.

Zeitoun, M. and Mirumachi, N. 2008. 'Transboundary Water Interaction I: Reconsidering Conflict and Cooperation', *International Environmental Agreements* 8: 297–316.

Zimlich, R. 2015. 'Regional Landfill Capacity Problems Do Not Equate to a National Shortage', waste360.com/operations/regional-landfill-capacity-problems-do-not-equate-national-shortage. Last accessed 16 December 2016.

Zuckerman, A. 2013. 'Rights and Responsibility: The Failure of Yasuní-ITT and What it Means for Ecuador's Indigenous Peoples', amazonwatch.org/news/2013/0825-rights-and-responsibility-the-failure-of-yasuni. Last accessed 9 March 2015.

# Index

acid rain, 50, 62, 245, 295
advertising, 70, 82, 200–201, 204, 298
Africa, 21, 45, 88, 186, 208, 253
  African commons systems, 28
agriculture, 67, 89, 91, 257, 261, 276–277, 289, 295
  agroecology, 275, 277, 279, 295, 305
  and environmental degradation, 225, 268–269, 271, 289
  and fossil fuels, 256, 268
  Cuba, 278–279
  environmental impact, 91, 263
  Food and Agriculture Organisation (FAO), 29, 113, 187
  food production, 91, 266–267, 269–270, 301
  food sovereignty, 273–274, 302, 305
  genetic engineering, 263–265, 303
  green revolution, 263, 304
  liberalisation, 266–267
  localism, 280, 306
  modernisation of, 262–264, 266
air pollution, 4, 175, 181, 201
  sulphur emissions, 48, 62
Antarctica, 30–31
Anthropocene, 1–3, 6–7, 16, 282–284, 293, 295, 316, 335, 339
Asia Pacific Partnership on Clean Development and Climate, 111, 157, 296
Australia, 87, 159, 272, 296

Basel Convention, 234, 248, 251, 296
  Basel Action Network, 242, 249, 252–253, 296
  Basel Ban, 235
  weaknesses and limitations, 248–249
biodiversity, xi, 3, 5, 34, 51, 58, 65, 118, 136, 168, 175–176, 180–182, 184, 193–195, 270–271, 276–277, 284–285, 295–296, 301, 339–340, 342

Brazil, 171, 175, 184, 212, 276
BRICS, 154
business, 10, 143, 155–156, 158, 161–163, 204, 262

Canada, 151, 153, 157, 203, 220, 248, 272
capitalism, 10, 60, 125, 164, 219, 257, 260, 299
  alienation, 64, 75, 295
  contradictions, 60–62, 71, 300
  ecological imperialism, 68, 75, 300
  metabolic and ecological rifts, 64–65, 67, 75, 300, 306
  natural capital, 71, 180–181, 307
  sustainable capitalism, 70–71, 311
carbon markets. See markets
Carson, Rachel, 224–225
chemicals and metals, 6, 205, 224–225, 289, 306, 308, 311, *see also Basel Convention*
  chemical industry, 225, 230, 232, 264
  environmental impact, 228, 232, 295
  e-waste, 248–252, 302
  global governance, 52, 133, 225, 233, 240–241
  hazardous waste, 52, 91, 205, 226–227, 234, 243, 248, 292, 296, 305, 310
  human impact, 6, 229, 231, 233, 252
  Khian Sea, 243, 305
  persistent organic pollutants, 233, 235
  Probo Koala, 250, 309
  role in modern life, 227–231
  types of, 225–227, 229, 231–232
China, 72, 99, 103, 154, 175, 197, 201–202, 212, 296
cities, 159
civil society, 9, 111, 124, 128, 130, 135, 141, 155–156, 162, 164, 171, 182, 192, 234, 257–258, 293, 297, 299, *see also social movements*
  World Wildlife Fund, 32, 160, 177, 188

climate change, 3, 65, 189, 267, 284, 290, 297,
    *see also markets*; *conflicts*; *finance*;
    transnational governance experiments
    common but differentiated responsibilities
        and respective capabilities (CBDR),
        150–151, 296
    adaptation, 161, 291
    bandwagoning, 156, 296
    Copenhagen Summit and Accord, 154
    flexible mechanisms, 152, 161
    greenhouse gas emissions, 3, 34, 141, 146,
        148, 158, 199, 306, 309
    Kyoto Protocol, 118, 151–153, 161, 305
    Paris Agreement, 154–155, 164, 171, 308
    risks and anticipated consequences, 91, 147,
        150, 268
    science, 146–148
    targets and timetables, 147, 151–153, 155
Club of Rome, 39–41, 297
commons, 20, 26, 310
    common pool resources, 22, 28–29, 33–34
    definition, 22
    global commons, 30–31, 303
    tragedy of the commons, 11, 19, 21, 23–26,
        35, 148, 298, 311
communal property, 27–28
conflict, 13, 72, 81–83, 99, 101, 193, 298,
    *see also* water
    and climate change, 103
    and natural resources, 56, 84, 104, 310
    civil conflict, 84
    definitions, 83
    greed and grievance, 87–88
    resource curse, 86–87
    sub-national conflicts, 100–101
    violent conflict, 83, 85–86
consumption, 51–52, 60, 68, 74, 91, 121,
        124–125, 132, 198, 200, 206–207, 211,
        219, 221, 289, 298–299, *see also*
        *individual responsibility*
    consuming class, 91, 185, 197–198,
        201–202, 298
    definitions of sustainable consumption,
        206–207, 311
    environmental impact, 197, 199, 202,
        204–205
    fashion, 204–205

greenwash, 160, 199, 217–218, 304
    luxury and subsistence consumption, 52,
        199, 306
    mobile phones, 202, 204
    planned obsolescence, 203, 249, 308
    UN initiatives, 207–208
    voluntary initiatives, 159, 288
counter-summits, 135, 274, 299

deforestation, 6, 32, 156, 183, 190, 285, 288,
        299, 305, 308, *see also finance*
    certification schemes, 32, 188–189, 297
    drivers of, 185–186
    Forest Stewardship Council (FSC), 32, 188,
        215, 303
    global forestry governance, 187, 288
    nature and scale of the problem, 167, 183
    REDD, 191–194, 292, 309
degrowth, 74, 299
dematerialisation, 71, 299
desertification, 85, 123, 131, 136, 138, 170,
        174–175, 196
developed countries, 9, 128, 135, 151, 153, 155,
        206, 251, *see also North*
developing countries, 9, 52–53, 120, 128, 135,
        151–152, 155, 167, 176, 183, 187, 249,
        251, 265, 267–268, *see also South*
development, 252–253
    health and human development, 40, 55
    human development, 114
    stages of development, 53

eco-development, 120, 300
ecological Marxism, 61
economic growth, 48–49, 51, 53, 55, 125,
        301–302, 304–305
ecosystem services, 5–6, 89, 180, 301
efficiency, 160, 173, 180, 182, 207, 262, 279,
        291, 305
Ehrlich, Paul and Anne, xv, 11, 39, 41, 47, 57,
        316, 319
emissions trading. See markets
energy, 3, 89, 162, 269
environmental degradation, 21, 55, 62, 67, 70,
        130, 134, 246, 299–300
Environmental Kuznets Curve, 48, 50, 52, 91,
        290, 302

environmental refugees, 84, 104, 284, 302
environmentalism, 12, 38, 56, 112, 118, 219

finance, 14, 168–169, 173, 288, 295
   aid as a financial commitment, 170, 302, 304
   debt-for-nature swaps, 167, 176–179, 299
   environmental aid, 167, 169, 172–173, 175
   environmental impact of aid, 171
   forestry, 183, 186–188, 190–192, 194–195
   Global Environment Facility, 170, 303
   payments for ecosystem services, 167,
      179–181, 183, 308
   promises, 171, 190
   traditional aid, 169–170
food security, 6, 143, 266, 268–269, 273,
   278–279, 302
fossil fuels, 148, 190, 307
fragmentation, 126, 129, 144–145, 163, 303
free market environmentalism, 24, 125

gender
   feminism, 56
   women, 42, 45
global governance, 30, 75, 111, 168, 282, 289,
   296, 303, 309
global warming, *see climate change*
globalisation, 32, 34, 67, 127, 140, 142, 204,
   246, 256, 260, 292
green economy, 134, 304

Hardin, Garrett, xv, 11, 19–21, 23–24, 26–27,
   29, 32, 35, 286, 290, 311, 323, 335,
   *see also commons; tragedy of the commons*
human security, 81, 95, 104, 116, 154

illegal activity, 249–250, 252
India, 129, 168, 171, 175, 197, 201, 212, 263,
   296
indigenous people, 182, 188, 192–193, 195,
   297
individual responsibility, 198, 209–210, 298
   carbon neutral schemes, 213
   eco-labels, 197, 214, 216, 300, 303
   ecological footprint, 34, 211, 300
   importance of, 209, 220–221
   limitations and critiques, 197, 215, 218, 222
   voluntary simplicity, 210

international law, 126, 155, 244
   hard and soft law, 34, 107, 119, 138, 187,
      287, 304

Jevons paradox, 50, 71, 305
justice, 290
   environmental justice and injustice, 4, 92,
      224, 242, 244, 246–247, 249–250, 290,
      292, 302, 309
   prior informed consent, 234–235, 309

Latin America, 178, 186, 275
liberal environmentalism, 164–165, 257, 305

Malthus, Thomas, 11–12, 37–38, 40, 47, 68,
   307, 317, 321
markets, 143, 156, 163, 181, 188, 194, 196,
   264, 266–267, 288
   carbon markets, 109, 153, 158, 191, 287,
      291, 296
   emissions offsetting, 10, 195, 214, 297,
      302
   emissions trading, 31, 152, 160
Marx, Karl, 11–12, 60–61, 63–65, 67, 72, 199,
   295, 306, 321, 328
Marxism, 59, 299–300, *see also socialism*
Millennium Development Goals, 128, 137,
   306
Minamata Convention, 239, 306
minilateralism, 107, 110–111, 118, 130, 154,
   306
multilateralism, 8, 13, 99, 107, 112, 116–117,
   126–128, 154, 173, 206, 234, 287, 298,
   307, 310
   definition, 109
   North-South divisions, 9, 14, 108, 115,
      168

negotiations, 10, 118, 123, 148, 152, *see also*
   multilateralism
   inequalities in participation, 123, 133
   international agreements, 107, 110
   Multilateral Environmental Agreements
      (MEAs), 13, 108, 115–117, 119, 133,
      171
neoliberalism, 140, 143, 257, 259, 261, 307
networks, 157, 171, 307

non-state actors, 14, 83, 111, 140–141, 143,
    156, 161, 163–164, 176, 287, 297, 303,
    307, *see also civil society*; *social
    movements*; *business*
North, 52, 68, 161, 170, 242, 248–249, 251,
    263, 296, 303, 307

O'Connor, James, 11, 62–63, 72, 331
ocean acidification, 3, 307–308
Ostrom, Elinor, 11–12, 26–29, 33–34, 165, 286,
    293, 319, 331, 333
ozone, 109, 306, 308, 312

planetary boundaries, 65, 308
pollution, 49–52, 56, 62, 85
pollution haven hypothesis, 52–53, 309
population, 3, 5, 20, 185, 291, 299, 307
    carrying capacity, 43
    distribution, 45
    population growth, 91–92
    poverty as a driver, 38, 46
poverty, 11, 37, 46–47, 50, 53, 59, 75, 115, 124,
    168, 185, 284
privatisation, 23, 143, 182
problem displacement, xvi, 15, 224–225, 242,
    245–247, 292, 299, 309
public awareness, 6–7, 132, 208, 224, 288

racism, 47
resource scarcity and depletion, 81–84, 86
Rotterdam Convention, 235, 310
Russia, 202, 212

securitisation, 83, 102–104, 310
sharing economy, 73
social movements, 15, 63, 256–257, 260, 266,
    272, 275, 289, 310
    Campesino a Campesino, 277
    La Via Campesina, 273, 279, 305
    Movimento dos Trabalhadores Rurais Sem
        Terra (MST), 276
    resistance, 15, 256, 258–259, 272, 274,
        276–277, 310
socialism, 23, 62
    eco-socialism, 59, 72–73, 301
South, 56, 68, 92, 127, 161, 169–170, 201, 242,
    249, 251, 263, 267, 296, 303–304, 310

sovereignty (consumer), 216, 298
sovereignty (state), 109, 141, 179, 187–188
states, 8, 82–83, 89, 92, 99, 103, 109–110,
    112–113, 119, 122, 125, 128, 132,
    134–135, 141, 143, 151, 153, 155,
    188, 193, 234, 247–248, 273,
    287–289, 303, 305
    newly independent states, 97
steady state economy, 74–75, 310
Stockholm Conference, (UN Conference on
    Environment and Development, 1972),
    114, 116, 120
sub-national actors, 14, 157, 303
sustainable development, 13, 47, 108, 122, 134,
    176, 180, 261, 285, 287, 311
    Commission on Sustainable Development
        (Rio, 1992), 123–124, 134, 298
    World Summit on Sustainable Development
        (2002), 127–128
    Agenda 21 (1992), 123–125, 206–207, 295
    Brundtland Commission, 47, 121, 296, 308
    Brundtland Report, 122
    definitions, 54, 120, 124, 126
    Earth Summit (UNCED) (1992), 122, 125,
        170, 206, 300
    Johannesburg Declaration on Sustainable
        Development, 128, 207
    Johannesburg Plan of Implementation,
        127–128
    Our Common Future, 47, 122, 307
    partnerships, 128–129, 207
    Rio+20 (2012), 89, 130, 133–134, 310
    Sustainable Development Goals, 136–137,
        285, 311

technology, 53, 66, 99, 112, 115, 135, 205, 207,
    252, 262, 270, 292
The European Union, 118, 134, 154, 181, 249
The Toronto Declaration, 150
transnational governance experiments, 14,
    140, 156, 293, 297, 311
    characteristics of climate governance
        experiments, 150
    defined, 157
    effectiveness, 153
    governance triangle, 143
    legitimacy, 145, 164

limitations and critiques, 153, 161, 163
orchestration, 145, 164, 307
private actors' motivations, 143
the rise of, 142–143
types of, 157–160
virtues, 162
what, 161
when, 160
who and where, 161

UN Conference on the Human Environment
    (1972), 47, 168, 310
UN Security Council, 103, 110
United Nations, 8–9, 29, 34, 91, 110, 187, 248,
    287, 296, 298, 306, 308
  UNEP, 3, 116, 121, 133–134, 240, 312
  UNESCO, 112
  UNFCCC, 151, 154, 170, 189–190, 312
United States, 116, 120, 134, 151, 154, 160,
    176, 200, 212, 249–250, 262, 272, 296

Barack Obama, 118, 166
Bill Clinton, 117, 244
George H.W. Bush, 125, 178
George W. Bush, 117
urbanisation, 92, 202

voluntary action, 32, 163, 287

waste. See chemicals and metals
water, 81, 88, 91, 156, 180, 286, 291
  Basins at Risk (BAR) scale, 98
  cooperation, 88, 95, 97, 99, 286
  transnational river basins, 89, 95–96,
    310
  water footprint, 91, 269
  water scarcity, 3, 6, 85, 91–92, 96, 100
  water uses, 3
  water wars, 13, 82, 92, 95, 100
wicked problems, 140, 142, 147–148, 312
World Bank, 48, 170–171, 181, 191, 266, 271

# Spectrophotometry
# & spectrofluorimetry

# TITLES PUBLISHED IN
# THE
# PRACTICAL APPROACH
# SERIES

Gel electrophoresis of proteins
Gel electrophoresis of nucleic acids
Iodinated density-gradient media
Centrifugation (2nd Edition)
Transcription and translation
Oligonucleotide synthesis
Microcomputers in biology
Mutagenicity testing
Affinity chromatography
Virology
DNA cloning
Plant cell culture
Immobilised cells and enzymes
Nucleic acid hybridisation
Animal cell culture
Human cytogenetics
Photosynthesis: energy transduction
Human cytogenetics
Drosophila
Human genetic diseases
H.p.l.c. of small molecules
Carbohydrate analysis
Biochemical toxicology
Electron microscopy in molecular biology
Nucleic acid and protein sequence analysis
Teratocarcinomas and embryonic stem cells